The Network Society

Social Aspects of New Media

Second edition

Jan A.G.M. van Dijk

SAGE Publications
London • Thousand Oaks • New Delhi

This edition first published 2006

First edition published 1999
Reprinted 2001, 2006 (twice)

First edition published 1991, *De netwerkmaatschappij*
© Bohn Staflen Van Loghum, Houten, The Netherlands

SAGE Publications Ltd
1 Oliver's Yard
55 City Road
London EC1Y 1SP

SAGE Publications Inc.
2455 Teller Road
Thousand Oaks, California 91320

SAGE Publications India Pvt Ltd
B-42, Panchsheel Enclave
Post Box 4109
New Delhi 110 017

British Library Cataloguing in Publication data

A catalogue record for this book is available
from the British Library

ISBN-13 978-1-4129-0867-2   ISBN-10 1-4129-0867-1
ISBN-13 978-1-4129-0868-9 (pbk)   ISBN-10 1-4129-0868-X (pbk)

Library of Congress Control Number available

Typeset by C&M Digitals (P) Ltd., Chennai, India
Printed on paper from sustainable resources
Printed in Great Britain by TJ Internnational, Padstow, Cornwall

The Network Society

ABOUT THE AUTHOR

Jan A.G.M. van Dijk is an internationally recognized expert in the field of communication, his specific interest being new media studies. He is the author of *The Deepening Divide, Inequality in the Information Society* (2005), co-editor with Keith L. Hacker of *Digital Democracy: Issues of Theory and Practice* (2000) and co-author with Harry Bouman, Bart van den Hooff and Lidwien van de Wijngaert of *Information and Communication Technology in Organizations* (2005), all published by SAGE Publications. As Professor of Communication Science at the University of Twente, van Dijk teaches and investigates the *Sociology of the Information Society*, in particular the social-cultural, political, and organizational aspects. He earned his PhD in the Social Sciences at the Radboud University of Nijmegen, the Netherlands. Van Dijk also is an advisor for the European Commission and a number of Dutch ministries.

His personal website contains more author information and background information for this book: http://www.gw.utwente.nl/vandijk

CONTENTS

1 **Introduction**   1
   A New Infrastructure for Society   1
   A Second Communications Revolution?   3
   Characteristics of the New Media   6
   Communication Capacities of the New Media   13
   The Nature and Design of this Book   17

2 **Networks: The Nervous System of Society**   19
   The Network Society and Other Classifications   19
   A Short History of the Human Web   21
   Networks at All Levels   24
   Causes of the Rise of Networks   29
   From Mass Society to Network Society   32
   Changing Relations in the Network Society   37

3 **Technology**   42
   Introduction   42
   Technical Foundations of the Network Society   43
   Telecommunication Networks   46
   Data Communication Networks   48
   Mass Communication Networks   51
   Integrated Networks   53
   Multimedia and Broadband Networks   55
   Future Trends   58

4 **Economy**   61
   Introduction   61
   Causes of the Current Communications Revolution   62
   A Flow Economy   65
   Markets, Hierarchies and Networks   72
   A New Economy?   76
   The Producers: From Infrastructure to Service Providers   81
   The Consumers: Pushers and Pulled   89
   Conclusions   93

5	**Politics and Power**	**95**
	Introduction	95
	The Vulnerability of Networks	96
	The Spread and Concentration of Politics	98
	The Claims of E-Government and Digital Democracy	103
	Power in the Organization	108
	Privacy and Personal Autonomy	112
	Conclusions	125

6	**Law**	**127**
	Introduction	127
	The Law Undermined by Networks	128
	Who Rules the Internet?	130
	Information and Communication Freedom	137
	Rights of Ownership	143
	The Right to Privacy	149
	Conclusions	154

7	**Social Structure**	**156**
	Introduction	156
	Space and Time in the Network Society	157
	The Blurring Spheres of Living	161
	Communities and Social Relations	165
	Unity and Fragmentation: A New Social Cohesion	171
	Networks and Social (In)equality	174
	The Digital Divide	177
	The Instability of the Network Society	186
	Conclusions	188

8	**Culture**	**190**
	Introduction	190
	Living in a Digital Culture	191
	The Quantity and Quality of New Media Content	199
	Changing Media Use	204
	Conclusions	208

9	**Psychology**	**210**
	Introduction	210
	Perception and the New Media	211
	Cognition and the New Media	217
	Learning with the New Media	224
	The Social Psychology of CMC	226
	Changes in the Human Personality?	233
	Conclusions	238

10 Conclusions and Policy Perspectives   240
    Introduction   240
    General Conclusions   240
    The Information and Network Society in North America,
    Europe, East Asia and the Third World   244
    Policy Perspectives for the Network Society   253

Glossary   264

References   272

Index   288

INTRODUCTION

1

A NEW INFRASTRUCTURE FOR SOCIETY

New roads are being built at tremendous speed and yet we hardly notice. After all, the countryside is not being cleared by bulldozers and covered with rails, canals or asphalt. These roads are for information and communication. Apparently they are part of an abstract, barely visible reality. We might see them as yet another cable running into our homes. We do not realize that they are making us dependent on yet another technology in our life. We are not only tied to roads, electricity cables, water pipes, gas lines, sewers, post-boxes, telephone wires and cable television, but also to computer networks such as the **Internet**.[1]

'Invisible' roads

Contemporary literature abounds with expressions such as 'we live in a connected world', 'a connected age', a 'human web' and a 'web society'. At first sight this seems rather peculiar because simultaneously there is much talk about individualization, social fragmentation, independence and freedom. On second thoughts this coincidence is not that strange because both tendencies might be two sides of the same coin. At least, that is argued in this book. 'The world may never have been freer, but it has also never been so interdependent and interconnected' (Mulgan, 1997: 1).

Networks everywhere

At the individual level the use of networks has come to dominate our lives. Counting the time spent on broadcast networks, telephony and the Internet we can add between five and seven hours of leisure time a day on average in a developed society. Not to mention the hours spent with them at work and at school. Observing social networking by individuals we could add several hours spent in all kinds of meetings. Individualization and smaller households packed with technology to make us more independent from others, have not made us less social human beings.

Almost every organization in the developed world has become completely dependent on networks of telephony and computers. When they break down, the organization simply stops working. Long before they became so dependent on these media networks organizations had already split in separate organizations, departments and teams that still worked together in an

---

1 Words in bold type in the text are explained in the Glossary.

extensive division of labour. These days organizations do not finish products or services all by themselves. This is done in cooperation and competition inside and between economic networks.

At the level of society and on a global scale we can see that media networks, social networks and economic networks reach into the farthest corners and edges of the world. Our world has become truly globally connected. With the swift spread of satellite TV, mobile telephony and the Internet, developing countries such as China and India rapidly transform from pre-industrial societies into industrial mass societies and partly even post-industrial network societies. The meaning of these terms will be fully explained below.

The age of networks

With little exaggeration, we may call the 21st century the age of networks. Networks are becoming the nervous system of our society, and we can expect this infrastructure to have more influence on our entire social and personal lives than did the construction of roads for the transportation of goods and people in the past. In this sense 'information highway' is an appropriate term. The design of such basic infrastructures is crucial for the opportunities and risks to follow. We did not foresee what the consequences would be of our choice in the early 20th century of predominantly small-scale private transportation instead of large-scale public transport. But now we are only too well aware of the consequences. Traffic congestion, environmental degradation and global warming are all too evident. The potential consequences of choosing a certain kind of communication infrastructure and embedding this infrastructure in our social and personal lives may be less visible, but it will be just as severe.

Continuing this line of argument, at stake here is not only the ecology of nature – that is, transportation of information and communication will partly replace transportation of goods and people – but also 'social ecology'. Therefore, when the new media arrived in the 1980s, some people were talking about the 'pollution' of our social environment by the new media penetrating our private lives. According to them, the new media were reducing, diminishing and even destroying the quality of face-to-face communications and were making relationships at work more formal (Kubicek, 1988). They would result in privacy reduction and total control from above. In the 1990s these *dystopian* views were replaced by *utopian* views of the new media substantially improving the quality of life and of communication. A 'new economy' and a new era of prosperity, freedom and online democracy was looming ahead.

In the first Dutch edition of this book (van Dijk, 1991), I championed a wide public debate about such presumed outcomes of the new media. This call was partly heeded. Especially between 1994 and 1998, a huge boost was given to discussion of the opportunities of the Internet and the perspective of the so-called electronic highway, a term introduced in the United States in 1993 as '**information superhighway**'. The discussion in those years was largely theoretical. Utopian and dystopian views were listed and opposed in an abstract and rather speculative manner.

In the first decade of the 21st century we are able to develop a more balanced or *syntopian* view (Katz and Rice, 2002) of new media development after more than 25 years of experience. This time we are able to draw conclusions based on facts and empirical investigations. This is the main objective of this book.

This book demonstrates how the most fundamental values of our society are at issue when it comes to the development of new information and communication technologies, in which networks are already setting the tone.

Values at stake

Social equality is at stake, since certain categories of people participate more than others in the information society. Some profit from its advantages, while others are deprived. Technology allows for a better distribution of knowledge. Its complexity and costs, however, may serve to intensify existing social inequalities, or even create large groups of 'misfits' – people who do not fit in with the information society.

The fact that the new media enable well-informed citizens, employees and consumers to have more direct communication with, and participation in, institutions of decision-making should, in principle, strengthen *democracy*. On the other hand, because the technology is susceptible to control from above, democracy could be threatened. Some would argue that *freedom*, for example the freedom of choice for consumers, will increase because of the interactivity offered by this technology. Others paint a more pessimistic picture, and predict that freedom will be endangered by a decrease in privacy for the individual as a registered citizen, a 'transparent' employee and a consumer screened for every personal characteristic, and by the growing opportunities for central control.

For certain groups of people (disabled, sick and elderly people) as well as for society as a whole, *safety* can be improved by all kinds of registration and alarm systems. At the same time, safety seems to decrease because we have become dependent on yet another type of technology. And a very vulnerable technology at that.

The *quantity and quality of social relationships* might improve if communication technology enables us to get in touch easily with almost everybody, even over long distances. On the other hand, they might decrease because they invite particular people to withdraw into computer communication and to interact only with safe, self-chosen social environments. In this way new media communication may become a complete substitute for face-to-face communication, causing the quality of communication to be diminished in certain respects.

The *richness of the human mind* may increase owing to the diversity of impressions we gather through these new media. On the other hand, it may also be reduced because these impressions are offered out of context in schematic, (pre-)programmed and fragmented frames. And because it is available in huge amounts, information can never be fully processed by the recipient.

A SECOND COMMUNICATIONS REVOLUTION?

Most descriptions of media history suggest an evolutionary development of a large number of new media in succession. In reality, media development in the last two centuries has been more like two concentrations of innovations, of

Media history

which the first can be placed roughly in the last decades of the 19th century and the early decades of the 20th century, and the second is to be observed in the last decade(s) of the 20th century and the first decades of the 21st century. James Beniger was the first to describe and analyse the first concentration and its background in his book *The Control Revolution* (1986); Frederick Williams first identified the second concentration in his book *The Communications Revolution* (1982). I dare to speak of the *first and second communications revolutions of the modern age*. 'Revolution' is a big word, all too readily referred to in the history of industry and technology, whether it is appropriate or not. Every so-called revolution in fact took decades to complete. For the major technological developments are seldom revolutionary; the technological process is usually much more evolutionary. Innovations are preceded by a long process of preparation. It would be misleading to suggest that new technologies arise suddenly. Rather they are a combination of techniques developed earlier. It would be wise to ask ourselves what exactly is new about the **new media** and why the term 'revolution' can be used here. If there was merely a considerable quantitative acceleration of the arrival of innovations in the two concentrations mentioned before, I would not dare to mention the word 'revolution'. *Structural changes* or *qualitative technical improvements* in mediated communications must take place in order for something to be called a revolution in communications.

Structural communications revolution
In the history of the media, several communications revolutions have taken place. These can be divided into structural and technical communications revolutions*.[2] In *structural* revolutions, fundamental changes take place in the coordinates of space and time. Media can be a form of communication fixed in space (in one place) or they may allow communications between different places. Furthermore, they can fix the moment of communication to a certain time or enable us to bridge time.

The switch from communication fixed in space and time to communication bridging space and time marks the two first communications revolutions in the (pre-)history of man: sending smoke, drum and fire signals over long distances, and sending messengers in order to bridge places. Time was transcended by making illustrations on pottery and inside caves – signs that passed to future generations.

The next and presumably most important structural communications revolution was the development of writing, which enabled humans to overcome both space and time. The most recent communications revolution – the subject of this book – is primarily a structural revolution. It signals an end to the distinction between media that are fixed in space and time and media that bridge these dimensions. The new media, after all, can be used for both purposes. Even though the purpose of bridging time and space is predominant, the new media can also be used in offline environments, for example in consulting a CD-ROM or **DVD**. The new media are a combination of online and offline media, such as computer networks and personal computers. They are a combination of transmission links and artificial memories (filled with text, data, images and/or sounds) that can also be installed in separate devices.

---

2 An asterisk indicates that the explanation of the term follows in the text itself.

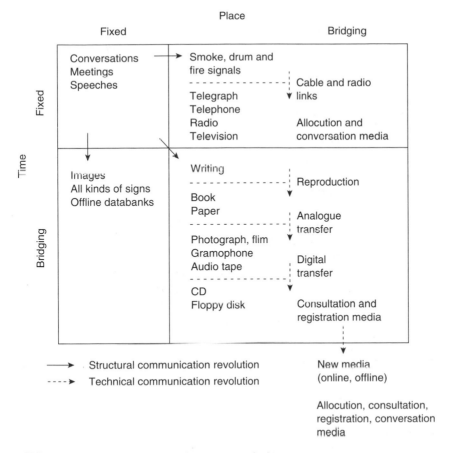

FIGURE 1.1 Communication revolutions in media history

Therefore, the new media require a step outside the scheme of revolutions that bridge space and time that have described media history until now (see Figure 1.1). The combination of online and offline applications of the new media, used both in traditional social environments fixed to a particular time and space and in online media environments bridging these dimensions, produces the structurally new characteristics of these media. This book will demonstrate that this combination helps to realize perhaps the most promising social perspective of the new media, which is not a replacement of local face-to-face communication by online mediated communication but a potentially fruitful interplay between them.

In a *technical* communications revolution, a fundamental change takes place in the structure of connections, artificial memories and/or the reproduction of their contents. The development of the printing press was a revolution in the reproduction of writing. In the second half of the 19th century a second revolution took place. It was mainly a technical revolution, based on the invention and construction of long-distance connections by cable and air, the introduction of new **analogue** artificial memories (photograph, film, gramophone record and audio recording tape) and new techniques for

**Technical
communications
revolution**

reproduction (the rotary press in particular). Qualitatively new was the development of media for a direct transfer of sound/speech, text/data and images by separate channels and over long distances. The *invention* of the telegraph and telephone date from a long time before the turn of the nineteenth to the twentieth century, and **telex**, radio and television from the years immediately after. Their *innovation**, meaning a first introduction in usable form, took place between 1890 and 1925. *Large-scale introduction* needed another 50 years. The most recent technical communications revolution is characterized by the introduction of **digital** artificial memories, and digital transmission and reproduction. The term 'digital revolution' is appropriate in this context.

Developments in the current communications revolution follow the same pattern. The inventions took place during the past 50 years. In the first decades after the Second World War, large mainframe computers, serving as number crunching machines or database processors, and satellite telecommunications were fabricated. Then, from the 1960s onwards smaller and yet more powerful computers were introduced that served as general symbolic machines concerned with the interactive manipulation of information and with communication and that were connected in networks. In the mean time we have passed the phase of innovations through the introduction of several generations of personal computers, computer networks, terminal equipment, programs and services. Currently, their large-scale introduction in workplaces, schools, households and public places is happening all over the world. This process will probably continue until about 2040.

Current communications revolution

Now we are able to answer the key question: how has quality improved in the current structural and technical communications revolution? It is not because the crucial coordinates of space and time seem to be reduced to insignificant proportions, or because it is possible to communicate with everyone all over the world within seconds if you have access to the means to do so. In other words, it is not the fact that 'the world is turning into a village', to use a popular phrase. This would simply mean an evolutionary development along the axes of space and time, which had already taken place with the communications revolution of the 19th century. It would 'merely' be an acceleration of this evolution. No, the essence of the current revolution can be summarized in the terms **digital code**, **integration** and **interactivity** as the defining characteristics of the new media.

CHARACTERISTICS OF THE NEW MEDIA

In this section I characterize the new media in three ways. First, I supply a definition of the new media as a combination of three characteristics. Then I discuss the typical patterns of information and communication to be observed in their application. Finally, I describe their strong and weak usage qualities, called **communication capacities**.

Integration

The most important *structural* new media characteristic is the integration of telecommunications, data communications and mass communications in

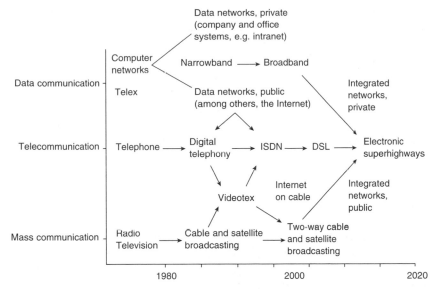

FIGURE 1.2 The integration of transmission in communications

a single medium. It is the process of *convergence*. For this reason, new media are often called multimedia. Integration can take place at one of the following levels:

1 infrastructure – for example combining the different transmission links and equipment for telephone and computer (data) communications;
2 transportation – for example Internet telephony and **web** TV riding on cable and satellite television;
3 management – for example a cable company that exploits telephone lines and a telephone company that exploits cable television;
4 services – for example the combination of information and communication services on the Internet;
5 types of data – putting together sounds, data, text and images.

This integration leads to a gradual merging of telecommunications, data communications and mass communications; the separate meanings of these terms will probably even disappear. We will use terms such as 'multimedia', 'broadband', 'the Internet' or 'the network'. Figure 1.2 shows the process of integration (Chapter 3 and the glossary offer more information on terminology). The figure demonstrates how public and private networks of data-, tele- and mass communication are flowing together to create multifunctional, high-speed networks that have been called electronic superhighways in the 1990s, but that nowadays usually carry the name of broadband (networks). This process of integration is enabled by two revolutionary techniques:

1 full digitalization of all media (the general use of digital code);
2 broadband transmission through all connections by cable and by air.

While the first technique enables a complete integration of telecommunications and data communications, the second is more relevant for the integration of mass communications in the process of convergence.

Interactivity   The second *structural* new media characteristic of the current communications revolution is the rise of interactive media. In a very general definition, interactivity is a sequence of action and reaction. It is remarkable how poorly this crucial concept is (further) defined and made operational for research in media and communication studies. Jensen (1999) has produced an exhaustive account of the laborious search by social and communication scientists for a suitable definition. Jensen himself wishes to reserve the concept of interactivity for mediated communication. Van Dijk and de Vos (2001) offer an operational definition that is supposed to be valid for face-to-face communication as well. These authors define interactivity at four accumulative levels, acknowledging, like many other authors, that this concept is a multidimensional construct. The levels of interactivity are supposed to be appropriate to define how interactive a particular digital medium is.

The most elementary level of interactivity is the possibility of establishing two-sided or multilateral communication. This is the *space* dimension. All digital media offer this possibility to a certain extent. However, most often, the downloaded link or the supply side of web sites, interactive television, and computer programs is much wider than the uplink or the retrieval made by their users.

The second level of interactivity is the degree of synchronicity. This is the *time* dimension. It is well known that an uninterrupted sequence of action and reaction usually improves the quality of interaction. However, some interactive media, such as electronic mail (email), are used for their lack of synchronicity. Producing and receiving messages can be done at self-chosen times and places, and one is allowed to think longer about a reply. Yet, this goes at the expense of immediate reactions and of the ability to send all kinds of verbal and nonverbal signs simultaneously.

When multilateral and synchronous communication are available, a higher level of control by the interacting parties is possible. So, the third level of interactivity is the extent of control exercised by the interacting parties. This *behavioural* dimension is defined as the ability of the sender and the receiver to switch roles at any moment. Furthermore, it is about the control over the events in the process of interaction. Interactivity in terms of control is the most important dimension in all interactivity definitions of media and communication studies (see Jensen, 1999). It means attention to the division of power in the interface of media and humans or between humans in both mediated and face-to-face communication. At this level, interactivity means, among other things, that the user is able to intervene into the program or representation itself and to make a difference. What the user does has to create a substantial change at the other side. Otherwise we cannot call the process fully interactive. As digital media are more interactive than traditional media, they enable a shift in the balance of power to the user and the side of demand. However, this potential is not fully realized in present uses of digital media in which a supply-side view still dominates the design of the medium.

The fourth and highest level of interactivity is acting and reacting with an understanding of meanings and contexts by all interactors involved. This *mental* dimension is a necessary condition for full interactivity, for example, in physical conversation and computer-mediated communication. Currently, this level of interactivity is reserved for mediated and face-to-face interaction between human beings and animals with a consciousness, except by those who have much confidence in interactions directed by artificial intelligence.

Digital code is a *technical* media characteristic only defining the form of new media operations. However, it has great substantial consequences for communication. Digital code means that in using computer technology, every item of information and communication can be transformed and transmitted in the form of strings of ones and zeros called bytes, with every single 1 or 0 being a bit. This artificial code replaces the natural codes of the analogue creation and transmission of items of information and communication (e.g. by beams of light and vibrations of sound).

Digital code

The first substantial effect of the transformation of all media contents in the same digital code is the uniformity and standardization of these contents. Form and substance cannot be separated as easily as many people think they can. Digital code is not a neutral form (see Chapter 8). It starts with initially cutting into pieces a number of undivided analogue items of information and communication (signs) and then recombining them in the digitized forms of images, sounds, texts, and numerical data. These forms are produced using not only the same basic code but also the same languages, such as **HTML** (hypertext mark-up language), a graphic code for pages of the **World Wide Web** (**www**). The resulting forms are known for their great similarities in menu and navigation structures when they are programmed in computer software. Another effect of using uniform digital code is the increase in the quantity of items of information and communication. This code makes their production, recording, and distribution much easier. Supported by the exponentially rising storage capacity of computers and their disks, unlimited amounts of items are produced. A final and perhaps most important effect of using digital code is the break-up of the traditional linear order of large units of information and communication, such as texts, images, sounds, and audiovisual programs, in such a way that they can be transformed into hyperlinks of items liable to be perceived and processed in the order that the reader, viewer, or listener wants. This transformation from linear to hypertext media would have been impossible without digital code. The social and cultural consequences of this 'revolution' in media production and use will be big. They will be fully described in this book, primarily in Chapters 8 and 9.

The new media are defined by all three characteristics simultaneously: they are *media which are both integrated and interactive and also use digital code at the turn of the 20th and 21st centuries*. It follows that their most common alternative names are multimedia, interactive media and digital media. Using this definition it is easy to identify media as old or new. For example, traditional television is integrated as it contains images, sound and text, but it is not interactive or based on digital code. The plain old telephone is interactive, but not integrated as it only transmits speech and sounds and it does not work with digital code. In contrast, the new medium of interactive television adds interactivity and digital code. Additionally, the new generations of mobile or fixed telephony are fully digitalized and integrated as they add text, pictures or video and they are connected to the Internet.

New media definition: All three characteristics

Information traffic patterns

As stated, the first level of interactivity is two-sided or multilateral communication. Bordewijk and Van Kaam (1982) had this concept in mind when they designed their typology of the four *information traffic patterns* of allocution, consultation, registration and conversation. They have proved very useful in social and communication science, as will be shown in this book. They illuminate the structures of communication and the aspects of power these structures contain. Finally, they show that the new media evolve from the pattern of allocution, characterizing the old media, to the patterns of consultation, registration and conversation. In this way they become more interactive and more integrated as they converge into fully integrated networks.

Allocution

In the twentieth century, the pattern of *allocution* has gained most importance in communication media. Radio, television and other mediated performances have come to the fore in this century of scale extension and massification. They perform important coordinating functions in society, because they are based on a pattern of allocution:* *the simultaneous distribution of information to an audience of local units by a centre that serves as the source of, and decision agency for, the information (in respect of its subject matter, time and speed)* (Figure 1.3a). The new media do not enhance this pattern. The only exceptions are where 'old' broadcasting media offer more opportunities of choice for viewers and listeners, such as by means of **pay-per-view** and home-video programming with feedback channels at freely chosen times. Here, within the limits and menus offered, the local unit is able to co-decide about the information to be received – the subject, the time the information is consumed, and the agenda of future broadcasting – by reactions to current programmes and by answers to questions posed. However, these innovations do more to damage the pattern of allocution than to enhance it. Therefore this pattern transforms into the next one in the new media environment.

Consultation

The pattern of *consultation* is enhanced by the new media. Consultation* is *the selection of information by (primarily) local units, which decide upon the subject matter, time and speed, at a centre which remains its source* (Figure 1.3b). Old consultative media are books, newspapers, magazines, audio and video. Examples of new consultative media are encyclopaedias on CD-ROM or DVD, teletext and other cable TV information services, interactive television and, of course, the numerous information sites on the Internet. Because they add new routes, these media are to be viewed as a basic improvement to the pattern of consultation. Often they are online connections enabling more consultation at the centre than the old media. Moreover, they are working at the expense of allocutive media, like audio and video equipment did with radio and television in the past.

Registration

The opportunities for *registration* also grow in the new media. Registration* is the *collection of information by a centre that determines the subject matter, time and speed of information sent by a number of local units, who are the sources of the information and sometimes take the initiative for this collection themselves (to realize a transaction or reservation)* (Figure 1.3c). In old media and data collection instruments, often the centre not only decides but also takes the initiative and requests the transfer of information. Examples of these media and instruments are enquiries, elections, examinations, archives

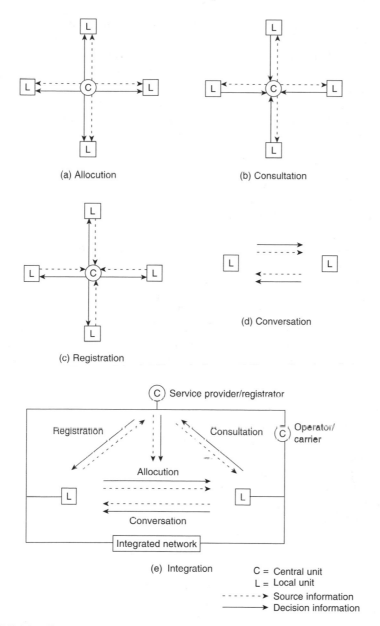

FIGURE 1.3 The integration of information traffic patterns in networks

and visual observation by cameras. To a large extent, these activities are already performed by old media. The new media offer even more opportunities. And the number of them grows with the diffusion of the new media: this certainly goes for online enquiries and online referenda. The new media, however, also offer more chances of registration by the centre at the initiative of the local units, for example in electronic reservations, teleshopping and telebanking. A more serious problem arises when the reverse is the case – when the registration initiative is taken by the centre, without the agreement of the local units. This might be the case with telemetry, electronic surveillance from a distance (such as electronic house arrest) or the observation of personal data without the individual concerned knowing or wanting it.

Conversation

The most fundamental change takes place in the pattern of *conversation*. Conversation* is an *exchange of information by two or more local units, addressing a shared medium instead of a centre and determining the subject matter, time and speed of information and communication themselves* (Figure 1.3d). The existing channels for conversation not only are enlarged, but can also contain more kinds of data. The old media (telegraph and telephone) only offered room for speech and a limited amount of data. Local computer networks and data communication over telephone lines caused an explosive growth in the capabilities for transporting data and text. The new media added a substantial new quality: the possibility to *combine* speech, data and text *in one message*. Then pictures could be added, and now we can even add moving images to these messages. This qualitative enlargement of the range of options for conversation requires broadband facilities, which until recently were available only in public networks of mass communications. From the 1990s onwards, integrated broadband networks for telecommunications, data communications and mass communications were added, first at the level of the organization and the larger scale of advanced or intelligent networks for research and defence institutions.

Integration of patterns

The birth of integrated networks implies a combination of allocution, consultation, registration and conversation in a single medium (Figure 1.3e). This would make such a medium important enough in social communications to enable us to speak of a communications revolution, the results of which will be the central theme of this book.

The evolution of the four information traffic patterns involves a clear shift of patterns towards local units. The new media cause a shift from allocution towards consultation, registration and conversation. The initiative and selection by local units, and the interactivity between these local units and the centre and between these local units themselves, have increased the opportunities in communications. But this does not mean that these opportunities will be taken up. That depends on the content and the context of the communication taking place. Opportunities for users can be enlarged by the combination of speech, text, data and images and by a firmer grip on the dimensions of space and time. On the other hand, they can be limited by new media management and supply. One-sided supply, limited access and increased possibilities for central control, manipulation and registration threatening privacy may just as easily result. One certainty is that these opportunities, and what is actually done with them, will cause a revolution in mediated communications, and perhaps even in all communications in our society. *For the first time in history, the new media will enable us to make a deliberate choice between mediated and face-to-face communication in a large number of social activities.* The implications of this choice will form a prime focus of this book.

COMMUNICATION CAPACITIES OF THE NEW MEDIA

In the last 25 years, a lot of research has been carried out on the opportunities and limitations of mediated communication as compared with face-to-face communication. In social-psychological experiments among small groups using different media, the modes of communication and the accomplishment of tasks have been investigated systematically. Two approaches are prevalent. The first takes the *objective* characteristics of media and channels as a point of departure. The second emphasizes the *(inter)subjective* characteristics of the use of them, mainly as a reaction to the first approach. In this book an *integrated* (objective and subjective) approach is taken to develop the concept of communication capacities. This concept is developed to answer the question of what can be done with the new media. What are their special characteristics compared with the old media? The general properties of integration and interactivity have been described in the previous section. Nine so-called communication capacities of the new media will now be introduced. First, the origin of the concept of communications capacities must be briefly explained.

The oldest social-psychological approach in this area mainly stresses the limitations of all media and channels as compared with face-to-face communication. Short et al. (1976) introduced the influential concept of **social presence**. It emphasizes the sociability, warmth, personal information and sensitivity of face-to-face communication that media are only able to transmit in a limited way. By means of these characteristics, presumed to be objective, all media and face-to-face communications produce a different experience of presence among communication partners. For example, the videophone offers more social presence than the audiophone.

An almost identical approach is the one that refers to the so-called *reduced social context cues* of the media of telecommunications and network computing (Kiesler and Sproull, 1992; Kiesler et al., 1984; Sproull and Kiesler, 1986, 1991). According to the psychologists concerned, media more or less lack the space for crucial nonverbal and contextual signs. In the somewhat further elaborated concept of **information richness**, Daft and Lengel (1984) have distinguished the following four objective characteristics of media: feedback capacity (immediate, fast, slow), channel used (audio, visual), nature of the source (personal, impersonal) and language richness (spoken, written and/or body language).

In the second half of the 1980s, this kind of classical social-psychological research was increasingly criticized. A large number of phenomena could not be explained using its objective approach. It appeared that media which are lacking in social presence and information richness, e.g. email and SMS-messaging, are frequently used for social-emotional and even erotic communications. The same phenomenon arose with phone sex and phone helplines. After a period of habituation, the quantity of informal and intimate communications in computer networks increases (Rice and Love, 1987; Walther, 1992). Eventually there arises a (sub)culture of electronic communication with new norms, language and behaviour.

Approaches to mediated communication

Objective characteristics first

**(Inter)subjective
characteristics**

In reaction to the social-psychological approaches just described, largely confining social reality to communication that is interpersonal and tied to place, a more social-cultural or sociological approach emphasizing (inter)subjective social construction processes has appeared. Fulk et al. (1987) were the first to develop a *social information processing model*. They wanted to know how the media are really used in daily practice and how humans shape them (inter)subjectively in their social information processing. This is supposed to be conditioned by the opinions about and attitudes towards media of people themselves and of others in their immediate social environment, most often colleagues at work, in the early phase of computer-mediated communications (CMC). See Fulk and Steinfield (1990) for a summary of this view.

Walther (1992; 1996) has presented a comparable approach. In his *relational perspective*, the media are used differently in relation to particular functions (tasks, goals) and contexts. According to the results of his experiments, after some time the quality of CMC approaches that of face-to-face communications. This conclusion is diametrically opposed to the claims of the social presence and reduced social context cues approaches.

The experiments of Spears and Lea (1992) support Walther's conclusion. According to their *social identity theory*, the reason for the approximate equivalence of mediated and face-to-face communication is that people take their whole social, cultural and personal identity with them as baggage into computer network communications. The smallest cue is then sufficient to compensate for the limitations of the medium, using the mental construction and imaginative power derived from this identity.

**Integrated
approach**

I have proposed an integrated approach, one that is both objective and (inter)subjective (van Dijk, 1993b). According to this view, it remains important to start the analysis with the structural, more or less objective properties of the media, old and new. Their (inter)subjective interpretation and their use in practice differ too much to allow any kind of generalization. Besides, the suggestion that media have no objective characteristics is incorrect. One event in an American computer discussion of women about intimate female affairs should be convincing enough (see Stone, 1991: 82ff.). When it transpired, after some time, that a male psychiatrist using the pseudonym 'Julie' had been taking part, the women were extremely shocked and insulted. In most other media this event just could not have happened.

So, media do have particular potentialities and limitations that cannot be removed (inter)subjectively. In this book they are called communication capacities, a concept which carries the connotation of both defining (objective) and enabling (subjective) features. Using the following nine communication capacities, we are able to compare old and new media in a systematic way: speed, reach, storage capacity, accuracy, selectivity, interactivity, stimuli richness, complexity and privacy protection. A short introduction to these capacities follows. Old and new media are compared in Table 1.1 in terms of these capacities.

The *speed* of bridging large distances in communication is one of the strongest capacities of the new media. In this respect they look like the telephone and broadcasting. Using the Internet and email, one is able to send

TABLE 1.1   Communication capacities of old and new media

Communication capacity	Old Media				New Media	
	Face-to-face	Print	Broadcasting	Telephone	Computer networks	Multimedia
Speed	Low	Low/medium	High	High	High	High
Reach (geographical)	Low	Medium	High[1]	High[1]	High[1]	Low
Reach (social)	Low	Medium	High[1]	High[1]	Low	Low
Storage capacity	Low	Medium	Medium	Low	High	High
Accuracy	Low	High	Low/medium	Low	High	High
Selectivity	Low	Low	Low	High	High	High
Interactivity	High	Low	Low	Medium	Medium	Medium
Stimuli richness	High	Low	Medium	Low	Low	Medium
Complexity	High	High	Medium	Medium	Low	Medium
Privacy protection	High	Medium	High	Medium	Low	Medium

[1] In developed countries only.

a message to the other side of the world within one minute. Face-to-face communication and print media are only able to connect quickly to proximate others.

The potential *geographical and social reach* of the new media is very large. The whole world might be connected to the converging networks of telecommunications, computer networks and broadcasting in the future. At present, every country and almost every region of the world is already linked to them, first via the telephone and the Internet. However, demographic reach lags behind as only about half the world population has ever used a telephone and only a small minority has access to the Internet.

Another strong quality of the new media is their huge *storage potential*. This potential is low in face-to-face communication, which depends on inadequate human memory. It was also low in telephony before the invention of answering devices. In digital media one can store much more than in printed media and analogue broadcast media.

The *accuracy* or exactness of the information transmitted is an important advantage of the new media as compared with the telephone and face-to-face communication. Signals in the latter media are often ambiguous. Historically, accuracy has also been an advantage of print media. The new media add the exactness of data or numbers and the informativeness of images. Both the storage capacity and the accuracy of the new media enable governments, politicians and managers to control the rising complexity of society and organizations. Without ICT, many processes would become out of control and bogged down in paperwork and bureaucracy (see p. 19 and Chapters 4 and 5).

The *selectivity* of messages and addresses is another strong capacity of the new media. This capacity is rather low in the face-to-face communication of groups and other collectives. Here individuals have to make appointments and separate themselves from each other. Much of the communication using print media is not addressed, except for personal letters of course. The same goes for broadcasting. The telephone was the first fully selective medium used to address people. The new media advance this capacity by enabling us to systematically select (parts of) groups using email lists and the like. In this way one can address very specific target groups. This is a capacity that is already used frequently in the corporate world (telemarketing) and American politics.

One refers to the new media as interactive, but actually their *interactivity* does not reach the high level that can be attained in face-to-face communication. The new media's general characteristic of interactivity described earlier has to be specified in terms of the concrete levels and types of interactive capacities to be observed in old and new media. Some new media do not offer anything more than two-way traffic and a central store-and-forward agency serving as some kind of answering device. Clearly this goes for email. In other new media like the interactive press and broadcasting, or digital information services, the user has very little control over content. The user does not (inter)act much; rather, (s)he chooses from menus and reacts. Moreover, fully fledged conversation in the new media is lacking. One is not able to exchange all the signals (often) desired. Even video conferences, which partly enable the participants to see each other, have their limitations. So-called kinaesthesis (the sense of movement) is largely absent and the sense of distance between conferencees is still present.

In terms of *stimuli richness*, no other medium is able to beat face-to-face communication. The reason is clear: all current new media are sensory poor. This is especially so for computer networks transmitting only lines of text and data. Multimedia offer a greater richness of stimuli, perhaps even an overload, in all kinds of combinations: images, sounds, data and text. However, the combination of these stimuli is not natural but artificial. Some stimuli can be strengthened while others recede, but there is still a clear lack of the movement and body language provided by someone who is close. So the most advanced kind of teleshopping will remain different from going to shop in town for a day.

As a consequence of the last two capacities described, the *complexity* that one is able to achieve collectively by using them is not high. Research indicates that one is able to make contacts, ask questions, exchange information and make appointments very well using computer networks, but it appears to be difficult to negotiate, decide, explain difficult issues and really get to know someone (see Rice, 1998).

A minus of the present design of the new media is the low capacity for *privacy protection* that they offer. Face-to-face communication can be secluded to a large degree. Current broadcasting and the press can be received anonymously. This does not apply for the new interactive broadcasting and electronic press media. In fact all usage, and often the personal characteristics of users, are registered in the new media. This is certainly the case for computer networks. For stand-alone computers and multimedia it is less so, because they are under the control of the user, but these media have internal memories which can be accessed.

THE NATURE AND DESIGN OF THIS BOOK

This book contains an outline of a large number of social aspects of the new media compiled in a particular framework. For the original first Dutch edition of this book, written at the end of the 1980s, an inventory was made of all social aspects that appeared to be relevant at that time. With every new edition the inventory was extended and reduced. At the time of writing (2005) it scarcely is possible anymore to be complete. The new media have so much merged in society that they touch about every aspect of it. So, this book is no encyclopaedia of new media social aspects. It is very comprehensive, but it does not discuss all the literature. That has been updated as compared to the first English edition, but the overview simply cannot be complete. A library full of books and articles on the topic of this book has been published in the past two decades.

Outline of social aspects

What I do attempt is to be extremely interdisciplinary in the treatment of social aspects. This is for fundamental reasons. I will explain that in the network society the so-called micro, meso and macro levels are closely connected and that many dividing lines between the fields of disciplines simply dissolve. To get a grip on the causes and consequences of the introduction and use of the new media in contemporary society one simply has to be interdisciplinary. Of course, this will provoke the comment of specialists in technology, economy, political science, law, culture and psychology that the treatment is not complete. I am prepared to take this risk for the benefit of reaching a better understanding of the whole picture.

Interdisciplinary

The outline is made against the background of a theoretical framework that has been made more explicit in this edition as compared to previous ones. This framework has found sources of inspiration in four theories of social and communication science.

Theoretical Framework

The first source of inspiration is *network theory*. This is known for decades now in social and communication science, but in the last five years it has made considerable progress. Social scientists have reached for the help of natural scientists and mathematicians in discovering the 'laws' or regularities of networks. The latest versions of network theory have made it possible to extend the framework linking the social aspects and to improve the coherence of the book. Here I defend a moderate network approach in social science. It is moderate because I not only focus on relations, but also on the characteristics of the units that are related in networks (people, groups, organizations, societies).

The second source is *(adaptive) structuration theory*. The axiom of this theory is that social structures and communicative action are mutually changing each other (structures are adapted continually). My general view of technology is that it is both defining and enabling, and that technologies and human beings are mutually shaping. These assumptions define another part of the nature of this book. Again and again both the opportunities and risks, optimistic and pessimistic views or utopian and dystopian perspectives of the new media for man, society and organization, are portrayed. The assumptions also explain why this book not only contains observation and analysis, but also policy perspectives based upon a number of explicit social values.

The third insight comes from so-called *medium theory* (inspired by Innis, Ong and Meyrowitz). This theory says that media and technologies in history are not only enabling but also defining. They have a number of objective characteristics that must have a particular influence on users in their social environments. The communication capacities elaborated above provide an example. The core argument is that media and technologies themselves are social environments. This clearly goes for media networks. The clearest case in this book is the Internet, which has become a society by itself. The growing integration of social and media networks becoming a single reality is one of the main statements in this book.

The final source of inspiration is contemporary *modernization theory*, not the one followed in the 1950s and 1960s hailing the superiority of western civilization. Current modernization theory rather observes the conflict of western and other cultures in the world (see for example Barber, 1996 and Castells, 1997, 1998). In this book, modernization theory appears in basic statements about networks linking global and local social relations and processes of scale extension and reduction in society.

Chapter division The book contains three parts. In the first part, comprising Chapters 1 to 3, basic terms and statements are explained. Chapter 1 contains the basic terms. Chapter 2 provides the most important part of the theoretical framework: network theory and an explanation of the network society concept. Chapter 3 describes the technological infrastructure of the network society. I have tried to do this in a manner that should be understandable for a non-technical readership.

The heart of the book is the exposition of the social aspects of the new media in several spheres and levels of society: the economy, politics, the law, the social infrastructure of society, culture and individuals (psychology). In this second English edition, I have added introductions and conclusions to the chapters of this second part. I hope this will improve the coherence and didactic quality of the book.

Every book I have published in this field contains policy perspectives at the end. I am not satisfied with only providing scientific analysis to my readers. I do not want them to feel helpless after they have grasped the overwhelming impact of the new media on their society. The opportunities of the new media for society can be taken and the risks can be reduced. The attention to policy perspectives is one of the features that distinguishes this book from its main competitor, the magnificent trilogy *The Information Age*, by Manuel Castells.

NETWORKS: THE NERVOUS SYSTEM OF SOCIETY

THE NETWORK SOCIETY AND OTHER CLASSIFICATIONS

Several concepts are available to indicate the type of society that evolves under the influence of the use of information and communication technology. The most popular concept is the information society. In this book that concept is used in combination with the concept network society to typify contemporary developed and modern societies marked by a high level of information exchange and use of information and communication technologies (ICTs). In the concept of an information society, the changing *substance* of activities and processes in these societies is emphasized. In the concept of a network society, attention shifts to the changing organizational *forms* and (infra)structures of these societies.

I start with my own complete definitions of these types of society and continue with a number of qualifications of these definitions and their relationships with other classifications such as capitalist society and (post-)modern society.

In an **information society** the information intensity of all activities becomes so high that this leads to:

Classifications of contemporary society

Information society definition

- an organization of society based on science, rationality and reflexivity;
- an economy with all values and sectors, even the agrarian and industrial sectors, increasingly characterized by information production;
- a labour market with a majority of functions largely or completely based on tasks of information processing requiring knowledge and higher education (hence, the alternative term *knowledge society*);
- a culture dominated by media and information products with their signs, symbols and meanings.

It is the intensity of information processing in all these spheres that allows us to describe it as a new type of society. The common denominator of the changes produced by the increasing information intensity of all activities is the semi-autonomous character of information processing. Most activities in contemporary society are dedicated to *means*, in this case means of processing and producing information. These activities tend to keep a distance from their ultimate aims and to gather their own momentum and reason to exist. Manuel

Castells (1996) even claims that information has become an independent source of productivity and power.

Network society definition

The **network society** concept emphasizes the form and organization of information processing and exchange. An infrastructure of social and media networks takes care of this. So the network society can be defined as a social formation with an infrastructure of **social and media networks** enabling its prime mode of organization at all levels (individual, group/organizational and societal). Increasingly, these networks link all units or parts of this formation (individuals, groups and organizations). In western societies, the individual linked by networks is becoming the basic unit of the network society. In eastern societies, this might still be the group (family, community, work team) linked by networks.

Mass society definition

This book compares the network society with the so-called mass society preceding it. The mass society can be defined as a social formation with an infrastructure of *groups, organizations and communities* ('masses') shaping its prime mode of organization at all levels (individual, group/organizational and societal). The basic units of this formation are all kinds of relatively large collectivities (masses) organizing individuals.

Qualifications

Later in this chapter, in the section From Mass Society to Network Society, and in the remaining chapters of this book I will elaborate the network and mass society concepts. Here I want to draw attention to a number of qualifications of the information and network society concepts. With good reasons, both concepts are contested. Webster (2001) concludes that all definitions of the information society refer to more *quantity* of information, information products, information occupations, communication means and so on, but are unable to identify the *qualitatively* new (system) character of this type of society. Manuel Castells (1996) also rejects the concept of information society as all societies in the past have been based on information. Instead, he proposes the concept of 'informational society': 'a specific form of social organization in which information generation, processing and transmission become the fundamental sources of productivity and power' (Castells, 1996: 21).

In the next section we see that all human societies since the invention of speech have been partly organized in networks. The idea of the network society as something particularly new has been called a fashionable and shallow concept with no theoretical basis. The fact that I try to improve the status does not deny that currently this statement is basically true.

Other classifications

These qualifications suggest that other classifications of contemporary society remain valid anyway. All of them are abstractions. Concrete human societies always are combinations of abstract relationships on several fields grasped with similar abstract concepts. From an economic point of view, almost every contemporary society is capitalist. The one type is called developed, the other developing. In political terms, a society is more or less democratic. Government might be called 'statist' as in the few remaining communist countries, a 'developmental state' such as in most East Asian countries, a welfare state such as in most European countries and a (neo)liberal state serving a market economy such as the United States. From a social and cultural perspective, present-day societies may be called modern, post-modern and late-modern, whatever term one prefers, or traditional. In ecological terms, contemporary societies may be more or less sustainable.

In this book the general classifications of information and network society will be related to these other classifications. For example, in Chapter 4 we will see that a network economy changes capitalism, in Chapter 5 it will be argued that a network state and digital democracy are able to alter government and in Chapter 7 and 8 that networks such as the Internet transform social living and culture in (post-)modern society. In several parts of the book it will be questioned whether ICT favours or harms a sustainable society.

A final qualification to add is that the information and network society concepts indicate long-term evolutionary processes of human society. They are not concrete societal forms with precise historical beginnings and ends. To clarify this one might say that the information society did not start in 1751 with the appearance of the first part of the *Encyclopédie* of Diderot and d'Alembert and the network society did not appear with the installation of the first telegraph line by Samuel Morse in 1844. In the 19th century, after the industrial revolution, modernizing western societies gradually became information societies (Beniger, 1986). In the twentieth century, their social structure, modes of organization and communication infrastructure together typifying a mass society progressively changed into a network society (Castells, 1996; Mulgan, 1991; van Dijk, 1991, 1993a). So, contemporary societies are in the process of becoming information and network societies. Developed, high-tech societies have gone further down this road than developing societies that still are in the stage of being mass societies. However, the history of human networking is much older than the last two centuries.

Long-term evolutions

A SHORT HISTORY OF THE HUMAN WEB

Social networks are as old as humanity. Human individuals have always communicated more with some people than with others since the time they lived in small bands and tribes. The bands and tribes of ancient human history consisted of a few dozen (bands) to hundreds (tribes) of people. This number was big enough to have people maintain very intensive relations with some members (direct family and kin) and less intensive relations with other members of the band or tribe. The obvious biological necessity was a scale of coupling and mating that prevented inbreeding.

According to the historians J.R. and W. McNeill (2003) the human web dates at least to the development of human speech. 'Our distant ancestors created social solidarity within small bands by talking together, and exchanging information and goods. Furthermore, bands interacted and communicated with one another, if only sporadically' (2003: 4). Their 'bird's eye view of world history' as a series of expanding and thickening webs, published in their brilliant book *The Human Web* (2003), is this section's guide.

Networks in ancient history

The McNeills portray world history as a succession of five worldwide webs. The extension of these webs was not only driven by biological necessity, but also by the need and desire to make new discoveries and material conquests to improve the conditions of life. In these webs, not only speech and information in general were exchanged, but also goods, technologies, ideas, crops, weeds, animals and diseases.

In the *first worldwide web*, human kind spread around the world in hunting and gathering tribes. The exchange of ideas and cultural expressions (song and dance), technologies (bows and arrows, the control of fire) and genes (exogamous marriages between members of different bands and tribes) swept across Africa, Asia, and Europe and into the Americas and Oceania. This first human web remained very loose until the invention of agriculture about 12 000 years ago. Settling enabled humans to sustain more continuous interactions among a larger number of people at a local level.

About 6000 years ago the local webs of settlements grew into *metropolitan or city webs*. They served as storehouses of information, goods and infections. In this way, the first civilizations of Mesopotamia, Egypt, the Indus, the Yellow River (China), Mexico and the Andes were created. These civilizations first established connections among thousands and then among millions of people. This was the first time in history that those connected actually remained strangers for each other. 'For the first time, key relationships and important everyday transactions routinely transcended the primary communities within which human beings had previously lived' (McNeill and McNeill, 2003: 41). These civilizations were connected by caravans of transport animals across land and by ships along sea coasts and rivers.

The third human web was the *Old World Web* that grew out of the contact between and partial fusion of civilizations in Eurasia and North Africa about 2000 years ago. It meant the rise of large bureaucratic empires in India, China, the Mediterranean (Greece and Rome), Mexico and the Andes. Transport and communication improved considerably with the invention and spread of hub and spoke wheels, better roads, ships with higher capacity and alphabetic writing. The first tensions in the worldwide web appeared as epidemics spread, religions clashed and different civilizations and their rural hinterlands not only borrowed ideas, habits and customs from each other, but also rejected them, defending their own.

From about 1450 onwards, oceanic navigation brought the Eurasian and American civilizations into contact with each other to produce a truly worldwide *cosmopolitan web*. It was a violent clash of European civilizations overruling the native American ones. The result was an exchange of everything these civilizations had to offer, including lethal diseases. Between 1450 and 1800 more and more people moved to cities and became enrolled in larger and larger social networks. The result was that information circulated faster and more cheaply than ever before. However, the majority of people in 1800 still lived on the land as farmers: 'they knew little about the world beyond their own experience, because they could not read and they only occasionally met strangers' (McNeill and McNeill, 2003: 212).

The fifth type of human web changed this last point: the *global web* that covers the last 160 years. This period is characterized by urbanization and population growth. The human web was not so much widening anymore, but thickening. The volume and velocity of communication increased markedly. The number and use of new means of transport and communication exploded with trains, automobiles and aeroplanes, together with telegraphs, telephones, radios, televisions and, finally, computers and networks.

In this book, the first period of this era of the global web is characterized as the mass society marked by mass communication networks. In the second period, the network society evolves. With the thickening of the global human web, it has turned inwards into society. It is no longer only quantitatively extending across the globe and becoming more voluminous, but it is also qualitatively changing the infrastructure and working of current societies. This comes to rest upon social and media networks of all kinds and at all levels of society.

Before I explain the role of networks and the characteristics of the network society in detail, I want to focus on the four important conclusions the McNeills have drawn from the history of the human web (McNeill and McNeill, 2003: 5–8). The first conclusion is that all webs have combined cooperation and competition. Communication sustains cooperation among people. Within a cooperative framework, specialization and division of labour are able to make a society richer and more powerful. They also make it more stratified and unequal. This inequality within society, together with the inequalities between societies, has always produced competition. Rivals share information too. It urges them to respond, for instance by cooperation with others.

Conclusions network history

The second conclusion is that the general direction of history has been toward greater social cooperation — both voluntary and compelled – driven by the realities of social competition. Groups and societies who cooperated most improved their competitive position and chances of survival. It gave them economic advantage (by the specialization of labour and exchange), military advantage (quantity and quality of warriors and the organization of armies) and epidemiological advantage (building immunities against diseases by close contact).

A third deduction from history is that, over time, the scale of human webs has tended to grow. So too has their influence on history. The current global web is truly worldwide. Practically no human society exists in isolation any more. The volume, velocity and importance of messages exchanged has become so large that their impact on contemporary society is incomparable to the effect of communication systems in ancient societies. This impact is a major reason for the emphasis of the network society concept in this book.

Finally, it has to be concluded that the power of human communication, both in its cooperative and competitive forms, has also affected the earth to an ever larger degree. Increasingly, economic and population growth, urbanization and technology have produced an ecological impact. 'We would not be 6 billion strong without the myriad of interconnections, the flows and exchanges of food, energy, technology, money that comprise the modern worldwide web' (2003: 7).

Definition of a network

What actually is a network? This question comes to mind after this broad description of networks in human history. After all, the concept appears in both natural and social sciences. Unfortunately, the following definition and account has to be rather abstract, but a precise definition and elaboration of the network concept here will enable better future understanding. A network can be defined as *a collection of links between elements of a unit*. The elements are called nodes. Units are often called systems. The smallest number of elements is three and the smallest number of links is two. A single link of two elements is called a relation(ship). Networks are a mode of organization of complex systems in nature and society.

In simple systems of nature and society, a static and hierarchical organization characterizes the relation of elements. For example, the relation between the elements or parts of atoms, molecules and chemical substances is fixed and has a particular order. Change means a transition to another (kind of) unit. When matter gets more complicated, especially when it becomes life, the elements have to be organized in more complicated ways. Life organizes these ways while it exchanges energy with the environment and adapts to this environment for survival. Networks are relatively complicated ways of organizing matter and living systems. They produce order out of chaos linking elements in a particular way. Chaotic situations always appear as soon as the elements of matter and living systems become less fixed.

Emphasizing the organization and the relation of elements entails less attention to the elements and units themselves. The characteristics of units and elements, among them human individuals, and the way they are made up, are not the focus of attention. Instead every network approach in the natural and social sciences stresses the relations of elements. It is opposed to atomistic views of reality and methodological individualism in research (measuring social reality by adding individual attributes).

Occurrence of networks in nature and society

So, networks occur both in complicated matter and in living systems at all levels (see Table 2.1). Buchanan (2002) mentions a couple of examples of physical networks. The first one is an ecosystem of earth surfaces, flora and fauna and the second one a river network organizing its downward water flow in branches adapting to the ground and all kinds of obstacles. Examples become more numerous in living systems. All organisms with many cells organize these cells in networks. When they become larger they create special (network) systems such as a nervous system and a blood stream. As a matter of fact, cells themselves contain networks. The most important one is the DNA string of genes (molecules). Nowadays it is common scientific understanding that the complexity of life is not determined by the number of genes but by their relationships.

The largest nervous system of organisms on earth is to be found in the human brain. An increasing number of neurobiologists and psychologists agree that the human mind works with neuronal networks that are organized on a higher level in mental 'maps' in particular regions of the brain. The

TABLE 2.1   Types of network

Physical networks	Natural systems of higher complexity: ecosystems, river networks
Organic networks	Organisms: nervous system, blood circulation, strings of DNA in cells
Neuronal networks	Mental systems: neuronal connections, mental maps
Social networks	Social systems with concrete ties in abstract relationships
Technical networks	Technical systems: roads, distribution networks, telecommunication and computer networks etc.
Media networks	Media systems connecting senders and receivers and filled with symbols and information

connection between these maps (themselves being neuronal networks) also reveals a network form. Gerald Edelman, one of the best known of these neurobiologists, argues that even human consciousness emerges from such connections of mental maps (Edelman and Tononi, 2000).

Human beings have created social networks at least since the invention of speech, as was explained in the previous section. In these networks, the elements are social agents (individuals, groups, organizations and even societies at large) and the links are created by communicative (inter)actions. Below I argue that social networks figure at all levels and subsystems of society. In the course of history, humans also have created a number of technical networks. Examples are roads, canals, all kinds of distribution networks and the telecommunication and computer networks that are an important subject matter in this book. When the latter networks are filled with symbols and information to connect human senders and receivers, they become media networks.

This book is about the relationship between social, technical and media networks. Together they shape the infrastructure of the network society. Even organic and neuronal networks receive some attention, for instance in Chapter 9, which discusses the psychology of new media use. However, the primary focus of attention is social networks supported by media networks.

Social networks supported by media networks are available at all levels and subsystems of society. Four levels can be distinguished. They are portrayed in Figure 2.1, which shows the first picture of the abstract concept of the network society in this book.

Networks at all social levels

The first and most basic level is the level of *individual relations*, not that of the individual because units and elements are not the prime focus of attention in a network perspective but relations (Brass, 1995; Wellman and Berkowitz, 1988). This level corresponds to the common sense meaning of (social) networking: individuals creating ties to family members, friends, acquaintances, neighbours, colleagues, fellow sportsmen, and so on. Currently, this level is supported and intensified by the rise of the media networks of the Internet (email) and mobile or fixed telephony.

The second level is that of *group and organizational relations*. Individuals create all kinds of groupings or collective agencies, some of them temporary and loose (such as project teams and mailing lists) and others permanent and fixed (institutions and corporations). All contemporary groupings are

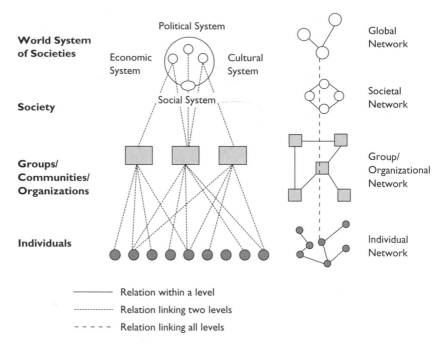

FIGURE 2.1   Four social units and levels linked by networks

supported by telecommunications and computer networks. They tend to loosen fixed group and organizational structures because they enable virtual organizing at every scale. Internally, many organizations have become network organizations of largely independent teams and projects. Externally, they assemble to form network organizations cooperating in the execution of a particular task. They may even become virtual organizations that are more or less independent from spatial, temporal and physical conditions as these conditions are substituted by networks of information and communication technology.

The third is the level of *societal relations*. Individuals, groups and organizations shape a society that is built on, and linked by, social and media networks. This goes for all subsystems of society. One increasingly uses the phrase 'network(ed) economy', which is sometimes called a 'new economy'. In politics, some people talk about a 'network state'. Internally, this state links the bodies and institutions of the government and the public administration at every level. Externally, it maintains strong relationships with organizations of citizens and with semi-autonomous or privatized public institutions (Castells, 1997; Fountain, 2001; Guéhenno, 1993; van Dijk, 2000a; Goldsmith and Eggers, 2004). In the cultural sphere, the Internet has created a vast hyperlink structure of sources and artefacts of human activity (de Kerckhove, 1998). Finally, the societal infrastructure of interpersonal and group relationships has been intensified by the ever-stronger links between social networks and telecommunication networks using email and mobile or fixed telephony (Katz and Rice, 2002; Wellman, 2001; Wellman and Haythornthwaite, 2002).

The final level is the level of *global relations* in the world system of societies and international organizations (Slaughter, 2004; Urry, 2003). We have entered the era of the global web as it was explained in the previous section. This is created by expanding international relations and a scale extension of organization. Both are strongly supported by international broadcasting, telecommunications and computer networking.

It is vital for the understanding of the network society to analyse it in terms of levels of networking. In their helpful overview of contemporary *Theories of Communication Networks* (2003), Monge and Contractor have made a strong argument for multilevel theories of networks. The word theory is used in the plural as they also defend a combination of theories to explain phenomena at the different levels distinguished. An important part of their argument is that the levels are linked themselves. They build their own theory relating statements at the level of the individual, the dyad, tryad, group, organization and at the interorganizational level.

Multilevel theory of networks

Previously, I also advocated a multilevel theory of the network society (van Dijk, 2001). This advocacy did not only lean on the historical rise of media networks that are used at every level, but also on basic views on the composition and (infra)structure of society. Such a basic view is developed in Kontopoulos' methodological and conceptual book *The Logics of Social Structure* (1993). According to him, the world must be analysed as a level structure. 'Levels are not juxtaposed layers; every level is rooted to lower levels, down to the chemical and physical ones. Therefore, same-level or intralevel analysis must be supplemented and enriched by cross-level or inter-level analysis' (1993: 63). At every level, particular properties emerge that only apply to that level (the individual, group, organization, society, world system). Examples of such properties are the personality of an individual, the measure of formality of a group, the extent of centralization of an organization and the phase of development of a society.

In this book about the network society, such a basic view is needed to explain the character of networks as a particular mode of social organization. Kontopoulos makes a distinction between hierarchical and heterarchical modes of organization of the world. Networks clearly belong to the last mode. In a hierarchical mode, the lower levels are fully included in the higher levels. The units at these levels are simply aggregated to form units at a higher level. Individuals add to groups and organizations and both add to society. A second property of the hierarchical mode is that the lower levels are superseded by the higher ones. This might mean that the higher level controls the lower one. This is the common meaning of the term hierarchy.

In a heterarchical mode of organization, the lower levels are only partially included in the higher levels. The units concerned contain relations and structures that overlap with those at higher levels. Networks belong to these relations and structures. They cut right through all levels, and they connect these levels (see Figure 2.1 again). Networks realize complex interactions within and between levels. In this way, they increase the flexibility of organization.

In terms of determination, the heterarchical mode means that neither the higher nor the lower levels are in control. Instead, a very complicated picture appears of determination from below, determination from above and determination at the semi-autonomous level in focus itself (1993: 55).

Examples of this cutting through all levels of networks are individuals who pass the borders of the units they belong to (families, groups, departments, organizations) to establish links with other individuals in groups, organizations and societies they do not belong to, in this way creating their own structures. The same goes for organizations passing the borders of their societies or nation states.

The use of telecommunication and computer networks strongly supports these practices. They also link the types and levels of interpersonal, organizational and mass communication. For the first time in history we have a medium, called the Internet, directly linking them simultaneously. Telephones, letters, documents, computer files and meetings served interpersonal and organizational communication, and mass communication was realized by broadcasting and the press. However, with the Internet, this traditional split has dissolved, as it is used for communication at all levels.

A moderate network approach   So, networks organize relations within and between levels or units of social reality. As has been argued before, every network approach stresses the importance of the relations as compared to the units that are linked. The traditional network approach defends this position in a radical way. It gives priority to forms instead of substances. The social network analysis following this approach emphasizes the morphology of ties and nodes to such an extent that it downplays the attributes of the social units and what happens inside or between them, that is, the communicative action of people who are using and creating rules, resources and meanings. In this book, I reject this formalistic and superficial approach. Instead, I defend a moderate notion of a network approach. This means that, first, not only are relations stressed, but also the characteristics of the units they link. The most interesting things occur when relations and the characteristics of units come into conflict. This happens, for example, when the new digital communication networks, with relations transcending space and time in the global 24-hour economy, collide with the limitations of the biological human organism (unit), with its daily rhythms and routines or needs for rest that cannot fulfil the expectations of the technology and economy concerned.

A second qualification of the radical network approach is that, in this book, networks are not supposed to be the basic units of contemporary society as they are in the view of Manuel Castells (1996, 2000, 2001). Instead, these basic units are held to be individuals, households, groups and organizations *increasingly linked by social and media networks*. In modern western societies, the individual is becoming the most important basic unit of society. In others, this frequently is the family, kinship group or local community. The combination of social and media networks produced by both organizational and technological innovation forms the all-embracing network structure of modern societies. This combination justifies the use of the strong metaphor of networks shaping the nervous system of advanced high-tech societies.

CAUSES OF THE RISE OF NETWORKS

What are the causes of the rise of networks in contemporary societies? It is relatively easy to describe a number of historical and social reasons. It is far more difficult to uncover the basic social infrastructures and modes of organization of societies explaining the rise of network structures. Let us start with the historical and social reasons. The McNeills would explain the current rise of information and communication networks as the last stage of the evolution of the global web. This web is no longer primarily widening, but it is thickening. Ever more persons, animals, plants, diseases, goods, services, pieces of information, messages, new ideas and innovations are exchanged globally and at ever faster rates.

Social explanations will emphasize the social need and appropriateness of the creation and use of networks at all levels. At the *individual* level we are witnessing the rise of networking as an explicit and increasingly systematic method of making contacts and improving social relations. Below, the concept of network individualization is used to describe this phenomenon. The use of networking is an evident social need in an individualizing society. Networks can be seen as the social counterparts of individualization. At the level of *organizations*, corporations and institutions are no longer working alone. They have become a part of a comprehensive division of labour. Increasingly, this division is organized in networks of cooperating organizations. Moreover, organizations have to open themselves more and more to their environment to survive in competition (business) and societal demand (government and non-profit organizations). Traditional internal structures of organizations are crumbling and external structures of communication are added to them. Acquiring new combinations of internal and external communication they are better equipped to adapt to a swiftly changing environment.

Networks also cause a comprehensive restructuring of *society at large*. They are breaking old modes of organization as they help organizations in their search for new scale levels, new markets and new ways to govern and control. Networks link the processes of scale extension and scale reduction occurring simultaneously in modern society. At the one side they support globalization and socialization and at the other side localization and individualization. In this way, they have accelerated modernization (Barber, 1996; Castells, 1996; van Dijk, 1993a).

All of these historical and social explanations are valid, but they fail to answer the question of why networks are built to satisfy these social needs. What is the presumed superior organizational quality of networks and networking? To answer these questions we have to dig deeper and consult network theory, a theory that has made considerable progress in the last five years. Unfortunately, this means that the exposition has to become fairly abstract again.

Networks are structures and they organize systems. Network theory is usually some kind of structural theory and systems theory. The most general one is systems theory. In terms of this theory a network can be defined as

Historical and social causes

Systems causes: Adaptation and evolution

a relatively open system linking at least three relatively closed systems. The relatively closed system is the unit. As we have seen, we need at least three of them to create a network. These units can be conceived as relatively closed systems because they contain elements that primarily act among themselves to reproduce the unit in a (pre)determined way. As soon as these closed units are forced, for one reason or another, to interact with their environment and to link themselves to other units in a network, they create an open system. In an open system, complete determination is lost and replaced by chance and random events. That allows change and new opportunities. This process of opening up closed systems is the secret of networks or networking as an organization principle.

This propensity of change is explained differently by two versions of systems theory that have inspired network theory. The first version has a biological inspiration and the second a physicist and mathematical inspiration. According to the biological inspiration, systems are conceived as organisms that have to adapt to a physical environment to survive (among others, Maturana and Varela, 1980, 1984; Prigogine and Stengers, 1984). This is the propensity of change here. In this reading, networks can be seen as adaptive systems. Our brain is a complex adaptive system. The same goes for our bodies. Increasingly our organizations and societies also are complex adaptive systems. All of them are relatively closed. However, they have to adapt to an ever more complex environment. Here they get the assistance of networks as relatively open systems. According to Axelrod and Cohen (1999), adaptation occurs in three successive processes they derive from evolution (systems) theory: variation, interaction and selection. However, I think the right order in this theory is interaction, variation, selection and retention and I will treat them in this order.

First there is interaction. Networks support interactions within and between system units. For example, inside organizations they help to break through the divisions of departments to enable the communication of more members than before in shifting teams and projects. This offers them opportunities for changing and (self-)steering the organization. Between organizations, networks, particularly telecommunication and computer networks, are reducing the limits of time and place that were formerly keeping their members' communicative (inter)actions apart.

Increasing or intensifying interaction leads to more variation. First of all, there is variation of scope as the reach of information retrieval and communication is enlarged by new network connections. Every one engaged in networking will recognize this idea: one has to break out of one's own small circle of people to obtain experiences and contacts outside, even when they are very superficial. Granovetter (1973) called this idea the strength of weak ties. Accepting the value of weak ties, one should not deny the importance of strong ties. Variation also reaches into depth. Our own familiar environment offers opportunities of interaction and information by means of intensive ties and high-quality communication. It is the combination of variation in scope and in depth that makes networks strong as relatively open systems emerging from relatively closed systems, but always remaining linked to them.

A person engaged in networking is not a roaming nomad, but someone who keeps a home base.

The final process is selection. Here the goal of networking is reached: choosing the most successful actions and actors. This serves the adaptation and survival of the particular system concerned: retention. For example, an unemployed individual gets a job, a company finds the best chain of suppliers and customers and a society adopts a particular policy, organization and provision to uphold itself in the process of globalization.

The second version of systems theory reveals a mathematical and physicist inspiration. Here systems are conceived as units, both in nature and in society, containing elements that can be connected in ordered (clustered) and disordered (random) ways. Here the propensity to change is the tendency of nature to produce order out of chaos. For ages now, networks have been studied as mathematical objects called graphs. Graphs depict the potential links between a collection of elements in a particular unit. A social-scientific application is the discovery by the psychologist Stanley Milgram (1967) that on average every inhabitant (element) of a given unit, in this case the United States, is linked by six intermediary persons, in the so-called *six degrees of separation*, to every other inhabitant. This peculiar fact can only be explained by the other fact that groups of people are closely linked and organized in clusters. These clusters are often linked by so-called weak ties, a phenomenon described by the sociologist Granovetter (see above). In the tradition of Milgram and Granovetter, a number of mathematicians and physicists have made their way to social science to produce important discoveries in network theory that will be represented in the sections and chapters that follow (Barabási, 2002; Barabási & Albert, 1999; Buchanan, 2002; Watts, 2003; Watts and Strogatz, 1998).

Systems causes: From chaos to order (complexity)

This version of network and systems theory tries to explain how randomly distributed elements of a unit or system link to each other in clusters and these clusters in a single whole (a particular order). In this way, a complex system is created, in this case a complex society that is highly adaptable to environmental change. The question remains how order appears in a system without a pre-existing centre but with a number of interacting equals. The answer is connectivity: at a critical point, a phase transition in the system, 'all parts of the system act *as if* they can communicate with each other, despite their interactions being purely local' (Watts, 2003: 63). This critical point appears as a sufficient number of (random) long-distance links connects a large number of local individual units ordered in all kinds of clusters (groups, communities, organizations). In this way a so-called *small world* is created within a large-scale or global environment. These small worlds have internal links and reveal order because two elements that are connected to a common third element are more likely to establish a link to each other than two elements picked at random. You will more easily get acquainted with the friend of your friend than with a stranger. Figure 2.2 portrays a network connecting a number of small worlds (clusters with strong ties) with long-distance (weak)ties.

Social and media networks in contemporary society increasingly create small worlds and clusters in such a way that any pair of individuals or

FIGURE 2.2   Picture of a network connecting small worlds (Clusters)

organizations can be connected via a short chain of intermediaries. This leads to statements, almost platitudes in the mean time, that we live in a connected world and that society is ever more connected. In short, that it is becoming a network society.

FROM MASS SOCIETY TO NETWORK SOCIETY

Comparison   Now we are ready to understand the main characteristics of the network society as compared to that of the mass society. This comparison is made in Table 2.2. It will serve as a summary of the argument in this section and an introduction to the following chapters where the network society is described in detail.

The mass society was defined earlier in this chapter as a social formation with an infrastructure of groups, organizations and communities ('masses') that shapes its prime mode of organization at all levels. The main components of this formation are all kinds of relatively large collectivities. Historically, the mass society characterizes the first phase of the era of the global web as it is called by the McNeills (2003). This society evolved during the industrial revolution when large concentrations of people came together in industrial towns and trading centres. Typical of these concentrations was that the traditional communities already existing in neighbourhoods and villages were largely maintained when they were combined on a larger scale in cities and nations.

TABLE 2.2   A typology of the mass society and the network society

Characteristics	Mass Society	Network Society
Main components	Collectivities (Groups, Organizations, Communities)	Individuals (linked by networks)
Nature of components	Homogeneous	Heterogeneous
Scale	Extended	Extended and Reduced
Scope	Local	'Glocal' (global and local)
Connectivity and Connectedness	High within components	High between components
Density	High	Lower
Centralization	High (few centres)	Lower (polycentric)
Inclusiveness	High	Lower
Type of community	Physical and unitary	Virtual and diverse
Type of organization	Bureaucracy Vertically integrated	Infocracy Horizontally differentiated
Type of household	Large with extended family	Small with diversity of family relations
Main type of communication	Face-to-face	Increasingly mediated
Kind of media	Broadcast mass media	Narrowcast interactive media
Number of media	Low	High

The basic components of mass society are large households and extended families in the rather tight communities of a village or a city neighbourhood. In large companies, other mass associations appear, such as closely cooperating shifts and departments. The basic components or units of the mass society are homogeneous. This does not mean that internal conflict or opposition is absent, but that all units concerned largely reveal the same characteristics and social structures. For example, the large households consist of standard nuclear families with a mother, father and many children. Local communities also are relatively homogeneous or unitary and they are marked by physical proximity.

The mass society is marked by scale extension. Corporations, governments and other organizations grow larger and larger and they become bureaucracies. They spread across nations and the world at large to create a global web of 19th-century empires and multinationals. However, the scope of the mass society remains local: the organization of its basic components is tied to particular places and communication is still overwhelmingly local. The mass society is an assembly and connection of relatively homogeneous separate local places.

These basic components or units of the mass society are marked by the physical co-presence of their members. This means high connectivity inside and relatively low connectivity outside. The mass society is very much clustered with strong ties of high density (in local communities and extended family structures) and it contains relatively few weak ties connecting these clusters at long distances in diffuse network structures.

The internal relations in the units of the mass society are centralized. Bureaucratic and vertically integrated modes of organization prevail. There

Mass society characteristics

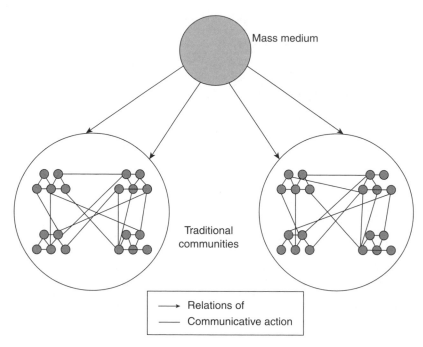

FIGURE 2.3   The structure of mass society

are relatively few very influential centres: the national, regional and local state, the army, a number of large corporations, churches or other cultural institutions and a limited number of mass media. The complement of centralization is that the inclusiveness of relations is high as well. The number of connected members is high and few of them are isolated or excluded. The mass society is marked more by solidarity than the network society.

In the mass society, every unit (community, household) has access to only one or perhaps a few of each type of mass media, such as one local newspaper, followed by one national newspaper and one or a few radio and television channels. So, the number of media is relatively low as compared to the current standards in network societies. Essentially, they are all broadcast media. However, generally speaking, face-to-face communication is much more important than mediated communication in the mass society.

In Figure 2.3 an attempt is made to depict the social and communicative structure of the mass society.

In the course of the 20th century, the structures of the mass society were gradually replaced by the structures of the network society. This happened first of all in developed or modern societies. The reasons for this replacement will be discussed in the following chapters, as they derive from problems of organization and communication in the economic, political and cultural systems and the general social infrastructure of these societies. The characteristics of the network society are described below in order to compare them with the mass society.

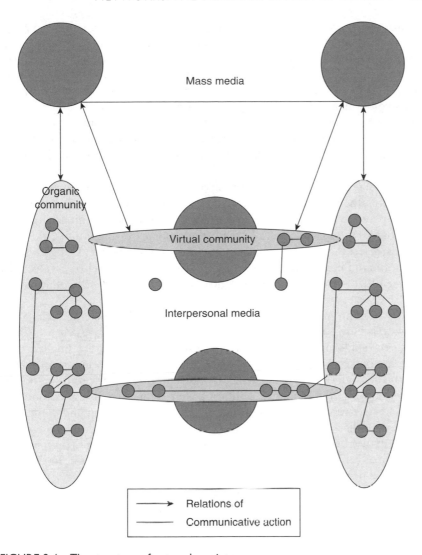

FIGURE 2.4   The structure of network society

As has been argued above, in the contemporary process of individualization, **Network** the basic unit of the network society has become the individual who is **society** linked by networks. Traditional local collectivities such as communities, **characteristics** extended families and large bureaucracies are fragmenting. This is caused by simultaneous scale extension (nationalization and internationalization) and scale reduction (smaller living and working environments). Other kinds of communities arise, consisting of people who on the one hand continue to live and work in their own families, neighbourhoods and organizations, but on the other hand frequently move around in large-scale social networks that are much more diffuse than the traditional ones. Daily living and working environments are getting smaller and more heterogeneous, while the range of the division of labour, interpersonal communications and mass media extends. So, the scale of the network society is both extended and reduced as compared to the mass society. The scope of the network society also is both global and local, sometimes indicated as 'glocal'. The organization of its components (individuals, groups, organizations) is no longer tied to particular times and places. Aided by information and communication technology, these coordinates of existence can be transcended to create virtual times and places and to simultaneously act, perceive and think in global and local terms.

The social units of the network society are fragmented and dispersed. This means that the density of contacts and ties *within* these units is relatively low as compared to traditional families, neighbourhoods, communities and organizations in the mass society. Instead, the elements of these units, the individuals, select their own contacts and ties *beyond* these units. Using all kinds of telecommunication they develop an extremely high level of connectivity between themselves as individuals and accordingly between the units of the network society of which they are a part.

Networks are relatively flat and horizontal, so-called heterarchical social structures. However, this does not mean that they do not have centres. Think about the spider in the web. Networks usually do not have a single centre. They are polycentric, as some nodes are (much) more important than others. For this reason, the network society is less centralized in the sense of having single centres in the economy, politics, government, culture and community life. They are replaced by a multitude of centres cooperating and competing with each other.

The network society is less inclusive than the mass society. You may be a member of some part of the mass society by birth or ascription. In the individualized network society you have to fight for a particular place. You have to show your value for every network. Otherwise you will be isolated in, or even excluded from, the network. In the network society, you have to stand firm as an individual. You are not that easily taken along in solidarity by proximate people.

In the network society, face-to-face communication remains the most important kind of communication in many ways. However, gradually it is also partly replaced and supplemented by mediated communication. A multitude of interpersonal and mass communication media are used for this purpose. Broadcast mass media reaching everyone are accompanied by, and partly replaced by, narrowcast interactive media reaching selected audiences. They lead to all kinds of new communication forms and groupings between interpersonal and mass communications, such as chat and instant messaging groups, virtual teams at work and virtual communities of interest. Virtual communities add to the thinned out physical communities of the network society with their small and diversely composed households. Figure 2.4 represents the complicated social and communicative structure of the network society.

CHANGING RELATIONS IN THE NETWORK SOCIETY

The advent of another structure of a society implies that the relations between its parts are changing. In the network society, both abstract relations and concrete ties between individuals, groups and organizations are transformed. By means of a summary of a large part of the argument in the chapters that follow, I now list ten perceivable trends as changes in these relations. I note that they have both technological and social causes and that they are backed by both media networks and social networks.

Often these changes run against popular views about social and media networks. For instance, one popular view is that networks are not a hierarchic but a 'flat' mode of organization. Most often, horizontal and flexible networks are opposed to vertical and ponderous columns of organizations. Some people even suggest that networks are democratic by nature. Or they suppose that they are more transparent than the institutions they partly replace. Another popular view is that networks are open and accessible to all, contrary to fixed and closed organizations with their memberships. A less positive popular connotation is that networks are breaking the social cohesion of modern societies. They cut right through existing institutions and everyone appears to communicate alongside each other in their own subcultural network. A final popular view is that computer networks are no longer tied to place, time and physical conditions and that they are offering us more freedom in this way. In this book, it is argued that these popular views are one-sided, to say the least. Networks are not necessarily more 'flat', democratic, open, free, accessible, physically unconditional or less socially coherent than other modes of organization and communication.

Popular, but wrong views of networks

The first, and most important trend is that in the network society the relations themselves are getting more important at the expense of the elements or units they are linking. I call this the articulated relation. Relations float to the surface in every subsystem of society. They are realized by a combination of social and media networks. Their effect substantially changes the economy, politics, government, culture and daily life.

Articulated relations

In Chapter 4, we will see that a network economy is created that is sometimes called a 'new economy'. The network relationships between producers in this economy are marked by a combination of cooperation and competition. This may fundamentally change the market as the prime medium of the economy. Anyway, networks in the economy are transforming the relationship between supply and demand. In Chapter 5, it will be observed that institutional politics and public administrations transfer power to other units directly getting into touch with each other via networks: transnational corporations, international bodies, nongovernmental organizations (NGOs), local corporations, individual citizens and their social and political organizations. In this way, the national state may be bypassed as the traditional centre of politics. Reacting to this shift of power, the state itself transforms into a 'network state' linking increasingly independent and privatized government agencies. In Chapter 6, we will find out that our current law system based on the notion of independent actors, acts and property items is undermined by networks. In Chapter 7, it will be established that we increasingly select and compose our own social relationships as a matter of network individualization. These relationships are less and less imposed by the social environment. Finally, in Chapter 8, we will observe the rise of a digital culture of hyper-linked creations that will completely transform our current reality of separate creations and media practices.

Substantial relations
A second trend is that, despite their articulation, all social relations in the network society remain inextricably bound up with units and physical environments. I call this the substantial relation. The trend is increasing tension between the rise of networks and the characteristics of units and environments that are relatively fixed and tied to particular places, times and physical conditions. Repeatedly, we will notice contradictions between properties of networks, such as their global scale and flexibility, and the properties of the humans of flesh and blood they are connecting, those poor creatures that are stuck to the biological needs of their bodies and the limits of mobility. For the understanding of this book, it is extremely important to bear in mind my notion of networks as forms and substances relating units or elements with particular attributes (see above). The traditional network approach tends to remove these attributes and the substance of relationships, such as the rules and resources entailed in communicative action, from the formal characteristics of networks as the quantity and quality of ties and media connections.

Direct relations
In the network society, individuals, groups and organizations are linked in increasingly direct relations, even across large distances. In the 1960s, Milgram estimated that on average Americans are only six intermediary steps separated from each other (1967). It is presumed that the six degrees of separation also hold worldwide; see Watts (2003). In the meantime, this number might have become smaller for several reasons. First, mobility and connectivity, both across large and small distances have increased substantially since the 1960s. Second, intermediary steps can be omitted, as ever more mass media and mailing lists are used to reach people simultaneously (the Milgram experiment organized a step-by-step individual procedure). Third, the use of the telephone and the Internet has considerably enlarged the number of direct relationships. The connections they offer are ever more short themselves. Albert et al. (1999) observed that the distance between one web site to another appeared to be only 19 clicks away on average in 1999. The explosive rise of the number of sites does not result in an equally fast increase in the number of links and degrees of separation. Just like people, sites and their pages are clustered.

The rise of connectivity in the network society has both social and technological reasons. The social reason is the scale extension of social relations in modern society with an increasing number of weak and strong ties across large distances. The technological reasons are the improvement of transport, the growth of the number and reach of mass media and the explosion of the use of telephony and email. The main consequence of these increasingly direct relations is the creation of a connected world that may become more organized, united and coherent in principle.

The fourth trend of the network society is that its relations are ever more realized by a combination of social and media networks. Fifteen years ago, the common opinion was that online activities would *replace* meetings. Those were the days of the electronic cottage as the perspective of future social life. Afterwards it was discovered that online communication *adds to* offline and face-to-face communication. Now the opinion is growing that both kinds of communication should not be separated and that they will be *combined* more and more. Chapters 7 through 9 will show that the future is to social and media networks that are linked and continually switching face-to-face and mediated communication. Probably this will be realized even more in mobile contexts than in electronic homes and places of work, study or leisure.

Online and offline relations linked

The combination of social and media networks will create a very strong new infrastructure of our society. Therefore, I am less afraid than most observers of a fragmentation of its public sphere by an increasing number of subcultures that communicate completely separately from each other in using the new media. In Chapter 8, it will be argued that the public sphere will become a *mosaic* of partly overlapping spheres that will keep common denominators.

The use of media to inform and to communicate in society and to realize social relationships is not without risk. Every medium has its own weight and properties such as communication capacities. The combination of social and media networks causes the media to become social environments themselves (Meyrowitz, 1985). Moreover, they are becoming important institutions of society with their own interests. Increasingly, mass media, the Internet included, are referring to themselves, discussing their own role in society and their own programmes or stars, and circulating information among themselves. This means that the relations of communication they realize and support tend to become self-referential.

Self-referential media relations

The media of the network society increasingly lean towards partiality concerning the views and interests they represent (mass media) and link (interactive media). In the mass society, the (mass) media were supposed to stand 'above' society, distributing information objectively and independently. In the network society, the mass and interactive media are embedded in society to a larger degree (compare Figures 2.3 and 2.4). They have difficulty upholding a particular independence and quality. Nonetheless, in forms adapted to the needs of their audiences and stakeholders, quality and objectivity remain important performance criteria of information supply in the network society, as will be argued in Chapter 8.

In the network society, social relations become increasingly interactive by the combination of social and media networks with multilateral communication. Compared to the 'mass society' with its one-way media and centralized institutions, the media and organizations of the network society tend to be more interactive and decentralized. Interactivity is a chain of action(s) and reaction(s). Presumably, it is the growth of interactive relations that has the greatest consequences for the structures of present and future society. In all spheres of society, one is able to observe a shift from the supply-side to the demand-side, from producer to consumer and from designer to user.

Interactive relations

This shift cannot be denied. However, it is also exaggerated by many observers who expect that social relationships will be turned upside-down completely. In fact, interactivity means an interplay of supply and demand. Selection, design and production remain with the suppliers; users mainly choose from preprogrammed menus. However, their choice affects the next supply and they may become suppliers themselves. Increasingly, businesses, governments and individuals alternately serve as the (co-)producers of goods, services or policies and as their consumers or executors.

Highly organized relations

The most important explanation for the rise of networks as a principle of organization is their combination of centralization and decentralization. In this way, the relations of the network society become better organized. In this book, it will be revealed that the 'secret' of networks is a very intelligent combination of openness and 'closedness', scale extension and scale reduction, decentralization and centralization of organization.

The use of networks as an organizational and media form is able to reduce more complexity than traditional centralist or mass media forms of organization. Therefore, old modes of bureaucratic organization and central coordination are disappearing. However, organizational control as such does not disappear. In Chapter 5 it will be argued that traditional bureaucracy is replaced by a so-called 'infocracy' that is based on ICT. We will see that networks are combining horizontal coordination and vertical control of activities.

Coded relations

As a consequence of rising complexity, uncertainty and vulnerability, social and media networks are more and more provided with programmed control and access codes. Networks of ICT in particular require all kinds of programming, codes and access barriers to prevent harmful use. This means that all relations in the network society are in fact programmed and coded more and more. This is quite the opposite of the popular view of networks as relatively informal modes of communication and decision-making. In this book, we will see that all codes used are contested and that none of them is technically neutral. Codes are instruments of power. Among others, they are defining the opportunities of personal autonomy and privacy, values that will receive much attention in Chapters 4 through 6.

Selective and exclusive relations

Among other reasons, the use of codes makes networks more selective in their operations, both inwards and outwards. Though they are appropriate to connect everybody and to spread information and communication in principle, they tend to lead to greater inequality in our present society and in organizations in practice. This is the trend of increasingly selective and exclusive relations in the network society.

There has always been inequality in social networks. When media networks are added to them, a new dimension of inequality is appended. The technology used is divided unequally considering physical access, the possession of digital skills and practical usage. This goes for the expensive, complex and multifunctional ICTs in particular. In the worst of cases, these digital divides (of physical access, skill and usage) might even turn into structural inequalities, as will be demonstrated in Chapter 7. Structural inequality means that differences in positions people occupy in society, in both social and media networks, become lasting and determine to a large degree whether they have any influence on decisions made in several fields of society.

The final trend to be summarized here is the increasing insecurity of the maintenance of relations. In Chapter 7, the instability of the network society will be highlighted. This society is marked by hypes, cascades of public mood and opinion and other sudden crises because it is changing so fast. Moreover, the use of media networks makes social relations vulnerable, technically and social-psychologically. Creating trust, commitment and sufficiently information-rich communication is both a condition and a problem for social and media networks. Networks of ICTs are particularly vulnerable as technical systems, as will be explained in Chapter 5. Vital functions of our risk societies and organizations are at stake because we have made ourselves completely dependent on new technologies while we cannot call back the old ones just like that.

Insecure relations

The use of communication networks does not only rely on vulnerable technology, but also on typically social and mental phenomena such as trust, commitment and richness of information exchanged. A lack of these characteristics also makes network communication insecure and is able to lead to its break-down. They should be available at a particular minimum level. A whole tradition of CMC research in the 1980s and 1990s, which is discussed in Chapters 7 through 9, supports this conclusion.

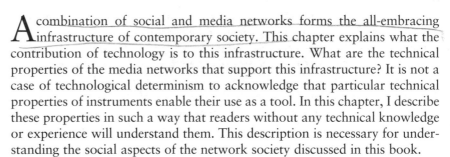

TECHNOLOGY 3

A combination of social and media networks forms the all-embracing infrastructure of contemporary society. This chapter explains what the contribution of technology is to this infrastructure. What are the technical properties of the media networks that support this infrastructure? It is not a case of technological determinism to acknowledge that particular technical properties of instruments enable their use as a tool. In this chapter, I describe these properties in such a way that readers without any technical knowledge or experience will understand them. This description is necessary for understanding the social aspects of the network society discussed in this book.

The contribution of technology to the network society is realized by telecommunication, data communication and mass communication networks. What is the share of the general infrastructure that each of these networks have? Is one of them perhaps dominant? It is evident that they are flowing together in a process called convergence. Integrated networks such as the Internet are produced. Convergence is the key word in this chapter. But how should it be understood? Will convergence be complete? Will there be a single connection to our homes for broadcasting, telephony and the Internet? Will all mobile uses of the new media be available on a single cellular phone? Or will we continue to be obliged to purchase several connections and a multitude of media to receive everything we need? The next question is whether convergence will be more than a technical integration that allows the use of a single infrastructure for all purposes. Will usage also be integrated? For example, will we send emails to our interactive television channel as a reply to programmes? Are we going to watch television on our multimedia mobile telephone? Will we use the Internet to make telephone calls? Or will we keep our traditional channels for their main purpose only, using the additional opportunities once in a while?

The last of these questions are answered at the end of this chapter. However, the chapter starts with the technical foundations of the infrastructure of the network society and the second communications revolution, as discussed in Chapter 1. These include developments such as the revolution in microelectronics, a complete digitalization of all signals and the creation of new connections by cable and by air.

The sections that follow describe the evolution of telecommunication networks, data communication networks and mass communication networks separately. The guiding line in the description of each of them is the gradual insertion of, for example, text and images in telephony, sound and video in data networks and speech or text replies in broadcasting. The ensuing section is dedicated to the logical next step in this evolution: the rise of integrated or multimedia networks such as the public Internet and the private broadband channels.

The last section provides perspectives of the future. A number of current technological trends, such as the rise of broadband and of wireless connections and the fusion of information and communication technology with other technologies of the 21st century (biotechnology and nanotechnology), are extended to depict an image of a fully integrated and all-embracing infrastructure of the network society.

TECHNICAL FOUNDATIONS OF THE NETWORK SOCIETY

The technical foundations of the network society and the second communications revolution were prepared in six revolutionary developments all happening in the last part of the 20th and the first part of the 21st century. The first, and most important, development was a series successive revolutions in micro-electronics. It led to five generations of computers in 35 years. This series was characterized mainly by a miniaturization of parts. The most important breakthrough was the invention of the integrated semiconductor, a chip consisting of hundreds of thousands of connections on a plate with a surface of just a few square millimetres. With these chips, microprocessors were developed for several different purposes: operating systems, artificial memories and processes linked to these. The capacity of chips increased exponentially; it doubled on average every 18 months. Chips enabled a complete computerization of telephone networks, from the central exchange to local switches and terminal equipment. At the same time, they caused a drastic decentralization of computer processing, turning data communication into an important phenomenon. Eventually, chips and processors were also used in audiovisual equipment for transmission and reception on a large scale. Thus, the foundation was laid for a uniform micro-electronic technology for telecommunications, data communications and mass communications. It is the basis for the improvement of the communication capacities of speed, storage capacity, accuracy, stimuli richness and complexity of operations in the new media, as discussed in Chapter 1.

Micro-electronics

The second foundation is inextricably linked to the first. Micro-electronics uses a uniform language for all signals exchanged in its components. This uniformity is the language of digital signals. Digitalization is the binding structure for all new media networks in tele-, data and mass communications. Telecommunications and mass communications have always used natural analogue signals for sound and images. Before transmission, these signals are

Digitalization

converted into electrical signals. At the receiving end, they are converted back to analogue signals. Although analogue signals are realistic, they are also open to flaws and misinterpretations. Therefore, switching is relatively slow and transmission causes some interference.

Digitalization means that all signals are chopped into little pieces, called bits, consisting of nothing but ones and zeros. With the aid of micro-electronics, these bits can be transported and connected fast and without interference. The best result is achieved when the entire link, from transmitter to receiver, consists of digital signals. Data are easily processed, texts are prepared for word processing and sounds and images achieve higher quality. Yet, this technical superiority is not the primary cause of the swift digitalization of all mediated communications. It is rather the need to assimilate the explosive growth of the entirely digitized data communications into the complete infrastructure of communications. The main boost for digitalization of the remaining infrastructure came from acute problems of data communication in transporting data via modems and analogue telephone lines with a limited capacity. With digitalization, data communication and computer technology become the dominant factors in all communication infrastructures.

Digitalization supports the communication capacities of accuracy, selectivity and stimuli richness of the new media. Its uniform language makes content more accurate: less faults and replication of mistakes and more opportunities for exact processing and calculation. It facilitates the selection of sources, contents and destinations as they are all framed and assembled in the same language. Finally, all data types (sound, text, numerical data and video) can be added in the same multimedia source to increase the stimuli richness of the new media.

Store and forward principle

The next technical foundation of the network society is the *store and forward principle** that is realized in digital micro-electronic equipment. This means the use of electronic memories and storage in **databases** of all types. Traditionally, the content of telephone calls could not be stored. Telephone operators in central exchanges simply switched the lines by hand. Only much later calls could be stored on the tapes of answering devices. Broadcast messages were only stored on tape. They were not accessible for both senders and receivers simultaneously. The storage of digitalized contents in electronic memories and databases, accessible by software programs, is a strong stimulus for all interactive media. They can be filled by producers and users and forwarded to all those connected to the medium. The insertion of the store and forward principle enriches telecommunications with a large number of new facilities and is the basis for all email use, all retrieval of web pages on the Internet, all use of computer software and all interactions with audiovisual multimedia programs. In short, it is the basis of all interfaces with online and offline new media.

The store and forward principle sustains the communication capacities of accuracy, selectivity and interactivity. Databases and electronic memories enable these capacities of control. However, they also are a potential threat to privacy protection, as every single action is registered and stored.

The fourth technical foundation of the network society is the layered organization of the technology of computers and computer networks. This characteristic is often unnoticed, but in this book it will become evident that it is extremely important for making choices and for information and communication freedom in the network society. The layered organization of computers is the distinction between hardware, software and applications. This distinction turns computers into multifunctional machines. Software is divided into operating systems and specific programs.

Layered organization

The use of software is becoming ever more important in tele-, data and mass communications. It offers increasing control over communication flows. These days, telephone exchanges are completely controlled by software. Data communication networks also are centrally controlled and secured with complex software, often so complex that they turn into technical networks themselves: so-called **value-added networks**. In mass communications, programmes are accessed, distributed and charged with **conditional access systems**, electronic program guides and billing systems.

Computer networks also reveal a layered organization. The least number of layers is three: the layer of network infrastructure, the layer of transport and operations and the layer of application services. According to the standard **open systems interconnection (OSI) model**, to be discussed below, computer networks can even have seven layers.

The layered organization of computers and their networks supports the capacities of selectivity and interactivity as choices can be made at every level. It offers the opportunity to both centralize and decentralize information and communication flows in networks. It offers the best opportunities for the management of computers and their networks. We will see that the division of labour in the operations of network layers also provides better opportunities for privacy protection.

The fifth technical foundation is improvements in the connections by cable and by air. They do not only concern the transmission capacity of the wires and beams used, but also the capacity of senders and reception equipment and all switchers and routers used in passing. In networks, the progress in microelectronics and digitalization cannot engender real changes until the connections are able to transport large amounts of digital signals. The transmission capacity of wires has considerably increased in the last century. The copper wires of telephony were accompanied by coaxial cables made of copper wires twisted into a bundle used for cable TV. For computer networks they were progressively replaced by *fibre-optic or plastic wires**. These are extremely thin wires made out of glass or new plastics, transporting light signals instead of electric signals. The capacity of fibre-optic wires increases up to four or five times the capacity of a six-wire-coaxial cable and many times the capacity of an ordinary copper wire. In the meantime, the capacity of connections by air has been improved by the use of higher frequencies. From the low frequencies used for radio and the medium frequencies used for television, the evolution was to high frequencies used for satellite broadcasting at a long distance and laser or infrared technology reaching short distances in broadband and wireless computer communications.

New connections

However, the capacity of transmitters, receivers and switchers is far more important. Gradually they have become computerized technology with ever stronger micro-electronic capacities. The embedded software is capable of compressing signals to such an extent that even the capacity of copper wires can be extended considerably. Another major improvement is the progress made in the optical transmission of satellites and antennas used for broadcasting, telephony and broadband computer traffic. In the future, all connections may consist of **optical computers**, fibre-optic wires or high-frequency transmission by air and satellites, all transporting signals of light (at the speed of light).

Obviously, better connections by cable and air improve the new media's communication capacities for speed and geographical reach. In the course of the 20th century, more and more different connections by cable and by air were interconnected to create a global system of telecommunications, computer networks and broadcasting.

Convergence   The last technical foundation to be called upon is the convergence of the technologies of telecommunication, data communication and mass communication to create one single digital communications infrastructure. This process rests upon all five foundations discussed above. It will guide the description in the sections that follow. Convergence has a major influence on the infrastructure of the network society. For the first time in history we will have a single communications infrastructure that links all activities in society. Online and offline communications will be linked in all kinds of ways. We will have the choice of conducting more and more activities either online or offline, or both: work, education, information retrieval, conversation, decision-making, cultural expression, entertainment and others. The convergence of communications will produce a tangible nervous system for society. It is time to explain how it has evolved.

TELECOMMUNICATION NETWORKS

Definition of telecommunication   In this book, telecommunication is defined as *a type of communication using technical media to exchange sound in the form of speech and text over (long) distances.* The telephone network forms the backbone of the existing telecommunications infrastructure. This network has surpassed and largely incorporated the old telegraph and telex networks.

Switching techniques   Telecommunication traditionally is based on circuit switching*. This means that a permanent link is kept open between those exchanging calls, text and data. With every new call, the link has to be switched on and off. Formerly this was done by the hands of human operators. Over the past 75 years, three types of automatic telephone exchange have been introduced. First, rotary switching made physical connections mechanically; then electromechanical **relays** were introduced. In the third type of automatic exchange, switching was realized by entirely different techniques, namely computers and software. This third step in the evolution of switching has been accompanied by the digitalization of the entire infrastructure, leading to a higher capacity and increasing the speed of the connections made.

Fixed telephony is the start of telecommunications development. This does not mean that no connections were used through the air using satellites and antennas for long distances. It means that, for reaching subscribers over shorter distances, copper wires were pulled through the ground on a massive scale and that people used telephone equipment that was fixed to particular places. The age of fixed telephony has lasted about a century. It brought relatively secure connections and increasing capacities. However, it was also rather expensive. Enormous investments and profits were made by telephone companies that acquired a (state) monopoly in their countries for about a century.

Fixed telephony

Since the 1980s, mobile telephony has gradually replaced fixed telephony. In developing countries, new telephone construction even starts with mobile telephony as it requires far less investment. The replacement started with the house cordless telephone and the car telephone. Before that time, mobile air telephony was used for long-distance communications in navigation and aviation and in radio transmissions. For these communications, signals are sent in all directions at a low frequency. Mobile or cellular telephony needs higher frequencies and bandwidths. So, intermediate stations have to be installed connecting so-called cells of cellular telephony.

Mobile telephony

Over the past 15 to 20 years, mobile telephony has already passed through several generations. The evolution started with the analogue cordless cellular phones and car phones. Since the 1990s, three generations of digital mobile telephony have appeared. They offer better quality and security, such as more protection against eavesdropping, and a lot of new facilities to be described below. The first digital generation comprises **GSM** (Global System for Mobile communications), which started in Europe, and comparable systems in other countries such as the United States. In 2005 there were already more than one billion GSM users worldwide. This highly successful type of digital mobile telephony has been accompanied by **GPRS** (General Packet Radio Service) since the year 2000. This so-called second generation type is five times as fast as GSM or comparable systems. It is particularly appropriate for sending and receiving data (such as text, picture, and web pages) in parallel to, or instead of, speech. One of the sources of this capacity is the use of packet switching* which stems from data communications. In this type of switching, no permanent link between callers is kept open, but connections are only used when space is available to send small packets of data with address tags. They not only contain speech, but also text, pictures and videos. The second generation not only offers much cheaper facilities for SMS (Short Message Service)*, that is text messages on mobile phones, but also MMS (Multi Media Messaging)* which means sending pictures and small videos on mobile phones, and Mobile Internet web pages.

The third generation of digital mobile telephony offers broadband communication. This means that streaming video of good quality and multimedia Internet applications are available on the mobile phone or laptop. The most familiar type is **UMTS** (Universal Mobile Telephone System) that started operations in 2004 in Japan and Europe. Several years before (mainly European) telecom operators had spent billions of dollars to acquire spectrum parts of the very high frequencies needed for this system. This was a very risky investment as it is still uncertain whether the system will be a success because large user needs in the short term are lacking and because competition is appearing from other wireless technologies originating from data communication, such as **WiFi** (Wireless Fidelity) (see below).

Digital telephony

It is probably not even these big improvements in terms of quantity and type of mobile telephony that will have the greatest effect for society and communication, but a number of other facilities that accompany digitalization under the heading of digital telephony* and that are offered with both mobile and fixed digital telephony, such as ISDN and DSL (see below). They were introduced in the United States in 1989 by AT&T and the regional Bell companies. When a line is occupied, 'automatic call-back' repeats the operation when the line is free again. With the system of 'calling line identification', the telephone number of the caller appears in a display. With 'distinctive ringing', the person called can hear who is calling before answering the telephone. With 'selective call rejection', a list of telephone numbers to be refused can be entered. Then there is 'customer originated trace' to identify unwelcome, for example obscene, callers. Finally, there are a number of facilities offering further refinement in answering equipment. The most important of these is voice mail*. This is a sort of spoken mail in which the sender enters one or more numbers and leaves a message. After entering the access code, the receiver is able to listen to this message on any telephone.

Computers and video move to the Telephone

The further increase in the capacity of the telephone network not only enables the transmission of pictures and videos on the mobile telephone, but also the serious introduction of the videophone and video or audio conferencing, first of all in fixed telephony. The videophone was introduced in 1964, but nobody seemed to need it. Following the appearance of images and videos on mobile phones, it will get a second chance. With mobile pictures and videos, the videophone and videoconferencing, the telephone is not only connected to the computer, but also to the audiovisual media. This contribution of telecommunications to the process of convergence is summarized in Figure 3.1.

DATA COMMUNICATION NETWORKS

Definition of data communication

Data communication can be defined as *a type of communication using technical media to exchange data and text in the form of computer language*. From connections within and between large computer centres, networks for data communication have changed mainly into connections between computers working on their own (PCs) or in local units (workstations or terminals). In this way networks of varying scales were constructed, from international data networks to house information systems.

Types of data networks

International data networks are private, public or semi-public. Private networks are used by transnational companies and military or security

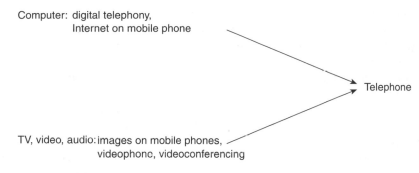

Computer: digital telephony,
Internet on mobile phone

Telephone

TV, video, audio: images on mobile phones,
videophone, videoconferencing

FIGURE 3.1   Convergence in telecommunications

organizations operating internationally. They require safe connections with high capacities. Companies and consumers transmitting relatively small amounts of data, mainly text and images, are using the public network of networks, the Internet. Semi-public networks are created by companies using rental lines on public telephone exchanges to dispatch large amounts of numerical data. They also need special security and capacity. Other semi-public international data networks are used in systems of transport by land, sea or air and by banks and other financial institutions. Having access to these networks is only useful for corporations working in the particular business involved and prepared to accept the particular technical standards.

On a *national* scale, the same division into public and private data networks can be seen. Public networks are the special data networks offered by national telephone companies and those used for local communication over the Internet. Semi-public networks are those for harbours and airports. Private networks are the internal networks of banks and public administrations and, in general, intranets (see below).

Large-scale (inter)national networks are called *wide area networks* (WANs). A WAN* is a network spanning a distance of at least 10 kilometres. It can either stand alone or connect several *local area networks* (LANs). A LAN* does not have a central exchange; it is controlled by servers and software. It is a small-scale network bridging a maximum of 10 kilometres, but usually it spans less than 100 metres, directly linking all terminals or stations that are part of it. At the beginning of the 1990s, LANs became the most important networks in data communication for companies and institutions. These networks consist of Personal Computers (PCs), **net PCs**, workstations and **network computers** (NCs), or any combination of these terminals.

A LAN has a decentralized structure: it has neither a centralized star structure nor a mesh structure, as a mesh network does have central exchanges and nodes. There are two ways in which data pass the terminals. In a *ring structure* data circulate through the entire network. The destination station copies the data and sends them back to the sender, which deletes them or sends them on to another address. In a *bus structure* all stations continuously 'listen' to what is being sent. Only the destination station copies the data. So the data no longer have to be deleted from the network. When a bus

Network topology

structure is expanded by putting more branches on the stem, it is called a *tree structure**. These network topologies are discussed in detail here to allow later explanation of the consequences for the balance of power in organizations using them (Chapter 5).

Just like telecommunication data, communication uses switching to connect and transmit. The switching techniques are circuit, packet and cell switching. Circuit switching, originating from telecommunications, is usually impracticable because the capacity of the existing lines is inadequate to maintain a permanent link for the transmission of data and text. For this reason, a series of ingenious packet-switching techniques has been developed. As has been explained, small 'parcels' of data are given address tags and they are sent when the connection has sufficient free space. After all, most data communication does not have to occur immediately and interactively since it usually involves bulk transport or transactions that can wait a while.

The latest switching technique is cell switching*. Data are sent not in parcels of varying size, but in very small cells of 53 bytes containing a message and an address. This makes switching even more flexible as the network can be divided into constantly changing subnetworks. The latest type of cell switching is **asynchronous transfer mode** (ATM) that can be used to create broadband communication. With this technique, the telephone companies have attempted to offer a broadband alternative to their biggest competitors, Internet companies using the Internet protocol (**TCP/IP**). This has become very popular for its flexibility and decentralized nature. By introducing ATM, the telephone companies are trying to recover the ground they lost to the Internet. The Internet used their connections but gained too much independence and became a competitor, for instance in offering Internet telephony called **Voice over IP**. This is a serious threat to the returns and profits of telephone companies. See Steinberg (1996) for the struggle behind the scenes between ATM and TCP/IP and the corporate interests backing them.

Network protocols   ATM and TCP/IP are so-called protocols. They serve as means for the standardization of network communications. Networks have to be constructed in the same way to enable internal and external communications. The leading standard is the **open systems interconnection** (OSI) model. By means of this standard, seven layers of a network are defined. The bottom two layers determine which hardware and which system software should be used to be able to communicate within the network. The next four layers determine the communication protocols (like ATM and TCP/IP). And the seventh and topmost layer defines what the whole thing is about: applications. The problem with these seven standard layers is that they are filled in differently by existing networks. Different switching techniques are used, to name just one of the problems. Therefore, the call for standardization of networks in so-called open systems* has grown. In an open system, network operators are able to connect to, and use, all layers of a network, except for the application layer, no matter who manufactured it.

Bandwidth   A narrowband network is sufficient for transmission of speech, and usually for data communications. However, network users have quickly reached the limits of the analogue telephone network. With the aid of modems converting digital signals to analogue ones and back, a speed of only 14 000 to 56 000 bit/s (bits per second) could be achieved. With the aid of complicated and expensive compression techniques, the capacity has been increased considerably, for both analogue and digital networks. However, only a complete digitalization of the telephone network finally creates more capacity. People connected do not need a modem anymore. The digital service **ISDN** (see later in this chapter) began with a basic narrowband capacity of twice 64 000 bit/s (in both directions) and a signalling channel of 16 000 bit/s. Soon this appeared to be insufficient for the transportation of large files. **DSL** (Digital Subscriber Line) was offered, providing much greater capacity in both directions. With this service, the transition is made to multimedia networks combining tele-, data and mass communication. Therefore, DSL is discussed below.

For the lack of other infrastructures in data communication, the computer had to be connected to the telephone network as a matter of necessity. As this is becoming completely digital and as it offers much more capacity than before, there is still room for growth. The computer is able to 'help' the telephone with certain programs that automatically call back, put conversations and data through to another telephone/monitor, and offer the opportunity for callers to temporarily break the conversation and consult someone at another telephone. The keys of a digital telephone can be used to collect data for computer processing, for instance when taking orders over the telephone. Telephone and computer were fully integrated in systems for buying and selling on the stock market a long time ago.

Telephony and video move to the computer

However, the limits of narrowband telecommunication were fully exposed in the transfer of moving images. The most elementary video images need a speed of 700 000 bit/s. Broadband LANs (see later in this chapter) cannot be linked through narrowband infrastructures of telephony, including ISDN. Therefore, DSL, UMTS, new compression techniques and the replacement of copper by fibre-optic wires had to be offered to transmit audiovisuals and multimedia web pages via telephone lines and to present them on computer and television screens. In this way data communication networks are able to incorporate the world of audiovisuals and television though they still use telephone lines. They could also offer data broadcasting* or 'datacasting', that is, central exchanges distributing large amounts of data such as oversized databases and television programmes to local terminals, for example transnational companies addressing their local departments. Figure 3.2 summarizes the trends described in this section.

MASS COMMUNICATION NETWORKS

Mass communication can be defined as *a type of communication using media to distribute sound, text and images among an audience*. Until recently, most networks used for this purpose were connections by air. It is obvious, though not essential, that radio broadcasting uses radio

Definition of mass communication

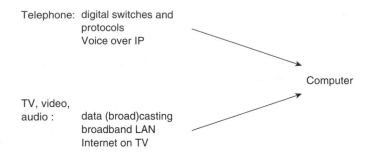

FIGURE 3.2   Convergence in data communications

communication in the 'ether'. However, FM radio and television need broader frequencies than ordinary radio. From the 1960s onwards, cable networks for broadcasting have been constructed in densely populated western countries. They were a solution for the problem of scarce frequencies in the 'ether'. This scarcity has always been a reason for governments to keep firm control over broadcasting.

Revival of atmospheric networks   However, the deregulation of broadcasting, the opportunities of direct broadcasting through powerful satellites and small dish antennas, and the limited infrastructure in large, poor and sparsely populated countries, have paradoxically led to a revival of connections by satellite and antenna as the leading global transmission media. A vast number of local and global atmospheric networks for mobile tele-, data and mass communications have been constructed. Some of them use satellites in geo-stationary orbits much lower than traditional ones.

Demise of centralized broadcasting   Networks of mass communications are still predominantly distribution networks. The structure of these networks is like a tree. A broadcasting corporation (the root) uses a transmitter (the trunk) to send sounds, images and text through carriers with ever smaller branches until they reach the recipient. However, these centralized broadcasting networks have reached their limits. This can be observed in five developments. First, broadcasting needed ever larger capacities. In the 1990s, the capacity offered by coaxial cable, about 30 channels, turned out to be insufficient. Compression techniques and fibreglass cables solved the problem. Since these cables are also used for the transmission of telephony and the Internet they are no longer pure networks for distribution. Second, the distribution of television programmes was increasingly accompanied by parallel flows of information, such as teletext. This was a transition from allocution to consultation as the need for two-way communication increased.

Rise of two-way TV   Two-way communication led to the third trend. Subscription TV and pay TV revealed a significant advantage over traditional one-way distribution. Two-way cable TV links also gave consumers the opportunity to respond to programmes. In this way, **interactive television*** (ITV) was born. This is defined as 'two-way TV in which the viewer can make programming choices and produce user input' by Jensen and Toscan (1999: 16). Van Dijk et al.

(2003) distinguish between set-top box ITV (connecting cable or satellite with a TV via a digital **set-top box**), Internet ITV (using streaming video on the Internet via cable or DSL) and hybrid ITV. In this case, a television channel is combined with the Internet (email or website) or telephony (SMS or telephone number) as separate return channels.

ITV is preceded by digital radio and television*. This means that radio and television channels and programmes are offered in a digital form. This provides a greater selection of channels and programmes than analogue radio or TV, but does not allow changes in or replies to programmes. Digital radio and TV are part of a fourth trend: the gradual digitalization of all audiovisual mass communications. The next steps are the complete digitalization of terminal equipment, such as the TV devices and video recorders (becoming DVD recorders and so on), and of television cameras using, for instance, high-definition television (**HDTV**)*. This means the creation of high-quality digital sound and very high-resolution images.

The fifth development breaking up centralized broadcasting is the rise of local, corporate and personal radio, television and web sites. These (inter)-personal and organizational media are turning the traditional centralized (inter)national distribution of mass communications upside down. Corporate TV, intranets or extranets for text and data and multimedia web sites with streaming video produced by businesses, government agencies, communities and individuals themselves have become actual applications in many cases. Computer gaming using high-quality audio and video is transplanted to the Internet in web-gaming. Inside and between organizations, videoconferencing has become a type of telecommunication in the audiovisual world. In this way, messages of mass communication can also be exchanged, albeit among groups that are small masses at best. | **Rise of private and personal TV**

This section has shown that the mass communication networks of TV and audiovisual media have moved to the world of telephony and computer networks. This trend is summarized in Figure 3.3. | **Telephony and the computer move to TV and video**

INTEGRATED NETWORKS

The previous sections described how the networks of tele-, data and mass communication grew towards each other. This process spurred the development of **integrated networks***. These are networks fulfilling the functions of all three of these communication types by themselves. They are able to do this because they are integrated from the bottom to the top: from infrastructure through transport and management to services. In other words, they are designed to offer integrated services. Most extensions described in the previous sections were spontaneous augmentations of functions and capacities. Integrated networks have been created at all levels. | **Integrated by themselves**

Most conspicuous are the macro-networks such as the Internet and ISDN. In telecommunications, it became apparent in the 1980s that telephony was not able to exchange the explosion in the amount of digital computer traffic | **Integrated macro-networks**

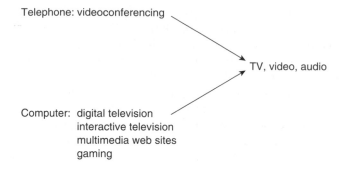

FIGURE 3.3   Convergence in audiovisual mass communications

using analogue modems only. The Integrated Services Digital Network (ISDN) was offered with the integrated services of digital telephony (enabling video or picture phone and the special digital services discussed above), extended file transfer and relatively fast Internet connections. ISDN started with a basic narrowband capacity of 64 000 bit/s in both directions and a signalling channel of 16 000 bit/s. ISDN is the first mature integration of tele- and data communication networks.

The Internet is an integration of data communication and mass communication. In the beginning it was just an extension of data communication with a massive number of pages of text to be diffused as public resources of information or as private message exchanges (email). After the introduction of the World Wide Web in 1991, the mass communicative character of the Internet became more visible with an explosion in the number of web sites in the shape of graphical interfaces. The Internet also improved the capacities of file transfer (data communication) and email attachments.

The third macro-network offering integrated services grew from satellite and cable TV. The capacity of digital satellites grew so much that hundreds of radio and television channels could be offered simultaneously for consumers and extended data-casting of large computer data and video program files for international corporations became a reality. In the home, set-top boxes, actually computers, were planted on television devices to couple interactive channel and programme selection services and traditional one-way broadcasting on cable.

Integrated meso-networks   Western companies were the first to extend integrated networks to improve internal data communications. Already in the 1980s, LANs and other local systems had been introduced to integrate corporate telecommunications into data communications, audiovisual services and archiving. The first pieces of equipment to be connected or integrated were the corporate telephone installations and computer systems. Then the capacity of the local network was increased to transport not only pictures and graphics, but also moving images. Thus, a document-archiving service, a system for video surveillance, a closed video-circuit and files of interactive video courses could be connected to a LAN.

Since 1996, so-called *intranets** have been installed in the computer systems of companies and public institutions. Intranets are private branches of the public Internet. They use the same protocols and browsers and they are especially suited for the transmission of text and images within an organization. When these intrancts are linked to the intranets of other companies, so-called *extranets** are created. They serve as resources for the employees of cooperating companies.

However, intranets and extranets usually are not the backbone of ICTs inside organizations. This comprises the much better protected and more powerful central administration systems and databases. The connection of these systems and databases in LANs is a matter of enterprise resource planning (ERP), document information systems (DIS) and workflow management systems for the execution of organizational tasks and executive information systems (EIS), management information systems (MIS) and decision support systems (DSS) for the management of these tasks. For the operations of big organizations, these systems still are far more important than Internet technology. The prospect created during the years of the Internet hype that all internal and external information and communication infrastructures of organizations would adopt Internet technology, is far from real. The systems listed above are proprietary, private systems that still are much safer and more powerful than the public infrastructure of the Internet.

The smallest integrated networks are standalone computer systems at home or at the workplace (a PC linked to a printer, a DVD or CD-player, a camera, a TV, a stereo, or whatever). They are becoming house systems*, also called 'smart house' or 'intelligent home'. Decades ago, futuristic designs were made for this integrated network, but consumers did not show much interest. It is to be expected that house systems will be introduced into our homes gradually and in clusters. The first cluster consists of audiovisual and computer equipment. The second probably will be the house power supply in general and the regulation of central heating systems, kitchen equipment and water supply in particular. The third cluster might consist of security equipment: burglar alarms and special devices for the sick, the elderly and disabled people. Telephone, cable and satellite will link these clusters to the outside world and to macro-networks. Still it will take a long time for all microprocessor-controlled equipment in our homes to be connected to a macro-network and to be controlled and monitored from single panels in a house.

Integrated micro-networks

MULTIMEDIA AND BROADBAND NETWORKS

The increasing need for integration and capacity revealed in all separate and integrated networks described above has led to **multimedia** and multimedia or broadband networks. In this book, multimedia are defined as offline hardware and software, while their online connections are called multimedia networks or broadband networks. Multimedia and their networks enable the

Definition of multimedia

creation, processing and transmission of all data types simultaneously, that is, text, numerical data, sound and video.

Multimedia* are links between *several* devices into one interactive medium, or links between several media into *one* interactive device. Applications with sound, text, data and images can be integrated in a combination of several devices or in a single device. The main characteristics of multimedia are the *integration of several types of data* and a *high-level of interactivity* enabled by the relatively high extent of control the user has over the interaction. The last characteristic is clearly perceivable in three other characteristics of the use of multimedia.

The first is the *stratification* of information. Users can find more information about a fact retrieved in the shape of explanations, figures, illustrations, photographs, videos, animations, sounds, and so on. So, the same information can be portrayed in several ways. The second characteristic is *modularity*: an information database is composed of pieces to be retrieved separately and combined in the way the user wants them. The final characteristic is the *manipulability* of information in multimedia, enabling the user to 'cut and paste' pieces of digital information.

In the sections that follow, I first give a short description of the different kinds of standalone multimedia equipment. These are multimedia desktop computers, multimedia disks, multimedia laptops and other portables and finally the ultimate multimedium: virtual reality. Then I discuss broadband networks.

Types of Multimedia In 1995, the *multimedia PC* made a breakthrough on the consumer market. Almost every PC sold nowadays is a multimedia PC. This is made possible by more powerful and cheaper micro-chips and by a further miniaturizing of audio and video connections and built-in CD or DVD players. The built-in player, at first mainly used for entertainment and education, has made the multimedia PC especially interesting for the general public. Between 1995 and 2005 ever more advanced features were introduced, for instance the possibility of editing video images and audio clips and connecting a microphone to make phone calls over the Internet or a web-cam to transmit moving images.

The *multimedia CD and DVD* in all their manifestations are likely to become the most important medium of multimedia storage and reproduction for the masses. Increasingly, they are used in all computers and audio-visual equipment. This technology is not primarily based on micro-electronics but on disc and laser-technology. Among the advantages of these CDs and DVDs are the autonomy and flexibility of using them, their relatively low cost and their suitability for a large public. However, there are three major disadvantages. First of all, despite the fast capacity increase of the successive CD and DVD generations, storage and processing capabilities remain rather limited. If one wants to consult large databases, one has to go online. The same goes for access to recent information. This may be realized on the Internet. Increasingly CD and DVD players are linked to Internet connections to add the latest information. Actually, a multimedia network is constructed this way (see below). A third deficiency of standalone multimedia is that they do not allow communication with others, for asking and replying to questions.

The same applications and capacities that are available for multimedia desktops and disks are expected in *multimedia laptops*. In *small portable digital devices* such as personal digital assistants, palmtop or handheld computers and personal communicators, or whatever they are called, only a few vital applications and small capacities are needed. Applications most used are an electronic agenda, email, telephony and SMS, limited word processing and calculating, and simple web-access. These devices are multimedia in a nutshell to be used both online and offline. They are available in all the types and sizes you can imagine. Applications and capacities just depend on the size of the screen and the other parts you want, and the weight you want to carry. Everything from a heavy multimedia desktop to a light mobile phone with video functions is available now as a portable multimedia device.

At the other end of the spectrum is **virtual reality media**. This is the ultimate multimedium, as it requires the connection of a large number of computers with high capacities for several functions to realize the most advanced applications. Virtual reality media create three-dimensional artificial environments to be perceived and experienced with a plurality of senses and offering the opportunity to interact with this simulated and pre-programmed environment. To achieve this the human body is surrounded with several input- and output-media enabling someone to see, hear, feel and move all at the same time. This all-embracing and mentally immersive technology is used for training (in aviation and surgery), design (architecture), research (visualization of complex data), film animation and games (perhaps the most important entertainment of the future).

The evolution of multimedia has gone much faster than the growth in capacity of the networks that were set up to transmit multimedia products, programs and files. Transmission of files via the analogue and first digital telephone modems could last for hours. The expanding graphics of the World Wide Web resulted in congestion of computer processing and downloads. For about a decade, substantial multimedia content had to be exchanged via CD-ROM and DVD. The only real solution for networks after the use of complicated compression techniques proved to be **broadband** networks. In fact, a capacity of 2 Mb/s in two directions is the minimum requirement for broadband. This is required to transmit high-quality moving pictures. (At least 750 Kb/s is needed for TV quality.) However, in 2003 most telecom operators and the International Telecommunication Union (ITU, 2003) called 256 Kb/s in two directions broadband. Anyway, in the year 2005, so-called broadband connections were offered by DSL on telephone lines (either Asynchronous DSL, which is broader downstream than upstream, or Synchronous DSL, which has equal capacities in two directions), by Internet on cable and satellite, by UMTS on the mobile phone and by Digital Video Broadcasting for television via cable and satellite.

Broadband networks

The broadband evolution started inside organizations requiring large capacities for their LANs and WANs. However, after the year 2000, broadband appeared in the consumer market. Consumers with a broadband connection take more advantage of the opportunities of the new media than other users. The actual usage, the usage time and the range of computer and

Internet applications are considerably extended. The second most important feature of broadband is, of course, greater bandwidth. This not only saves waiting time in operations, but also enables a large number of new applications requiring video streams. For the first time in history, telework, telestudy, telegames and the use of the videophone and videoconferencing are becoming real alternatives to their offline counterparts.

FUTURE TRENDS

Miniaturization

Extending the trends in tele-, data and mass communication discussed in this chapter, the image of a fully integrated and all-embracing technical infrastructure of the network society appears. A number of future trends described above are creating this infrastructure. The first, and undoubtedly most important, is the trend towards the further miniaturization of information and communication technology. In 1965, Gordon Moore published a general conclusion that has become known as *Moore's Law**: every 18 months the memory and processing capacity of chips doubles. This 'law' still holds and will continue to work in the near future. Eventually, we will reach the limits of electrical currents that can run on the smallest amount of physical material used for chips, but then the optical computer might appear, working with small beams of light instead of electricity. A further prospect is the integration of *nanotechnology**, the science of building devices at the molecular and atomic level. This would lead to the smallest chips, computers and communication devices you can imagine, built-in almost everywhere, from objects to human bodies and brains. Perhaps the chips will even be linked to human cells. In this way, ICT will be integrated with the other two great technologies of the first part of the 21st century: biotechnology and nanotechnology.

In terms of networking, miniaturization means that the potential elements or units to be linked are getting smaller. This goes for both social and media networks. In this book, it is argued that computer and telephone networks support the process of network individualization, which means social scale reduction. When the new media are miniaturized they will become available and portable everywhere. Social and media networks will be fully integrated together producing a network society, the basic theme of this book.

Embedded technology

Miniaturization enables so-called embedded technology. Currently, chips are not only a part of computers and electronic communication devices, but also of an increasing number of other devices and physical objects, from watches to cars, houses and clothing. The most familiar example is the refrigerator that sends signals to the supermarket that the milk is almost finished, prompting a new delivery. The built-in chips can be processors, but they can also act as small transmitters of signals to other devices. The result is called *ubiquitous computing**. In the future, both people and their physical objects will use information processing and transmitting technologies almost everywhere. A general term for this is information appliances. According to

Donald Norman (1999) information appliances should serve as invisible computers.

Embedded technology means an enormous extension of the scale of networking. Increasingly, not only are people connected, but also objects that are able to exchange signals without human intervention. When human intervention occurs, we also have a connection between people and objects. In this way we create an all-embracing network infrastructure.

The third trend is the transition from ICT that is tied to fixed devices or places and uses wires for transmission to a technology that is used when we are going mobile and that uses atmospheric beams for transmission. In mass communication, there has been a return to atmospheric (satellite) networks after the dominance of cable in many developed societies. In telecommunications, fixed telephony is partly replaced by cellular telephony; in developing countries, large-scale telephone distribution even starts in wireless formats. Finally, data communication is increasingly exchanging computer cables for wireless connections, first in local house or office environments and subsequently in mobile and wide area space.

Mobile and wireless technology

However, in this chapter we have seen that wide area wireless communication is limited. First, broadband cable is still far superior in terms of potential capacity as compared to wireless connections. A second limitation is the scarcity of frequencies in the air and a third the problem of keeping the increasing number of atmospheric connections apart. So, the combination that is most likely to appear is the connection of long-distance cable with access points of wireless communication in neighbourhoods, organizations and public centres.

The significance of the rise of mobile and wireless communication in terms of networking is the considerable extension and expansion of it. First there is the expansion of geographical reach. Rural areas in developed countries and all territories of developing countries acquire relatively easy and cheap access to telephony, satellite broadcasting and the Internet. Second is the extension of use from homes and workplaces to uses in transport and in leisure time. In all these environments, the room to move and to use the technology will no longer be limited by wires and fixed access points. This will significantly increase the scale and scope of networking. This is important, because at a particular moment connectivity accelerates. This will happen when a critical mass of about one-third of potential users has been reached. According to (Robert) *Metcalfe's Law**, the usefulness, or utility, of a network equals the square of the number of users. Mobile and wireless technology will spread the network society to the most remote places and the deepest pores of the world.

The final trend that creates the technical foundation for a fully developed network society is the advance of broadband connections. The multimedia PC power and applications provided in the 1990s are gradually extended and distributed ten years later in broadband connections by cable and by air. George Guilder even maintains in the so-called *Guilder's Law* that bandwidth grows at least three times faster than computer power. This means that if computer power doubles every 18 months, communications power doubles every 6 months.

Broadband technology

Whether this is true or not, broadband has an enormous influence on the daily use of computers and their networks. New usage patterns appear and a new lifestyle is developed according to surveys of the Pew Internet & American Life Project (Horrigan and Rainie, 2002) and the UCLA *Internet Report* (UCLA, 2003). Gradually the use of computers and the Internet is becoming embedded in everyday life. With the 'always on' feature of broadband, people do not have to worry about the cost of connection time any more. The result is that the connection is used for the smallest occasions to inform and to communicate. A 'broadband elite' has appeared that uses this connection for at least ten different applications a day (Horrigan and Rainie, 2002). Not only the elite, but also average users are increasingly online all of the day. Moreover, they use more network applications in general and more applications that substitute for offline activities and particular environments. So, broadband will also extend the scale and scope of networking in society.

ECONOMY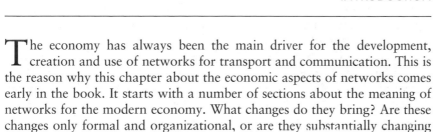

The economy has always been the main driver for the development, creation and use of networks for transport and communication. This is the reason why this chapter about the economic aspects of networks comes early in the book. It starts with a number of sections about the meaning of networks for the modern economy. What changes do they bring? Are these changes only formal and organizational, or are they substantially changing the relations of production, distribution and consumption? Some people claim that a new economy has appeared.

The next section searches for an explanation of the steeply rising demand for all kinds of communication in the contemporary economy. In Chapter 1, it was argued that we are witnessing a second communication revolution. What are the causes of this revolution? What solutions do the new media offer for current problems of communication in the economy?

The third section deals with the appearance of the network economy. Every economic activity appears to go faster and faster. Place does not seem to be relevant any more in the age of globalization. A type of flow economy emerges from the congestion and bureaucracies of traditional business and government. How is this flow economy organized? Is it really replacing organizations that are hierarchical and vertically integrated from the top to the bottom with network organizations that are flat and horizontally differentiated? Who controls these network organizations? Some of these organizations turn into so-called virtual organizations. They are supposed to be independent from temporal, spatial and physical constraints, as they only work online. Is such an organization able to survive?

Networks are considered to be a new form of economic organization next to traditional markets and hierarchies (of governments and corporations). In the fourth section, the characteristics of this new form are discussed. If it really is a viable form of economic organization, the consequences could be far-reaching for future economies. It could expand the space of mixed economies between the free market economy on the one side and the hierarchical planned economy on the other.

This possibility is not equal to the chances of the so-called new economy that appeared as a perspective in the 1990s. The claims of this perspective are discussed in the fifth section. Is the new economy an altogether new economy, or are the revolutionary changes this concept indicates aspects of the older information and network economy?

The last sections of this chapter deal with the place in the economy of networks themselves. All the actors engaged with the supply and demand of networks are described. Network producers range from manufacturers of infrastructure to service providers. Network consumers vary from corporations and governments to individual users. Network producers face the complicated and converging market of networks. The formerly independent business columns of the telephone, computer and broadcast networks are merging to create integrated networks (Chapter 3). The layers of networks, from the infrastructure below to the services on top, have to be coordinated. It appears that the network producers face this situation with concentrations and mergers. What does this mean for freedom, competition and regulation in the media sector of the economy?

It is noteworthy that until the mid 1990s, household consumers were lagging far behind corporations and governments in the adoption of the new media. Most of them failed in the consumer market. What is the reason for this failure? Why have the new media only fairly recently been adopted on a massive scale by the consumers of developed countries?

CAUSES OF THE CURRENT COMMUNICATIONS REVOLUTION

Accelerating communication demand

In *telecommunications*, the number of telephone lines in western countries grew 10 per cent every year in the 1960s and 1970s. In the 1980s and the early 1990s, growth decreased. However, growth percentages remained high, considering the saturated demand for first telephone connections in ordinary households. The highest increase was observed in long-distance and international calls. In the second part of the 1990s, the demand for mobile telephony started to grow faster and faster and to replace the demand for fixed lines, especially in developing countries without a traditional infrastructure.

If we separate *data communications* from telecommunications, we will see not an acceleration but a virtual explosion. The demand for data communications has appeared to exceed supply on many occasions. This has regularly caused problems in corporate tele- and data communications.

A strong increase in the supply of media, channels and broadcasters is to be observed in *mass communications*. Over the past few years, many technical, political and legal issues obstructing supply have been removed. In most western countries, one is able to choose from dozens of new channels, programs and subscription services. At first sight, supply seems to exceed demand. This observation would be correct, but it would not acknowledge the lack of choice opportunities available over the past decades, the strongly increasing needs for cultural differentiation and social individualization and the lack of specific channels for companies to advertise on. And demand is still growing. The total money spent by households on media continues to rise, partly because the new media do not replace the old media but are added to them (See the regular Communications Outlooks of the OECD, OECD, 2003).

General background

The acceleration, in some cases even the explosion, in demand for communication media over the past two or three decades cannot be explained simply by looking at *general* tendencies in society, economy and culture or at the availability of new technologies (van Dijk, 1993b). Saunders and Warford (1983) and Metcalfe (1986) were among the first to identify the following factors governing the increasing need for information and communication media in developed economies:

1 scale extension in production processes;
2 an increase in the division of labour and the complexity of organization;
3 a rise in standards of living;
4 information production gaining its own dynamics.

This list is not entirely correct (in this book, scale reduction is stressed in addition to scale extension) and it is not complete either, because it is mainly based on economic aspects. For example, it omits the social-cultural aspects of individualization and the reduction of household size, which have a direct influence on the need for communication media. However, the most important objections to an explanation using these factors are the lack of historical specification – even from an economic point of view – and the assumption of linear evolution. Contrary to this, I will describe a combination of several background factors that produce their effects with varying speed and strength in the long, medium and short term. The American scientist James Beniger initiated such a description in a detailed, historic-economic analysis of technological developments in the United States in the 19th and early 20th centuries (*The Control Revolution*, 1986). And since I want to apply his argument to the current state of affairs, it is important to briefly repeat his account.

First communications revolution

Beniger demonstrates that, during the period just mentioned, a veritable information and communications revolution took place. He considers it to have been a reaction to the faltering industrial revolution owing to its poor infrastructure. Many points of friction arose halfway through the 19th century. Together they produced a *control crisis*. This term describes a period in which the organizational and communication means of control lagged behind the size, speed and complexity of physical production, energy extraction and transportation. Beniger describes the control crisis in the industrial revolution as follows: 'Suddenly – owing to the harnessing of steam power – goods could be moved at the full speed of industrial production, night and day and under virtually any conditions, not only from town to town but across entire continents and around the world' (1986: 12). The crisis was visible in numerous frictions: problems of coordination in factories, in mass transportation (trains colliding, mistakes made in freight transfers, missing vehicles, divergent timetables) and in the distribution and sale of bulk goods in department stores. In the second half of the 19th century, the crisis was solved by a *control revolution* marked by the following three series of innovations:

1 *bureaucratic organization*: the rise of bureaucratic functions, sharp task divisions and hierarchies, rationalization by formal procedures, preparations (for example paper forms) and time synchronization;

2 *a new infrastructure* of transportation and communication (paved roads, trains, telegraph, telephone and so on) to handle the explosive growth in mass transportation of goods and people;

3 *mass communication and mass research* (national press, film, radio, advertising, market research, opinion polls) as ways to reach and map an elusive new mass of consumers.

Beniger describes the rapid development, within a lifetime, of a whole series of new communication means still controlling everyday life. He lists: photography and telegraphy (1830–40), the rotary press (1840–50), the typewriter (1860–70), the transatlantic cable (1866), the telephone (1876), film (1894), wireless telegraphy (1895), magnetic tape recording (1899), radio (1906) and, somewhat later, television (1923). Beniger considers them to be the means of a (very broadly defined) control revolution. Considering the list supplied, we prefer to speak of the *first communications revolution* of the modern age, for the innovations of the control revolution are much more than simply new means or media: they also contain basic techniques of organization and programming.

All the means mentioned were invented, developed and introduced on a small scale in the period indicated. In the decades between 1920 and 1970, they were diffused on a large scale as the main technologies of an economic age characterized by mass production and mass consumption.

A similar, but shorter, period of invention, development and innovation, with the computer as its central medium, resulted from the Second World War and the race in arms and in space that followed. With a staggering speed of development, computers are already in their fifth generation since 1950. With their miniaturization and chip technology, the third and fourth generations (from 1965 onwards) were the most important. They paved the way for large-scale digitalization and integration of communication media.

According to Beniger, the computer has replaced bureaucracy as the most important instrument of control since the Second World War. He considers the introduction of the computer, the revolution in micro-electronics and the information society in general to be only a new – albeit much faster – phase in the control revolution of modern times (1986: 427). To us this is an underestimation of the meaning of current innovations. However, it is productive to apply Beniger's analysis to the present situation, defending the thesis that we are now going through a *second* control crisis which is partly being solved using the media of a *second communications revolution*. For we can see that the three series of innovations, which Beniger considers to be the solution to the control revolution, have run their course. They have even become impediments to present development. This applies to certain bureaucratic modes of organization, to the congesting and polluting system of the transportation of goods and people, to the fragmented types of mass communication and to the growing problems for mass research and marketing in an individualizing and differentiating society. New media networks can be important *means* to solve these problems. They are able to support the flexibility, efficiency and productivity of organizations, to improve all kinds of logistic processes, to replace transportation of goods and people by transportation of information, and to reach effectively a segmented public of communicating consumers.

The question arises as to whether this technology is not just as much a reaction to the frictions and congestions in processes of production, distribution and consumption as nineteenth-century technology was to the control revolution of those days.

A FLOW ECONOMY

In the United States, the turning point in the scale extension of production processes had already been reached before the Second World War (Jerome, 1934). Up to that time, production had been concentrated in ever larger units. Since World War II companies have slowly started decreasing in size, not only in the United States, but also in other Western countries. This should not overshadow a second process that has been going on simultaneously: the centralization of capital and strategic control over production processes (Castells, 1996; Harrison, 1994). These trends appear in the growth of international corporations and conglomerates of financial capital, and in the tendencies towards business monopolization or oligopolization, which are dealt with in this chapter. A present-day example of the convergence of both trends is the concentration of media in the hands of tycoons like Murdoch, Berlusconi, Malone and Bertelsmann. These people have no wish to merge the media they appropriate: on the contrary, more often they are diversifying them in order to gain a larger share of a growth market.

Decentralization of production and centralization of capital and control

If the all-embracing parent company of the past is taken as a starting point, the decentralization of production can be portrayed as in Figure 4.1. The first phase of this process was the spread of western transnational corporations over the rest of the world. Subsequently, a division in depth took place in the western countries themselves: a split in formally independent and regional departments first and in subcontracting business activities afterwards.

Network structure between corporations

Over the past 15 years, decentralization of executive power has also taken place inside western governments and public administrations, by means of a regional spread of activities, privatization and subcontracting. In contrast to this, the commercial service sector has always been marked by small-scale organizations. In recent times, the emphasis has shifted to scale extension. For example, cleaning agencies, IT companies and other service organizations are getting bigger. However, activities are still performed locally.

Behind these trends of predominant decentralization are specific *economic* motives that become more urgent in times of economic recession: rationalization and redistribution of added value towards the place(s) where all the money is concentrated (see below). A more general reason is the necessity to

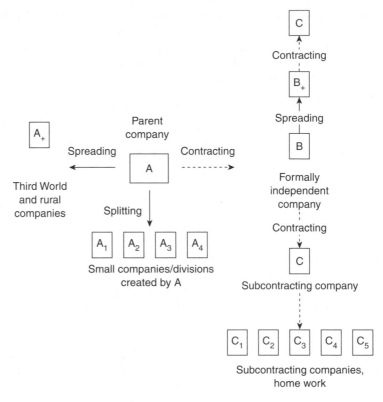

FIGURE 4.1   Network structure between companies (inspired by Murray, 1983)

control the extending scale and organization of large corporations. This is also related to increasing *geographical restraints*. Formerly, centralization of production led to high costs of establishment, traffic congestion and other problems with regard to transportation.

Decentralized economic organization was a reaction to all these organizational and financial problems. However, the result was a huge increase in the need for communications, and thus capacity problems in existing infrastructures (Palvia et al., 1992). The lack of capacity and flexibility in public networks has been the most important reason for large companies to construct their own (inter)national networks and to install advanced private branch exchanges, for which they have been willing to make large investments. This comes as no surprise if one realizes how many *strategic opportunities of choice* are created by this technology. Companies are able to choose the best place for all their specific activities of production, distribution, information, management, support and maintenance. So, production can take place in regions/countries with the best trained and most reliable personnel available. Subsequently, assembly is located in low-wage countries or near markets; distribution is based on the best infrastructure; and information is concentrated in centres of high technology. The preferred place for management, which requires high-quality internal communication and support services, is a metropolitan area close to financial centres. Thus, a spread of activities can be combined with extreme centralization and specialization (Castells, 1989, 1994, 1996; Harrison, 1994; Nicol, 1985). The spatial proximity of business activities appears to have lost its importance. A geography of places is replaced by a geography of flows (Castells, 1989, 1996; Martin, 1978). The conclusion is obvious: this corporate network structure, representing both scale extension and scale reduction, can exist only with the help of advanced communication networks.

The conclusion reached in the previous paragraph is underlined by trends *within* separate corporate departments, that is, production processes. Within companies, a network structure of functions, tasks and activities also arises. This is a fundamental transformation described variously as a movement 'from just-in-case to just-in-time production' (Sayer, 1986), 'from mass production to flexible specialization' (Piore and Sabel, 1984) and 'from **Fordism** to post-Fordism' (Aglietta, 1979). The first part of these distinctions refers to the modern industrial production process based on **Taylorism** and the system of assembly lines that was predominant in industrialized countries until recently. Here, the goal was to achieve the highest production at the greatest speed. Machines had to work for as long as possible on a single (part of a) mass product. A high level of specialization between and within divisions was prevalent. Assembly lines and other systems of transportation took care of transit. Parts, components and personnel had to be kept in store ('just-in-case') to keep production going during breakdowns. However, this system, so devoted to the speed of continuous mass production, in fact suffered delays in almost every link (De Sitter, 1994). The linear structure had too many phases and links working at different speeds. So, numerous **logistical** problems were created. The structure was vulnerable to the smallest malfunction. An extensive hierarchical line structure was needed to coordinate all the processes and divisions. The more complicated the end product, the longer and more complicated the route between all the divisions. The results were long and unreliable delivery times. Only two decades ago a (part of a) product was processed only 5 percent of the time it spent in the factory; 30 percent of production costs were used for storage, coordination and transportation inside the factory (Balance and Sinclair, 1983: 148). To summarize: this type of production process was characterized by optimizing *partial aspects*, to allow separate machines and workers to work faster. The advancing complexity of products and differentiation of demand slowed this process and reduced the growth of productivity in the 1960s. However, it took the economic crisis of the 1970s and the model of the Japanese economic system to make manufacturers face the facts.

The alternative, developed in large Japanese assembly companies, optimized the production process *as a whole*. The process was not split into stations, tasks and activities but in parallel streams in which entire products and components, all similar to each other, were produced. Of course, the phases in these streams were divided into segments too, but these segments were homogeneous and they were supported by production groups working relatively independently. These production groups were multifunctional; they

Flexible automation of production: reorganization of labour processes

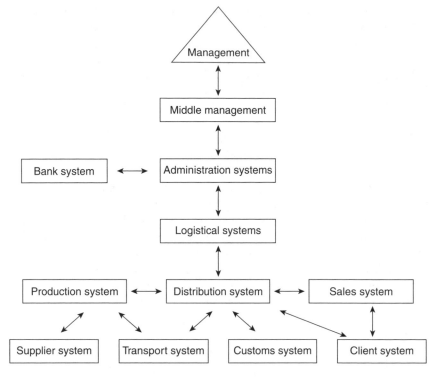

FIGURE 4.2   Network structure inside companies

constantly improved their work and were charged with quality control of their own products. Hence the name 'quality circles'. The number of segments was limited and they could be coordinated by a small staff 'recruited' from the quality circles themselves. In order to make this system succeed, the work done in the segments had to fit closely ('just-in-time'). Waiting periods were unacceptable. Information always had to be where it was needed. Therefore, direct communication between production groups was vital. However, soon production processes became so complicated, and distances increased so much, that media networks became indispensable for the integration of all types of communication required. They were needed to integrate computer-aided design and computer-aided manufacturing in a single cybernetic system: computer-integrated manufacturing. In turn, this system had to be connected to distribution and supply systems, office systems, personnel information systems and management information systems (see Figure 4.2).

Over the past 20 years, this method of flexible specialization mediated by information and communication networks has spread across the world and become the dominant mode of production. The next step was a transition to the world of distribution, circulation and consumption. The first thing required was a transformation of office work and the processing of information and knowledge.

Even though it is hard to measure and compare differences in productivity in factories and offices, it is well known that, during the 20th century, productivity in factories increased far more than productivity in offices (for data see Gershuny and Miles, 1983). The difference was experienced as a growing economic problem: whereas the costs per single product gradually decreased, the share of administration and management in the total costs kept increasing both in absolute and in relative figures. The reasons are obvious: office work is, and always has been, highly informal, unstructured and little mechanized or automated. But this has rapidly changed in the last 15 to 20 years. Traditional office work has been automated, in fits and starts, and with many organizational problems. The Italian computer manufacturer Carlo de Benedetti early expressed a clear view of this process: 'Essentially, information technology is a technology of control and coordination of workers – in particular white-collar workers – not yet reached by Taylorism' (cited in Rada, 1980: 106). Soon it became evident that a more Tayloristic, or even a factory-like, organization could be created for office work when an office is viewed as a *system of information processing* passing through stages of generating, producing, collecting, processing, multiplying, distributing, storing, retrieving and interpreting data (see Hawryskiewicz, 1996).

Streamlined offices

Such a concept of office work is necessary in order to first structure and then formalize and standardize this particular type of work. This will enable automation as soon as the necessary techniques are available. High-grade technology for offices is still a fairly new phenomenon. Take, for example, the copier: this was introduced only 35 years ago. Clearly, several separate phases of the above-mentioned process have been automated through ICT in the past 15 to 20 years. But in the average office, this has not yet produced an increase in productivity that can be measured. The changes seem to have been too basic and introduced too swiftly for personnel and organization to respond to them adequately. Much more information is processed and many more communication channels and sources are used, but it is questionable whether the quality of office products has increased and real savings in terms of resources have been made. Anyway, the 'paperless office' will continue to be a utopia for some time.

The office as an information processing system

The really fundamental changes will be brought about by network technology. One should not expect major changes in the productivity, efficiency and structure of office work until either integrated office systems are introduced or all existing equipment and software are connected in networks. The first step in this process will be to connect activities such as word processing and graphical design to databases and documentary systems or electronic supply management. The next step is very aptly called *workflow automation*. The entire administrative procedure of an office is divided into separate tasks to be performed successively by the departments/workers in the network. A list of tasks for the day is displayed in a window on the monitor. All tasks performed are marked and passed on to the next station in the network. The process of office streamlining will not be completed until it is extended to the office environment of suppliers and customers by means of integrated tele- and data communication networks. The network will be the assembly line of

The office assembly line

the office, an assembly line not stopping at the door, but continuing outside to be connected to other lines. Therefore, the effects of networks in offices will be even greater than the effects that assembly lines had in factories.

Of course this does not mean that networks will lead to the same standardization and division of tasks that occurred in factories. It will still be possible to work in teams and on all-round sets of activities. Special programs have been developed for *groupware* or *computer-supported cooperative work* emphasizing cooperation (see Greiff, 1988; Hawryskiewicz, 1996). Furthermore, activities like generating, producing, collecting and, above all, interpreting office information are difficult to formalize. Therefore, the network as the assembly line of the office can have different consequences for various groups of office employees: those who keep managing and communicating informally and those whose tasks are formalized in a factory-like way.

Knowledge networks Gradually, flows of information and communication have become more important to the modern economy than flows of physical products. Initially, they only accompanied the flows of physical products in transport and assisted in their coordination, but later they became increasingly independent. All developed countries now have a so-called service and knowledge economy. In this economy, information exchange and communication are predominant economic activities. Detailed and timely information has to be available for all operations at every level of economic activity. Increasingly, electronic networks are used to accomplish this. A particular kind of network specializes in the creation, distribution and exchange of a certain type of information: knowledge networks*. They are ICT networks designed for the creation, accumulation, distribution, exchange and use of knowledge.

Knowledge is a distinct form of information because it is produced and processed following particular rules. For instance, the rules of scientific method assist in the production of scientific knowledge. Knowledge* can be defined as a collection of facts and relations of cause and effect that explain how things work and how we can use them. See Chapter 8 for the distinction between knowledge, data, information and wisdom.

Knowledge networks actually consist of people who use both social and media networks to create, exchange and apply all kinds of knowledge. Knowledge that can be exchanged easily is so-called migratory knowledge, to be distinguished from embedded knowledge (Badaracco, 1991). Migratory knowledge is the explicit and codified knowledge contained in books, reports, designs, programs, databases and other files. ICT has made the creation, exchange and use of this type of knowledge in digital and accessible formats much easier.

It is a lot more difficult to use knowledge networks for embedded knowledge, also called tacit knowledge. This is the accumulated know how, unique individual skill, craftsmanship and group expertise that rests with people, in this case with employees. This type of knowledge is not becoming less, but more important in the complex flow economy based on cooperation. Here, knowledge creation is less and less an individual and increasingly a social affair of communities of practice and learning (Brown and Duguid, 2000).

Moreover, knowledge production is not a static thing, but a process (Hakken, 2003). Finally, knowledge exchange is mostly informal, not using official channels but informal social networking (Davenport and Prusak, 1997).

Social, changeable and informally embedded or tacit knowledge has to be extracted with special effort. This is attempted by knowledge management* in organizations. It uses ICT and ICT networks, in particular computer-supported collaborative work (**CSCW**) and **online learning communities**, to create expert systems and knowledge databases extracting and making explicit all the professional knowledge of available employees. This requires the cooperation of these employees. They have to be motivated to pass their main asset as individual professional workers, their explicit knowledge and implicit skill and expertise, to the collectivity of the organization. For this purpose, all kinds of material and immaterial rewards are appearing, from bonuses and career advancement to status increase and corporate identity or job satisfaction (Thomas, 1996). However, a fundamental problem is that the flow economy of flexible jobs and subcontracting reduces attachment to the organization and the motivation to pass on one's personal expertise (Nonaka and Takeuchi, 1995).

Knowledge management

Networking within and between organizations raises the prospect of the so-called virtual organization (Davidow and Malone, 1992; Mowshowitz, 1994, 1997). Unfortunately, this is a loose concept with several meanings. Most often, it is a mixture of the following organizational and technological principles.

Virtual organizations?

In the first place it refers to the *internal network organization* described above. Here, the growing importance of teamwork in so-called business redesign is stressed: autonomously working and often shifting multidisciplinary groups cross the old divisions and departments of organizations.

The concept is also used to depict the growth of the *external network organization*. In this case, it emphasizes the modern practice of splitting and cutting off parts of the (mother) organization by privatization, subcontracting and a search for partnerships, while keeping these parts together by networking. It also stresses the growing practice of cooperation, forging federations and alliances between formerly independent companies.

A common third interpretation is the *flexible organization* of the labour process and labour conditions. In this way, old limits of time, place and other conditions of labour are transcended as well.

A fourth interpretation emphasizes the decisive *role of ICT* in the virtual organization. This interpretation is favoured in this book. Here, the virtual organization is defined as *an association that is predominantly based on ICT and tries to work relatively independently of the constraints of time, place and physical conditions*. To paraphrase the words of a popular AT&T commercial in the 1990s: it is an organization that works anytime, anywhere and anyhow. It should be stressed that the first three meanings of the virtual organization concept described above may be realized without any use of ICT; they are just new principles of organization. Of course, the adoption of ICT substantially helps them, as was explained above. However, the core of the term 'virtual' is the possibility of doing things without the constraints of

Definition of the virtual organization

time, place and physical conditions. It means an increase in the opportunities for choice by continually switching the organizational means one uses to reach the goals, where both means and goals are defined in the most abstract way (Mowshowitz, 1997).

The virtual organization is the most abstract type of association we know. The ideal type of it is a web organization. This might be a temporary network of experts working together on a particular job at a distance using the Internet, perhaps not knowing each other, but reaching a potential world market. Most organizations making significant use of ICT are not predominantly virtual organizations. Doing telework or telestudy for a couple of days a week does not make an organization virtual. The backbone of the organization still rests on time, place and physical conditions. A few aspects of virtuality, like more choice and opportunities for switching, are just added.

Viability   The big question is whether a virtual organization, in the sense of the fourth meaning given, is able to survive. It is not only an abstract type of association, it is extremely volatile as well. It runs the risk of a short life or perpetual splitting. The latest experience of using ICT in teleworking and offices without fixed working places proves that it can work as long as virtual ways of working are *added* to the traditional or organic ones. When virtual methods *replace* traditional methods completely, we get an ideal type of virtual organization which will not last for long and is not actually able to work according to this ideal. After all, a greater choice among time and place constraints does not mean that they do not exist any more. On the contrary, the application of ICT radicalizes the importance of time and place in all our activities, as it helps to increase our needs (see Chapter 7). Finally, even a web organization is still tied to many physical conditions, for example the hardware and software of communication systems, using the international telephone system (the largest machine in history), and the minds and bodies of its own employees or independent professionals.

MARKETS, HIERARCHIES AND NETWORKS

In the flow economy described above, ICT networks are used as *channels* to exchange goods and services. In this section, the question to be answered is whether they also help to create a new *form of economic organization*. The next section will discuss whether they create an altogether new economy, as was claimed in the 1990s.

Networks between markets and hierarchies   In 1990, Walter Powell published a well-known article called *Neither Market Nor Hierarchy: Network forms of organization*. In this article, he compared three typical forms of contemporary economic organization: markets, hierarchies and networks. This comparison will serve as a source of inspiration for this section. It will be claimed that networks are a form of economic organization that is not new, as networks of production, trade, circulation and distribution have evolved in human history over thousands of years (McNeill and McNeill, 2003), but that they are now coming to the fore

TABLE 4.1   Forms of economic organization (adapted from Powell (1990))

Characteristics	Forms		
	Markets	**Networks**	**Hierarchies**
Organizational basis	Contracts, property rights	Complementary strengths	Employment relationship
Relation of actors	Independent	Interdependent	Dependent
Goals of organization	Profits	Reciprocal gains	Careers
Means of organization	Prices	Relationships	Routines
Mode of organization	Competition	Competition and cooperation	Cooperation
Control	Horizontal	Horizontal and vertical	Vertical
Coordination	Horizontal	Horizontal and vertical	Vertical
Conflict resolution	Dealing, going to court	Trust, reputation	Administrative fiat, supervision
Flexibility	High	Medium	Low

as a form of organization and technology that takes its place between the forms that have dominated the economy since the industrial revolution: markets and hierarchies. I want to locate this form *between* markets and hierarchies, even though it is distinctively different (Powell, 1990: 299). These three forms are ideal types. Real economies are combinations of these three forms. In my view, they also characterize whole economies from the organizational point of view. A communist or so-called command economy is dominated by hierarchies, and a free-market economy by markets. In the so-called 'mixed economy', networks achieve special importance. However, these simplifications require several qualifications.

I have adapted Powell's typology and made it more general and appropriate to the argument in this chapter. The result is summarized in Table 4.1.

Organizational basis

The organizational basis of markets is a free exchange of values between independent actors. This exchange can only survive under a law that gives the actors property rights and binds them to the agreements made in contracts of buying and selling. In a hierarchy, actors are no longer independent. They are employed and become part of a relationship between employers and employed. They are dependent on each other. In networks, actors make agreements and more or less freely engage in associations. They cooperate on the basis of complementary strengths and they become *inter*dependent.

Relation of actors

After the industrial revolution, independent producers (farmers, craftsmen) and traders were increasingly subsumed under a wage condition in the ever larger hierarchies of corporations and government agencies. In communist societies, this even was/is the rule for everybody. The rise of networks as an economic form entails that more and more actors become semi-independent as they both have an employment relationship and their own business. Clear examples are freelance workers, semi-autonomous professionals and subcontracting firms.

Goals of organization

The primary goal of the market form of economic organization is to make profits. This is realized by particular means of production, distribution, circulation and trade that are ruled by prices. Hierarchies are forms of organization that have departed from this goal in the general social division of labour in order to manage necessary tasks and conditions separately. Their familiar names are management and government. Here, the actual goals of the actors engaged shift to their own personal advancement in the organization, that is to say their careers. Their actions are not ruled by prices, but by organizational routines. The rise of networks fulfills the growing organizational need to achieve common goals in a division of labour that has gone very far. However, this is not realized by the invisible hand of the market and its prices, nor by the visible hand of management and its routines, but by reciprocal gains to be achieved in conscious agreements of interdependent actors and their relationships. This is considered to be an ideal compromise between freedom and control in an increasingly complex environment.

Means and modes of organization

The history of the human web has always been a combination of cooperation and competition (see Chapter 2). Contemporary networks of organization and communication in the economy bring this combination to perfection. The modern capitalist economy is a mixture of strategic alliances, federations, oligopolies and even monopolies on the one side and heavy competition on the other. The free market of independent producers and traders manufacturing and exchanging a single product all by themselves has ceased to exist, if it has ever existed. Production and trade have become parts of an extensive value chain that requires a sharp division of labour and a smooth cooperation of all those concerned. Competition only exists in sections of this value chain, most often sections close to consumers. Auctions, stock markets and all kinds of retail markets are still highly competitive. However, the large chains of production and distribution are ruled by strategic alliances and divisions of labour based on cooperation in relations of contracting and subcontracting. The previous section explained that networks between and inside corporations have contributed to this trend. In the sections below, we see that the modern capitalist economy, among others the media sector itself, remains highly organized and regulated, despite all calls for liberalization and deregulation to bring more competition; except that this organization increasingly adopts a network form.

Control and coordination

All forms of economic organization reveal a particular type of control and coordination. Control is the management of economic processes by decisions to allocate resources. It requires power, authority and accountability. Coordination is the division and synchronization of tasks. It involves the operation, communication and consent of those engaged. A common theme in the literature on new organizational forms is that a reduction in vertical *control* mechanisms is linked to an increase in horizontal *coordination* mechanisms (Fulk and DeSanctis, 1999: 18). This link is attributed to networks as they are considered to be 'flat' horizontal structures. However, I think this partly is a mistake. All organizational forms require both control and coordination. There is no shift from control to coordination. Only the types of control and coordination are changing.

In markets, control is achieved by contracts and coordination is realized by prices. Both are horizontal as, in principle, all actors are equal. However, they do involve so-called transaction costs. Historically, the hierarchy of corporations and government departments has traded transaction costs between actors on the market for coordination costs within these organizations (Watts, 2003: 263). 'The visible hand of management supplants the invisible hand of the market in coordinating supply and demand' (Powell, 1990: 303).

In hierarchies, management attempts control by command, authority and supervision. This often means centralization of decision-making. Coordination is achieved by formalization, standardization and specialization of tasks in a sharp division of labour. The resources of the organization and the skills and time of employees are allocated according to fixed schemes. This combination of vertical control and coordination is called bureaucracy.

The network form of organization is a smart combination of both horizontal and vertical control and coordination. It is no surprise that in the previous section, a combination of decentralization of production and centralization of capital and control was established. In a labour survey of more than 500 managers from firms of all sizes located throughout the world, Lynda Applegate (1999) observed that ICTs permit simultaneous centralization and decentralization. Hierarchical reporting and authority structures between top-management and employees were maintained, but middle-management layers were removed. The span of control of top-management increased. All kinds of incentives and boundary systems (limits of action) for employees remained. At the same time, organizations became more flexible, adaptive and locally responsive because the employees and the remaining line managers were provided with powerful information systems. These systems enabled them to coordinate and control operations locally themselves, albeit within clearly defined limits. Additionally, the 'adoption of a more information-intensive approach to control resulted in a shift in emphasis from standardization and supervision to learning' (Applegate, 1999: 43).

Information and communication networks enable new types of combined vertical and horizontal control in organizations. Human supervision is replaced by the technical control of information systems. Infocracy takes the place of bureaucracy (see Chapter 5 for an explanation of the concept of infocracy). Coordination is achieved by communication and knowledge networks. They have both horizontal and vertical characteristics. Horizontal are all kinds of cross-functional and virtual teams within and across organizational units, computer-supported collaborative work (CSCW) and so-called concurrent engineering (working in parallel instead of linearly). Vertical are identity and performance controls, personnel registration systems and password-protected databases.

Forms of economic organization should not be viewed in a narrow economic sense: they have a number of social, ethical and juridical ramifications. For instance, conflict resolution happens in different ways. When normal procedures for dealing in markets do not work anymore, because the parties engaged do not agree, they can only go to court or to another mediation agency. In hierarchies, conflicts are solved by administrative fiat, which

**Conflict
resolution**

means a higher level supervising a lower one. In networks, the parties engaged have to solve their own problems. Cooperation emerges out of mutual interests and is guided by common standards. These standards are built during a long process of generating reputations and mutual trust. With these means, the actors in networks try to prevent conflicts and solve problems more quickly than in markets and hierarchies. Trust and reputation are vital in networks.

Flexibility   The last characteristic of the three forms of economic organization is flexibility. The gradual replacement of markets by hierarchies in the economic development of the last two centuries has produced a bureaucratic organization with low flexibility. This increasingly became a problem when the environments of corporations changed ever faster and when demand and supply revealed sharp fluctuations. A new control crisis appeared (see above). Compared to hierarchies, networks are much more flexible because they combine centralization and decentralization, as we have seen several times now. Markets are the most flexible form of organization, as they quickly react to changing prices. However, the simple price mechanism is no longer sufficient to rule the extremely complex contemporary economy. Other mechanisms of adaptation have been added to run a kind of mixed economy on a capitalist basis. Networks are a form of organization that serves this interest.

In fact, a particular combination of markets, hierarchies and networks rules all contemporary economies. In some economies, markets are prevalent, in others hierarchies. In network societies, networks come forward as increasingly important forms of economic organization.

A NEW ECONOMY?

Does this combination of organizational forms lead to an altogether new economy? Is the flow economy also a 'new economy'? This expression became quite popular in a short period of time in the year 1999. Unfortunately, the term is rather loose, as it expresses several meanings. It points to the growth of ICT business (of hardware, software and services). It indicates the transformation of other businesses (the 'old economy') into corporations increasingly using computer technology and online communications. Finally, it means an economy working in a completely different way to the 'old economy'.

Strong and   Under the label 'new economy', both strong and weak claims are made.
weak claims A strong claim is the statement that this economy causes a permanent rise of labour productivity and economic growth without recessions or high unemployment and high inflation. The assumption is that this economy will push aside the 'old economy' in a short period of time (Kelly, 1998). A weak claim is that the 'new economy' temporarily increases economic growth and that it launches a wave of innovations that first make the processes in our economy faster and more efficient (a 'flow economy') and afterwards, perhaps, cause

a breakthrough of new products. According to this claim, the economy keeps working according to the old rules of capitalism. This means periods of downturns in economic growth, rising unemployment, recessions and inflation. Those who defend this weak claim prefer not to use the term 'new economy', but terms such as 'information economy' and 'network economy' (Shapiro and Varian, 1999). In this section, it is argued that the strong claim has to be rejected and that the weak claim might be justified.

For a long time it was unclear whether ICT affected productivity and economic growth at all. This phenomenon is known as the *productivity paradox* of ICT: considerable investments in ICT are made but the returns arc not clearly perceptible or measurable (it is difficult to measure the productivity of ICT anyway). In the second half of the 1990s, ICT was observed to have a surprisingly high influence in the statistics of economic growth and productivity (see OECD, 2000 for a global overview). According to the *EU-Economy 2003 Review* (European Commission, 2004: 123), ICT accounted for about 60 percent of US labour productivity growth over the second half of the 1990s, compared with 40 percent in the European Union (EU). This seems to be a big contribution for a sector only contributing a 2.6 percent share of total economic output in the EU and 3.3 percent in the US in the narrow sense of ICT manufacturers and ICT service providers, and 17.6 percent (EU) and 22.4 percent (US) in the broad sense of service and manufacturing industries intensively using IT. The latter are financial services and trade organizations (ibid.: 119). However, it appears that the ICT manufacturing industries reveal the highest productivity growth rates between 1996 and 2000 (17 percent in the EU and 26 percent in the US), followed by the ICT service industries (6.8 percent in the EU and 0.8 percent in the US) and the service industries intensively using ICT (2.1 percent in the EU and 5.3 percent in the US); see ibid.: 118. Therefore, the biggest contribution to productivity growth comes from the ICT industry itself, which produces increasingly powerful hardware and software for declining prices. These are causing a steep increase in ICT investments. However, in 1999, their share in the total costs of the gross national product (GNP) was still higher than their returns: a share of investment almost equal to 7 percent and a total added value of 4.2 percent in the EU (ibid.: 17). So, the productivity paradox continues. Most likely, the biggest impact of ICT on the economy has yet to come (see below).

A first conclusion is that it is impossible for a sector of less than 4 percent of the total economy (narrow count) or 17 to 22 percent (broad count) to push aside the other sectors (the 'old economy'). I am not talking here about the delusions of the day ruling the stock markets and the mass media. On the stock markets, the rates of ICT shares were grossly inflated between March 1999 and March 2000 only to burst like a bubble shortly afterwards. I would like to consider a number of fundamental characteristics attributed to the 'new economy' that, in my opinion, actually are aspects of a much older information and network economy.

In the first place, the products of the information economy are characterized by *high development costs* and *low (re)production costs*. The major part of labour is spent in the development and design of products such as software

ICT and productivity

Characteristics of the 'new economy'

and information files. Creating many digital copies of them takes only a small effort. This is the opposite of goods in the material economy that can be designed, developed and produced much faster, but require additional labour, capital, raw material and transport when (re)production is increased. This characteristic causes a further shift towards an information services economy, already appearing in the 'old economy'.

A second attribute of the information economy is that information is an *experience good*. One first has to taste or know something of this good to ensure that it has sufficient worth to purchase it, in this case that it offers useful information. The only alternative is to trust in advance that the supplier is a provider of useful information. This is the main reason why so many services are given away free on the Internet and through other channels and the reason why building a reputation for providing quality has become a prerequisite for any information business.

Thirdly, *information is a special good or product* because the producer is able to sell and transfer the good to a purchaser without losing it himself. Information is shared by producer and consumers. In a digital shape, it is easy to copy nowadays. This explains the current problem of safeguarding intellectual property rights in a digital environment and the frenetic efforts of the owners to maintain these rights (see Chapter 6).

The fourth and fifth characteristics belong to a network economy. They are a consequence of the most important attribute of networks: being a system of elements with links and some coherence. Networks create information *systems*, combining devices (nodes and terminals), connections and information flows inside. This attribute first of all leads to *high switching costs* in cases where users want to change systems as products. Switching from Apple to Microsoft means a replacement of all programs, files and operating skills. This attribute explains all the fighting over *standards* and the continuous threat of *monopolization* in the sector of ICT (see the next section). Standards are necessary in a system; moreover, they are very useful for most users. This is the main reason why, perhaps unwillingly, the Microsoft standards are so popular among users.

The fifth and last characteristic is the existence of *network effects*, also called network externalities. A network becomes both less expensive and more effective when more units or people are connected. The more people have access to the Internet and email, the more valuable these media become for those connected. At a particular time a new medium reaches the stage of so-called *critical mass*, from that moment onwards the medium seems to diffuse as a matter of course until all potential users are connected. This characteristic explains why telephone, cable and Internet companies long to have the highest potential number of subscribers or clients and to get them as quickly as possible. It is a prime reason for the current wave of fusions and take-overs in the new media sector and the immediate reason why new media companies run into high debts to acquire a strong position in the networks concerned.

New characteristics?   In fact, these five characteristics are not new (Shapiro and Varian, 1999). The 'old economy' also makes information products (e.g. broadcasting and the press), experience goods (if only a piece of cake tasted before purchasing) and network systems (railways, telephony). However, the characteristics do become increasingly important in the information and network economy.

Only two characteristics of the network economy can really be called new. The first one is the so-called *reversal of the value chain*. This is a process running from production via distribution and marketing to consumption. In the network economy, the traditional preponderance of supply shifts to demand and the value chain is reversed (Rayport and Sviokla, 1999). Increasingly, consumers give the first signals and producers deliver on demand. It also becomes easier for consumers to make large-scale price comparisons with the aid of software on the Internet. Moreover, they are able to organize electronically as groups of purchasers to push down prices and to command conditions, for example, by means of rating and filtering systems (see Chapter 6). On the other hand, producers also get the opportunity to organize and to collectively buy parts of their products online. Besides, they are able to reach much more understanding of their own opportunities to sell and the patterns of spending among individual consumers.

A fundamental consequence of the reversal might be that stocks can get smaller and that the periodic crises of overproduction in capitalism will be mitigated. Opposed to this, we more often observe the destabilizing effects of increasingly fast and massive buying and selling in electronic markets. Clearly, the rapid exchanges enabled by electronic networks are partly responsible for the continuous yo-yo movements on the stock markets. They boost financial speculation and proliferate crises and upturns. See Watts (2003: 195–219) for the social and psychological backgrounds of sudden shifts on markets using networks as channels.

A second fundamental change is a continuing *division and dematerialization of the value chain* (Rayport and Sviokla, 1999). Increasingly, all available information about the production, distribution and consumption process is detached from the process itself, both with material and immaterial products. This information is processed electronically and sold separately. In this way, the information-based organization of the different parts of the value chain can be split in many parts, detached from the process of material production and handled purely electronically by different companies. This is the core of e-commerce. For example, the Internet shop Amazon.com is able to uncouple the most profitable part of, among others, the book industry – marketing and selling – from the largely material process of producing, printing and distributing books and other goods. Amazon.com itself only possesses an electronic catalogue, a database of customers and suppliers and distribution houses with small stocks of popular books. It mainly uses the stocks of other companies.

In an increasing number of value chains of the network economy, the organization and the information of the production process can be detached. In this way, the most profitable parts are creamed off. However, the material process and the production or distribution companies do not disappear at all. As many traders in e-commerce have learned the hard way, they are extremely dependent on the fast and reliable supply of their products to keep their customers satisfied and to guarantee their success. An important consequence of this division and dematerialization is the partial disappearance of traditional distributive trade to be replaced by all kinds of information brokers. The result is an increasing shift in the economy from material to informational goods. One of the problems with this shift is the difficulty of private appropriation of information, as we will see in Chapter 6. This explains the intensifying struggle for copyright, standards, codes and regulations (see the next section).

These two characteristics of the network economy might have a large impact on the capitalist economy of the future. However, they will not cause the end of crises, recessions, inflation, unemployment and exploitation. The flow economy, with the growing support of ICT, has led to all kinds of *process innovation* enabling the economy to recover from the crises of the 1970s and 1980s and to remove a long list of bottlenecks in production, distribution and consumption (see, among others, van Tulder and Junne, 1988). In the 1980s, direct cutbacks in production costs had the highest priority; in the 1990s, the emphasis shifted towards improvements in the efficiency and effectiveness of production and a better strategic control of production.

Long waves of the economy
Possibly, ICT has assisted in the gradual recovery of the world economy in the 1990s through better organization of the production process. This conjecture would match very well with the *theory of long waves of economic development* particularly known through the work of the Russian economist Kondratieff (1929) and extended by very different economists, from the Marxist Mandel (1980) to mainstream economists like Forrester (1976) and van Duijn (1979). According to this theory, the economy not only reveals short trade cycles between five and seven years long, but also long waves of about 50 years with an upturn and a downturn phase that are mainly launched by the arrival of new technologies. In the last two centuries, we have witnessed four waves dominated by:

1 the steam engine (roughly 1800–50);
2 electricity and the media of the first communication revolution (1850–1900);
3 oil, steel, chemicals and the combustion engine (1900–50); and finally
4 electronically controlled machines followed by the transistor and the computer (1950–2000).

All these technologies had a great and lasting impact on production, transport and communications. However, not until decades after their first application did they appear to have a clear influence on economic growth and labour productivity. Apparently, technology has to be incorporated and domesticated in organizations and households before it has a greater impact. The same seems to be happening at this very moment, with the introduction of ICT. The computer has existed for a long time, but only after its miniaturization, exponential capacity growth and connection in networks is it entering organizations and households on a massive scale. Here, the computer is helping them to remove bottlenecks and to develop all kinds of new products and applications.

The last long wave in the world economy started after the Second World War with an upturn that lasted until the early 1970s, when it changed into a downturn. In the middle of the 1990s, a new upturn appeared. Perhaps this will launch a new long wave that is stimulated by ICT in general and network technology in particular and, to a lesser degree (yet), by biotechnology. In the upturn phase of a long wave, periods of boom are long and they reach high growth figures, while recessions are relatively mild and short. The upturn is characterized by numerous innovations, as has been emphasized by Schumpeter (1942), another advocate of long waves in the economy. According to him, the history of capitalism is a long succession of destruction and innovation. In the innovative upturn, young, creative entrepreneurs start a series of daring innovations that will be partly adopted by the whole economy later on. It is not difficult to recognize this process in the advent of Internet companies and the Internet hype, and their successive partial adoption by the mainstream of the economy and society.

THE PRODUCERS: FROM INFRASTRUCTURE TO SERVICE PROVIDERS

This section discusses how the 'communication branch' of the economy takes advantage of the technological and economic developments discussed earlier. Since activities in this sector are extremely divergent, it is important to make a clear distinction between the five parties engaged in networks. They are the manufacturers of infrastructure; those who construct and maintain the infrastructure; the carriers and managers of both public and private networks; the service providers; and the consumers of networks. The last of these parties is discussed in the next section.

In order to understand what is going on in the media sector in general and in the production of networks in particular, it is necessary to make a distinction between the vertical columns of the various networks – of telephone, computer and broadcasting – and the horizontal layers of the functions performed by them. This distinction is made in Figure 4.3.

Kinds and functions of network producers

Manufacturers of infrastructure

These days, the highest turnover of capital takes place at the level of material infrastructure. Total turnovers in tele-, data and mass communication equipment worldwide are about 100 billion dollars a year. Clearly there

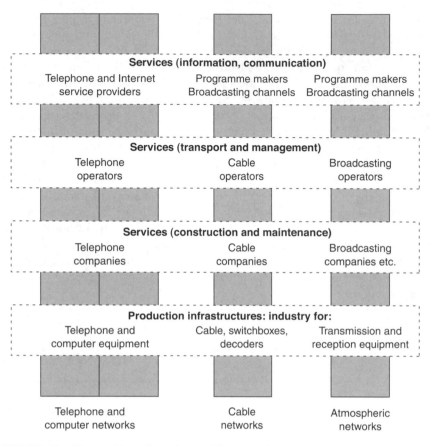

FIGURE 4.3   Composition of supply in public networks

are strong links with the micro-electronics industry, particularly in components and terminal equipment. The largest sums are spent on nodes and exchanges: telephone exchanges, powerful mainframes and servers in data communications and recording, and transmission and receiving devices in mass communications. Sales of cables, switches and transmitters flourish every time a new network is constructed. Then a shift takes place toward terminal equipment – from single devices to complete company and house systems.

Horizontal concentration and oligopolization

For some decades now, a strong *horizontal concentration* – that is, concentration on the same level in the production chain (see the rows in Figure 4.3) – has been apparent in both tele- and data communications. In the last two decades, the world market for telecommunications and computer network equipment has been largely controlled by ten companies. Important names in this context are Alcatel, Siemens Nixdorf, AT&T, Cisco, NEC and Fujitsu. A new round of mergers has started, and analysts expect that only five or six multinational giants will remain after these mergers.

The companies involved have to make extraordinarily capital-intensive investments and they have extremely high research and development costs. Therefore, high turnovers and profits are required. In order to survive, a company needs a vast and solid international market. So, capital and control are being concentrated more than in any other field, although there is some outsourcing to national subsidiaries. The corporations concerned have been privatized almost completely.

In 2004, the old giant computer manufacturer IBM halted and sold its production lines, but years earlier we could see new 'giants' appearing, such as Dell, Compaq, Hewlett-Packard, Siemens Fujitsu, Hitachi and Samsung. Two facts are striking. In the first place, the most dominant producers on the computer hardware market are American and East Asian. However, the software market is only controlled by American companies (Microsoft, Computer Associates, Oracle, Silicon Graphics and others). With its almost perfect monopoly in PC operating systems and web-browsers Microsoft, in practice, determines what software is used by the overwhelming part of the market.

Traditionally, the production of *mass communication* equipment is closely linked to that of telecommunications. The same companies dominate. This situation has been only slightly changed by the appearance of satellite manufacturers emerging from the space and arms industry.

Network operators and carriers

The construction and maintenance of networks are tasks largely performed or contracted out by network operators and carriers, especially when national telecommunication companies are involved. To simplify matters, these parties are treated as one party here. In the next subsection they will be separated again.

A strong tendency to oligopolization is noticeable in infrastructure manufacturing. But in the branches of the most important customers of equipment – network operators and carriers – an opposite tendency can be discerned: one of eroding monopolies. Public networks have lost their exclusive rights of transmission to private networks.

Eroding public monopolies

Public network operators and carriers originally created a *natural monopoly* of great social significance. This means there are many reasons to concentrate management and carriage:

Significance of natural monopoly

1 The services are of general social interest.
2 They are part of a combined system of carriage and communication.
3 They have to get as close to the customers as possible.
4 They experience peak hours and moments of unutilized capacity.
5 Demand is not flexible.
6 Competition is bound to technical constraints (standardization is desirable).

7 Using a single system usually offers advantages.
8 High continuous investments are needed.

The persistent validity of these reasons was unable to prevent the decline of existing public monopolies in telephony and broadcasting. The decline was caused by technical factors (insufficient capacity) and economic-ideological factors (desirability of competition, deregulation and privatization).

The decline of public monopolies and the rise of private operators and carriers has created an altogether new situation: a multiplication of infrastructure with the same facilities being constructed side by side. One of its manifestations is the construction of three or four information superhighways largely designed for the same applications (they are described in detail below). This will lead to an overcapacity outside peak hours. This is a waste from the perspective of society as a whole. In the near future, we will face countless conflicts between companies about the interconnectivity of their networks.

In *mass* communication, public broadcasting has eroded swiftly (Tracey, 1998). On a national and local level, the public broadcasting corporations have had to accept the competition of a growing number of commercial channels. Subsequently, they were overtaken by lightly regulated international satellite broadcasting. Meanwhile, public broadcasting corporations can only maintain their position by government protection or by commercializing themselves.

From differentiation to private concentration

Initially, the decline of public broadcasting has enabled a considerable differentiation in supply. The new services offer room for large numbers of new broadcasting channels. But initial experience already indicates that within a short period a concentration of ownership and organization is taking place. As long as there is tough (inter)national competition, the number of channels does not have to be reduced. However, new (inter)national broadcasting corporations have been founded or swiftly taken over by large media companies such as Time Warner, Murdoch, Bertelsmann, Hersant and the channels of Berlusconi. In this field also, five to ten media giants are taking control of the world market. The first in line were Time Warner with America Online and Disney with Capital Cities ABC. They appeared in major mergers of the 1990s.

From public monopolies to private oligopolies

The trend in all sectors of communication goes from public monopolies to private oligopolies. It is important to note that both are able to manage a natural monopoly. The public monopoly does or did so on a national scale. Private oligopolies operate on an international level. There are no complete monopolies on the market – basically, there is competition – but they can split the world market among themselves, fix prices and benefit from international regulations on standardization and interconnectivity. Increasingly, large international telephone companies cooperate and merge. A handful of conglomerates are preparing to divide the world market. The final result will be a replacement of government-controlled public monopoly without competition by a small number of private oligopolies with limited competition but no democratic supervision.

Service providers

Network services are divided into four categories: purely technical and **Network** organizational tele- and data communication services, transaction services, **services:** communication services and substantial information services. Services of car- **categories** riage, construction and maintenance were discussed in the previous subsection.

When speaking of *tele- and data communication services*, I refer to general services such as operating systems for computers (Windows and Linux) and browsers for the Internet (Internet Explorer and Netscape) and special services that are needed for the development and support of infrastructures. For instance, they offer security services and the supply of back-up facilities for large companies and institutes. Furthermore, they help companies with the development, maintenance and support of integrated business systems.

Transaction services vary from highly specialized financial activities for enterprises, banks and investment companies to simple transmissions of payments, orders, reservations and other online commercial services on the Internet.

Using open networks, *communication services* offer new exchange facilities for speech, data, text and image exchange to a wide range of businesses and consumers. These facilities include the services of so-called digital telephony (see Chapter 3), Internet access, Voice over IP, email, instant messaging, videophone and videoconferencing.

Information services are various. First, there are information search engines for the Internet such as Google and Yahoo. Then there are services offering the storage and processing of data (databanks, databases and data processors). Subsequently there are services for creating, editing and distributing data. 'Creating' is done by all kinds of professional consultants who have discovered 'networking': scientific, legal, accounting and architects' agencies. Involved in editing are developers of network software. Distribution is taken care of by database distributors, all kinds of electronic libraries or videothèques and Internet publishers. Finally there are the broadcasting corporations, which offer their audiovisual programs and other services in new shapes (channel bouquets and subscriptions) and channels (the Internet).

Except for public communication services, most of these services are completely commercial and deregulated. Although they increasingly use the Internet for their services, they are by no means confined to this channel. On the contrary, traditionally they have offered their own private tele- and data-communication channels with higher capacity and better security.

Concentrations

A trend towards *horizontal concentration* has been described, that is, among **Horizontal** network producers and, to a lesser extent, service providers. This means **and vertical** mergers and collaborations between companies with similar activities, on the **concentration** same level of the production chain. When we take a step further and relate the three levels discussed, we will observe important impulses towards *vertical concentration*, that is, integration of different levels in the production chain (see Figure 4.3): (a) manufacturing of infrastructure; (b) network management; and (c) service provision.

At the moment, the relationships between (b) and (c) are strongest. Operators and carriers try to become or to remain the most important service provider on their own network. This is easier to accomplish in a fragmented broadcasting system (independent broadcasters with their own TV programmes). In tele- and data communication networks, the opposite happens because of current privatization policies. Operators and carriers have to accept services of competitors on their own networks. Here, network operators are losing ground with their own services. They will have to compete if they want to concentrate management, carriage and service providing. From the second half of the 1990s, this is what telecommunication companies and cable operators in particular have tried to do. They are working on both horizontal and vertical integration. Telephone companies have started to distribute broadcasting programmes and Internet services, while cable companies are offering telephony and Internet services as well. They are doing this on the networks they manage themselves (vertical concentration). For both kinds of concentration, they buy or merge with each other's networks.

Effects on communication policy   In present-day economies, concentration is a logical reaction to the technical integration or convergence in the communication field as a whole. Still, it might have political consequences which are neither logical nor desirable. The companies involved can get too tight a hold on a country's communication policy. And, more specifically, they might acquire a strong influence on (inter)national standards and prices (levels and differentiation of prices for local and long-distance calls) and on technical facilities for security and the protection of privacy. In delivering integrated business systems and their operating systems or other software, they might gain disproportionately large control of the structure of organizations.

One example will be instructive enough. In 1996, Time Warner was sued by News Corporation (owned by media tycoon Murdoch). Time Warner refused to transmit News Corporation's 24-hour news channel FCC on its cable networks. The reason is evident: Time Warner owns its own news channel, called CNN.

In 1993, the breakthrough of the information superhighway perspective in the United States, Japan and Europe has accelerated these concentration processes. Many telephone, computer, electronics, software and media companies started to cooperate and to merge. Ultimately, the information superhighways will represent the peak in the horizontal concentration of telephone, data, cable and broadcasting networks in the shape of broadband networks. They are also an extra stimulus for vertical concentration. After the liberalization of infrastructure, manufacturers of this infrastructure decided to construct and manage their own networks. Operators of telephony, data, cable and atmospheric networks started to offer services themselves.

However, at the end of the 1990s and the end of the hype about the Internet, many companies realized they had been too hasty in proclaiming themselves general media companies. Shares in neighbouring columns and rows in the communication branch (see Figure 4.3) were resold and mergers cancelled. Most companies have since gone back to their core businesses. However, the concentration and integration described here are lasting facts. The shifts are driven by continuing processes of technical convergence and economic concentration of (financial) capital.

From deregulation to reregulation

The end of public monopolies was brought about by a series of liberalizations that are called *deregulation*. The reason for this fundamental change in communications policy is the supposition that all parties will benefit from competition: increased freedom of choice and lower prices, based on real costs. But the communication sector with all its natural monopolies is not a normal economic sector. The supposition of the beneficial effects of competition is not unequivocal here. Robin Mansell (1993) even claims it is based on an *idealist model* that does not correspond with the facts. These are more suited to a *strategic model*. Oligopolies control their markets according to carefully planned strategies. In some ways they work together, in others they compete.

Competition and control

An oligopoly does not end a monopoly. On the contrary, the companies involved protect their markets, enforcing their own standards, keeping strict control of the most profitable so-called intelligent parts of networks, designing smart price policies and making deals with their rivals. According to Mansell (1993: 210), telecommunication competition exists only in certain segments of the market, such as the production of peripherals and the supply of international communication services. She reaches the conclusion that the increasing costs of adapting networks, provided initially for the benefit of large or specialized transnational corporations, are passed on by the oligopolies to small companies and households (1993: 213–31).

Now it seems the same thing is going to happen with the broadband extension of a number of integrated networks (the different information highways to be described below) that will be constructed in parallel and will be partly interconnected. It remains to be seen whether their owners will compete with one another. They all have an interest in letting their customers pay for the huge investments.

With the need to counteract these moves towards oligopolization and to organize the rising complexity of this sector, the number of regulations quickly turned out to be increasing instead of decreasing. Institutions charged with the organization of a privatized supply on public networks have been established in all countries liberalizing telecommunications. In these countries, books with regulations and standards are piling up in the regulatory offices. Clearly, *reregulation* is taking place. This is very understandable. An increasing number of networks, operators and service providers in an environment requiring a lot of organization and fine-tuning simply has to lead to more rules, for it is easier to regulate one public monopoly than a handful of private oligopolies. Furthermore, a number of social, economic and cultural values have to be safeguarded in this complex situation, such as universal service and affordable access to public networks, free competition and the protection of cultural values from outside interference. The coexistence of partially or completely integrated networks requires agreement on interconnectivity, standards, subscriber numbers, rates, rights of ownership and so forth (Noam, 1992).

Information highways and regulation

The necessity for reregulation will show up again in the construction of several information superhighways side by side. So far, we have the perspective of at least three types of superhighway currently offered as broadband networks. The first is constructed from digitalized and broadened fibre-optic *public telephone networks* extended with mobile telephony. The PTOs (Public Telephone Operators) are currently spending fortunes to complete digitalization, to broaden infrastructure and to create new interactive services, for instance Internet services with DSL connections. Their competitors are doing the same, partly hiring their infrastructure.

The second type of information superhighway is developed by *cable networks*, which are extremely important in countries with high cable density such as the Netherlands and Belgium. Operators of cable TV systems are concentrating their efforts on being able to afford the high investments needed for the adaptation of their distribution networks. Usually they already have broadband capacity, but they have to be adapted to enable two-way traffic and they require the construction or lease of expensive digital switching nodes and exchanges. Here, the need for cooperation with Internet service providers and telephone companies is obvious – for an important goal is to offer Internet access and telephony.

The third type of superhighway is constructed in the 'ether'. These are the digital *satellite and mobile communication networks* springing from (commercial) TV or from telephony and data communications. Global systems of satellites close to the earth or high in space and terrestrial antennas are offered as complete alternatives to terrestrial connections by cable. This third type will prevail in countries with few existing fixed lines, such as Third World countries in general and rapidly growing economies like China and India in particular.

In theory, these three types of superhighway or broadband connection offer the same facilities: telephony, Internet, broadcasting and special audiovisual services. In practice, they will probably concentrate on one or two of these activities, most often telephony and Internet or broadcasting and Internet.

Access systems and regulation

One of the most important facilities to (re)regulate is the access systems for computer networks and interactive broadcasting. The control of these systems will decide who will be in power on the future information superhighway. Regulation must safeguard open access for producers and consumers and prevent gatekeeping and other oligopolistic practices. The first test has already appeared in computer networks. The inclusion of Microsoft's own **browser** Internet Explorer into its operating system Windows has launched a hot legal dispute in the United States and elsewhere. The fear is that Microsoft is using its predominant position in operating systems to favour its browser, search engine and other software or services. Comparable contests in digital broadcasting have appeared. Several suppliers have developed and presented their own set-top boxes (hardware) with application programming interfaces (operating systems for interactive broadcasting), electronic programme guides (comparable to Internet browsers), TV programme bouquets and **web portals**. Just as Microsoft is trying to control the supply of software and services, so a few big interactive broadcast corporations (like Time Warner, Disney, News Corporation, Microsoft NBC, Bertelsmann and Canal+) are trying to control the gateways, instruments of selection and programme supply in the digital radio, television, audio and video of the future. These instances of vertical integration must be controlled by new (inter)national regulation for open access, interconnectivity and non-proprietary standards.

CONSUMERS: PUSHERS AND PULLED

Governments and corporations

The owners and hirers of private networks and the participants in special public networks are the most important driving forces behind the technological and economic supply of networks. Most owners can be found among the (quasi-)government bodies (defence agencies, population administrations and universities) and transnational corporations.

Some decades ago, the largest and most advanced networks were constructed for military applications and for space travel. As early as 1970, the American global defence network AUTOVON already had cable connections of the same length as the entire American telephone network in the 1950s. It already integrated speech and data and had numerous facilities for regulating the priority of what was sent (Martin, 1978). It could withstand a nuclear attack and was equipped with several back-up facilities. Therefore it is no surprise that most breakthroughs in tele- and data communications, such as packet switching, sprung from this industry. Space travel has played an important role in the development of the satellite technology required for fast international connections.

Defence and space Industry

The second pioneer in the introduction of networks is the financial sector (Castells, 1996; Reagan, 1989). The present world economy, trading monetary values representing about 50 times the value of goods every day, cannot exist without the global networks connecting stock exchanges, large transnational corporations, banks and investment funds. The large international banks, insurance companies and credit card companies were among the first to invest billions in private networks connected by satellites or, if necessary, by terrestrial rental lines. The networks in this sphere of activity have stimulated technical innovation in transmission and in processing large quantities of structured data.

Financial sector

Transnational corporations

The third series of pioneers consists of international industry, transportation companies and audiovisual media (Palvia et al., 1992). They are responsible for innovations in logistics, the integration of heterogeneous connections and broadband transmission.

Databanks

The large databanks and databases, sometimes connected to networks of universities or libraries, are the fourth pioneer in the development of networks. They broke new ground in the sphere of consultation and in the accessibility and interconnectivity of files with different structures.

Applications in production and distribution

The increasing power and miniaturization of computer equipment, the perfection of intelligent terminals, and the accelerating speed of packet-switched transmission enable a true revolution in data processing in industrial, financial, trade and transport companies. The need for large central computer divisions is reduced by increasing use of *distributed data processing*.

A second series of applications is *monitor systems*. These systems perform measurements, analyse, organize and report. The use of process control systems in the chemical industry, heavy industry, the graphics industry and the food industry is long established. Today there is a swift development in all kinds of safety and signalling systems.

However, the fastest developments are taking place in transactions of goods, services and personnel. This branch benefits most from the connections between registration systems that once used to be separate. This offers qualitatively new facilities such as fully automated booking and stock-keeping and electronic registration and control of employees.

The final series of applications in the sphere of production and distribution is *database systems*. The most important types offer marketing and credit information, legal and bibliographical reference and economic or financial news.

Applications in administration

In the meantime, networks in offices are created by connecting formerly separated functions, equipment and workplaces (see the section earlier in this chapter about the streamlined office). The oldest applications are accounting and administration, both very suitable for computerization. But automation of the lifeblood of an office, that is, word processing, is the greatest leap forward. Connecting formerly unattached word processors and documentary systems in a network is the most important step towards the streamlined office. It gives access to applications such as email, electronic meetings and digital archives. These, in their turn, are a welcome addition to management information systems. More and more often these management information systems will be connected to the systems mentioned above, thus turning them into the nerve centre of the organization (see Hawryskiewicz, 1996). All this results from the convergence of process automation, logistics and office automation, which in large companies has been going on for at least 25 years.

Households and individuals

Demand catching up

Initially, in the 1980s and early 1990s, the demand for computer networks, hardware, software and services by small and medium enterprises (SMEs) and households or individual consumers lagged far behind the demand by big (trans)national corporations. Clearly, this illustrated the general pattern of adoption of the new media: first the large enterprises; then their professional employees and people working in departments of higher education; afterwards the SMEs; and finally, a long way behind, the mass of households and individual consumers. However, the adoption of the new media by the last group is essential to pay for the high investments in large-scale infrastructures. This explains the desperate scramble by the IT industry in the 1980s and 1990s to bring on to the market one new medium after another. As almost all of them failed until the middle of the 1990s, these attempts may be termed *technology push*.

In the 1980s and the first half of the 1990s, there was an impressive series of (consumer) market failures in the supply of new media devices and services: the videophone, the videodisk, videotex, **CD-I**, the first generation of personal digital assistants and the systems of (home) video on demand, to mention just the most important.

Market failures

Only since the middle of the 1990s have we witnessed a partial breakthrough of PCs, digital and mobile telephony and, later on, Internet connections in households. It is partial, because the general diffusion of these new media is still confined to North America, Western Europe and some countries in East Asia. Here, the 2005 average household penetration of PCs reached between 60 and 85 percent and between 50 and 70 percent for Internet connections. In the rest of the world, the diffusion of these new media is much lower, creating a so-called digital divide (Norris, 2001; van Dijk, 2005; Warschauer, 2003). In the 1990s, the introduction of so-called full service networks – integrated networks of broadcasting, information, transaction and interpersonal communication services for households (see Baldwin et al., 1996) appeared to be a bridge too far in North America and Western Europe (see Fidler, 1997). They were cancelled or substantially cut back to a few successful single services.

What are the main reasons for these evident past and present failures of the new media on the consumer market? To answer this question one has to appreciate that the introduction of new technologies is a matter of *design by producers* and *domestication by consumers* (Silverstone and Hadden, 1996). Domestication is the appropriation of new technologies by consumers in households, workplaces and other private places, making them acceptable in their own familiar everyday lives. Domestication is anticipated in design, and design is completed in domestication (ibid.: 46). So, it appears that design and domestication have become separated in the recent drive for adoption of the new media by households and individual consumers. Three interrelated characteristics are responsible for this mismatch.

Reasons for the mismatch of design and demand

First, a *supply-side view* dominates design, production and marketing of the new media. They are held to be so superior in features like speed, mobility, comfort and other benefits or communication capacities, like those described in Chapter 1, that their demand is taken for granted when their prices drop to a reasonable level. Therefore, unprejudiced market research before and after introduction is scarce. Rarely are user groups invited to participate in design. Of course, the new media are designed and constructed with users in mind. But putting them on the market remains a matter of trial and error instead of real and valid experiment. When a new medium appears to be reasonably successful, all bets are placed on it; when it does not catch on, it is simply dropped. In both cases there is insufficient learning about the causes of success or failure.

The second characteristic of the introduction of the new media is the dominance of *technical* design. Technicians develop most hardware and software. They are so devoted to the presumed splendid technical capabilities of their artefacts that they neglect real user perspectives and pay insufficient attention to user-friendliness. They simply cannot imagine that a particular target group will not use their technically superior products. It would not be rational to refuse them. They do not realize that the adoption of new technologies is a social and cultural affair as well. Many consumers will stick to their old habits, daily routines and emotional attachments to old technologies for personal and social reasons, which go much deeper than simple utilitarian, rational objectives.

Here we encounter the third and most basic reason for the mismatch between design and domestication. In the offer of new media products, a *device perspective* (hardware) or *service perspective* (software) is taken instead of a social and contextual perspective. A good example is the technical convergence of the computer and the television. Technically speaking, it will become easy to watch TV on a multimedia computer and to use computer services like the Internet on TV screens. However, this does not mean that these will become dominant social and personal practices in the real settings and daily routines of households. Computer use is mainly an individual affair, with people working and playing close to small screens with extended keyboards, usually in a study. TV viewing is both an individual and a collective activity, with people entertaining themselves watching large screens using a limited remote control, most often in the living room, kitchen or bedroom.

The simple technical availability of multifunctional computers and TVs does not mean that they will be accepted in the social settings and relationships of households. This is the heart of domestication. The same goes for information, communication, entertainment and transaction services, which are believed by their designers to be superior in use and enjoyment, but do not manage to become embedded in the daily routines of households and individual consumers. Surprisingly little attention is given to research into the social and contextual environments where the new media are supposed to work. The spatial characteristics and usage patterns in living, working and cultural places are neglected, as are the social relationships of gender, generation, status and power in households (see Morley, 1986; Silverstone and Hadden, 1996).

However, the main reason for the failure of most new media on the consumer market, at least until the middle of the 1990s, is the very rational reason that they have simply offered insufficient *surplus value* as compared with the old media. These days, most observers take it for granted that the new media will not replace the old ones completely, but will be added to them. This is one of the most striking effects of media history in the 20th century. It means that new media should have a particular surplus value of their own. At the time of writing, it appears that consumers are fairly satisfied with the old media of broadcasting, the press and telephony and a new medium such as the Internet, all of them used separately. Moreover, they can be improved and adapted to enable more comfort, more selectivity and more interactivity. They offer so much diversity in themselves that the opportunities of choice appear to be satisfactory to the majority of consumers.

All these rather sceptical perspectives do not imply that present and future new media will continue to fail on the consumer market. They just mean that success will take considerably longer than the new media industry would like. Moreover, the final adoption of the new media by the mass of consumers might be different from that expected now. This is another striking feature of media history. For example, the telephone was designed to be a medium for business and emergencies, not for social talk between people, especially women (Moyal, 1992). Radio users were expected to become broadcasters at the beginning of the 20th century, but they ended up as listeners. Computers were designed to calculate or process data and certainly not to play games with. The most important type of application of the new media in households is not yet known either. The continuing dominance of business and professional uses makes one part of industry think that information (services) and transaction (electronic commerce and ordering things) will be the so-called 'trigger applications' of the new media for the mass of households as well. Another part, primarily the vested interests in the media industry and telecommunications, expects that it will be primarily entertainment and communication, since they correspond to the mass applications of broadcasting, the press and telephony in the 20th century.

The main reason for a more successful current and future introduction of the new media is the opportunity for differentiation, individualization or personalization of demand they offer. Users are much better able to choose the time, place and kind of application according to their own individual needs for information and communication than with the old media. These diverging needs fit the selections that individuals in the network society want to make. The differentiation of information and communication patterns in households makes the removal of the mismatch between design and domestication all the more necessary, as the contexts of consumption become more complicated.

Expected and actual applications

CONCLUSIONS

- The rise of the new media networks should be explained by the needs of control in the complex organization, production, distribution, consumption and communication of the contemporary economy. These networks are able to support the flexibility, efficiency and productivity of organizations, to improve all kinds of logistic processes, to replace transportation of goods and people by the exchange of information, and to reach a segmented public of consumers.

- These networks help to create a flow economy that links scale extensions and scale reductions in production, circulation and consumption. Production is decentralized, while capital and control are centralized. Increasingly, economic flows are immaterial processes with exchanges of information and knowledge.
- New particular types of organization appear: networked and virtual. Networks, in general, are a new form of organization between traditional markets and hierarchies. They are a compromise between (market) freedom and control (planning) in an increasingly complex environment.
- The networked economy is only a 'new economy' in a limited sense, as all 'laws' or rules of capitalism remain. The only new aspects are a partial reversal of the value chain and a far-reaching dematerialization of the information economy. Computer networking and the embedding of computers in all activities of human life seem to have started a new long wave of economic development in the 1990s.
- The producers of communication networks operate on a market that is characterized by a convergence of formerly independent networks of tele-, data and mass communication that stimulates horizontal concentrations. The distinctive layers of these networks (infrastructure, transport and services) spur attempts of vertical concentrations by general media companies.
- Initially, the consumers of communication networks were businesses and governments engaged in process innovation. From the second part of the 1990s onwards household consumers have adopted the new media on a massive scale after the hardware and software were made sufficiently accessible, useful and user-friendly in product innovation.

POLITICS AND POWER

The central theme of this chapter is power. The division of power is one of the most important social aspects in the design and use of communication networks. These media are by no means technically or politically neutral. The structure of a network enables both centralization and decentralization. The centre, nodes and terminals can be connected in several ways. In the future, the central or peripheral position of people inside communication networks, or their exclusion from these networks, will largely determine their position in society. Compared with this, the content transmitted through networks is of secondary importance. This shows how deceptive the popular phrases 'information is power' or 'knowledge is power' really are. It is not just having access to information or knowledge that is important, but also being in the right position to use it. Few would consider the outstanding creators and processors of knowledge and information in our society – scientists, information experts and journalists – to be the people in control of it. One thing is for certain: people who do not have access to the new communication networks, nor the skill to use them or to process and select the information distributed by them, will be powerless.

I start this chapter to discuss the most general level. People often tend to forget that we may all lose power when we become dependent on networks. Computer networks, at least, appear to be extremely vulnerable technologies. How should this vulnerability be reduced to make computer networks viable communication structures for everybody?

In the past 20 years, the democratic potential of the new media has been hailed by many people; they would be empowering for citizens, consumers and users in other contexts and they promised a reinvigorated, more direct type of democracy that everyone could easily engage in. So, what is the result of 15 to 20 years of so-called digital democracy and e-government? Three claims have been made: they would provide more and better political and government information, they would enable online public debate and they would bring more (direct) participation in decision-making. Which of these claims has been realized?

In the second section, I move to the organizational level to see whether networks are changing the relationship of power inside organizations. The popular idea is that networks are flattening organizations and that they help to transform bureaucratic, top-down organizations into efficient, horizontal types of organization based on teamwork and cooperation. Is this really true, or will more complex combinations of horizontal and vertical coordination and control be established?

In the last two sections of the chapter, I go down to the level of the individual to see what happens to the privacy and personal autonomy of network users. A serious loss of privacy has been called the most negative effect of the new media. In the last five years dozens of books have appeared with (sub)titles announcing the end of privacy. Is the situation really that bad? What could be done to protect privacy in a computer network environment? Conversely, a potential positive effect of the new media is the popular expectation that they will bring more personal autonomy, providing more choice for consumers, citizens and users in general. Is the situation really that rosy or does this freedom of choice only exist on the surface?

THE VULNERABILITY OF NETWORKS

Everybody knows by now that things can go wrong with computer networks. We are informed again and again of yet another hack, virus, criminal offence, violation of privacy and system breakdown. In the last two decades, countless congresses and seminars about the security of information systems have been offered. And in spite of, or perhaps as a result of, the problems being reduced to concrete technical, organizational and legal proportions, fully satisfactory solutions remain to be found.

Technical and social vulnerability
It is remarkable how the problem of network vulnerability is reduced to aspects of technical security and the protection of confidentiality and privacy. In fact, vulnerability is a much broader problem. It is about *the stability of the entire social system* working with new ICTs. The system is making itself dependent on powers over which it has no (complete) control. When technology fails, the system cannot function any more, or only continues to function with problems, sometimes even big ones. Furthermore, it can generate internal forces opposing the use of technology, resisting the effects or even destroying them. This can happen when certain social groups or classes feel they are deprived of certain rights or pushed to the margins of society as some kind of 'misfits' in the network society. Finally, the power of the system as a whole can be threatened from outside by units that have a wider reach. Thus, in most countries, national sovereignty is at stake because nations are conceding their grip on their own economy, culture and political policy to the networks of international broadcasting, the Internet, global industry and, most important of all, financial trade.

The broad idea of vulnerability developed here applies to information technology in general. But it applies to networks in particular. They possess certain *characteristics enhancing their vulnerability in daily usage*, as shown below.

Size is a network's most important characteristic. A network's reach largely determines its power and usability. At the same time, the network becomes harder for the network management to control. The chances of something going wrong increase. More than separate machines and applications, a network depends on the quality of hardware and software.

Integration of central and local sources or carriers of information, and their *multifunctionality* are also strong features of networks. However, precisely these features cause a – direct or indirect – effect across the entire network if there is a failure in one section. Clear examples are computer viruses and computer hackers; most often they can 'travel' unhindered within and between networks. A network's technical design is able to minimize the failures caused by them, but only at the expense of accessibility, flexibility and efficiency.

Another characteristic is that many networks are *patchworks*. In order to increase interconnectivity, hybrid combinations of advanced and well-protected business and government networks with less advanced and less secure public networks based on the regular telephone infrastructure are created. The lesser security of the latter spoils the security of the whole system.

Accessibility for many interconnected users is one of the strong features of a network, but at the same time one of its weaknesses. The chances of ignorant and unauthorized people having access to the network increase proportionally.

Networks enhance the *complexity* of information systems in comparison with separate units. Numerous new communication problems arise. Furthermore, complexity increases as local units (intelligent terminals or PCs) become able to do more by themselves. As a network becomes more complex, the chances of failure increase in proportion. And the origin of such failures becomes harder to trace and solve.

Increasing complexity usually leads to *dependence on a few experts*: technicians and network operators. The potential drop-out or unreliability of these experts – caused by illness, a strike, incompetence or fraud – make these networks vulnerable.

A common though avoidable feature of networks is the speed of updating by the producers of their operating systems and other network software. *Immature network technologies* are pushed on the market with an endless series of security updates coming afterwards. The almost daily updates of Microsoft's operating systems are a familiar example. Users are willing to take the risks as they usually opt for the latest update and the highest capacity or they are more or less forced to adopt them according to contract or when they buy a new computer (Anderson, 2002: 193).

Another avoidable feature of networks is the *absence or deterioration of back-up facilities*. When there is a failure, there is no old equipment, software or storage to fall back on. A related problem, more fundamental and harder to avoid, is the fact that old knowledge and (manual) methods and procedures will eventually disappear from workers' memories. For example, many retired designers and programmers had to be summoned back to the job to solve the so-called year 2000 problem (in former decades they had programmed computers not recognizing the date 2000).

Solutions? Most solutions to these problems in fact limit the positive features of networks. Some strategic options have far-reaching consequences: should networks be reduced in size or made less functional, integrated and interconnected? This can be achieved by installing smaller networks for one purpose which can be interconnected, but do not have to be. Interconnections can be made more or less complex and secure. Furthermore, the connection itself can be kept as 'basic' as possible. This means 'intelligence' is stored at the centre and in the terminal equipment alone.

Companies often try to reduce complexity by purchasing ready-made systems instead of using a hybrid combination of old and new equipment or several standalone devices. Furthermore, they strive for standardization and compatibility. Access for all is the most tangible feature. It was also the first feature to be restricted. Most existing technical and organizational security is based on restrictions. Yet many experts say foolproof security of networks can never be realized. They should not support this claim solely by stating that security relies on people. The user-friendliness of a network – which everyone wants – is achieved through its size, multifunctionality and interconnectivity, and these automatically increase the chances of failure and unauthorized access. Besides, any limitation of accessibility conflicts with the distribution of knowledge and power which safeguards against dependence on a few experts.

Installing back-up facilities for hardware, software and storage capacity is a very costly process. The same goes for preserving old technology, methods of organization and operating procedures. Soon back-up is accorded a lower priority. In many cases, keeping complete and adequate facilities in reserve would make installation of a network unprofitable.

The preceding list shows how most solutions limit or even nullify the usability of networks. Some solutions increase vulnerability in new directions. This means that the result must be some kind of compromise between the security and the freedom or usefulness of networks.

THE SPREAD AND CONCENTRATION OF POLITICS

The support of democracy and civil rights Without doubt, the diffusion of communication media and an increasing level of education have been the most important factors in the worldwide revival of the movements for civil rights and democracy during the 1980s and 1990s. The spread of international networks of mass communication and telecommunication had a big impact on the collapse of the communist regimes in Eastern Europe and on the rise of movements fighting for democracy in developing countries. It may be said that, owing to the daily broadcasts of western radio and television programmes and the increase in international telephone calls, the fall of the Berlin Wall and the collapse of the Soviet Union were inevitable in the long run. Even relatively 'closed' countries such as Romania, Albania or the southern Soviet republics, and a large number of developing countries weak in democracy turned out to be susceptible to the influences of international media of communication.

The thesis of information and communication technologies presenting a 'lethal' threat to *traditional* totalitarian political systems, based on the centralization and control of all information and communication in a particular territory, can easily be defended. It is impossible to centrally register and control all individual activities of small-scale production and large-scale distribution across any border using these technologies. No traditional totalitarian regime can remain in power after the massive introduction of PCs, diskettes, faxes and all sorts of new audiovisual equipment. On the other hand, several new types of rule with a totalitarian flavour are conceivable using this new technology, as one of its capacities is to enable central management, surveillance and control (see Beniger, 1996; Burnham, 1983; Gandy, 1994; Lyon, 1995; Mulgan, 1991). Especially after September 11 in the year 2001, the day of the terrorist attack on the World Trade Centre and other US targets, many governments have stepped up surveillance for so-called security reasons (see O'Harrow, 2005; Lyon, 2003). To get a true view of these new types of rule, one should abandon the idea that they need *direct* supervision (in the Orwellian sense) or *total* control of every level of production and distribution of information. Central political and economic power only has to be wielded when citizens, workers or consumers cross one of the carefully chosen lines guarded electronically by large-scale, interconnected systems of registration and surveillance. There are methods of checking on people and their activities that are much more efficient than direct supervision, whether electronic or by eye. They allow plenty of room and freedom, but when a certain line is crossed, a 'red alarm' is triggered at some central control. See the final section of this chapter for further discussion of this dark perspective.

Totalitarianism: Old and new forms

In view of the contrast presented in the previous paragraph, it is no surprise that there are opposing views concerning the effects of ICT on freedom, democracy and organization. To some, ICT is a *technology of freedom* since it enhances the freedom of choice for individuals and intensifies horizontal (bottom-up) relations in networks of organizations and individuals (Pool, 1983). Others claim that, since the design and introduction of ICT is determined by leaders in governments, public administrations, businesses and other organizations, it is primarily a technology of central registration, surveillance and control. They are accused of using ICT to get a firmer grip on their organizations and subordinates (Burnham, 1983; Gandy, 1994; Garfinkel, 2000; Loudon, 1986; Lyon, 2001; Zuurmond, 1994).

Technology of freedom or control?

I want to concentrate on the actual development in governments and public administrations before getting embroiled in this ideological discussion. This development can be mapped. The relations between all actors involved in political activities in the widest sense can be subsumed in a comprehensive model of the political system (see Figure 5.1). In the previous chapter, the manifestation of the infrastructure of the network society in the economy was described in terms of networks within and between companies. Goldsmith and Eggers (2004) have demonstrated that government is increasingly shaped through networks. Figure 5.1 shows that even politics in general are organized in a network structure. All the relations between the different actors of the political system – governments, parliaments and public

Network structure in the political system

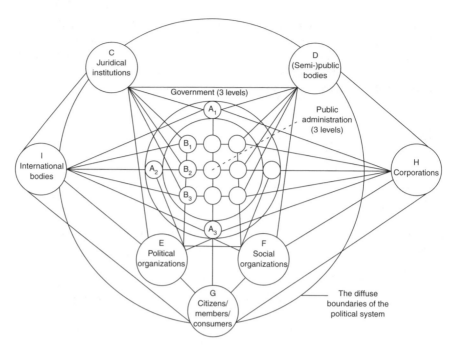

FIGURE 5.1   Network structure of the political system

administrations on a national, regional and local level, political parties and organizations in civil society, international bodies, legal authorities, (semi-) public institutions, corporations and individual citizens – can be interpreted both as political relations (of power) and as relations of information and communication. Media networks and their applications increasingly organize and shape these relations. Figure 5.1 should be seen as a model of the political system, able to show how some relations and actors achieve central importance while others drop out or become peripheral.

Spread of politics   In one of the chapters of the book *Digital Democracy*, I reached the conclusion that ICT enables both a spread and a concentration of politics (van Dijk, 2000a). The use of ICT enhances existing centrifugal forces in the political system, because in the heart of the system, institutional political forces have to give up some of their powers in favour of international bodies, (inter)national companies, legal institutions, privatized agencies and individual citizens and corporations sharply calculating according to their own interests. With the aid of a public network, they can start their own relations of information and communication and spheres of influence and management. Thus, they can shape a politics of their own and bypass the government's coordinating role in a given territory. Unlike a state, a computer network has no frontiers.

Concentration of politics   On the other hand, networks enable attempts at total registration of the citizenry by governments and public administrations. Moreover, they help to strengthen the power of civil servants over parliaments as these servants are in control of the information systems of government. So, ICT also supports attempts to concentrate politics (van Dijk, 2000a). Departments of the government and the public administration are among the first to introduce ICTs on a large scale. It is obvious that they use this technology for their own primary tasks of governing, coordinating and collecting taxes rather than for the improvement of the representation of citizens and parliaments.

Nevertheless, the analysis of those expecting a strong government of total registration and control to arise is as one-sided as the analysis of those who think the state will wither away or even dissolve into virtual relationships of horizontal types of organization appearing on the Internet. Frissen (1999) has perceived the rise of a *virtual state* and the disappearance of traditional politics into the margins of society. Along the same lines, Guéhenno (1993) has predicted the *end of politics and democracy*. According to him, they will be replaced by a system of informal relations and networks without a clear centre:

One-sided visions

> in the age of networks, the relationship between citizens and the body politic competes with the infinite number of connections citizens make outside this body. Politics is far from being the prime organizer of the life of people and society; instead it appears as a second-rate activity, an artificial construction no longer able to solve practical problems in a changing world. (1993: 37–8, my translation from the French)

Both visions are one-sided, since networks consist not only of (horizontal) connections but also of (vertical) centres and nodes. Furthermore, they do not float in the air. They connect actors of flesh and blood (people) and material resources (in households and organizations). In a network society, networks do not replace society, but they increasingly connect and organize its constituents. So, the state still belongs to the strongest (assembly of) actors in society. Therefore, politics and democracy, primarily operating at the level of society, are not doomed. As Slaughter (2004) has argued, the state is not disappearing, but disaggregating into its component institutions linked by networks. However, the state, politics and democracy have to be supported or corrected by political and democratic forces outside institutional politics, among other things with the aid of ICT.

Authors like Guéhenno (1993) and Mowshowitz (1992) have demonstrated why the development of ICT is not necessarily in the interests of democracy. Power might shift to less democratic or even undemocratic forces. Furthermore, the presumed positive influence of ICT on democracy completely depends on what view one has of democracy (see Abrahamson et al., 1988). There are at least six views of democracy in this respect. The first five are coined by Held (1987) as *models of democracy*. Their supporters appear to have different preferences for applying ICT in the political system (van Dijk, 1996; 2000a).

ICT and views of democracy

The first two views on democracy lead to the use of ICT for the *reinforcement of institutional politics*, that is the centre of the political system (see Figure 5.1, A and B, the actors of the government and the public administration). With the spread of politics and with the erosion of the national state

ICT and the reinforcement of institutional politics

compared with other (inter)national forces, institutional politics have ended up in a perilous position, which will only be aggravated by ICT. Yet, the most dominant political forces in Western democracies are striking back, using ICT to fortify the positions of the state. The so-called '9/11' and other terrorist attacks give them the occasion to prioritize security issues and to organize a strong state. The classical western view on democracy supporting this move is *legalist democracy* – a so-called procedural view of democracy, regarding the constitution and other laws and rules as the foundations of democracy. The three basic principles are: separation of powers (legislative and executive power, the judiciary); a system of checks and balances between the government, the public administration and the judiciary; and representation. In this view, the lack of information gathered by the state is currently the most important problem to be solved with the aid of ICT. So, ICT has to bring about an effective administration of government, a strong state and more security. Furthermore, it can help to improve public support for the government and the administration by offering more and better information in both directions.

The second conception of democracy is called *competitive democracy*. It is mainly supported in countries with a two-party or a presidential system. According to this view, parties and leaders compete for the support of the electorate. This rather elitist view of democracy emphasizes representation and efficient decision-making by leaders. ICT is first and foremost used for information campaigns and election campaigns. In the United States, a lot of experience has been gained with this use of ICT (Newman, 1994; Rash, 1997; Selnow, 1994; Sunstein, 2001). Public information systems and telepolling can help voters in their choice of the best leaders and policies.

ICT and the socialization of politics The other four views of democracy have a completely different strategic orientation. Supporters of these views fight for a *socialization of politics* – a further dispersion of politics through the system as a whole (referring to the actors around the outside of the model in Figure 5.1). This implies a more prominent role for social organizations and individual citizens. The assumption is that ICT will enable them to have a direct influence on politics, and even to bypass institutional politics or replace it with their own political relations. Figure 5.1 clearly shows that their relations can be created in this way (bypassing the centre). While views intending to strengthen institutional politics are mainly supported by politicians and administrators, these alternative views are defended by many social organizations and intellectuals.

The most radical view concerning existing political practice is *plebiscitary democracy*. According to this view, political decisions have to be made through referenda or plebiscites. This implies a preference for direct democracy instead of representative democracy. The opportunities offered by ICT to hold telepolls or telereferenda and to have electronic discussions have had an immediate appeal to the supporters of this view. They are said to revive direct democracy as practised in the Athenian agora. The term 'teledemocracy'* has been introduced (Arterton, 1987; Barber, 1984; Becker, 1981), which means that citizens and social organizations are able to directly determine at a distance, using ICT, what goes on at the political heart of the political system. See

Arterton (1987), Becker and Slaton (2000), Barber (1984) and van Dijk (2000a), on the possibilities and limitations.

Another alternative view is *pluralist democracy*. In this view, opinion formation within and between social organizations is emphasized. Democracy is not the will of the majority but that of a constantly changing coalition of minorities. Its most important value is pluralism in social and political discussion and in the media. It is a combination of direct and representative democracy, since representation is exercised not only by politicians but also by social organizations. ICT offers numerous opportunities for pluralism in public debates, among them Internet debates, and for discussions within social organizations, for example by using an intranet.

The fifth view discussed here is *participatory democracy*. Its supporters promote a socialization of politics, encouraging active citizenship. The emphasis lies on the broadest possible opinion formation about political affairs and on a particular combination of direct and representative democracy. Its most important instruments are public debates, public education and citizen participation in general. If the new media are to play a positive role in enabling these instruments, access for all is vital.

The last view on democracy has appeared as a dominant model among the pioneers of the Internet community. This does not mean that the political views behind it are entirely new. Many observers have noticed the affinity of the Internet pioneers to the radical social movements of the 1960s and 1970s in most western countries. These views range from classical anarchism and left-wing socialism to all kinds of libertarianism. The last are most important in the 1990s. The *libertarian view* is close to the pluralist and plebiscitarian views in several respects, as the opportunities for (virtual) community, telepolling and teleconversation are proclaimed. Specific to libertarianism is the emphasis on autonomous politics by citizens in their own associations using the horizontal communication capabilities of ICT in general and the Internet in particular. In its most extreme form, institutional politics is held to be obsolete and to be superseded by a new political reality collectively created in networks. The basic problem to be solved, according to this view, is that the centralism, bureaucracy and backwardness of institutional politics are such that it fails to live up to expectations (the primacy of politics) and is unable to solve the most important problems of modern society. A combination of Internet democracy and a free-market economy will serve as a replacement (see Jon Katz, 1997).

The preference for Internet applications such as electronic debate, virtual community building and telepolling implies that the libertarian model is both a substantial and a procedural conception of democracy and that it is much closer to direct than to representative democracy.

THE CLAIMS OF E-GOVERNMENT AND DIGITAL DEMOCRACY

The potential applications of ICT in government, in the public administration and in the parliamentary process of representation have spurred new

Definitions

concepts, perspectives and claims of government, administration and political representation. The most popular concepts are e-government and digital democracy. In my (broad) definition *e-government* comprises all processes of information processing, communication and transaction that pertain to the tasks of the government (the political and public administration) and that are realized by a particular application of ICT. *Digital democracy* is a broader concept in my view. It can be defined as an attempt to practice democracy without the limits of time, space and other physical conditions, using digital means, as an addition, not a replacement for traditional 'analogue' political practices (Hacker and van Dijk, 2000: 1). Democracy can be understood in one or more of the six views summarized above.

In the 1990s, optimist perspectives of the opportunities of e-government and digital democracy prevailed. Many observers thought that an altogether new type of government and democracy mediated by the Internet loomed on the horizon. Pessimists repeated that undemocratic power of governments and public administrations would only increase with the registration and control potential of ICTs. According to them, there would not be more but less participation of citizens in political processes through information technology as it was conceived to be unattractive, difficult and expensive. In this discussion, I have taken the skeptical position: there are opportunities and risks; let's wait and see (van Dijk, 2000a).

Claims and results
After 15 to 20 years of experience with e-government and digital democracy, it is time to strike a first balance. I will do this by a comparison of the claims that the advocates made in the 1990s and the results that we were able to observe. The claims were first made and evaluated by authors such as Arterton (1987) and Abrahamson et al. (1988). At the end of the 1990s, three strong advocates of digital democracy, Bryan, Tsagarousianou and Tambini listed these claims (Bryan et al., 1998; Tsagarousianou, 1999). Their digital democracy list can also be applied to e-government:

1 Digital democracy and e-government improve political *information retrieval and exchange* between governments, public administrations, representatives, political and community organizations and individual citizens.
2 Digital democracy and e-government support *public debate, deliberation and community formation.*
3 Digital democracy and e-government enhance *participation in political decision-making* by citizens.

Information provision, retrieval and exchange
The greatest achievement of digital democracy and e-government at the time of writing (2005) is much better political and government information provision, retrieval and exchange. An enormous stock of relevant information is available to citizens with access to the new media. When they have the skills required, they can freely select from this body of knowledge themselves, instead of being dependent on traditional preprogrammed government and mass media supply. Of course, journalists and all kinds of information brokers have benefited most from these opportunities, but sufficiently educated and

experienced net users are also able to do this with the aid of some tools such as search engines and special software.

Almost every local, regional and national government and their public administrations, practically all political parties, citizen organizations and political pressure groups in countries with high Internet penetration now offer *web sites* with political and other public information. Some of them are *portals* with extended options to search particular files or pieces of information. Others are linked to advanced *public information systems* containing databases of government and political information.

Parties and candidates in elections offer *campaign sites* that gain importance in comparison to broadcasting and the press with every new election. Television is still far more important than the Internet for politics, but among young voters, the Internet has started to catch up with the old media.

The mass media extend the content of *online newspapers, journals and broadcast channels* with sections that contain political news and government documents not published in their regular editions. Organizations of citizens, voters and pressure groups add their own *independent sources of online information* and search instruments such as *voter guides* for elections.

In this way citizens and voters can be much better informed than they used to be. Additionally, they are able to react to these online sources by email and web postings and to create their own political information. Accessible, reliable and valid information is a necessary condition of viable government and a healthy democracy. However, it is not, I think, a sufficient condition. There are a number of qualifications to this success story. First, there are a number of steps between retrieving information and having any impact on decision-making. Information has to be selected and processed from an abundance of data sources. The result of these mental steps is unpredictable and it strongly depends on individual skills and preferences.

The next question is what is actually done with the information. Is it transformed into political action? This is a matter of motivation and ability to change. After all, the effects of potential action on actual decision-making in a democracy crucially depend on relationships of power in the political system and in the media. Even when the stage of decision-making is reached, it does not follow that more information enhances democracy. According to John Street (1997: 31), 'decisions are not necessarily improved by the simple expedient of acquiring more data. All decisions are ultimately matters of judgment, and the art of judgment may, in fact be hampered by an excess of information (Dennett, 1986; Vickers, 1965)'. Psychologists know that people reach decisions with few factors and pieces of factual information simultaneously processed in their mind and that they are also relying on needs, emotions, norms and values.

Another objection is that government and political representatives may become more *approachable* for citizens and voters but not more *accessible* in practice. It is easy to send an email to the President, but chances are small that the President will read it or deputies will pass it on. Actually, governments and political representatives often use the new media as a buffer. Research indicates that they present themselves in more or less open ways on web sites and that they enable and manage the feedback of citizens and voters very differently (La Porte, 1999; La Porte et al., 1999). The potential interactivity of the Internet is hardly used on government and political web sites.

A final qualification is derived from the quantity and speed of political and government information exchanged on the Internet. Both quantity and speed are so high that they put a strong pressure on the political system of government and representation. Who is able to assess the quality of the exploding number of statements, questions, rumours and accusations published on the Internet? The threshold for the offer of information on the Internet is very low. Moreover, the speed of rotation of political news on this network is so high (24 hours a day) that all kinds of hypes and so-called *cyber-cascades* of rumours, scandals and outbursts of public opinion increasingly dominate the political news (Sunstein, 2001). Politicians and government representatives are forced to react immediately and probably less appropriately compared to when they were able to inform themselves, to consult people and to deliberate on the issues.

Debate and community building

Perhaps the valuable information created in the *electronic debates of newsgroups and online forums or communities*, the second main claim attached to digital democracy, offers better chances of being transformed into action and to result in well-prepared decision-making. This claim is based upon the capacity for interactivity of the new media (Chapter 1). Unfortunately, many observers such as Jankowski and van Selm (2000), Norris (2001) and Rojo and Ragsdale (1997) have shown that the communication of equals in Internet debates is weak in terms of interactivity. The debates they analysed contained no extensive exchanges between contributors. Most people appeared to simply read the contributions of others and not contribute themselves. When they did, the people most often addressed were political representatives. Frequently, debate was dominated by a few persons. Finally, there was not much pressure to come to a conclusion, let alone reach consensus in electronic debates as compared to face-to-face discussions. There were only weak attempts to resolve a collectively perceived problem.

However, this does not mean that all claims of the benefits of electronic debates are untenable. The quality and equality of these debates pose serious problems indeed (see Schneider, 1997). But the diversity of inputs and the (limited) reciprocity of contributors are promising. Otherwise, one could not explain their enormous popularity as there are tens of thousands of political discussion lists and news groups on the Internet. They are not simply exhaust valves. The exchange of opinions must have some influence on the consciousness of the participants and hence on their online and offline political behaviour. In this way, political communities are built and maintained. Undoubtedly, electronic debates will cover large parts of all future public spheres and communities. The big problem, however, is that there is no perceivable effect of debate on decision-making of institutional politics at the time of writing. Here we touch the third claim of digital democracy.

Participation and political decision-making

Contrary to popular expectations in the 1990s, the Internet is not drawing more people into the political process (Boogers and Voerman, 2002; Delli Carpini and Keeter, 2003; Katz and Rice, 2002: 148; Quan-Haase et al.,

2002: 312; Wilhelm, 2003). However, it does provide a platform for additional forms of political activity that are more difficult to realize in the offline world: additional opportunities to find political information and to create political interaction. Familiar examples are sending and receiving email to and from the government and candidates, using email to support or oppose a candidate, taking part in online polls and participating in online discussions. By far the most popular activity is browsing to find information about political parties or candidates, about their voting behaviour and about elections and political news (Boogers and Voerman, 2002; Cornfield et al., 2003; Katz and Rice, 2002). Information is much more popular than online discussion and campaigning (Cornfield et al., 2003).

In the United States and most other countries with data about political uses of the Internet, it appears that between a tenth and a fifth of Internet users were engaged in some kind of online political activity at the end of the 1990s (see Katz and Rice, 2002: 138). The total number of users of political information and news on the Internet is rising. In the United States, it rose to 46 million or 39.4 percent of the online population in 2002 (Cornfield et al., 2003). In the Netherlands, there were 2 million users of the electronic voting compass called *Stemwijzer* among an electorate of approximately 7 million Dutch in the 2002 elections (Boogers and Voerman, 2002). However, those already politically involved and those with high levels of education are much more likely to use these new forms of political information retrieval and activity than those who are less involved and have a low level of education (Boogers and Voerman, 2002; Robinson et al., 2003; Wilhelm, 2003). The only exception is a part of the younger generation that was less politically engaged in many western countries during the 1980s and 1990s, but which has now been attracted to politics via the practice of web browsing (Boogers and Voerman, 2002; Katz and Rice, 2002; Cornfield et al., 2003).

So, while the mass of the population that is scarcely or moderately interested in politics does not benefit from the new media opportunities of participation, the political elite does. The already politically involved obtain a new powerful tool that reinforces their activity and their capacity to influence politics. Slowly but surely, the politically active on the Internet and those using computers are getting better informed than those who only read papers or watch TV. Moreover, they can be more influential sending emails to politicians and public administrators and participating in electronic pressure groups. Conversely, those who obtain access to the Internet but who are not sufficiently motivated for political participation will not suddenly become more involved. There is no technological fix for a basic lack of political motivation (Hacker and van Dijk, 2000: 210).

Another basic claim of digital democracy in the 1990s is that *electronic polls, electronic referenda* and *electronic voting* would bring an era of direct democracy resembling citizen participation in the Athenian agora with modern means. This perspective is primarily defended by the proponents of a plebiscitary and libertarian democracy. However, experience so far indicates that large-scale Internet activity in online forums, polls, communities and pressure groups is able to flourish without any influence on decision-making in official politics. The representative system is barely touched. Television and the press and face-to-face political communication are still far more influential.

Probably this will change in the future when the era of Internet or network politics really makes its breakthrough. Then, electronic polls, referenda and voting will be more influential. They will put the traditional representative system under growing pressure.

On this issue, some political theorists claim that a system of direct democracy will overtake the system of political representation with the help of ICT. Unfortunately, a system of direct democracy, digital or otherwise, oversimplifies the complexity of contemporary political systems and the societies they are supposed to serve (McLean, 1989; Hacker and van Dijk, 2000). Perhaps all those electronic polls and referenda will produce contradictory results and make political decisions even more difficult. Possibly they will create a simplified *market* of opinions, candidacies and votes instead of a viable *forum* of discussion and deliberation weighing increasingly complex issues.

My own expectation is that the rise of political and computer networking and the growing use of ICTs will introduce a number of instruments with the potential for direct democratic influence of citizens in a political system of representation that tries to incorporate them more or less successfully. The future might be some combination of direct and representative modes of democracy, combinations varying across political systems and cultures, as they do today.

POWER IN THE ORGANIZATION

Modernizing bureaucracy The previous chapter explained how networks can be used to change the *superstructure* of a (large) business organization. They turned out to support a combination of concentrating power, finance and control and decentralizing production and execution. The *structure within* organizations is also fundamentally changed by the introduction of networks. Here I am talking about changes in management. In the previous chapter, I described how bureaucracy turned out to be an obstacle instead of an innovation for organizations. By modernizing bureaucracy, ICT can help to get rid of this obstacle. According to Max Weber (1922) bureaucracy has five features:

1 hierarchy of authority;
2 centralization of decision-making;
3 formalization of rules;
4 specialization of tasks;
5 standardization of actions.

The use of ICT does not make these features disappear. On the contrary, they are integrated in this technology. Frissen (1989) has demonstrated the close relationship between bureaucracy and ICT. This is obvious for three of the features just mentioned. ICT offers much better opportunities for formalizing rules, specializing tasks and standardizing actions than did the old techniques. In using computers and networks, traditional procedures are formalized by programming them in software or even in hardware. Informal solutions have to be rejected as much as possible. People are restricted to their specific tasks more strictly than before, because they know everything they do is registered. Finally, the use of computers and networks leads to an extensive standardization of actions. After all, their use supposes fixed and detailed procedures and strict fine-tuning before one is able to start cooperation through networks.

The relationship between bureaucracy and ICT is less obvious for the first two features mentioned. Many think ICT 'flattens' organizations, as the distribution of network operations requires less hierarchy and centralization of decision-making. So, these features need more detailed explanation.

After having conducted an investigation in a number of Dutch social service departments, Zuurmond (1994) reached the conclusion that hierarchy, centralization, formalization and specialization in these services were decreasing. In some respects, these organizations had become 'flatter'. More teamwork took place at several levels. Civil servants less frequently recorded every step by writing it down. They acquired broader job responsibilities. Even the fifth feature of bureaucracy, standardization, was adapted. Within certain boundaries, civil servants were allowed to produce 'made-to-measure' work in the service. However, the extent of freedom for this work was strictly limited by computerization. Staff were given fewer opportunities to take important decisions themselves than before. Zuurmond has claimed with great emphasis that, in spite of requiring fewer traditional bureaucratic procedures, ICT causes an increase in (central) control over organization:

> Thus, an organization can create more horizontal structures, take out hierarchical levels, cancel checks and eliminate paper-devouring file guiding systems because information architecture can take care of these things. In particular, (routine) coordination and (routine) communication are being taken over by information systems. Management no longer has to control this coordination and communication: very strict procedures, designed to guide these actions, are allowed to 'disappear'. Now they are inside the system. (1994: 300–1, my translation from the Dutch)

So, the main part of traditional management's tasks is integrated in information systems. Modern management *selects* and *steers* these systems. Zuurmond calls his type of management *infocracy*, the successor of bureaucracy (see Zuurmond, 1998 for an elaboration of this concept in English).

Claiming that (central) control over organizations is increasing, while traditional hierarchical and bureaucratic procedures are declining, seems contradictory. What does it really mean? In the previous chapter, I argued that networks combine horizontal and vertical types of control and coordination. As further explanation, I want to make a clear distinction between the following aspects of the *infrastructure of organizations*:

From bureaucracy to infocracy

- a structure of *control*, regulation and information coordinating decision-making within and between organizational layers; this requires a structure of *authority* in a number of organizational layers;
- a *division of labour* distributing functions and tasks within the organization that necessitate *coordination*.

Control and Authority

Centralized or decentralized control?

The *control of decisions* in networks has to meet high demands. One can meet these demands by both centralization and decentralization. Mintzberg (1979) makes a distinction between a horizontal dimension (within one organizational level) and a vertical dimension (between organizational levels). Applying these concepts here, the following possibilities arise:

- *Horizontal centralization*: the highest level of management takes complete control (see above); the most important decisions are taken away from staff members, whose only job now is to shape the information network to enable the development of manageable options.
- *Horizontal decentralization*: increasingly complex information processes give staff functionaries more authority in the organization's management: the so-called 'line structure' (management) loses some of its influence to the 'technostructure'.
- *Vertical centralization*: the top layers in management take decisions away from the lower levels and even from employees at the base by means of standardization, formalization and increasing routine; inevitably, lines are shorter and parts of middle management become redundant.
- *Vertical decentralization*: standardization, formalization and increasing routine allow a transfer of decision-making power to the operational levels. They also allow a swift and flexible reaction to changes in the company's environment, an important benefit in the market and in direct relations between personnel and customers or clients.

It is important to note that all four tendencies are technically enabled by the introduction of networks. Which tendency will predominate depends not only on the balance of power within the organization, but also on the type and size of the organization, its diversity and the extent of its computerization. An increase in centralization is to be expected in offices which have had a low level of automation until recently. But most organizations will have to deal with a combination of the four tendencies described. Horizontal and vertical decentralization within a centralizing framework will be the most likely combination, as it is clearly enabled by networks of ICT.

Flat organizations?

Developments in the structure of *organizational authority* can be shown more clearly. It is common knowledge that the introduction of networks causes a decrease in the number of hierarchical levels. The network 'itself' takes over some of the supervising personnel's coordination tasks. Coordination and supervision are partly replaced by network operations. The work left for supervisors is to watch over and maintain the network instead of supervising and coordinating personnel. Lower and middle management have to give up some of their authority to higher management and staff functionaries on the one hand, and to operatives working independently with the aid of computer programs on the other. From these trends, many people have drawn the conclusion that organizations are getting flatter. But this does not have to be the case at all. It would be more true to say that the line between the top and the base is being 'thinned out'. The distance that communications have to bridge is decreasing; the difference in control and authority is not.

Division of labour and coordination

The *division of labour within organizations* that are supported by computer networks may lead to the integration of tasks (task broadening and even task enrichment) as much as to further specialization (task division and even task erosion). As claimed before, integration of tasks is most likely using ICT. Opening a multitude of programs at one terminal is made easier. Furthermore, task exchanges are supported: it is easier for a person to substitute for someone or to take over for a while. Technology will help to increase the organization's internal flexibility. Looking at things from this angle, we will see tasks *broaden*. Whether this will lead to task *enrichment* for the employee involved depends on the extent of power, education and freedom of action within the programs available. With unchanged policies of task divisions within organizations, the standardization and computer programming of traditional craft or expert knowledge often leads to task *erosion*. Task broadening could serve as a compensation.

Integration or specialization?

The same network technology, however, may lead to unprecedented task *division* in administrative and industrial organizations: tasks are standardized in programs that assign them to specific functions much more strictly than before. The computer system's access registration controls whether this really happens. Subsequently, the system 'itself' determines the observance of the procedures prescribed.

All this shows that network techniques are not power neutral. They are a clear matter of design, for instance in network architecture. Therefore, let us take a closer look at the *technical options* available in network design. The most important questions in this respect are:

- Will the main processing capacity be placed in a central or a local position?
- Will a workstation have its own connection to a central computer or a shared one?
- Who is able/allowed to communicate with whom over the network?
- Which programs and files can be used by the various categories of personnel?

The answer to most of these questions is largely determined by the network's technical typology and topology, programmed in the construction and the organization of the OSI standard network layers (see Chapter 3).

PRIVACY AND PERSONAL AUTONOMY

Now we reach the level of the individual. The use of networks can have major consequences for the power of individuals. Their privacy and their personal autonomy can be violated, but they can use the same techniques to protect themselves and to increase their freedom of choice.

We make a distinction between privacy and personal autonomy. Privacy is a freedom. It is a freedom of *individuals*, not of groups or organizations. Personal autonomy is a characteristic of an individual's *relations to others*. It determines the individual's opportunities to gain and protect freedom. Personal autonomy is a synonym for the power of the individual. Here, freedom becomes freedom of choice and control – in this case in the use of ICT. Privacy is a precondition of personal autonomy. Without an individual's freedom in general, any freedom of choice is restricted. Therefore this section begins with a discussion of privacy. First, the meaning of privacy is explained. Subsequently, the threats to privacy caused by the use of ICT are discussed. Finally, there is a treatise on existing possibilities to protect a person's privacy.

What is privacy?

Privacy definitions Privacy is an abstract concept bearing many meanings. It is so intangible that many people do not realize its importance. Popular descriptions are expressions such as 'privacy is the individual's right to determine whether and to what extent one is willing to expose oneself to others' and 'privacy is the right to be left alone'. A scientifically justifiable definition, however, has to be based on concepts and notions accepted in legal theory, in history or in social science.

Historical and anthropological research have shown that the value attached to privacy varies significantly in social and cultural terms, but that some aspects of privacy may be universal (Roberts and Gregor, 1971). At the end of extensive comparative historical research of ancient cultures, Barrington Moore (1984) reached the conclusion that the *need* for privacy, defined as the need to seclude one's intimate behaviour, to be alone occasionally and not to (have to) show certain views and behaviour to a group or community, is universal. However, *in historical practice* this need is often subordinated to a primitive social organization and technology, according to Moore. In this book, I want to add that, at the beginning of the 21st century, the individual is subordinated rather to *advanced* social organization and technology.

In legal theory, privacy is a particular right of freedom. It is a right of no interference, in this case of private life. Nabben and van de Luytgaarden (1996) even went so far as to call this right the *ultimate freedom*, not to be transferred on to a community and to be weighed against other interests.

The social philosopher Holmes produced one of the best definitions, in my view: 'Freedom from intrusion into areas of one's own life that one has not explicitly or implicitly opened to others' (1995: 18). In this definition of privacy, and in many others, spatial and informational dimensions are evident. Privacy is about the *spatial seclusion* of certain areas, starting with the body and its direct surroundings (private life) which are not to be interfered with. Added to this, *phases of information processing* often recur in definitions: the perception, registration and disclosure of the characteristics and behaviour of individuals.

Following Westin (1987), a distinction is often made between relational and informational privacy. Even though I argue that these two types of privacy often mingle, particularly in the context of networks, I maintain this division and even add a third type: physical privacy. In fact, the body and its immediate physical surroundings are the ultimate private area. This is the main reason why the act of rape is among the greatest possible violations of one's privacy.

Physical privacy

Physical privacy is the *right to selective intimacy*. This applies to the inviolability of the body and the fulfilment of intimate human needs, allowing the presence of only a very small selection of other persons or no other people at all. This may not seem to have relevance to ICT. But, in fact, biotechnology and information technology are increasingly intertwined. The most important link between them is the information code of life: DNA. Charting all genes of the human species and holding DNA tests have everything to do with a registration of personal data. In the future, DNA will probably produce the most important personal data. They will be recorded with the aid of ICT, which will also be used to link DNA data with other kinds of personal data.

Another potential threat to physical privacy is so-called biometrics. These are first of all identity checks (such as eye, face, finger and voice recognition) and entrance checks (screening sensors placed on the body). In addition, analogue and digital video cameras intrude into intimate physical spheres of personal life. For instance, cases are known of employers using cameras to store and process images centrally, to control whether employees spend too much time going to the toilet.

Relational privacy

Most of the time, camera checks will affect relational privacy: the *right to make contacts selectively*. This is about relationships and behaviour in one's (semi-)private life at home, at work, in forms of transportation (including one's own car) and other less reserved spaces. Being able to determine one's own personal relationships and conduct without other people observing and interfering with them is a fundamental right of freedom. This right might be threatened by the use of communication networks and information systems registering behaviour and relationships at a distance. Electronic house arrest and cameras in (semi-)public places serve as good examples of the registration of behaviour. Recording digital telephone conversations and tracking traffic between telephone numbers, electronic mailboxes and Internet addresses are examples of the registration of relationships.

Informational privacy

The last type of privacy is informational privacy: *the right to selective disclosure*. In a primitive sense, this type of privacy is as old as mankind (gossip) or writing (the first registers), but the introduction of ICT has made it much more relevant. Information privacy is about the grip the individual has and keeps over his or her personal data and over the information or decisions based on these data. Unfortunately, the concept of personal data has narrowed the common notions of privacy. The protection of privacy has been replaced by the protection of personal **data**, and it is sometimes even turned into the *security* of these data. For obvious reasons, most attention in this book is directed to informational privacy, but the most important links to relational and physical privacy are taken into account as much as possible. I describe the integration of these three types of privacy. For instance, the words 'traceability' and 'transparency', to be used below, show the close link between relational, informational and physical privacy.

Threats to privacy

More than all previous phases in the development of ICT, the introduction of networks is a threat to all types of privacy. The threats to informational privacy are most obvious, but relational and physical privacy are endangered as well when the spatial and physical spheres of personal life are opened up.

Traceability

The danger of the *traceability* of all actions of public network users is what scares people most. It can become a real danger, as the development of services throughout history shows. Financial services, for instance, went through a process starting with the circulation of coins, continuing through payments by cheques and printed accounts, and finally reaching electronic payment. Along this road, service providers have obtained increasing amounts of information about their clients. In electronic transactions, the bank is informed of the exact place, time and nature of every transaction and the client receives bank statements of these data. In transaction services, a similar shift from cash to electronic registration is occurring. Intelligent cash registers, point-of-sale terminals, 'road pricing', email orders and reservations provide ever greater details and personal information about the consumer. This is a golden opportunity for market research, marketing and advertising. On the Internet, every step in information and conversation services is recorded by so-called *tracking technologies*. If they want to, webmasters can follow every entry to, and every 'click' on, their sites. They have two ways to do this. First, log files are kept of every step made on the Internet. These log files consist of large series of numbers containing information about the computer and the web browser used and the country they are from. Increasingly, hardware such as processors, and software such as word-processing programs, contain numbers and even the names of their owners. Often the user's email address is added to this information. This information turns log files into collections of personal data. Analysing them without advanced programs would be extremely labour-intensive. Very often, therefore, a second means is used: the user is offered an invisible *cookie**. A small file containing data on the visitor to a site is created automatically, sent back to the user's web browser and stored on the hard disk without the user knowing it. Every time the user visits this particular site, the file is retrieved automatically. Thus, after some time, a user profile is created. All this takes place without the knowledge of users. The users are often helpful in filling in all sorts of questionnaires before using a particular service. Unsuspecting users do not know that the questionnaire actually completes the user profile.

It is obvious that registration and consultation services cause the greatest danger to privacy because they have a powerful centre that is 'hungry' for personal data. But with the rise of digital communication networks using registration software, privacy in decentralized conversation is also at stake. For example, tapping and reading someone else's email is fairly simple. This danger not only springs from people breaking into a registration centre (such as hackers); increasingly, the threat comes from the centre itself. For example, managers may want to (be able to) read all of the email of their employees – although more often they are satisfied with just checking the addresses they visit and the services they use. As the role of central exchanges in decentralized conversation grows, the capacity for these checks increases. In software controlled digital electronic exchanges and switches, the duration and the cost of the connection and the number of the sender and the receiver are always registered. **Checks on decentralized conversation**

The next consideration is a much more open use of the subscriber's number in digital networks. Especially important in this respect is calling line identification (CLI). The display of (digital) telephones shows the number of the caller. From a privacy protection point of view, the most important advantage is the shift in power from the caller to the called. Ever since the introduction of automatic telephony, the caller has had disproportionate power in the process of making contact. CLI makes it harder for callers to get away with unwelcome calls, such as obscene calls and fake emergency calls. **Calling line identification**

This brings us to the risks for relational privacy. There is pressure in all communications technology to *be within reach at any time and place*. If new facilities such as 'follow-me switches', answering machines and voice mailboxes will not see to this, mobile and cellular telephony will. The explosive demand for these kinds of facilities proves how much people have adjusted to continuous communication, but at the same time it causes the individual to be traceable to the deepest crevices of the social fabric and in all environments. Almost every place becomes a social space. It is becoming hard to avoid being accessible at any time and place. And even if one tries and succeeds in using blocking options, the chances of having to *justify* oneself are increasing. This is a threat to personal autonomy (discussed below). Our natural space to withdraw (though this space is not divided equally in social **Total reachability** terms) and to be left alone is shrinking. Yet this space has always been useful to the efficiency of communication. Being accessible at any time and place will lead to a sharp increase in the quantity of communication appearing to be (almost) irrelevant afterwards.

Central control

Not only are spaces of private life in the house and the car opened up by computer networks, but also private space at work. This is fixed to particular places when people have to work at desktop computers or terminals. In this case, not only the employee's achievements but also his/her spatial behaviour can be traced by management. Free movement across the department, through the building or on the road is registered and controlled. Through all kinds of passes and check cards, every movement is traceable. All in all, management and technology increasingly decide on the right of employees to make contacts selectively, even at work. Some managers and employers deny any right of employees to privacy at work. In any case, private space at work is changing into a more collective space.

Data intelligence

The next threat to privacy is the establishment of relationships between data that cause no harm if they are used separately. There are many ways for information technology to help establish relations between personal data within and between files. First, relations within files are discussed. Next, relations between files, also known as links or couplings, are described.

Within files: Data warehouses and data mining

Most database files are created to establish relations between individual records and fields (characteristics) in a matrix. This produces information about individuals. As a next step, databases are created to establish overviews of all records and fields or a selection of them. Thus, strategic information is obtained about groups of people – for instance the purchasing behaviour of various groups of people at various times of the day. In most cases, the information can be traced back to an individual. Enabling a company to use all these possibilities, data from several sources are brought together in one database and checked for correctness (a clearing operation). These data collections are called *data warehouses*. Filling these warehouses with large amounts of data to be used in various contexts has become an industry on its own. Accompanying search techniques are called *knowledge discovery in databases* (KDD).

The next step is *data mining*: the extraction of implicitly present, formerly unknown, but potentially usable information from data. All kinds of new search techniques are developed for this purpose, based on a combination of statistics and artificial intelligence.

Data warehouses and data mining help to produce strategically significant information on persons. The people involved are usually not aware of this. They leave their tracks everywhere, for instance in using customer cards, savings cards and chip cards, or by filling out reply forms, thinking this will not be of any consequence to their privacy. Then, suddenly, the data deposited everywhere return to the person concerned like a boomerang. Many institutions turn out to have a surprisingly wide knowledge of an individual and appear to be able to take decisions, and not always the right ones, for the customer, employee or citizen. This knowledge can result in very interesting offers, but can also result in being turned down for a job interview, in not being granted a loan, or in having an income tax return refused.

More possibilities appear in the production of links between data in several different files – a process known as *file coupling*. This process can vary from simple comparisons to the actual coupling of files, enabling the use of KDD's advanced search techniques.

Combining two or more files may lead to a complete integration of these files in one file. This integration can help to make *profiles* of a person (and a group or organization). These profiles are created using behavioural psychology and statistics to estimate the chance that someone with specific characteristics will do certain things (Rothfelder, 1992).

These profiles become more and more influential in personnel information systems and in management and marketing information systems. In all these systems, the distance between combined data and the source is great. In the combination of data, in fact, new data are created (often for a different purpose from that of the original registration) and are immediately interpreted by these systems as information. The person involved is hardly ever informed of these adaptations and new purposes. It is strategic information. Yet, mistakes and inaccurate presuppositions are easily made.

The elusiveness of file combination and adaptation in networks means that the distance between the reality of individuals, the data on these individuals and the decisions based on them is increasing, and the influence of individuals on the total process is decreasing accordingly.

Between files: File coupling and making profiles

Defences of privacy

Without protective measures, the introduction of networks will lead to a serious threat to individual privacy. One does not need to suffer from paranoia to say this. The applications offered by networks are clearly attractive to the people in control of politics and the economy. On this occasion, I am not even talking about the potential rise of a more or less totalitarian administration, that is offered a perfect infrastructure, or about the real conceivable expansion of electronic surveillance after the terrorist attacks of September 11, 2001. For the first time in history, the network phase in computerization more or less justifies the popular spectre of a 'big brother society' characterized by far-reaching traceability and controllability of the individual (O'Harrow, 2005). The difference is that we are not dealing with a single 'big brother' here, but with a whole series of 'little brothers'. Furthermore, most often we are not dealing with direct supervision through monitors and screens, but with indirect traceability and control. However, this is at least as efficient and effective, because (a) it can be based on summarized data and information and (b) it is totally unapparent to the victims, causing them to adjust mentally to ever-present supervision, or to become indifferent to it.

Fortunately, there are numerous ways to protect privacy in networks as well. They can be summarized in four categories:

Ways to protect privacy

1   legal protection;
2   social protection: refusal of or participation in the supply of new services and techniques by consumers and codes of conduct adopted by producers;
3   system-technical and organizational protection;
4   technical alternatives.

So far, 1 and 3 have received the most attention. However, according to the analysis below, more protection is to be expected from 2 and 4 in the short term.

Legal protection   Legal protection of privacy in media networks is necessary as a framework and a backbone for the other three kinds of protection. Unfortunately, legal protection is still very inadequate. Almost all of the countries in the world have either a constitutional or a legal right to privacy. A country can have legal privacy protection at three levels: the constitution, specific privacy law and common law (this is law based upon decisions of judges and customs instead of written law). The legal protection of privacy is inadequate, in particular with regard to networks, for several reasons.

Weaknesses   First, privacy regulation and legislation are at a low level of development and effectiveness. Constitutions are very broad. They have no immediate and indisputable practical implications. In the United States, the part of the constitution concerned, the Fourth Amendment, is both broad and narrow, as it only protects against government infringement of a person's privacy. On the other hand, privacy laws are often very specific. For instance, the United States has adopted an impressive series of privacy acts at the federal and state levels. This has produced a complete fragmentation of privacy legislation, making it weak and capable of being mastered by juridical experts only (Perritt, 1996). By contrast, the EU has developed very comprehensive and ambitious privacy legislation, based upon the long-standing principles and guidelines of the OECD and the Council of Europe. However, the execution of the comprehensive European privacy laws takes so much effort and social support that they are difficult to put into practice. Moreover, the effectiveness of all privacy legislation is uncertain as personal data in networks are transferred across borders with different jurisdictions and because the legislation has a rather low status: it is most often civil law and common law rather than criminal law. So, prosecution and punishment for privacy offences are rare.

This brings us to a second reason. Privacy is not viewed as an absolute right of individuals. It is always weighed against other rights and interests, primarily the information and communication freedom of others and the security rights of the government. More and more, privacy regulation is overruled by other laws and by national security or emergency regulation.

The third weakness of legal privacy protection is that it still deals almost exclusively with informational privacy. It is a matter of *data* protection. However, ICT in general and media networks in particular increasingly enter the areas of relational and physical privacy. As a result, applications such as email, calling line identification, video surveillance with storage of recordings, and all kinds of monitoring of Internet use, are poorly protected (see Chapter 6). The same goes for physical privacy, which might be threatened by biometrics and DNA testing using new media (see Davies, 1994).

Finally, the most important weakness of legal privacy protection is that it always lags behind the development of technology, as do so many laws. In the 1980s, laws were made in which computer registration was assumed to be a static affair of producing and consulting fixed files managed by controllers who could be identified and alerted to their legal obligations. In the 1990s, it was discovered that registration in computer networks is a dynamic affair of continually collecting, processing, editing, changing, consulting, using and transferring data. The European Directive of 1995 took this dynamic process as its main point of departure in the adaptation of privacy law (European Commission, 1995). Shortly afterwards, new technological difficulties appeared: encryption, diverging international standards, monitoring on the Internet and the qualification of video registration. These problems are discussed in Chapter 6.

The flaws in privacy legislation make the perspective of self-regulation by individuals and interest groups more attractive, although legislation remains necessary to guide self-regulation and to prevent the law of the jungle. After all, self-regulation favours the strongest parties involved. There are two types of self-regulation: individual and social. | **Self-regulation**

Individual self-regulation consists of the attempts of ICT users to safeguard privacy themselves using their own expertise, actions and technical means such as filtering with software and using browsers to help them negotiate their personal data with online service providers. The Platform for Privacy Preferences (P3) and TRUSTe are names for this kind of means. They are considered in Chapter 6. | **Individual**

Some users with less technical expertise simply refuse to fill out names and credit card numbers on the Internet or leave false ones instead. Privacy is a growing concern to individual Internet users according to many surveys. In practice, however, these users also appear to be very careless in protecting their privacy while using Internet applications. Software instruments offered for the encryption of email, for anonymous surfing, for filtering sites with poor privacy protection and for the elimination of **cookies** and **spyware** are rarely used. Perhaps their application is too difficult or laborious. However, a lack of trust leading to simple refusals is more effective than one might expect. It is one of the reasons for the disappointing start of electronic commerce in the 1990s and the early years of the 21st century. So, offering privacy guarantees will become one of the most important quality standards of services in networks. Many producers have prepared codes of conduct and codes of good practice on their own initiative, in an attempt to convince consumers.

Often social self-regulation has to step in to support individual users. Increasingly, consumer organizations, user groups, trade unions and civil organizations negotiate with producers, employers and public administrations about the privacy conditions of using personal data in computer files and networks. They might be able to prevent misuse, instead of trying to cure things afterwards. | **Collective**

When trade unions and consumer organizations are allowed to participate in the design, construction and introduction of networks in advance, this will produce earlier and better results – broadly supported decisions in favour of or against particular solutions – than will legislation and technical or organizational measures of protection afterwards. For instance, apart from an occasional judicial decision, personnel assessment and personnel information systems, which often needlessly threaten privacy, at present can only be stopped or changed by collective agreements between employers and trade unions or works councils. Organizations of employees are able to point out how these systems may have negative effects on achievements as well, such as too much attention being directed to the quantity of production, and the stimulation of all kinds of informal resistance and escape.

System-technical and organizational protection

Often the suggestion is made that privacy is sufficiently protected by privacy regulations and reliable personal data protection. Yet, it should be clear by now how vulnerable networks are. They simply *cannot* be secured 100 percent. Besides, privacy cannot be protected by security alone. This is often regarded as a series of impartial technical measures in which social processes and clashes of interest do not play a part. In the professional literature on this issue, three terms are confused with each other: security, protection of confidentiality and protection of privacy.

Security, confidentiality and privacy

Security is a necessary but not a sufficient condition for the protection of confidential and sensitive data. Until now, most attention has been given to the system-technical and physical security of networks – things such as guarding, locking, and using access cards and the safe technical construction of networks. This kind of security almost by definition is not foolproof, for connections by cable cannot be secured as long as they are not made of fibre-optic wires. And in connections with fibre-optic wires, it is still possible to tap switches, nodes and central exchanges. Worse still, the quickest way to break security is not via connections and switches, but simply 'through the front door' by hacking access codes.

Since the late 1990s, calls for procedural and organizational security have become louder. For instance, files containing personal data are left to certain functionaries who alone are allowed access to these files, whereas everyone else is denied it. These procedures are recorded in scenarios and regulations concerning access. This type of security requires training for personnel that pays a lot of attention to aspects of security and the stimulation of an organizational structure in which the protection of (personal) data, programs and equipment is a point of particular salience in daily routine.

Confidentiality should not be confused with privacy either. Privacy is better reserved for individuals, whereas confidentiality has to do with the data and behaviour of groups or (departments of) an organization. When people who are registered demand access to the procedures used in the information system or to the contents of their own files, they often meet with the argument that these procedures and data are confidential. In some cases, those registered have virtually no rights at all, for instance when trying to gain access to the registers of the police and security agencies.

My conclusion is that the protection of *individual privacy* involves more than security and the protection of confidentiality. Even though they are based upon the power, interests and divisions of labour within organizations, the measures taken often fail to allow for conflicts of interest. When reading professional literature on technology and organizations, one might get the impression that the people responsible for keeping and securing a register themselves cannot violate the privacy of the registered, most often their own employees – as if the violators were automatically outsiders, that is, criminals and unauthorized persons. Legislation and self-regulation are of vital importance to the protection of privacy. The interests of the individual or groups of individuals have to be weighed against the interests of other individuals or groups and organizations.

Developing technical alternatives might be the best structural solution to the problems concerning privacy. In fact, a small number of scientists and technicians have been working hard on such alternatives from the 1990s onwards. They base their work on four alternative network characteristics: local control, concentration of intelligence in terminals, more offline equipment and privacy-enhancing technologies. Local control means that smaller networks are constructed, one each for every organization or department, that are able to protect their own files containing personal data. Concentration of intelligence in network terminals or standalone machines enables more unregistered use of computers. Using more offline equipment for personal registration, such as chip cards or smart cards instead of large online databases, also offers more privacy protection. However, user control of these means remains necessary because most often smart or chip cards are simply plugged into computer networks and their central registrations. The fourth alternative, privacy-enhancing technologies, seems to be the most promising concerning privacy protection. This is the reason why I will now go deeper into these technologies.

Technical alternatives

The same techniques that cause risks to privacy can also be used to protect it. In the 1990s, we saw the breakthrough of all sorts of techniques to encrypt information and communication in networks. Defenders of the right to privacy increasingly consider these *privacy-enhancing technologies* to be their most important weapons. But that is only after it has been determined that the registration of personal data is necessary anyway.

Basic principles of privacy-enhancing technologies

The observation that the identity of the individual is of no importance to the greater part of the process of registration is the basic principle of these techniques. Individuals can be given a pseudo-identity that replaces their real identity in the process of registration. In registration by ICT systems, the following phases usually follow each other:

1   authorization (permission to 'enter' the system);
2   identification and authentication;
3   access control (in particular applications);
4   auditing (check and justification of the use of the system);
5   accounting.

According to a report by the Dutch and the Canadian official data registrars (van Rossum et al., 1995a and 1995b), the user's true identity is needed only in particular cases at the beginning (authorization) and at the end (payment). However, in all cases (when desired) and in all intermediate phases, both of them can be replaced by a pseudo-identity protecting the true identity. The following privacy techniques are used for this purpose.

Digital signature The digital signature is the digital alternative to the written signature. A digital signature cannot be copied, since it consists of the unique combination of a private key, known only to the owner, and a public key, known to the other party involved, for instance a service provider. The private key is not some sort of personal identification number (PIN) code, since this code is known by other parties – at least by the distributor (the bank, for instance). The private key is compiled by the user from a unique series of randomly chosen numbers. The private key and the public key are combined when a certain process requires identification of the individual by an institution. This combination is another key. When the combination is decoded by the institution concerned using the public key, the authenticity of the signature is confirmed. At that point in the process, it is not necessary to know to whom the signature actually belongs.

Digital pseudonym The second technique is the digital pseudonym. By using the same combination as used for digital signatures, users can take a pseudonym authorizing them to receive a certain amount of services from service providers. The providers are paid for the amount as a whole. A different pseudonym can be used for every service and service provider. Thus, registration and exchange of individual sales data by service providers is made impossible (consult van Rossum et al., 1995b for technical details on digital signatures and pseudonyms).

Encryption The techniques mentioned above do not have to be used until some sort of identification or authorization is needed, for example in a transaction or in an electronic payment system (Chaum, 1992, 1994). They can be used to protect both *transfers* and the *contents* of messages and transactions. In the latter case, they block access to a message for everyone but the addressee. These codes or *encryptions* have been designed for email, for instance. Until well into the 1990s, messages by email could be opened by others fairly easily. Pretty Good Privacy (PGP), designed by Phil Zimmermann, was among the first techniques for encrypting email. Zimmermann was prosecuted by the American government for his illegal export of 'defence technology'. In fact, the American government had been trying to gain control of the distribution of encryption for years. First, it forced hardware manufacturers to build in a so-called clipper chip, enabling the police and intelligence services to decode for criminal investigations. Later it ordered one copy of the key to be handed over to the Department of Justice. These measures led to a wave of criticism from business and private users of the Internet. In Europe, the proposals to hand over one key to the Ministry of Justice were relaxed after a few years, and it was suggested that this copy could be delivered to a trusted third party. This third party would be authorized to pass on a copy of the key to the Ministry of Justice under strict conditions, for example in the case of an official legal investigation, to decode communications by criminals, terrorists, racists and producers of child pornography.

The latest techniques for encryption are extremely hard to track and decode. **Steganography**
They can also be used for privacy protection. Some of them are based on *steganography*. This technique enables the user to make a message invisible by hiding it in another message. Seemingly harmless texts, videos and audio sources may contain criminal messages written 'between the lines'. In this case, the police and security organizations do not even know where to look for them. The rise of these new techniques proves that the authorities' preferred solutions – the demands to build in chips and to deliver copies of keys – are actually rearguard actions. It will be harder and harder to intercept illegal communication in transit. Gradually, the solution will be to search at the source and at the destination – the sender and the receiver of messages – where the encrypted or hidden messages are bound to disappear from, and reappear in, the analogue world. Photographs of child pornography have to be taken somewhere. Racist electronic statements are compiled, stored and printed on local computers, media and printers. Criminal deals and the theft of digital money will leave traces or lead to actions in nonvirtual reality.

The most important conclusion concerning the four means used in the pro- **Integrated**
tection of privacy is that none of them can be omitted. They presuppose each **protection**
other. Legislation will not be effective without the practice of self-regulation and the security of data. Conversely, self-regulation and social protection will be unrestrained without a legal framework of enforceable rights: they will promote a culture of the 'survival of the fittest'. I have also argued that organizational and system-technical measures are a necessary but not a sufficient condition for privacy protection. Finally, the conclusion has to be drawn that technical solutions will not cure all evils either. They have to be embedded in legislation, self-regulation (such as participation of employees and clients) and managerial practices. Most solutions are two-edged swords. They can just as easily endanger as protect privacy. Encryption can be used equally by the Ministry of Justice, by criminals and by respectable citizens. The association between the means to defend privacy shows once more that networks are not neutral technical means. In all kinds of ways, they are related to power in society, in organizations and between individuals.

Personal autonomy

The conclusion just reached will be even more evident when we take the step from privacy to the personal autonomy of individuals in the choices they have to make when dealing with networks.

Networks define the character of a system. They connect several end points **Networks are**
or terminals. At these points, human individuals are working, studying and **systems**
living. These simple remarks evoke the most fundamental questions concerning power in networks. To what extent do individuals, as members of an

organization, as citizens, employees, clients or consumers, have a say in whether or not they are *connected* to the network, and how much influence do they have on the *use* of the network once they have been connected?

The questions above concern the control human beings have over their technical means. However, a network cannot be compared with a machine one decides to purchase. A network is *not a standalone instrument* just replacing or simplifying human communication and activity. A network is *a medium with a system character*. It links separate machines and their human operators and it streamlines their communications and activities. Kubicek and Rolf (1985) have claimed the necessity for an entirely different approach to get a grip on network technology. The traditional approach stems from a *machine* model: hardware and software are considered to be detached and locally or functionally confined instruments. Their effects can be calculated and changed directly. This model no longer works in network technology. It has to be replaced by a *system* model. This model not only assesses all nodes, connections, protocols, terminals and programs separately, but also their *combinations in a system* and especially their *implementation in existing organizational and social processes*. It turns out that most often the whole organization or other social unit will change, in both their internal and external relations. Many corporations and administrations have discovered that the network phase of automation means more radical changes than the preceding phases when only separate machines were installed. The consequences are harder to foresee and calculate. They often cross borders that the organization itself has not yet crossed. This can be the case when companies are connected to a common network. This makes this technology almost intangible to works councils and other organizations of employees. For individuals, the distance to places where decisions are made becomes even greater. For them, this technology usually appears to be extremely large scale, opaque and intangible. However, from the following list it appears that networks have both positive and negative consequences for personal autonomy.

Individual autonomy of:

Citizens

As *citizens*, individuals have become completely dependent upon their political representatives and governors concerning decisions on whether and how the government will record data on their use of networks. At best, they will get rights of access to, and correction of, their data. Police and intelligence agents are able to ignore privacy legislation on many issues and to shut off their networks from political control. On the other hand, citizens are able to use networks such as the Internet to learn about their government, public administration and political representatives. And they can express their own opinions in electronic discussions and televotes (teledemocracy).

Employees

As *employees*, individuals have to accept their workplaces being integrated in a company network, perhaps abolishing any autonomy they possessed. Trade unions and other organizations of employees are not able to stop these fundamental changes, even if they want to. Usually, they lack the power and knowledge. The network's system character and its radical consequences for work and organization force employers' representatives to specialize in fields unknown to them and sometimes to retrain completely. Management and personnel information systems increase the power of executives. On the other hand, employees are able to use organizational networks for task extension and enrichment through vertical decentralization (see above) or for better and more empowering communication with their colleagues.

As *clients* of a company or government institution, individuals simply have to accept that services are now offered and registered electronically. After a short period of transition, access will be granted only after entering a pass and a PIN code. This can be used to transfer personal details automatically and on a larger scale than ever before. Another consequence will be the replacement of traditional services, based on more or less informal processes of negotiation between persons, by electronic services working with fixed, pre-programmed instructions leaving less room for negotiation. On the other hand, clients are able to address multifunctional or one-stop services of the government and private providers where all information and services are gathered. On the Internet, the position of clients and consumers is strengthened by software enabling them to compare the price and quality of various sites in electronic commerce.

Clients

Finally, as *consumers*, individuals face the constant pressure of a 'technology push' to buy electronic products. As long as the majority has not yet bought the products, the customer seems to be king. But when theatre performances and aeroplane flights are being booked mostly or wholly electronically, the potential customer of electronic services will no longer feel free to say no to them. And this freedom to say no will probably disappear completely when the vast majority has been connected. Then the crucial question will arise: will non-electronic and analogue techniques be kept in supply? For instance, as in some countries, will consumers be forced to buy digital television sets and decoders to replace their old analogue equipment?

Consumers

CONCLUSIONS

- When social networks reach for the support of media networks, some people may win and others may lose power. Media networks are not neutral technical instruments.
- However, all people may lose power on occasions because networks constitute a vulnerable technology that is liable to break down. The apparent solution, more security, tends to reduce the usefulness and freedom of networking. Some kind of compromise is needed.
- Computer networks can concentrate and spread politics in and from its institutional core: governments, parliaments and public administrations. They can help to create a strong state that is able to support security and effective government, and a weak state that gives way to (inter)national business power and civil societies.
- The spread and concentration of politics also depend on the views of the democracy that political actors support in using computer networks. Some views favour more direct democracy, while other views prefer better representation.

- Among the three claims of digital democracy and e-government: better political information retrieval and exchange, more and better public debates or community building and more participation in political decision-making, only the first (regarding information) has been realized sufficiently.
- The power in the organization shifts from bureaucracy to infocracy. Both horizontal and vertical types of control and coordination are installed in organizational information systems. In this way, organizations are not necessarily getting flatter: the distance of communication between all members of the organization is reduced, not the distance of control and authority.
- Without protective measures, computer networks will lead to a serious threat to privacy. The vast registration capacity, traceability, reachability and visibility (on video files) of people and behaviour together with the integration of biometrics deeply touch our informational, relational and physical privacy.
- The three main protections of privacy: legislation, self-regulation and technological solutions, are only effective in combination.
- The personal autonomy of network users is also at stake because computer networks are not devices under direct individual control, but systems. They are relational constructs of many individual agents that try to realize their own choices, but also have to accept the choices of others and the design of the technological system or program as a whole. The advance and reduction of personal autonomy are decided in a struggle for power over networks.

LAW

In the last two chapters we saw how the introduction and utilization of networks may change the balance of power at every level. The social unit as a whole becomes more vulnerable. The risks are growing. Computer networks are a very vulnerable technology. Liberty and equality may also be threatened. Networks are both used and abused by surveilling governments and criminals, terrorists, racists or child pornographers. We would expect the law to offer some protection, for the law is a sort of legitimized power. It is supposed to regulate power, or at least to prevent excesses. But the tragedy is that the law itself, particularly existing legislation, is itself being undermined by network technology. Better protection is needed; inadequate protection is the situation at present.

The prevailing principle in applying the law to networks is that what goes offline should go online. This seems to be a safe principle when technology is new, but does it manage to do justice to online reality? Many online actions create a virtual reality and they are a mixture of public and private behaviour. Current law has difficulties in grasping this and offering solutions that not only control but also help online actions to move in the right direction. One of the first questions this chapter addresses is who actually rules the Internet? Is it the law and governments, the public interest, corporate interests, the Internet community or network technology?

In the subsequent sections, I discuss the most important juridical issues that are related to social affairs in general and the network society in particular. They are rights (and duties) of information and communication freedom, intellectual property rights and privacy rights. With all these rights I will ask whether the adaptation of legislation is sufficient for protection. Self-regulation is on the rise because it can react much quicker than legislation to new technological realities and because it is appropriate for societies with less government influence than there used to be. Another alternative is technological protection in the form of encryption, technical blocks and warning systems. Which of these three protection modes is the most successful in safeguarding rights and duties?

Law, justice and technology

The law and justice have lagged behind new technology in almost every period in history. This is understandable, as new technology must become established in society before legislation can be applied to it. Furthermore, the consequences of new technology are not always clear right away. That is why the legal answer usually has the character of a reaction or an adjustment of existing principles. In civil society, this character is enhanced by the principle of civil law, in which individuals initially act freely and the law subsequently makes corrections. Legislation in advance, for instance to stimulate or halt the development of a particular new technology, would be state planning. This idea does not fit well with the principle of free initiative in technological development in capitalist societies. Justice in general, and legislation in particular, increasingly lag behind micro-electronic technological development. In 2005, even the most basic terms such as 'information', 'data', 'program' and 'communication' were not yet defined unambiguously and fixed in legislation. Jurisprudence is the most important weapon against misuse of these new technologies. It is created by judges who often tend to make things easy for themselves by simply declaring existing legal terminology applicable to new technical realities. Before legislation has dealt with any phase in computerization, the next phase is already happening. More than any preceding technology, networks test existing legislation. This happens for at least seven fundamental reasons.

Challenges of network technology

The first challenge, as preceding chapters have stressed, is the intangible, geographically free and continuously changing character of information and communication in networks. By contrast, existing legislation depends on *clearly demonstrable, localizable and liable legal persons and ownership titles*. Information and evidence have to be, or must be able to be, set down on a data carrier that still has to be comparable to printed paper.

Second, when legislators have managed to develop and lay down new legislation for the utilization of networks, the problem of *implementing these laws* arises. Networks are connected to other networks and they are not terminated by frontiers. This causes three essential problems:

- *perception* of the violation of the law, an offence or a crime: activities in networks are non-transparent and hard to trace;
- *evidence* of such activities: evidence can easily be destroyed, changed or hidden in networks;
- *prosecution*: jurisprudence differs across countries and the accuser and the accused may come from different jurisdictions, especially when international crime is involved.

Third, network technology has become international very quickly. Laws, on the other hand, are mainly national, particularly with regard to the actual prosecution and punishment of crime. International regulation usually stops at general declarations and basic principles agreed upon by international institutions. No matter how important these declarations and principles are as an impetus to international legislation, they do not themselves have any real practical meaning. Moreover, they are usually pretexts for international political action and economic protectionism, rather than genuine protection against the unacceptable consequences of a new technology.

Fourth, existing legislation is still bound to the material reality of the industrial revolution and the first communications revolution, or even pre-industrial trade and craft. This explains why some juridical discussions are still about whether information is a commodity and whether communication by computers can be treated as equivalent to a 'conversation'. However, the network phase already represents the culmination of a revolution in micro-electronics that has supported the rise of tertiary and quarternary services and has submitted them to processes of industrialization and rationalization. Furthermore, as we have seen, the network phase is the basis for a second communications revolution. Without a thorough (re)definition of basic terms such as 'information', 'data', 'program', 'electronic communications', 'information service', 'file', 'owner', 'editor', 'controller' or 'processor' of (personal) data, and so forth, any legal grip on the consequences of network technology is bound to fail.

Fifth, existing legislation is still tied to preceding phases in economic development, the phases of free competition and monopolization, state regulation and the beginning of internationalization. However, the international concentration of capital and power, combined with decentralization of production, the creation of a global 'flow economy' and the enormous growth of an elusive financial sphere, together cause a new economic reality to arise. It can hardly be controlled with existing means, and certainly not with existing legislation.

Sixth, around the turn of the millennium, existing legislation was still based on rapidly obsolete technological boundaries. Network technology ends the old divisions between tele-, data and mass communications and between the various media within these types of communications. Separate legislation is no longer adequate for integrated networks. For instance, the separation of press and broadcasting legislation had already started to become outdated with the appearance of cable TV information services decades ago. Obviously, a *general framework of communication and information legislation* is needed. This will have to be based no longer on concrete material technical differences, but on much more abstract distinctions of information and communication, such as the information traffic patterns discussed in Chapter 1 and the network layers dealt with in Chapters 2, 3 and 4. The information traffic patterns, based on relationships of (rightful) power and other basic rights in communication and information (which are discussed later in this chapter), can provide a useful beginning. The network layers of a technical kind (the OSI layers described in Chapter 3) and of an economic kind (the levels of infrastructure production, network management and application services discussed in Chapter 4) also provide useful distinctions for the general framework required. They put together related activities that should be regulated in a similar way.

Seventh, most new legislation is characterized by fragmentary adjustments and by (often) contradictory jurisprudence. There is no integral readjustment. Instead, detailed alterations are made to existing legislation including technical definitions that will soon be outdated. For the larger part, they are economic emergency regulation in copyright, contract law, certification or authentication law (concerning orders and payments), legal responsibility and the like. The only non-economic legislation of any importance consists of freedom of information or communication and privacy acts in some countries. Fragmentary adjustments to legislation are not suitable for the regulation of large-scale networks and their far-reaching consequences to individuals and society at large. Here, the failure to reach conclusions in current social and political discussion about new communication technology is felt. Such conclusions are necessary for any future framework legislation, to be worked out subsequently in more specific legislation and self-regulation.

What goes offline should go online? The main principle for governments and other authorities in adapting current legislation is that rules that go offline should also be(come) valid online. This seems to be a sensible and wise principle in the first development stages of a new technology. Indeed, it has served as a way to fill the main lacunae of existing legislation concerning ICT. However, I do not think it will work in the long term. This conservative principle does not take into account the fundamental differences between offline and online environments such as those discussed in this book. And it does not take sufficiently seriously the special problems characteristic of a network such as the Internet. Fundamental differences are derived from: the fact that one environment is virtual and the other physical or material, that the distinction between public and private is blurred in online environments, that the accountability of things that happen in these environments cannot clearly be ascribed to the technology or to human effort, that the division between collective and individual property rights in networks is not easily made, and many other characteristics of public computer networks to be dealt with in this and the chapters that follow. Difficult-to-solve problems are derived from the peculiar hardware and software architecture of the Internet with its network layers and codes, which are discussed in the next section.

Framework legislation To solve the legal problems of the online environment in a really fundamental way, new legislation has to be designed that does not depend on particular technologies and their characteristics but on basic principles of law in contemporary high-tech societies. To combine these principles, legislators could prepare framework legislation that covers a broad range of laws. The main point of departure should be the constitution of a country, which contains the basic rights of information and communication freedom, rights of protection (among others privacy rights) and property rights that all have to be balanced. Framework legislation does not consist of concrete pieces or articles of law but of political-legal documents proposed by governments and parliaments. Once a country agrees on the framework, concrete laws can be made or changed.

WHO RULES THE INTERNET?

States and politics losing their grip As has been stated, legislation cannot keep pace with technological and economic development, just at a time when we are confronted with new risks.

The same can be said about 'politics'. Nationally and internationally states are losing their grip on information policy owing to three tendencies which took place at the end of the 20th century:

- media networks increasingly crossing borders;
- the growth of a world market of transnational corporations, operating freely and communicating through their own networks, allowing hardly any influence by international regulatory organizations;
- current policies of privatization and deregulation of public goods and services.

This state of affairs reveals that individual governments have only weak control over the Internet. However, this does not mean that this network of networks is not ruled by other actors or instruments. This section shows that a fierce struggle is going on between government, corporate, technological and self-regulatory control of the Internet. As it is considered to be the most important media network of the future, the Internet will be the focus of my attention.

First, I want to compare the regulation of the Internet to the regulation of older media such as broadcasting, the press and telecommunications. McQuail and Windahl (1993: 211) have compared the broadcasting model, the press model and the telecommunications model of regulation of public media, among others, with the help of the information traffic patterns discussed in Chapter 1. I want to start the discussion in this section by adding the Internet model of regulation (see Figure 6.1). It appears from this figure that the regulation of the Internet has more similarities with the press model and the telecommunications model than with the broadcasting model. As the Internet combines public and private communication, it looks like the press model considering public communication (web sites) and like the telecommunications model regarding private communication (such as email). Traditionally, broadcasting meets strong regulation. Both infrastructure and content have high levels of regulation. The access of senders (channels) has always been controlled by governments and regulatory committees. In the past, the reasons for control were the powerful role of the centre (the channels and their programmes), the scarcity of frequencies and the pressures of particular cultural policies. For example, TV is considered to be a penetrating visual medium with potential negative effects such as those caused by violence in programmes. In undemocratic societies, the reason for regulating broadcasting was political censorship.

The Internet looks like a relatively free press model because publication of Internet content is just as open as that of press media and because this content is scarcely controlled by media law. Later in this chapter, I will discuss why governments and media law have no effective grip on Internet content. However, contrary to the press, the Internet meets with high infrastructure regulation and access limitations for receivers. The Internet rides on the heavily regulated infrastructure of telecommunication and cable networks. As it is also used for private communication, it has to offer

Models of media regulation

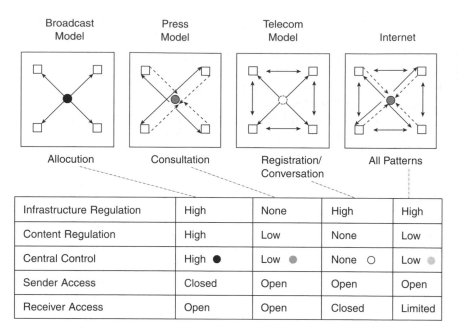

	Broadcast Model	Press Model	Telecom Model	Internet
	Allocution	Consultation	Registration/ Conversation	All Patterns
Infrastructure Regulation	High	None	High	High
Content Regulation	High	Low	None	Low
Central Control	High ●	Low ●	None ○	Low ●
Sender Access	Closed	Open	Open	Open
Receiver Access	Open	Open	Closed	Limited

FIGURE 6.1 Four contemporary models of media regulation in democratic societies.

the same level of protection as telephony. Moreover, conditional access (payment, subscriptions, memberships) limits the admission of all users to every service.

Four constraints of the internet

The limitations discussed above will grow. When broadcasting is integrated in the Internet and broadband use increases, powerful centres (portals, large commercial and public services previously only offered offline) will also appear on the Internet. Governments and corporations will step up their attempts to control all activities on this network. To understand this trend, it is important to list all actors and forces that are able to control the Internet. In his book *Code, and other Laws of Cyberspace* Lawrence Lessig has listed four constraints of all Internet activities: the law, the norms of the Internet organizing committees and user communities, the market and the whole technological architecture of the Internet summarized under the name 'code' (Lessig, 1999: 87–90). I will adopt his list to answer the question: who rules the Internet? I will argue that in the first decade of the 21st century, control is shifting from the law and the Internet community to the market and the technical standards that are all but neutral technologies, both of them backed by new legislation.

Legal control

For reasons discussed above, legislation has only weak direct control on Internet activities. The following sections give numerous examples illustrating computer abuse, international property rights, privacy laws and juridical aspects of information and communication freedom. Generally, control is confined to national jurisdictions. To rule the Internet flows of information and communication across borders, governments have to forge international agreements. These appear to be difficult to create, maintain and enact (discussion follows). Increasingly, governments try to exert indirect control calling in the help of market actors, such as Internet service providers (ISPs), hardware producers and software agencies. The major part of new legislation addresses these actors, for example, ISPs acting as surveyors on behalf of governments, or backs the technological standards and security instruments proposed by producers.

Within their borders, less democratic governments try to exert control on free Internet exchanges, ordering ISPs to filter and block oppositional sites and email messages, manipulating access in public places and surveying all exchanges by security agencies. However, often these attempts are far from effective. A large part of Internet use slips through the hands of the surveyors.

It is a widespread mistake that the Internet has no central organization and that it has to be controlled from outside. The Internet started as a decentralized network for academics and for the American Departments of Defense and Commerce who initiated its design, operation and organization. Internet design (architecture), organization and technical standards have been enforced through self-regulation by the pioneers – mainly technicians and academics – of the Internet community under the supervision of these American departments.

Internet community control

The most important organization is the Internet Engineering Task Force (IETF). This committee of more than 100 working groups takes care of the Internet protocols such as TCP/IP and other standards. Membership is open to all Internet users in principle. However, members of its leading body, the Internet Architecture Board (IAB) are nominated and appointed according to the expertise they have demonstrated. The second most important organization is the Internet Corporation for Assigned Names and Numbers (ICANN) that decides which domain names and IP addresses can be used and that registers these names worldwide. The third organization is the Internet Society (ISOC), founded in 1992, which is intended to be the future 'government' or 'United Nations' of the global Internet community. In 2004, there were more than 150 national Internet Societies. They are NGOs with both individual and organizational membership. The ISOC deals with all policy aspects of the Internet concerning technical, juridical, economic and tax issues and it advises national governments on these issues.

The mission of these self-regulatory bodies is to work only in the interest of the Internet and its users. They mainly take technical decisions to manage the exploding growth of this medium, to keep it working and to defend security. Since the end of the 1990s, they have gradually been pulled away from the umbrella of the American departments.

However, the Internet community does not only consist of these self-regulatory bodies. Millions of newsgroups, online forums, virtual communities, peer-to-peer networks and regular organizational web sites rule their own matters of content with comparatively great freedom. In the 1990s, many participants of these online groups or their spokespersons and Internet ideologues held the view that the Internet was creating a new democracy in the media and society at large. The arrival of commercial interests and governmental controls on the Internet was considered to be a threat.

Market control   In the meantime, these interests and controls have arrived and extended their influence on most Internet activities. The rise of e-commerce requires secure payments and conditional access. The increasing criminal abuses of the Internet make governments want to cut back on freedom of information, communication, privacy and personal autonomy, both in the general and the business interest. Free downloads and copies of source material with copyright urge both businesses and governments to protect intellectual property rights with technical means and legislation.

Yet it is not these evident attempts of corporate control, backed by legislation, that should have the main focus of attention in describing the growing market control of the Internet. This would have to be the partly hidden influence of the hardware and software manufacturers and the commercial services on this network. The influence of operating systems, Internet browsers, search engines and application software is the most visible. They are not neutral technical tools; all of them have a substantial influence on Internet activity and content.

It is barely possible to overrate the impact of Microsoft on the Internet. The basis is the operating system Windows that is integrated with Microsoft's browser Internet Explorer, both used by about 90 percent of Internet users. All software producers and software providers have to adapt to Microsoft's technical standards. The special characteristics and the speed of software development by Microsoft, particularly for Windows and the email program Outlook, has a crucial impact on the chances of computer hacking and the spread of viruses. From a social and cultural point of view, it can be maintained that Microsoft's office and operating system software is mirrored by American office culture (just think of the terminology used when talking about desktops, files and presentations!). From the point of view of free competition, Microsoft is able to favour its own supply of software catering for all needs. This leads to an endless number of cases in court all over the world. It also has led to an open source movement that is trying to regain control over the Internet and all other computer applications for individual and organizational users.

Search engines such as Google and Yahoo are not really neutral instruments either. They favour not necessarily the best, but the most popular web sites by the methods they use to select and order the list of hits to be presented. Thus, the most popular web sites are getting more popular (and the others less popular) – this often means the most commercially viable web sites, which are always able to pay for advertising space on the first page. As about 85 percent of users only look at the first page (Silverstein et al., 1999; Spink et al., 2002), they have a considerable influence on the search behaviour and search results of Internet users.

Internet access or service providers have extended their influence on Internet behaviour, as they are increasingly engaged with security management, the operation of personal web sites and the execution of tasks imposed by legislation. These are tasks such as storing all their clients' traffic data for security agencies, filtering web sites on the request of clients or censoring governments and watching for the infringement intellectual property rights. With the transition to broadband services, these tasks grow even more. The days of simple dial-up and connection are gone. This gives the access and service providers more room for their own policies and preferences within the limits of growing external pressures.

Network operators, such as telecom and cable companies, and producers of computer and network hardware are also exerting more control than before. The patchwork of networks constituting the Internet is ever more vulnerable and requires a higher level of technological protection that is built into the hardware and controlled by security software. With this observation, we have encountered the fourth source of Internet control.

The architecture of the Internet is not a neutral communication infrastructure; it is the central nervous system of this network that defines its character. The core of the Internet is the TCP/IP protocol that enables its decentralized structure of end-to-end exchange and peer-to-peer networking. This architecture becomes increasingly important and it is contested by all parties that are trying to achieve a bigger control of the Internet. According to Lawrence Lessig, a shift of regulatory power over the Internet is occurring that goes 'from law to code, from sovereigns to software' (Lessig, 1999: 206). With 'code' he means all apparently neutral technical standards and protocols that are ruling Internet activity. In fact, these technical means are manipulated by all parties to get a bigger grip on the Internet. However, these means comprise more than code; they also contain particular hardware options at the bottom and application software control at the top. The OSI-model of network layers described in Chapter 3 is able to serve as an analytic tool to list them all (see Table 6.1). I will describe the most important Internet control instruments following this model from the bottom to the top.

Technological control

At the *physical* layer of networks, all kinds of options to connect computers and other terminals and to get access to them and the network are built into the hardware of terminals, routers, switchers and central exchanges. Currently, we are heading towards a next phase with an emphasis on access devices for terminals and networks. Most often they are smart card devices and other means to turn on a computer using passwords. This will be extended by devices using biometrics (electronic fingerprints, iris scans or face and voice recognition). Implementing these technical means on a massive scale will have an enormous effect on potential privacy, personal autonomy and freedom on the Internet.

At the *data link* layer, enabling computers to 'talk' with each other as they use the same so-called 'frames', we find protocols that are built into the hardware such as ATM (see Chapter 3). This is a favourite tool of the telecom companies and local area network (LAN) operators as it enables much more central control than the present decentralized and hardware independent TCP/IP protocol that is installed on the two layers above the physical and data link layers. These parties would love to change TCP/IP for ATM or any other protocol offering more central control (see Chapter 3).

However, the TCP/IP protocol at the *network and transport* layers *is* the Internet as we know it. Without this protocol the relatively free and

TABLE 6.1 Network layers and control instruments

Nature	Network Layer	Control Instruments
Content	Application	Software control: proprietary versus open sources
	Presentation	All translations: encryption, conversion, compression
Code	Session	ID: username + password; digital signatures and certificates; Public Key Infrastructure; electronic payment systems; digital rights management systems; 'cookies'; log files (Internet traffic data)
	Transport	Transmission Control Protocol: decentralized routing of packages
	Network	Internet Protocol: end-to-end principle
Basis	Data link	among others : Asynchronous Transfer Mode
	Physical	Hardware features (e.g. installed blocking chips and switches, biometric access devices)

potentially anonymous decentralized exchange of information and messages on the Internet would be impossible. For example, it is the basis of email and all peer-to-peer networks that exchange music, videos, chat messages and other texts. This protocol follows the end-to-end principle: the shortest and most efficient route is chosen with TCP to connect IP-addresses of computers and other terminals at every end. It allows for little intelligence inside the network and much intelligence in terminals.

Most likely this situation will change. The architecture of the Internet is incorporating traits of the traditional telecom networks with central traffic control (Hain, 2000). The IP protocol Version 4 is in the process of being replaced by Version 6, which contains much more intelligence and options for central control. For example, it contains *IP Sec(urity)*, which enables better encryption of the packages of Internet data streams and also labels them with numbers that allow operators and security agencies to identify the packages, to steer them and to tap their senders and receivers. Since 2000, ardent discussions have been going on in the working groups of the IETF about ways to reconcile this version with the end-to-end principle of the Internet (see www.ietf.org/html.charters/wg-dir.html). The result will be decisive for the character of the Internet as we know it.

Presently, government, corporate and other private interests that try to control Internet traffic have to rely on the codes of the *session* layer. These codes enable user identification and message authentication. Every Internet user knows the screens that request user name and password for identification. To secure the message authenticity, a codification system of digital signatures and certifications with an optional use of a Public Key Infrastructure has been created (see 'Rights of Ownership' below for an explanation). Subsequently, electronic payment systems and digital rights management systems have been installed that debit the personal accounts of users and consumers. All these codes at the session layer are visible for users. This does not go for the hidden session codes contained in **log files** and cookies. They allow businesses, governments, service providers and network operators to trace all

Internet use. Some organizations take a further step using spyware, software that secretly gathers Internet user information without users' knowledge. However, at the *presentation* layer the user is able to hide internet messages using encryption.

On the *application* layer, numerous other instances of software control of Internet use could be discussed. I will just mention the examples of the obligation imposed by Microsoft to register software and its technical decision to assign user names to files, such as word processing files.

Taken together, these ways of technological control of the Internet are shaping powerful tools. They might change the character of the Internet from a relatively free, public and user-controlled medium into an instrument of corporate, government and private control. All in all, there is a shift from early government initiative and Internet community rule to technological and market rule of the Internet backed by new legislation. This can be done for good and bad purposes, as we will see in the following sections.

INFORMATION AND COMMUNICATION FREEDOM

Citizens' right to information and communication freedom have been established in the constitutions of democratic states and in general international declarations such as the Declaration of Human Rights. In most constitutions, this freedom is confined to a freedom of *expression* by means of a ban on government censorship. For instance, the famous First Amendment of the American constitution ('Congress shall make no law ... abridging the freedom of speech or the press') only protects against interference of the government or a public institution performing state action, not against private interference (Perritt, 1996: 263ff.). A logical corollary would be that the freedom to *receive* expressions should be protected as well. Constitutions and declarations are less clear about this legal principle. In practice, there is no guarantee, as regulatory bodies, cable operators and other service providers decide what channels, programmes and services can be received. **What freedom?**

So, it is important to observe that current legal rights of information and communication freedom offer a passive protection (against interference) and not an active protection (supply of conditions). Further, they mainly protect against government interference, not against intrusions by private conduct. This means that the infringement of this freedom in new media practice, for example by increasing information inequalities or gatekeeping media monopolies, is not covered by them. These problems have to be confronted by other laws (of privacy and free competition, for instance) and by public information services.

A second point is that information and communication freedom is not an absolute right. The right to information and communication freedom is not absolute where individual and state autonomy are concerned. At the individual level, one person's freedom of speech and right to reception ends where another person's right to privacy, security, identity, dignity **Conflicting rights** ('reputation') and personal material interest begins. At the state level, the right to entirely free (inter)national information traffic conflicts with a state's right to sovereignty, national security, public order, cultural identity and economic interests.

Law and state autonomy undermined

These conflicts are inevitable and can never be resolved completely. This is even expressed in the essence of the descriptions of information and communication freedom, all of which reveal at least some internal tension. Thus in the discussion on international traffic of data, jurists use expressions like a 'free *and balanced* flow of information' (Freese, 1979) and 'everyone is free to ... as long as this does not ...'. This means values have to be weighed against each other in legislation. Such considerations can be made in national legislation. Internationally, legislation can have little effect, while international declarations of human rights are too general and their sanctions are too weak to provide a solution. The biggest problem is that the right to state autonomy is being undermined by the free flow of information in cross-border networks. In addition to the legal aspects, this right also has economic, political, military and cultural aspects, as described below.

First, in the *legal* sphere, international networks can be instruments to evade national legislation. They enable not only extremely fast file transfers from one country to another, but also a division of the parts of information processing between the most advantageous countries – which means the cheapest and least regulated countries. Data are gathered in one country, edited and stored in another, and distributed and used as information in yet another country, thus avoiding taxes, rights of ownership and privacy legislation. Some countries are already known as *data paradises* or *data-free havens*. One just picks a country where there is little or no sanction against a particular wrongful act, or even a crime, and makes sure one has access to an international network.

Second, in the *economic* sphere, states increasingly miss out on income because taxes are imposed only on data carriers and not on the content and the production of these data, which are usually worth a lot more than the carriers. It is impossible to install 'gateways' to serve as a kind of customs in every network at the point where it crosses a border. In the past, Brazil tried to do this, but very soon had to give up its attempts.

Material goods (CDs, books, etc.) ordered over the Internet are not the biggest problem. They have to 'surface' (out of the virtual economy into the material one) once they are imported or delivered. Then, import duty and VAT might be collected. Intangible services, on the other hand (digital information, transaction services), offer simpler ways to evade taxes.

Third, in the *political* sphere, the (exclusive) use of information can be of great interest to a country. Most countries want to have crucial information stored on their own territory to make sure they are not completely dependent on others in cases of emergency. Many developing countries in debt discover the importance of the exclusive use a country has over its own data at the moment when the IMF or the World Bank presents an austerity plan based on far more advanced processing of a country's own data than it is capable of doing itself.

Fourth, the *military* importance of a country's information sovereignty closely relates to the political. Passing on confidential data can cause a threat to national safety. What is more, international information networks are gaining importance as military instruments. At this point, the United States has taken the lead. The networks controlled by the Pentagon, the Central Intelligence Agency (CIA) and the National Security Agency (NSA) are vastly superior to anything else that exists in this field. The 2003 war in Iraq has been called *network warfare*, as the Coalition's battle forces on the ground were fully directed and supported by satellites, aircraft and rockets, all of them integrated in a single network system. Defence experts expect that future wars will increasingly be *network wars* or *infowars*. Networks have become so important for a country, and at the same time so vulnerable, that putting them down will prove to be a decisive military action.

Fifth, the *cultural* identity of poor or less developed countries and of closed communities is seriously threatened by broadcasting satellites, international computer networks such as the Internet, and the powerful databanks and databases of the rich western countries (see Hamelink, 1994).

A country's autonomy should not be absolute either. This would oppose the information freedom and material interests of other countries and, in particular, the country's own inhabitants. In order to disguise this opposition, countries often use false arguments. For instance, countries regularly use arguments about the protection of national sovereignty and culture as a reason to restrict the information and communication freedom of their own citizens. Pure economic protectionism often hides behind claims of legal, political or technological sovereignty.

The rash and uncontrolled development of the new media, the Internet in particular, appears to offer a refuge for anyone who wants to escape prosecution for offences against information and communication law. That is why it is viewed suspiciously by governments, security organizations, regulatory bodies and all kinds of interest groups. The conduct of criminals, terrorists, slanderers, racists and (child) pornographers is more or less controlled in the old media. How should one try to regulate the same conduct in the new media? The groups mentioned are among the heavy users of the Internet. Evidently, they threaten the freedom and safety of others and of society at large. There is a growing consensus that the law should apply to both old and new media, including the Internet as a public mass medium. What are the problems, then, with this application? Some of them are fundamental. The most important follow.

Other problems implementing the law

First, what is the character of the new media? They are in a process of convergence, blurring many of the distinctions between the old media. Should the new media be modelled on the press model, the common carrier (telephone) model or the broadcasting model (see the previous section)? By the end of the 1990s, most governments in the western world and east Asia had tended to accept the press model for economic freedom (on the market) and the common carrier or broadcasting model for social, cultural and political freedoms in the new media environment. These governments try very hard to stimulate global electronic commerce while at the same time trying to implement new restrictions, or to apply existing ones to the social and cultural uses of the Internet.

Blurred character of new media

A related problem in applying current legislation is that many words for the old media are used in laws and even in constitutions. For instance, the First Amendment mentions (only) 'speech' and 'the press'. Some legal experts say words for new media should be added or more general expressions invented. Others claim the old expressions remain valid and only require a broader interpretation.

Blurred public–private distinction

The second problem is that the new media blur the distinctions not only between media themselves but between social spheres of living as well, especially the public–private distinction. This blurring of spheres of living is analysed in Chapters 7 and 8. It has immediate consequences for new media legislation. The Internet is both a mass medium and an interpersonal medium. In offering web sites, it is a mass medium, and in the facility of email, it is an interpersonal medium. But what about the increasing list of Internet applications having both public and private functions: more or less closed news lists, electronic billboards, chat rooms, erotic web-cam services and multi-user dungeons (MUDs)? They operate somewhere between mass and interpersonal communications.

Traditionally, the regulation of information and communication freedom in mass and interpersonal communication has been rather different. What is left free in private and personal communication, for instance obscenity, may not be allowed in mass communication. The question is how the different applications of the Internet should be rated. There is no difficulty in treating web sites and news or discussion lists, billboards and MUDs with open access as mass communication. The email between persons will probably be treated as private communications, although there is (as yet) no legal right to confidentiality of email in many countries. But what about completely closed discussion lists, erotic web-cam sessions, chat rooms or private mailing lists? A large number of norms and observable facts have to be invented to specify things like membership, accounts, passwords and encryption as indicators of the private or public character of these applications.

The last problem to be mentioned here is that of the extremely volatile, dynamic and perhaps encrypted nature of network communication crossing many borders and jurisdictions. This makes criminal behaviour of all kinds, obscene, indecent and defamatory expressions, violations of human rights like privacy and other offences extremely difficult to trace, investigate, prosecute and prove. These activities are very time-consuming for the police and security agencies. So even when an offence is detected, the chances are small that someone will be charged and convicted.

Three kinds of solutions

There are three kinds of solutions to these problems, which have already been mentioned in Chapter 5 and reappear several times in the next sections: legal solutions, self-regulation and technological protection. It is one of the most important claims of this chapter that they are only effective when used in combination. Table 6.2 shows a list of instruments to choose in realizing these solutions.

Adaptation of legislation

The adaptation of legislation and other regulations in the field of ICT remains necessary, however great the difficulties mentioned. It produces a legal framework and protection for all the more or less voluntary solutions

TABLE 6.2   Types of solution for legal ICT problems

Legal solutions
    Adaptation of laws and regulations
    Product standardization

Self-regulation
    Codes of conduct and good practice
    Hot lines (reporting offences)
    Market regulation: licensees, public domain software, relationship marketing, advertising
    Mediation (civil conflict resolution)
    Information agents (self-service)
    Rating and filtering systems (self-service)

Technical solutions
    Rating and filtering systems (software)
    Built-in hardware: Violence chips, etc.
    Embedded software, scrambling and coding techniques
    Encryption: encoding messages, digital signatures, pseudonyms and watermarks
    Data metering and digital rights management systems
    Monitoring and tracking (log files, cookies)

---

to be described below. This will take considerable time, as the technology in question and its uses in daily practice are still maturing. However, some governments have been seized by panic, observing the apparently anarchic nature of Internet use. They have hastily adopted emergency legislation. A clear case was the Communications Decency Act signed by President Clinton in 1996. The aim of adopting this act was to limit access to, and prosecute offences in, expressions of violence and obscenity on cable broadcasting, the Internet and online computer services. It subjected these media to more severe prohibitions than those existing in traditional media like free-to-air broadcasting and the press. Only one year later the act was overruled as being unconstitutional by a judgement of the U.S. Supreme Court. It is interesting to observe that the court stressed the right of freedom of interpersonal communication on the Internet as protected by the First Amendment, while the Decency Act primarily classified the Internet as a medium of mass communication. Restrictions on the freedom of communication on the Internet have been made by east Asian governments as well. The EU has adopted a *Directive on the Protection of Minors* and a *Resolution on Illegal and Harmful Content of the Internet*, that have forced the member states to adapt their laws for Internet regulation accordingly.

The emergency legislation adopted in the last ten years has often led to more restrictions on information and communication freedom in the new online world than in the old offline world. Generally, this legislation backed the technological modes of protection and the market- or self-regulation of businesses and service providers on the Internet (Lessig, 1999, 2001). In this way, ISPs were forced to store and open the traffic data of their clients or to filter web sites and their contents with rating systems. Existing fair use rights of CDs, DVDs and web services were taken away by built-in protection codes backed by the law. These opportunities were not available in the comparable old media.

An infringement on the information and communication freedom of Internet users themselves is the massive posting of unsolicited online messages (in email, SMS or chat), a phenomenon called **spam**. After some time legislation has been adopted that intends to drive back this phenomenon. In the United States, the federal CAN-SPAM Act of 2003 works on the basis of the *opt-out* principle of unsolicited messages by users. Spam senders have to stop when receivers ask for it in return. The Act also prohibits the use of deceptive subject lines and false headers in messages. Every message has to be labelled (though not by a standard method). In the EU Spam Directive of 2002 the more severe *opt-in* principle is enacted: unsolicited messages are only allowed after previous permissions of receivers. Other countries in the world also choose between legislation on the basis of the opt-in or opt-out principles. However, the biggest problem is poor maintenance and prosecution after the adoption of anti-spam laws. Therefore, the self-regulation of codes of conduct by advertising agencies and the like and the technological protections offered by software companies and ISPs are increasingly popular (partial) solutions.

Self-regulation In view of the fundamental problems with the adaptation of legislation mentioned above, it is no surprise that for the time being the two other classes of solutions have received more attention: self-regulation and technological alternatives. Urging some kind of self-regulation, but in fact trying to use them as an extension of the law, the authorities have approached service providers on the Internet and cable networks concerning their presumed liability in controlling and surveying all traffic on their networks. Many of them react by saying that they are not the police. Most access providers assert that they have no control over the messages they carry, just as the telephone companies do. They claim not to be editors or suppliers of cable programmes. However, for the service providers that offer content, the claims must be different: consensus is growing that they are liable for the content of their services.

The access and service providers themselves propose self-regulation as the best solution, offering codes of conduct and self-censorship in refusing subscribers, sites, programs and files which might get them into trouble. Moreover, they introduce special addresses serving as *hot lines* for their own clients to report child pornography, racism and other potential violations of the law.

Rating and filtering systems By the end of the 1990s, so-called *rating and filtering systems* had emerged as (perhaps) the most important protectors against illegal and harmful content on computer networks in the coming decades. In fact, these systems are a combination of self-regulation and technology. Rating systems mean either a self-rating of content by providers themselves or an assessment by professional rating services specializing in particular sectors of content. The quantity and quality of items such as sex or violence are rated on a scale that is attached to a service or site to be rated and is presented in browsers. Then the software of the filtering systems installed by the users themselves is able to offer whatever nature and level of protection are required by parents, educators and in fact any other kind of authority. Future users will be able to include them in their personal information selections.

The best-known organizer of rating systems is the Platform of Internet Content Selection (PICS) offered by the World Wide Web Consortium. Well-known filtering systems received the meaningful names of Net Nanny, Cybersitter, Net Shepherd, Surf Watch and Cyber Patrol. The government of the United States and the European Commission increasingly put their faith in these solutions after the disaster of the Decency Act and the problems they had with adapting and executing legislation. From a libertarian point of view, they are strongly supported by Internet experts like Esther Dyson (1997). She opposes government regulation of the net and offers self-regulation by means of rating and filtering systems as the most important alternative. She expects these systems will become the most important quality standards of service providers. Unfortunately, in giving this support, she neglects any relationship of power in society and on the Internet. Governments and other authorities may well enforce the use of these systems of a specified nature and quality. At the time of writing, the governments of China, Vietnam, Cuba, Singapore and other countries screen sites on the Internet using filter systems on a massive scale. American parents demand in court that schools install them on their networks to censor the information available to their children. Moreover, the supply and design of rating and filtering systems will most likely be controlled by all kinds of vested interests. Minority interests might become marginal or blocked entirely. So, the adaptation of legislation remains necessary to protect the information and communication freedom of all. Another disadvantage of these systems is that they are easy to escape by the target group, especially children. They just go to friends, neighbours or public places offering a lower level of protection in filtering. Or they will use one of the many small mobile devices offering easy access to the Internet in the near future.

For this reason, and others, still more effective solutions are being looked for in technology. Some observers are very optimistic about this. For example, the American law professor Reidenberg has proposed a *Lex Informatica* that would be able to solve most problems discussed in this chapter by technological means such as encryptions and other codes of protection (Reidenberg, 1998). As a matter of fact, rating and filtering systems are included in operating systems, search engines and other software and they might even be programmed in hardware. The introduction of the so-called 'violence chip' in TV sets was a precursor to this option. Scrambling messages in programs or blocking them by some kind of code are increasingly 'popular' techniques. However, just like self-regulation these technological solutions are a two-edged sword. They both protect and threaten information and communication freedoms. They are indispensable as solutions, but to strike a balance in using them in a right, justified and equal way the adaptation of legislation remains vital.

Technical solutions

RIGHTS OF OWNERSHIP

Information and communication freedom does not only clash with limitations of public communication and autonomy, but also with rights of ownership. The latter conflict is even harder to resolve than the former. On the

Information freedom versus ownership rights

one hand, many people consider information to be a social product that should not be exclusively appropriated by private interests. On the other hand, information has become one of the most important economic products in the modern economy and it should therefore be submitted to the principles of the market economy like any other good. This contrast can be derived from four special characteristics of a more or less fixed kind of information: *knowledge as a product*. (See Chapter 8 for the difference between knowledge and information.)

Special characteristics of knowledge

- The production of knowledge demands far greater investment than its distribution and use. Knowledge is produced once, but it can be used endlessly. The use of networks reinforces this characteristic.
- Every time knowledge is produced or used, risks are taken: one can never be 100 percent certain about producing useful results. This is why scientific research is subsidized by the government and why the reliability of a knowledge supplier is crucial to the consumer.
- Knowledge is an intangible product. Unlike a material good, it cannot be transferred from one owner to another, giving the new owner the exclusive permission to use it. On the contrary, knowledge is shared. After transfer, knowledge is owned by both senders and receivers. A person is able to 'acquire knowledge' without the producer losing any of his own. This characteristic is also reinforced by networks.
- Knowledge is a result of both individual and social labour. It is hard to place a dividing line between them. For this reason, the protection of individual achievements is a problem and solutions are always temporary. Because networks link individuals and their contribution in a social exchange, they highlight this characteristic too.

Problem: The socialization of knowledge

These four characteristics offer arguments for both the production of knowledge as a property (the first two) and the free disposal of knowledge (the second two). The existence of networks weakens the arguments of the first two and strengthens those of the second two. Networks simplify and expand the possibilities for exchanging and duplicating knowledge. Knowledge in networks (data, programs, information) is at the disposal of numerous users without losing any quality or intellectual value. Increasingly, it is passed on to multiple users in licence agreements (passing on the right to use the information), and decreasingly it is transferred in strict sale agreements or hire agreements (passing on ownership). *Without doubt, networks add to the socialization of knowledge*. This makes it even harder to protect the ownership of knowledge passed on in networks. Most legal instruments to do so are faulty and outdated (see below).

The socialization of knowledge, and the problem of its private appropriation in digital environments in general and networks in particular, explain the enormous efforts made by governments to protect the billion-dollar interests of the copyright industry and to adapt the legislation of intellectual property rights accordingly. They tend to make it even more rigid than it used to be in the analogue environment.

Legal adaptation is the first kind of solution to the problem of protecting intellectual and material property rights in the use of the new media. The others are, once again, self-regulation or self-organization on the market and technological solutions.

Legal solutions

Let's deal with the problems of intellectual property rights first; later we discuss material property rights. Intellectual property rights consist of three basic parts: the right of *publication* of a work of unique creative effort (authors' right), the right of *reproduction* (copyright) and the right of *distribution* (for instance in broadcasting and on stage). We must recognize that continental European legislation is more concerned to protect (cultural) authors' rights, while American and English legislation tends to put (economic) copyright first. That is why the American law is called the Copyright Act, while the Dutch law is called the Auteurswet (Authors' Law).

Intellectual property rights

The most important fact concerning new media intellectual property rights is that communication in computer networks links the acts of publication, reproduction and distribution. It is the process that becomes central. For example, making a web site with hyperlinks and files to be copied blurs their distinction. Therefore, the question arises, which of the three rights mentioned will be emphasized in new legislation?. For fundamental reasons concerning the development of authors' rights in a digital environment (see above and below) and for historical reasons, that is the rise of corporate power and privatization, it is very likely that reproduction and distribution rights will be defended most. The rights of authors as the protectors of creative effort will be threatened (Lessig, 2001). There are fundamental difficulties in protecting them in the digital network environment.

Copyright and authors' right in a digital environment

First, authors' right and copyright only protect the *form* of an idea, concept, procedure, method of operation or discovery, not the *content*, that is the facts and ideas embodied (see Perritt, 1996: 421ff.). In content, one encounters the cultural heritage of society: one never knows exactly where this heritage ends and the original expression of creators begins. This was already a basic problem for works created in analogue media. Using digital media, the problem appears to be insoluble for the following two reasons. First, in digital environments the content changes continuously and it soon acquires a general public character. The recognizable artistic content of the age of simple commodity production, clearly visible in paintings, sculptures and books, is lost in digital signs which are very easy to manipulate, reproduce and exchange. Moreover, the form can be changed just as easily. Computer programs are adapted continuously, both by producers and by users. Databanks contain more or less automatic summaries and abstracts of forms and pieces of information. For these reasons, infringements of authors' right and copyright are extremely difficult to prove.

Second, all existing laws of intellectual property right only protect works that are *fixed*, enabling their originals to be copied and multiplied. In the dynamic digital environment of computer networks, this point of departure is untenable. As has been argued above, the process of creation, re-creation and reproduction will replace fixed forms.

These fundamental problems lead to the conclusion that any authors' rights solely based on the protection of the unique creativity of products of the

Judicial solutions

mind will become untenable in digital environments. A clear case is the problem of computers creating computer programs themselves. The rights to these programs are granted to the owners of the technologies concerned. Other cases are judicial decisions mentioning the added or surplus value of new computer programs, the new composition or reworking of data in databanks or the production of new information out of existing data. More and more, judges and lawyers speak about the protection of *labour* effort instead of creative effort. In this way, authors' rights move from a cultural into an economic sphere. This is an essential change, unnoticed by many people.

In the practice of using software and information services, this evolution of intellectual property towards economic property goes yet further. Here one can observe the shift from property right to *usage right*. All kinds of licences and contracts between producers and business or household consumers become ever more important. In these cases, one buys not a copy of the original but a licence to use it.

Contemporary legislation In the American and European intellectual property rights legislation of the late 1990s, the fundamental shifts mentioned above were reflected. European proposals moved in the direction of the basic American assumptions of an economic conception of intellectual property rights. Both American and European proposals tried to meet the terms of digital technology. However, I will argue that they did this so zealously and so much influenced by economic interests that essential freedoms of information and communication have been at risk.

In 1998, the Digital Millennium Copyright Act (DMCA) was adopted in the United States (US Copyright Office, 1998). This Act extended the existing Copyright Act to the digital media and gave copyright owners control over every publication, reproduction and distribution of works in a digital form. For example, service providers on the Internet are expected to remove material from users' web sites that appears to constitute copyright infringement. Fair use rights traditionally attached to intellectual property rights, such as personal use and use by libraries and schools, are strictly curbed to allow licensed use only. Everyday personal uses, such as making copies of software to use on a second household computer and copying tracks from purchased CDs to make a personal compilation, are not allowed in principle either. Another traditional right of the user, the so-called first-sale right of a book, for instance, meaning the right to use and forward the copy purchased as long as this does not harm the commercial interests of the producer, is also cancelled. So, many technically protected CDs and DVDs do not allow a single copy.

To prevent digital copying and to track every use of protected works, so-called *digital rights management systems* and protections by means of encryption are backed by this Act. With a few exceptions, attempts to circumvent these technological solutions have become illegal. Online service providers are held to be responsible for the report of these offences and for the protection of pay-per-use rules.

Simultaneously, the European Commission adopted the *Directive on Certain Aspects of Copyright and Related Rights in the Information Society*

(European Commission, 2001) an obligation to adapt copyrights and authors' rights by the member states that is fairly similar to the DMCA. It was a bit less severe in fair use rights to be allowed and it still mentioned 'related rights' – referring to authors' rights that were in fact swallowed by copyright in this Directive – but its basic assumptions were the same.

There has been considerable opposition to this legislation in the U.S. Congress, in the European Parliament and by civil liberties groups, free-speech advocates and digital equipment manufacturers. Critics have called attention to the fundamental shift they introduce into intellectual property rights (Catinat, 1997; Lessig, 1999, 2001; Miller, 1996; Samuelson, 1996). The balance in existing legislation between creators' and copyright owners' interests on the one side, and the public interest in the diffusion of ideas in fair use and limited copying on the other, has clearly shifted to the benefit of the former, the copyright owners, in the first place. Perritt argues that 'the justification for copyright is to reward new contributions, not merely to increase the revenue for old contributions' (1996: 423). The latter will happen when (fair) individual users, libraries, schools and research institutions will have to pay for uses that were free until now on a non-commercial basis.

With this legislation, the groundwork is laid for extensive and unprecedented tolling on the Internet. This is especially so because the technological solutions to unlimited copying of digital works – all kinds of encryption and rights management software – are strongly backed by this legislation. However, at the time of writing, all countries, both American, European and others with similar new copyright legislation, exhibit several juridical proposals to revise the laws and numerous court cases that deal with inconsistencies and omissions in the new laws.

In the meantime, the second type of solution is increasing in the daily practice of new media use. With the transformation of property rights into usage rights described above, all kinds of self-regulation or self-organization appear on the market of intellectual value. All kinds of public domain software, freeware and shareware are appearing, the use of which is more or less free. Public domain software is free for distribution and for change. It is also called **open code** under a so-called General Public License. The operating system Linux is the most familiar current example. Freeware is called free, but in fact exploitation and change are not allowed. Freeware means that the source code of the software must be made available to other users, not necessarily free of charge. A synonym of freeware is **open source**. Finally, shareware is software that is free until it is actually used; then a licence is to be obtained. Generally, licences have become the prime type of transaction in the new media market of intellectual value.

Another method is advertising. Increasingly, software and other information services are paid for by advertisements. According to Esther Dyson (1995), intellectual ownership on the net is being gradually replaced by advertisements for intellectual services and products that really are profitable: all kinds of support; advanced services in searching, collecting and processing scattered information; and, last but not least, selling the latest version of a program. The provider's main occupation is (customer) *relationship*

Self-regulatory solutions

management, which will be the service provider's main source of profit for the future. In this way, the information sector increasingly organizes its own business without appealing to copyright.

Another example of self-regulatory protection of intellectual property rights is the free adoption of codes of conduct or codes of good practice by service providers themselves. Sometimes they promise to assist property owners in searching and charging violators of their rights. To an increasing degree, they are able to use search engines and software screening for content and for broken conditions of access to, and usage of, protected works. These information agents will serve as the private and public 'copyright police' of the future.

Technical solutions

However, probably the most effective solutions to the problem of illegal appropriation of digital works are technological ones. The copyright industry and the producers of encryption software are working hard to develop and introduce all kinds of technical means to control any access and usage of these works. To begin with, they can be encrypted like any electronic message. In this case, one only gets a key after payment. A special kind of encryption is a *digital watermark**: a product is equipped with invisible codes which scramble the image in the event of unauthorized use. Again, hardware players (multimedia computers, CD players) have been developed that can no longer make illegal copies: they automatically register what rights a particular user has to use a certain product, and allow access only by payment. For instance, listening to a CD on the Internet might cost the user 25 cents, whereas to buy a copy would cost $5. This solution comes pretty close to so-called *data metering**: a built-in chip or a small device connected to a television or a computer registers the use of a certain product in the same way as an electricity meter. Chip cards are a means of payment. However, data metering might become another great threat to privacy, since all use can (also) be registered in central processors and files.

When these technological solutions are backed up by legal enforcement, such as that envisaged in the American and European proposals for legislation, the present situation on the Internet and in other new media of uncontrolled illegal copying on a massive scale will be completely reversed (Catinat, 1997; Lessig, 2001; Miller, 1996). No longer will the rights of copyright owners be in danger, but instead the rights of (fair) users, authors (except for the financial protection by their publishers) and the public at large will be at risk. The balance between owners' rights and legitimate public usage will be lost and the scale will tip towards the former. So, while in principle computer networks support an unprecedented distribution and socialization of information, and although technological means are able to protect both owners and users, the practice of our free-market economy will lead information into an (attempted) level of private appropriation as never before.

Material property rights

The material property right at stake through the use of information technology has been safeguarded much earlier than the intellectual property right. It is so crucial to our economic system in the digital age that it is defended by every means. This has been done right from the beginning. All kinds of statutes about computer fraud and abuses have been adopted in criminal law. It is no surprise that the range of electronic services, electronic trade and electronic payments is marked by increasingly strong legal and contractual protection. However, problems remain as network transactions increase in size and quality. The problems are greatest in information services. Here we find problems such as the liability of databanks (see Perritt, 1996). Other remaining problems of electronic trade are: fixing online agreements; providing evidence in electronic messages and claiming responsibility for mistakes made in them; enforcing the use of particular standards; and exacting the rules and obligations in message storage. In other words, the main issues of contract law, certification and authentication law, liability legislation, laws of open competition and storage obligations are at stake. These problems are all caused by the replacement of paper by other carriers of data. An increasing amount of data is never recorded on paper. However, the faith of the law and judges in paper is not completely unfounded. It is easier to demonstrate manipulation of data on paper than manipulation of data stored in computers or on networks. And what is more, data on paper can never be moved from one piece of paper to another.

THE RIGHT TO PRIVACY

The legal framework for the protection of privacy consists of the following three parts:

Legal framework

- national legislation;
- international legislation and treaties;
- codes of conduct and professional codes.

On a national level, the right to privacy is covered in most constitutions. On an international level it is described in the Treaties of Rome and Strasbourg (European Council) and the Treaty on Civil Rights and Political Rights (UN). To them we can add more general declarations such as the Universal Declaration of Human Rights, and more specific and locally valid ones such as OECD and European Commission guidelines.

Codes of conduct as a result of organizational self-regulation are available in electronic banking or information services and in collective agreements between employers and trade unions or between producers and consumer organizations. Professional codes are made for researchers and information workers or for medical staff and social workers. Both kinds of codes are a valuable addition to legislation. In times of fast technological change, they serve as a buffer or as emergency legislation for some time.

First, we will discuss the legislative protection of informational privacy. Legislation and self-regulation in this field are often guided by the eight principles formulated by the OECD and the European Council as early as 1980. The following four are the most important of these:

Legal protection

- The *use limitation principle*: the smallest possible amount of personal data should be gathered and used for the purpose given.
- The *principle of purpose specification*: only personal data for strictly specified purposes should be collected and processed.
- *Quality*: the personal data must be correct, complete and up to date. Furthermore, they have to be well protected by means of security.
- The *principle of transparency or openness*: the people involved have the right to know what personal data are collected, to what purpose, who has access to these data, what will happen to these data when they are passed on to others, and to whom they are passed on.

National legislation

The EU Directive called *The Protection of Individuals with Regard to the Processing of Personal Data and the Free Movement of Such Data* (European Commission, 1995) is based on these principles. At the turn of the century, all EU member states have adopted privacy laws founded on this directive. The United States has no general and comprehensive privacy (federal or state) law and no other legislation following these principles.

United States

The United States has an impressive number of privacy-related acts dealing with specific issues only (see Perritt, 1996: Chapter 3). The Electronic Communications Privacy Act (ECPA) is the broadest of the federal statutes that focuses on communication. Then there are Computer Fraud and Abuse Acts, dealing only with intrusions that cause certain harm after they have happened. These forbid certain actions of intruders and eavesdroppers in computers and their networks, but impose no duties on controllers and processors of personal data (1996: 88). The federal and state privacy acts impose these duties only on government agencies.

The fragmented nature of American privacy legislation leads to a number of weaknesses and loopholes. For example, medical records are not protected. Most often one has to appeal to the constitution in general or to common law. The results in court are unpredictable.

According to Michel Catinat:

> most of the attempts to improve the legal environment fall short because of the lobbying of businesses including the marketing industry, federal intelligence and law enforcement agencies, and others. All these actors have diverse interests in maintaining easy access to individual data. (1997: 53)

The EU finds American privacy legislation so defective that, according to the directive mentioned above, no export of personal data to that country is allowed. This may force the United States and the EU to adopt legislation protecting their international business interests.

Europe

The EU directive on personal data protection (European Commission, 1995) is the most stringent in the world. This does not mean that it is an unconditional defence of the civil and human rights concerned. Not for nothing does its long name carry the expression 'and the free movement of such data'. The directive tries to balance the economic interests of global, primarily European, commerce and human or civil rights. According to some critics, it even legitimizes current economic practices of handling personal data with a large potential for privacy intrusion. The economic interest of free movement of data, including personal data, is suspected to be the prime motivation. The directive only afterwards offers some safeguards.

Four essential characteristics of this piece of EU legislation are worth mentioning here.

First, it is technologically appropriate, as it takes the processing of data in networks as the main point of departure. The directive covers the 'collection, recording, organization, storage, adaptation or alteration, retrieval, consultation, use, disclosure by transmission, dissemination or otherwise making available, alignment or combination, blocking, erasure or destruction of all personal data' (European Commission, 1995: Article 2). Personal data 'mean any information relating to an identified or identifiable natural person ... directly or indirectly' (Article 2). This dynamic approach is considerably better for computer networks than the static approach of taking the existence of single computer files and their exchange as the main assumption for data protection legislation. This static approach marked the first generation of European privacy laws. Moreover, the broad definition of personal data just mentioned makes the new legislation valid for all multimedia registration as video (camera) and audio recording are protected as well. The same goes for biometrics.

Assets of EU privacy legislation

A second advantage of the European directive is the full application of the OECD principles of use limitation, purpose specification, openness and quality of personal data referred to earlier. These data may only be 'collected for specified, explicit and legitimate purposes and not further processed in a way incompatible with these purposes'. The data should be 'adequate, relevant and not excessive in relation to the purposes' and they should be kept up to date (Article 6). A controller is held to be responsible: a controller is any agency or body determining the purposes and means of processing personal data. Controllers have to take care of all the actions of processors processing data by technical means on their behalf.

The openness of personal data registration is supported by the demand for prior consent by the so-called 'data subjects' concerned. They have to be informed about the purpose of, and all events subsequent to, the registration, such as passing the data on to third parties. Prior consent is not required when there is a legal obligation or when the registration is part of a contract to which the 'data subject' is a party. However, in any case there is the right of access to one's own data (Article 12).

A third advantage of the directive is that the strong obligations it imposes on controllers and processors are enforced not by governments but by independent supervisory authorities such as national data protection registrars (Article 28). Controllers have to notify these authorities about the purpose and other features of their processing activities. They are bodies of consultation, investigation and legal intervention or redress. Although the directive is supposed to be a sound legal solution by itself, it strongly encourages self-regulation by codes of conduct and good practice and by the appointment of independent protection officers inside organizations.

A fourth plus-point is the list of special categories of personal data that one is not allowed to process at all. They are 'data revealing racial or ethnic origin, political opinions, religions or philosophical beliefs, trade-union membership, and the processing of data concerning health or sex life' (Article 8: also see this article for exemptions). Although it is not the category of personal data per se that makes it more sensitive than others, but the combination of categories and the context of appropriation, this list is very instructive, as these kinds of personal data are those most misused.

Shortcomings of EU privacy legislation

However, there are a number of shortcomings to this directive and the national laws based on it. First, its most decisive assumption, the principle of purpose specification for processing personal data, makes it vulnerable. Marking out separate registrations with their own purposes is its Achilles' heel. Controllers will either have great difficulty putting this into practice, or they will prove to be very creative in defining divisions and combinations of purposes that circumvent the meaning of the law and its principle of specification. They may control several registrations or appoint other controllers instead of themselves.

A second weakness is the protection of personal data in international networks crossing borders of jurisdiction. Of course, European legislation is only valid in member states of the EU. Many networks, the Internet in particular, move through numerous countries. The prohibition of a transfer of personal data to countries outside the EU which have no adequate level of protection (European Commission, 1995: Article 25) – the United States is considered to be such a country – is difficult to enforce. In 2003 and 2004, there was a dispute between the United States and the EU about the registration of personal data of European travellers on American airlines that was imposed by the American government for security reasons. It ended in some kind of compromise.

The laws derived from the EU directive are applicable to data protection issues across the Internet because domain names or email addresses are identifiable personal data and because Internet access providers are both controllers and processors, while content providers are controllers and network providers are processors (see Walden, 1997). However, the directive does not apply where a user of European personal data is not established in an EU member state or does not use a server in such a state – perhaps only passing nodes on their territories in technical transmission, which is allowed (1997: 53).

The greatest disadvantage of the EU directive is that it is very difficult and expensive to put into practice and easily leads to bureaucracy. There is much complaint about this among European controllers and processors. This piece of legislation will therefore only work with the help of organizations supplementing it with self-regulation and 'data subjects' being conscious about their assets and defending their own personal data. So, here, self-regulation is a necessary counterpart of the legal framework.

Individual self-regulation

At the level of individual solutions, we have the development of privacy rating systems by special software like P3 and TRUSTe (see Chapter 5). These show great promise. Nevertheless, they also have disadvantages. Individual responsibility assumes a level of knowledge about the extremely complicated affairs of data protection in networks, which cannot be expected from most people. Organizations offering personal help and information in this regard are not well established.

At the level of collective solutions, one can observe a large number of codes of conduct in the business of electronic banking, direct marketing, personnel information systems and specific information and communication systems. Let us take the last of these as an example. The best solution for (self-)regulation in information and communication systems is to make sure that a clear division exists between the tasks and responsibilities of the carrier; the system operator; the service provider; and the bank or other financial account provider. The more these tasks and responsibilities coincide, the bigger the potential threat to privacy. For instance, a provider of information who manages the network with the databank *and* charges users is able to apply both user details and data on the use of the network to create full profiles.

Collective self-regulation

The laws and self-regulation mentioned have been directed almost exclusively at informational privacy. Even though *relational privacy* is covered by most constitutions in a very general sense, in the context of networks it is not (adequately) supported by specific legislation concerning, for instance, trespassing, and secrecy of telephone conversations and posted mail. The legislation concerned is based upon the technical possibilities of the past. 'Entering' someone's home through interactive media, telemetrics or electronic house arrest is not considered to be trespassing, as the law presupposes only a physical entering of the home. And what is more, the law assumes the resident has given permission to enter after accepting the installation of equipment. (Of course, this does not apply to electronic house arrest.)

Regulation of relational privacy

The confidentiality of electronic conversation is not sufficiently protected, as usually the exchange of digital messages is not treated as an equivalent to telephone speech conversation, and making contact with a computer system is not considered to be equal to addressing another person. In most countries, it is not clear yet whether the confidentiality of traditional mail and telephone conversations covers email, or when this will be the case.

Relational privacy in digital telephony and in company networks electronically tracking employees is only protected by most constitutions in a very general sense. There is hardly any jurisprudence. This type of privacy is still scarcely discussed. It is just another example of a technology slowly and secretly changing relations between people. The sociological and psychological aspects concerned are barely known. Apparently, they are so abstract that their importance is not recognized – all the more reason to explain them in the chapters that follow.

Finally, we have the technical solutions for privacy protection described in the previous chapter. Cryptographic techniques show great promise for privacy protection. In the field of digital cash, privacy-enhancing systems are offered, although they are not yet adopted by banking on a massive scale. Another encryption technique, designed for all messages, is Pretty Good Privacy (PGP). Other ways of message protection are so-called anonymous remailers (services forwarding your mail anonymously) and anonymous

Technical solutions

access by means of public Internet terminals, anonymous email addresses and prepaid access cards.

These means put the question of the right to anonymity in electronic environments on the agenda. Anonymity is (ab)used by all kinds of criminals and networkers displaying improper behaviour. So, these technological solutions are a two-edged sword, as has been explained before. However, according to the Working Party on the Protection of Individuals with Regard to Processing of Personal Data (1997), a body advising on data protection registrars to the European Commission, the right to anonymity should preserve the same level of protection in online as in offline environments. So, anonymously sending messages, browsing web sites, purchasing goods or services and telephoning should be as possible on the Internet as it is in the offline world of sending letters, looking in shop windows, buying with cash and calling anonymously.

The further advice of the Working Party was to adopt the same careful balance between the fundamental rights of privacy and freedom of expression on the one hand, and the prevention of crime on the other, as we aspire to in offline environments. After all, since the end of the 1990s, and particularly after September 11, 2001, we observe all kinds of overreactions of governments adopting measures of control affecting the right of anonymity and freedom of expression on public computer networks.

I would like to add my prediction that current government attempts to confront or to break into encryption systems to combat crime will prove to be rearguard actions, as encryption techniques, like steganography (see Chapter 5), are progressing much faster than the countermeasures of the authorities. It is better to reorient the search methods of the police and security agencies to traffic analysis (tracking the use of electronic networks in log files, among others) and to investigations at the source and destination where criminal actions go into the digital underworld and have to return to the analogue surface. Most police officers investigating child pornography know that the images concerned – which are less of a problem than the acts of production, where irreversible harm is done to children – are difficult to trace on the Internet when they are encrypted. Most often, this is not even the case. Therefore these officers first analyse the sources of images, the persons on them, and their destinations and distribution lines (pictures and videos).

Reductions in privacy protection All the solutions described scarcely address any type of privacy other than informational privacy. It has been argued that privacy protection is reduced to the protection of personal data, if not the technical security of these data. Relational privacy and physical privacy are neglected, while their importance in communication networks, video surveillance and biometrics increases by the day.

CONCLUSIONS

- The law that should protect against abuses of network technology is itself undermined by this technology. It is largely out of government control, respects no borders, and is continually changing and overly complex because so many actors and techniques are involved. To get a better grip on network technology, general framework legislation has to be conceived that is based on legitimate principles of power in networking and that takes account of the individual characteristics of networks. Until the time appropriate legislation is adopted, the safest principle is to accept that what goes offline should also go online. This should be backed by international agreements.

- The first network to be considered is the Internet. Here, regulation has shifted from early attempts to rule the Internet by (mainly American) government departments and Internet communities to technological control (architecture and codes) and market rule both backed by legislation. This means a shift from public and self-regulatory rule to private and juridical rule.

- The most common opinion is that the current law for the old mass media should also apply to the public applications of the Internet. However, problems are posed by the private and semi-public applications on the Internet that are difficult to separate from the public ones, but that should be ruled by private law.

- Public computer networks such as the Internet offer both an advance and a threat to information and communication freedom. Freedoms cannot only be defended by legislation. Self-regulation and technological protection are necessary to prevent the censorships of governments and others.

- Networks add to the socialization of knowledge. Therefore it is difficult to protect intellectual property rights in networks. In the American Copyright Act and the European Directive on Copyright, digital intellectual property rights are defended so zealously that the balance between the copyright owners' interests on the one side and the public interest of the diffusion of ideas in fair use and limited copying on the other is lost to the benefit of the former. However, intellectual copyrights cannot be defended by legislation only. Self-regulation that is marked by new business models in the market of intellectual value (advertising, more or less free software and relationship management) and technological solutions, such as digital encryption of pay-per-view products, should be added to legislation.

- The same combination is required for privacy protection. Privacy legislation of a level of protection that is at least equal to the EU privacy directive should be the framework for self-regulatory solutions and technological protection (encryption and anonymous computer and Internet use). Privacy is perhaps the most threatened value in network communications; it should be considered as a basic freedom underlying many others that should not be opposed to, and sacrificed for, security so easily.

SOCIAL STRUCTURE

This chapter is about the infrastructure of society. One of the core arguments of this book is that this infrastructure is changing under the influence of communication networks. However, the opposite also holds: the changing social infrastructure of society shapes communication technology. These mutual shaping processes create the network society.

Social (infra)structures can be seen in a number of dimensions. The most basic ones are the space and time dimensions. The new media in general and communication networks in particular are supposed to eliminate constraints of space and time in societies. There is much talk about the death of distance and the 24-hour economy. However, are space and time really no longer important in the network society? In the first section below, I defend the opposite view: in a particular way, the importance of these basic categories increases.

The third dimension is about depth. A part of social structure is the connection of social spaces. They are, among others, the spheres of living and the public versus the private sphere. In the network society, these divisions appear to blur. Networks are directly connecting them and an increasing number of activities that traditionally took place in a particular sphere of life can now be done almost everywhere. I am talking about telework, telestudy and other tele-activities. What are the prospects for these activities? Are the spheres of life and of society (public and private) merging as easily as they are supposed to be? Conversely, is the fear of many observers that the public sphere will be completely fragmented by all kinds of subcultures and special interest groups communicating only among each other justified?

In the network society, new social structures seem to fill the void (depth) of traditional communities and associations that are lost in modern society. All kinds of new communication groups between mass and interpersonal communication, such as chat and messaging groups and personal websites or web-logs, and a colourful collection of online communities are created. Are they reshaping community and association in new ways, or are they causing society to fall apart? On a more general level, will computer networks like the Internet increase our sociability or will they add to the loneliness of people in modern society?

The next dimension is the high versus low dimension of social structure. Will social inequality increase or decrease in the network society? Networks facilitate the spread of knowledge and other resources. But what about the large inequalities of access to digital technology that have been observed in the first phases of the introduction of the new media? Is the so-called digital divide widening or closing?

The chapter's final section brings all the dimensions together: how coherent and stable are the structures of the network society as a whole? These structures appear to be very flexible, but this might be at the cost of rising instability. The prices of stocks, currencies and other economic values, the popularity of politicians and media stars and the attention to particular cultural items appears to rise and fall faster and faster. Crises, news items, rumours, fashions and crazes spread with accelerating speeds. Is this instability an inescapable feature of network use?

SPACE AND TIME IN THE NETWORK SOCIETY

This section shows how the use of media networks is linked to several fundamental social changes taking place in modern society at the beginning of the 21st century. We are talking about processes such as individualization, privatization and socialization, which together shape society's new infrastructure. The importance of networks for this infrastructure can be shown on several levels of abstraction and generality. Unfortunately, the account that follows has to be fairly abstract.

One of the most abstract and general historical processes is *time–space distantiation*. Anthony Giddens (1984, 1991a, 1991b) uses this term to show that human and social time and space dimensions tend to widen in the course of history. Traditional society is based on direct interaction between people living close to each other. Modern societies stretch further and further across time and space. Barriers of time are broken by the spread of customs or traditions. Information is stored to be used later or to be passed on to future generations. Barriers of space are broken by the increasing reach of communication and transportation.

Time–space distantiation

With the introduction of global networks reaching into every home, the process of time–space distantiation seems to be approaching its limit, at least in developed societies. Many take it for granted that we have a 'global village'. Distance and time seem to lose any relevance. Some have spoken about the 'death of distance' (Cairncross, 2001), others about 'timeless time' (Castells, 1996). These popular ideas are partly wrong, however. All in all, the process of time–space distantiation is marked not only by the extension of space and time, but also by the contraction of space and the compression of time. As a result, time and space in some respects gain importance, instead of losing relevance. Their meaning has radicalized. The technological capabilities of bridging space and time enable people to be more *selective* in choosing coordinates of space and time than ever before in history.

Many examples can be given to support this statement (see also Ferguson, 1990). The enormous growth in telephony and the explosive increase of demand for data communication already show that more value is being placed on bridging distances of space and time. Nobody will deny the extreme relevance of (clock) time in the most advanced nerve centres of ICT, the stock markets. Hesitating for a second or failing to make a fast connection to another financial market can mean the difference between profit and loss. In companies, the coordination of labour by means of ICT leads to an increase of the relevance of logistics and time registration. In mass communication, the importance of time schedules for broadcasters of programmes and commercials is still increasing, for they want to reach very specific target audiences. The dimension of time is becoming more important for viewers as well, as new concepts of global time (produced by satellite TV and Internet communication) overlie the old ones (marked by local, daily rhythms and routines) (Ferguson, 1990: 155).

In the dimension of space, the same applies to all the fields we have just mentioned. In Chapter 4, it was stressed how selective transnational corporations have become. They are extremely careful in strategically choosing the right places for their departments and computer network nodes in the world, assigning them particular functions. Increasing control over space enables them to choose between the quality of particular places (Graham and Marvin, 1996; Harvey, 1989: 294ff.).

So, expansion and compression of space and time are two sides of the same coin. They represent the most general expression of the idea of the unity of scale extension and reduction, one of the key threads running through this book. Increased control over space and time in a local context by a small social unit can only exist thanks to increased control of space and time over long distances by a larger social unit. In Chapter 1, I pointed out that the privatization of local units to become smaller units has always been enabled by means of large-scale infrastructures for the supply and transportation of energy, matter and people. The need for communication and information flows by media networks is now added to this list. In households, the need for these infrastructures has grown with the development of four dimensions of privatization:

- decreasing housing density (settlement);
- increasing size of a single house with more individual rooms;
- decreasing household size;
- a cultural process of spending more time at home and in family life.

In companies, the combination of decentralizing production and centralizing control described in Chapter 2 causes an increase in the need for all kinds of communication channels. Both at home and in companies, the expansion of communication and of information processing over long distances goes hand in hand with an increasing intensity of information activities in local contexts (using an 'intelligent home', an 'intelligent' workstation or a local network). The historical process of both socialization and individualization of space and time in society runs side by side with the scale extensions and scale reductions mentioned above. The spatial dimension was aptly described by Burgers (1988) as 'the detachment of society from geography'. The natural environment as a relevant context is replaced by, or interwoven with, social environments constructed by people. Simultaneously, natural time is outstripped by the increasing importance of clock time constructed by society (Bolter, 1984; Rifkin, 1987). Communication and information networks more or less complete these processes (Meyrowitz, 1985).

In the temporal dimension, global media networks add different levels of fragmented temporality on top of the continuous local level. We were already familiar with the fragments of 24 time zones across the globe. In 1998, the first attempt was made to replace clock time by a unitary computer and network time. The Swiss watchmaker Swatch from Biel proposed Biel Mean Time (BMT) as a global Internet time consisting of 1000 beats of 1 minute and 26.4 seconds a day. Of course, the British did not want to lag behind; in 2002 they tried to rescue GMT with the proposal of Greenwich Electronic Time (GeT) (www.get-time.org). Both Internet time systems allow only one time to be used in a global web exchange; the computer system then translates this time to the requested local times. According to the Thai philosopher Hongladarom (2002), they enable both the coexistence of different conceptions of time across cultures in the world and a return to a 'medieval' conception of unitary time, currently appearing as 'glocal' (global and local) time.

In computer networks, transmission takes place in 'real time' and messages can be sent and received at any moment. With the shifting limits of natural time, the meaning of socially constructed time becomes increasingly important. The Internet times described above are just the latest example. Even the socialization of time seems to have become complete, as people think time is no longer relevant in the new media environment. So it seems – but in reality the natural (for instance biological) substratum will continue to exist, of course. The consequences and tensions produced by the combination of all these temporal regimes (natural, social and media time) have a large social, cultural and mental impact (Green, 2002; Hongladarom, 2002; Lee and Liebenau, 2000; Lee and Whitley, 2002). This will be demonstrated in the chapters that follow.

In the spatial dimension, global media networks spatially enlarge society – in the past centuries mainly western society – and they reduce the size of the world. In the following pages, I consider this dimension, forgetting the time dimension for a moment.

A first observation about space is that an *upgrading* of the social environment is going on. Although individual environments remain decisive for individuals, of course, people acknowledge the shrinking relevance of their own environment in the world. *Life is Elsewhere*, as the title of a Milan Kundera (1986) novel says. Burgers (1988: 17, my translation from Dutch) has expressed it this way:

Socialization of space

The moment the world is brought into the home via the mass media, the relevance of individual experiences seems to shrink to insignificant proportions.

Viewed from the perspective of modern society, the ups and downs of individual life are less and less important and the individual is well aware of this. In relation to the physical environment this means that really important events seem to be taking place elsewhere.

Second, the social environment is made more *objective*. The social environments made by humans increasingly adopt the character of a natural environment. Individuals therefore feel that they face an anonymous, opaque, inaccessible and uncontrollable reality. Symptoms of alienation and uprooting are widespread. Social and economic crises begin to resemble natural disasters. Media networks, which enable more direct communications between the micro-level and the institutions of the macro-level, do not reduce these experiences. On the contrary, I have argued that computer networks both subjectively and objectively tend to enhance opaque and uncontrollable processes. A network breakdown is like a natural disaster.

In the third place, a *fragmentation* of social environments can be observed. They comprise fewer concrete, continuous and collectively used areas, and more abstract, dispersed areas used for special purposes. And what is more, homogeneous communities are being gradually replaced by all kinds of diffuse social networks. This is discussed in greater detail later, for the communication capacities of media networks seem to fit perfectly with these trends.

Finally, we perceive a *generalization and a standardization* of social environments. 'Human activities seem to become more uniform after the scale extension of social communications; the same activities are happening in ever more places' (Burgers, 1988: 21). The exchange of experiences through networks on a global level has led to a general diffusion of western urban culture. It is made dominant by western economic and technological strength and it has produced a loss of the particularity and identity of other, less materially strong cultures (Barber, 1996; Castells, 1997). On the other hand, elements of the latter cultures are adopted by western culture (see Chapter 8).

Socialization and individualization of space and time

In the 20th century, this general socialization of space was pursued within a particular dialectical process, that is a unity of opposing tendencies: a particular socialization of individual space on the one hand, and a particular individualization of social space on the other. One social scientist will emphasize the first development, whereas another will emphasize the second, but in fact both processes are active simultaneously and both are supported by media networks. Again we are dealing with an expression of the unity of scale extension and scale reduction. The second tendency suggests individualization and privatization – social processes visible to everyone in modern western society. A nice description in this respect was given by Burgers: 'It seems as if a process of detachment of society from geography "in the second degree" is taking place: we try to detach ourselves from our direct social environment in the same way as we have liberated ourselves from our "natural" environment' (1988: 21). Instead, solitary individuals are withdrawing into their own (ever smaller) households and are participating in all kinds of 'communities without propinquity'. This term is from Webber (1963) and refers to the multifarious, more or less diffused and large-scale social networks of modern society. The result of this process is a strong *erosion of public space* as we know it. Instead, we find a completely different type of public space, to a large extent realized by media networks. This is discussed in one of the next sections. Well-known analyses of individualizing public space have been made by Richard Sennett in *The Fall of Public Man* (1974) and Christopher Lasch in *Heaven in a Heartless World* (1977).

The often neglected opposite tendency is a particular socialization of individual space. Some critical, emancipatory or liberal social scientists speak about 'colonization of the world of daily life by the system' (Habermas, 1981) or about the increasing intrusion into private life by the authorities and by fellow citizens (Shils, 1975). Usually, they describe these tendencies as linear historical processes produced by public authorities and private corporations, previously operating from a distance and now increasingly penetrating the private life of (for instance) households. When these tendencies are solely described as a linear process, it is hard to understand how a socialization of individual space can go hand in hand with an individualization of social space. There is no reason to call the conditions of the 19th century a 'golden age of privacy'. In the close-knit, socially controlled communities of those days, the privacy of citizens among themselves and in relation to local authorities was not considered to be relevant. Only in the 20th century has the penetration of authorities and market organizations into the private life of households and other more or less private spaces increasingly run contrary to the process of privatization and the attempts to protect these households and other spaces. This conflict has made privacy an increasingly important value to modern western people.

It is extremely important to understand that media networks offer an infrastructure for both the tendencies described above. They are a potential social threat to privacy in private life, and at the same time they are a condition for the fulfilment of the need for social communication and information in the same spheres of privatized life. This contrast is a fertile breeding ground for future social conflicts.

THE BLURRING SPHERES OF LIVING

As already has become evident in the previous section, one of the network society's most important characteristics is the dissolving of boundaries between the macro-, meso- and micro-levels of social life, between the public and the private sphere and between the spheres of living, working, studying, recreation and travelling. Therefore, telework and telestudy are among the most discussed applications of the new media. So far, these tele-activities have not yet proved themselves. The overestimation of their adoption is caused not so much by a lower than expected introduction of the infrastructure required, but by an inaccurate view of existing relations between spheres of living and by a strong underestimation of the social and organizational

Multifunctional or connected spheres of living?

difficulties involved in tele-activity. Most people assume that the spheres of living, the domestic sphere in particular, will become *multifunctional*. At the same time, it is assumed that people want to perform their activities *in a single place* (except for travelling, of course), preferably at home. Both assumptions are only partly correct. The dissolving of boundaries between the spheres of living, described earlier, is caused not so much by the multifunctional use of spaces enabled by communication technology, but by the *linking of spaces that remain and are used primarily for special purposes*. Therefore we are witnessing more increases of tele-activity in mobile environments than in homes and other private places. A network's most fundamental technical characteristic is the connections it makes. That enables the combination of multifunctionality and specialization everywhere; but this opportunity will only be taken when it is desired.

The opportunity for an increasing multifunctional use of *spaces* in spheres of living cannot be denied. The same applies to the multifunctional use of *time* for that matter. The new media enable working, studying and entertaining oneself at home at every hour of the day. In the meantime, workplaces are also provided with opportunities for study, entertainment and mediated conversation with friends, acquaintances and relatives at a distance (although there is a limited chance that this will be allowed). Direct links to companies will enable students to gain work experience while sitting at the school desk. And people will be able to work and have conversations while travelling and being entertained (by way of portable PC, mobile phone or car telephone, and audiovisual equipment). Finally, the workaholics among us will be able to work while having a holiday (for instance by taking a laptop to the beach).

Telework   However, there are several limitations to a predominantly multifunctional use of space and time. But before these limitations are discussed, we will briefly survey the first experiences with telework and telestudy, which already show these limitations. At the start of the 21st century, the number of real teleworkers must be rather disappointing to the advocates of this type of work. In most developed countries, it is less than ten percent and the majority of this proportion only telecommutes one day a week. According to IDC (1996), real teleworkers are employees having a formal agreement with their employers that allows them to spend some part of the working week at some location other than the bureau/office (for instance at home or at a telework office) using ICT. So, teleworkers are not simply people who have always worked at home, who were mobile workers before, or who have a business of their own. On the one hand, teleworkers are professionals usually working independently (such as programmers, consultants and system designers); and on the other hand, they are functional workers undertaking activities such as data entry, data processing and selling goods and services. Finally, there is a group of professionals often working at home, and most often working overtime.

Advantages and   The advantages of telework are obvious. Employees need to travel less and
disadvantages   they are able to plan their own days. Moreover, telework can be combined with other activities such as household work and looking after children.

However, the disadvantages appear to be numerous in the first experimental phase of teleworking. They can be summarized as follows:

- The *conditions of labour* for (in particular) teleworkers having functional tasks are poor. Like all people working at home in flexible labour relationships, they have little protection. They have almost no chance of making a career within the organization. Trained professionals often work overtime without receiving any extra payment.
- *Impoverished communication* with management and co-workers affects the quality of the tasks to be performed. The work is routine and it lacks informality and crucial non-verbal aspects. In Chapter 9, I argue that online communication can be richer and more social than people expected in the early days of computer networking. However, telework and telestudy in advanced jobs and training require very complex types of exchange often not available in online communication.
- A consequence, disadvantageous to both management and functional personnel, is that *little support can be given* by management. Not only is supervision unsatisfactory, but there is little opportunity for suggestions (for improvements) and coordination between colleagues. This seems to be the main reason why telework in organizations is growing so slowly.
- *Social isolation* of employees working at home is considered to be the most important problem. It can reduce productivity to such an extent that it is noticed by management as well. This is why, in some cases, companies decide to start local telework centres.
- Doing telework at home makes it *hard to separate work* from other domestic activities. A teleworker is required to have strong self discipline. When several members of one household spend more time at home than before, tensions may arise.

The advantages of *telestudy* can be compared with those of telework: less time spent travelling, being able to plan one's own day, and the possibility of combining activities. Furthermore, teachers can correct and grade assignments sooner and sometimes even faster. In the late 1990s, however, the practice of distance education was confined to an elite of people in higher education having some experience with computers and used to working independently. The disadvantages of telestudy also resemble those of telework:

Telestudy: advantages and disadvantages

- Telestudents *completely depend* upon communication with the educational department offering this facility. It is much more difficult for them to consult other students if they have study problems requiring collective action. Telestudents work more individually than traditional students, though they may send each other messages by email.
- In fact, *interaction* between teachers and students reaches such a *low level* that the quality of education completely depends on the programme, which has to be repeatedly tested and improved.

- Many students cannot handle the *independence* and *self-discipline* required. Direct supervision and help, beyond instruction at a distance, are sorely missed. Drop-out rates in distance education will be at least as high as in present-day correspondence and lifelong learning courses.
- Telestudy is a *socially isolated activity* as well. Students can only lean on their fellow students with online communication. A traditional educational institution serves as a meeting place, a place of socialization and a means of creating a daily study routine. It is therefore highly unlikely that distance education will become the predominant way to educate children and adolescents.
- As is the case with telework, separating study from *other domestic activities* is extremely difficult. This division has to be enforced by, for instance, putting the PC in the attic, which can have negative effects on living together. Both too many and too few contacts may lead to tensions in a modern household.

General problems of tele-activity
These disadvantages of both telework and telestudy involve a number of structural limitations to tele-activity and the multifunctional use of spaces in general:

- In practice, tele-activities are still bound to certain places, even though they can be performed in numerous places in theory and by technical means.
- They remain dependent upon an external centre.
- They encounter difficulties concerning the separation of activities.
- They have to deal with a limited quality of communication.

In part, these disadvantages are the same as the limitations of traditional work and study at home. However, mediated tele-activities considerably intensify these limitations because the demands are much more ambitious and because the number and complexity of distance activities increase. People think activities formerly performed in centralized and face-to-face situations can now be performed locally and in mediated contexts. Furthermore, adequate and frequent or even permanent communication between the centre and the local units is assumed to exist. And finally, the local units are expected to make unhindered use of their own multifunctional spaces and terminals. These assumptions are realized only in a limited number of cases, as is shown by the following series of problems.

First, all tele-activity except mobile networking is actually tied to one place and leads to symptoms of social isolation. This applies not only to telework and telestudy, but also to working at a terminal in general. So far, most labour has been carried out in face-to-face or telephone conversations with colleagues and by moving around the company and meeting colleagues everywhere. In computer work, it seems that the terminal has become the closest colleague and the nearest partner in conversations. In Chapter 9, it will be argued that people do not stop being social when they are working alone in front of a computer. However, when social life, work and education are *reduced* to online communication, people feel isolated and miss particular social information and rewards.

Second, the fact that most tele-activities are tied to a particular place conflicts not only with the need for social contact, but also with the *need for mobility*. Daily travel to work, school and shops and regular trips to meetings are not undertaken merely to get there. They also fulfil the need for a change of scene, for chance encounters or impressions – and for adventure. An accumulation of several types of tele-activity can stop these needs from being fulfilled sufficiently.

Third, dependence on a centrally controlled and integrated medium of communication that does not respond to all individual needs directly *clashes with the pursuit of individualization* in present-day western culture. People not only want more control over their work, their study and their spare time, instead of less, but also want more space of their own, with a telephone, a TV, and so on. Those who do want a room to be used multifunctionally, want this room to be an individual place. In the light of most current situations at work and school or in the home, it will be impossible to fulfil this need. The dependence described also counters the wish of modern individuals to manage extremely heterogeneous activities and contacts in their own times and places.

Fourth, a multifunctional use of all times and places does not provide people with the daily routines and rhythms needed to *distinguish and coordinate activities*. It is not without reason that most people want to do one activity in one place and another elsewhere, or one activity at one time and another at another time.

So, the reluctance of managers to stimulate telework and of teachers to experiment with distance education is no surprise. Their resistance is not merely based on conservatism or a wish to save their own jobs and to keep workers and students under supervision and control. They really do have legitimate problems, as the quality of communication required for advanced tasks of formal labour and education is still lacking in current tele-activities.

One can reach the conclusion that there are so many limitations and contradictions attached to tele-activities that they are not likely to dominate work, study, travel and recreation in the near future. So, the blurring of the spheres of living will not result in their disappearance. These spheres will keep being used for specific purposes (of domestic life, work, study, travel and leisure time) predominantly. *Additions* of other activities and *connections* with other spaces are increasingly realized by means of mobile equipment. This explains the explosive growth of this equipment in new media use.

Tele-activity: Replacement or addition?

COMMUNITIES AND SOCIAL RELATIONS

The history of the 20th century reveals a disintegration of traditional communities such as families, neighbourhoods and groups of workers, into associations which on the one hand are declining in size (caused by privatization and individualization) and on the other hand are extending as they become more diffused and spread over greater distances. In the eyes of many social scientists, planners and citizens, we are dealing with a 'lost community'; see Putnam (2000) in particular.

'Lost' communities and the perspective of virtual communities

After the second World War, town planners tried to create a counter-balance to this presumed social uprooting by saving communities and (re-) creating them ('saved communities' in the terms of Wellman and Leighton, 1979). In the first decade of the 21st century, these attempts are dropped far more easily. Most people accept the strong trend towards privatization and individualization and the rise of diffuse communities. The introduction of the new media, in particular the Internet with all its sites and discussion groups, has raised hopes for a recovery of community in electronic environments. So-called **virtual communities** were considered to be a renaissance of lost community by the early adopters and advocates of the Internet (see de Kerckhove, 1998; Lévy, 1997 and Rheingold, 1993a and 1993b in particular). The reality of such virtual community building can be judged by comparing these communities systematically with **organic** or *physical* **communities** (see van Dijk, 1997a).

Virtual and organic communities compared

Virtual communities are associations of people not tied to time, place and physical or material circumstances, other than those of the people and media enabling them. They are created in electronic environments with the aid of mediated communications. Organic communities are bound to time, place and natural environments because they depend on the physical contact of human organisms together shaping a 'social body' that is called a community. So, they are mainly based on face-to-face communication. Every community has its own particular structure and activities, a social organization, a language and modes of interaction, and finally its own culture and identity.

Composition

An organic or physical community (in a neighbourhood, quarter, extended family or workplace) is a relatively stable unit with many short and overlapping communication lines and joint activities (see Figure 2.3). Virtual communities, on the other hand, are loose affiliations of people that can fall apart at any moment. For instance, leaving a group on the Internet is simple and may hardly be noticed. Virtual communities consist of people with a particular interest or range of activities. Therefore, they are called *communities of interest*.

Social organization

A virtual community's social organization is not bound to a particular time, place and material environment. Many think these fundamental coordinates of life are redundant in virtual communities. This is a misunderstanding. The content of communication in networks, and therefore in virtual communities, is largely determined by the reality of the organic communities with which one is familiar. This is the origin of the many expressions containing 'virtual this' and 'digital that'. People take the reality they know with them, as a kind of baggage, when they surf the Internet and take part in virtual communities. The constitution of people is shaped entirely by their physical and mental condition and environment. Furthermore, we have just seen that the importance of place and time in using networks is increasing instead of decreasing. Attempts to ignore time, place and other physical conditions result in the extremely fragile organization of most virtual communities. Some think leadership and coordination are unnecessary in such communities, because technology enables all members to participate at the same time. This supposition is also false, as social-psychological research has made perfectly clear (see

Chapter 9). Electronic discussion and interaction require more organization and coordination than face-to-face discussion, not less.

One of the reasons for this requirement is that for the time being almost all signals in the communication of virtual communities are restricted to verbal utterances of a particular type (texts on a screen). The rich potential of verbal and non-verbal communication in organic communities is sorely missed. This is compensated for by consciously using artificial paralanguage such as smileys (tokens of emotion added to the keyboard, such as ☺) and asynchronous types of interaction (the language of the answering machine). See Chapter 9 for further information.

Language and interaction

Members of a virtual community usually have only one thing in common: the interest that brought them together. They are heterogeneous in everything else. In an organic community, on the other hand, people have several interests in common, which makes such a community relatively homogeneous. This provides an organic community with better chances of building and maintaining its own culture and identity than a virtual community.

Culture and identity

From this short comparison (see van Dijk, 1997a for an extended one), we can draw the conclusion that virtual communities cannot make up for the loss of traditional community. They cannot replace organic communities, because they are too limited and unstable to exist without them. However, increasingly they will become added to traditional communities. The bridge between them is created by so-called *communities online*, that is organic communities with a virtual counterpart on the Internet. They should be distinguished from *online communities*, that is, complete virtual communities only 'living' on the Internet. A mutual improvement and reinforcement of online communities, communities online and organic communities will be the real challenge for the future.

Communities online and online communities

The partial shift from organic to virtual communities has spurred an ardent debate about the question whether the virtual communities created on the Internet reduce or enhance sociability. In the 1990s, the following related fears about the Internet were frequent among the observers of this new medium:

The Internet reduces sociability?

- High Internet use leads to social isolation and even loneliness or depression as strong face-to-face relations with proximate people maintained for a diversity of purposes are replaced by weak mediated relations with people far away that are only used for special interests (Kraut et al., 1998).
- High Internet use leads to less real-life involvement producing loners, 'computer nerds' and even computer or Internet addicts (Nie and Erbring, 2000).
- High Internet use impoverishes social interaction as rich face-to-face interactions are replaced by poor, shallow, deceiving and transient online interactions (Nie, 2001).

From the end of the 1990s onwards a large number of social surveys and time-diary studies were published that both supported and denied the rightfulness of these fears. The problem is that studies measuring Internet use at a single moment in time cannot prove causal relationships. We do not know for sure whether Internet use is the cause of these phenomena or previously existing social and psychological characteristics of users. Nie et al. (2002: 224) observed that 'for each minute spent on the Internet during the last 24 hours there is a reduction of approximately one-third of a minute spent with family members' in the United States. They also found that for every minute on the Internet the average American user spends 7 seconds less with friends and 11 less with colleagues. Finally, they measured that 'for every minute spent on the Internet, there is an additional 45 seconds of time spent alone' (pp. 224–225).

Apparently, these investigators consider Internet use as an isolated activity. 'One simply cannot be engaged with others while being engaged on the Internet' (Nie et al., 2002: 230). For several reasons, this statement is wrong. First, it denies multitasking: talking to proximate others while being online. Second, every Internet user knows that it is possible to start, develop and maintain social relations online. Face-to-face contact is only one way to realize them. Online and offline social contact can reinforce each other. Exchanging basic information online can increase the quality time of meetings, as some facts no longer have to be revealed. Moreover, online contact is a convenient way to make appointments. Increasingly, it will be wrong to strictly separate online and offline social relations.

Network individualization

Another basic reason why Nie et al. are wrong is that they do not recognize the phenomenon of 'network individualism' (Wellman, 2000), which I would prefer to call *network individualization*. This means that the individual is becoming the most important node in the network society and not a particular place, group or organization. The social and cultural process of individualization, which appeared long before the Internet, particularly in western societies, is strongly supported by the rise of social and media networks. Networks are the social counterpart of individualization. Using them, the individual creates a very mobile lifestyle and a criss-cross of geographically dispersed relations. Inevitably, it means that individuals will spend more time alone accompanied by technology (transport and communication means) and that they will spend more time being online. However, being online may be fully social.

The Internet enhances sociability?

In the first decade of the 21st century, more and more social surveys are being published revealing that the fears discussed above should be moderated and qualified. Of course, every medium is employed for social and personal escape and can be used excessively by particular users with social and psychological problems. The medium is not to blame for this. Most North American social surveys summarized in Wellman and Haythornthwaite (2002) and Katz and Rice (2002) demonstrate that the Internet can also result in the opposite. They show that the use of computers and the Internet can increase so-called 'social capital' in terms of social contact, civic engagement and sense of community (Katz and Rice, 2002; Quan-Haase et al., 2002). 'The Internet complements and even strengthens offline interactions, provides frequent uses for social interaction and extends communication with family and friends.' (Katz and Rice, 2002: 326).

A number of the social surveys referred to above also show that the Internet provides increased contact with distant friends and relatives (Boneva and Kraut, 2002; Kavanaugh and Patterson, 2002; Kraut et al., 1998). Others add that those ties previously 'just out of reach' geographically experience the greatest increase in contact by means of the Internet (Hampton and Wellman, 2002). Finally, it has been observed that the Internet and email even increase the communication with nearby kin, friends and neighbors (Quan-Haase et al., 2002; Chen et al., 2002). Conversely, most studies, at least in western countries, agree that face-to-face contact with family members and with direct colleagues at work is decreasing and partly shifting to email and telephone contact. This, however, may be a part of network individualization.

As has been argued before, the Internet does not replace existing communication modes but supplements them. The Internet adds new forms of social capital to the traditional ones (dinner parties, sporting events, club meetings, local bars, or dances, etc.). These are forms of selecting and contacting complete strangers with particular characteristics, types of online conversation, and the initiative to act both online and offline. More than a tenth of Internet users in the United States had established friendships via the Internet by the year 2000 (Katz and Rice, 2002: 327). A comparable number is known to be engaged in online dating in a number of countries.

While the evidence in favour of more or less sociability as a result of Internet use is mixed, one thing is fairly sure. The Internet is a powerful tool that supports both those who are rich and poor in so-called social capital. It supports those already strong in social contact, civic engagement and sense of community and it enables those weak in these things to further isolate themselves and to be excluded from the many opportunities the new media have to offer (Cummings et al., 2002; Robinson and Nie, 2002; Robinson et al., 2003; van Dijk, 2005). Some people have access to this new tool and others don't. In this way, some people are capable of maintaining and extending their social networks while others see these networks crumble if they cannot compensate for the increasing difficulties of maintaining pure offline social relationships in an individualizing and busy urbanized society. This refers to the problem of the digital divide that will be discussed below. A related problem is that those who already have developed a large and dense social network through face-to-face communication, the telephone, and writing are more likely to extend this network with Internet use than those who have only a small network, even though they also use the Internet. 'Those who are more active offline are more active online – and vice versa' (Quan-Haase et al., 2002: 320).

The Internet reinforces differences of sociability

It is also certain that the support given by networks and the rise of all kinds of weak ties along with the traditional strong ties create new communication groups, and even new types of communities. They have at least one thing in common: *they fill the field between interpersonal communication and mass communication*. These groups and types can be analysed by placing them along the dimensions of public versus private and sender versus receiver, for they exist between one extreme, a combination of public sender and public receiver, and the other, a combination of private transmitter and private receiver (see Figure 7.1).

New communication groups

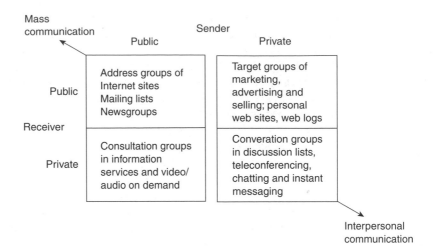

FIGURE 7.1   Online groups between interpersonal and mass communication

Receiver groups   In the mass communication relationship between public sender and public receiver, a clear *segmentation of public receiver groups* can be perceived. This means that these groups acquire a more private character. This trend is discussed in Chapter 8, where the question is posed as to whether this means the end of mass communication.

Consultation groups   Segmentation of the public is completed in new media *connecting public senders to private receivers*. The dominant pattern is consultation. I am referring to video and audio on demand and to information services. But one can also identify phenomena springing from the segmentation just mentioned. James Beniger (1987) has referred to the strong tendency in current mass communications to create or suggest a 'personal' relation to receivers. He has shown the correspondence with the boom in 'personal' direct mail and in marketing backed by research into special consumer groups. In this way 'pseudo-communities' are created, according to Beniger.

Target groups   In the Fordist age of mass production, communication between *private senders and public receivers* expanded enormously (see Beniger, 1986). I am referring to target groups in public relations, advertising and all kinds of propaganda. In the current age of specialized production, this type of communication is enhanced and directed towards *semi-public* reception aimed at specific target groups. The new media offer all the necessary facilities. And, in fact, they do not provide these facilities merely for commercial and party political purposes. The number of networks for experts, hobbyists and activists is increasing rapidly. For instance, networks of medical experts, computer hackers and environmentalists are multiplying. The same goes for the number of personal web sites and web logs being offered.

Conversation groups   The latter phenomenon also creates new and improved opportunities for communication between *private senders and public receivers*. In contemporary computer networks, people can talk and exchange text, audio and video almost simultaneously while everybody that has been granted access watches, listens, reads and occasionally gives feedback. This happens with (semi-) private senders and receivers in online news and discussion groups, or in groups that open other new communication forums, such as groups for chatting and (semi-) public instant messaging (Herring, 2004).

All the initiatives mentioned above indicate the birth of more or less new types of communication and community operating *between* interpersonal and mass communication.

UNITY AND FRAGMENTATION: A NEW SOCIAL COHESION

Now we shift to the level of society as a whole. Previously, it was argued that scale extensions and scale reductions, including socialization and individualization, are two sides of the coin of modernity. This *duality of social structure* has been noted by many theorists of high modernity or postmodernity, notably Barber (1996); Castells (1996; 1997); Featherstone et al. (1995); Giddens (1991a); Lash and Urry (1994); and van Dijk (1993a). Modern society simultaneously reveals aspects of growing homogeneity and heterogeneity, integration and differentiation, unity and fragmentation. This is not some kind of compromise position of social scientists who refuse to take a stand. It really is characteristic of all spheres of modern society, as is shown by the authors just mentioned, and as is claimed in this book in the context of the role of the new media in society. Usually social scientists have to argue in favour of the existence of homogeneity, integration and unity and against simplistic notions of a fragmenting society. It seems as if the sociologist's classic nightmare of a society falling apart returns with every modern and technological development.

Against people expecting a break-up of American society into subcultural clusters of race, religion, ethnicity and gender – a process supposedly reinforced by a fragmented media system of countless cable channels, pay-per-view programmes and Internet sites – Meyrowitz and Maguire contend that 'the current trend is towards integration of all groups into a relatively common experiential sphere – with a new recognition of the special needs and idiosyncrasies of individuals' (1993: 43). According to them, television and other electronic media have made the divisions between social groups more visible and permeable. 'Current media, then, continue a trend towards greater homogenization in one way and greater fragmentation in another. Traditional groups are bypassed in both directions: individuals experience more diversity and choice, but traditional group cultures are overlapping, losing identity and blurring into each other' (p. 45). This goes for broadcasting as well as for (new media) narrowcasting. Television has bridged the lives of people living in different physical and informational spheres. The Internet goes even further in offering the opportunity to connect by direct interaction both people of the same origin and different people or environments.

So, we may observe a *duality of media structure* closely corresponding to the duality of social structure in society. According to 'medium theory' (Meyrowitz, 1985, 1997) media have their own characteristics, producing social contexts that foster certain forms of interaction and social identity.

Social unity and fragmentation

Media unity and fragmentation

They are both defining and enabling, just like the communication capacities described in Chapter 1. Meyrowitz claims that oral media in traditional societies fostered a homogenization of relatively small communities ('us against them'). Opposed to this, the diversity of print media in early modern societies produced a compartmentalization and specialization of social groups and simultaneously supported the unification of nations by a single official language. This duality returns in the history of broadcasting. At first, radio and TV unified national and local societies with a single or a few network(s). After the multiplication of channels and the advent of pay TV, audiences became fragmented again, while keeping many similarities and overlaps. For example, audiences actually choose a handful of broadcasting channels among a much larger number, and broadcasters or advertisers still prefer the mass market (the common denominator).

Duality increases In the new media, the duality of media structure increases once again. They are both mass and interpersonal media and they offer new types of media in between: the so-called virtual communities or new associations of communication analysed in the previous section. They are media of allocution, consultation, registration and conversation in a system of integration or convergence. The new media are individualizing media, mainly because they are based upon individual human–computer interaction, and they are media to be used collectively as these computers are connected in networks. This huge plurality of potential applications enables both divisions and commonalities among users and audiences. So, the actual result of the duality of media structure is defined by the unifying and fragmenting trends in society, that is the duality of social structure.

The divisions of marketing Both dualities are eagerly adopted by electronic traders on the Internet who have discovered the concept of virtual community and are translating it into new opportunities for commercial relationships. Hagel and Armstrong (1997), for example, make a number of proposals to exploit people's desire to congregate on the net for basic needs of (common) interest, relationship, fantasy and transaction in their book *Net Gain*. This definition of virtual communities as new types of association fits with that supplied above. The authors claim that the more a community can be split or segmented, resulting in smaller electronic groups, the better it is for the depth, coherence and commercial exploitability of this community. So, they start with a complete fragmentation of potential communities along so-called 'vectors' (differences in geography, demography, topics of interest and business functions or categories) from the point of view of the marketer. However, these are the abstract conceptual inventions of marketing, not of the concrete organic groups trying to organize themselves online and offline.

A widely held view is that the narrowcasting of the new media based upon these techniques of categorizing and direct marketing, trying to reach extremely specific groups in advertising and sales, will (further) divide society. That is why Joseph Turow (1997) has called his book *Breaking up America*. Turow claims that direct marketing with new media exploits growing social divisions and exacerbates them. According to Meyrowitz and Maguire (1993: 43–4), this is wrong. The target groups that narrowcasters and direct marketers are trying to reach are 'thin age/sex bands (such as pre-teen girls, nine to twelve) or "lifestyle clusters" based on interests, tastes, values, attitudes and consumption patterns'. They are conceptual categories constructed by marketing people, not organic groups of social class, race, ethnicity and gender acting and organizing themselves and (still) having a number of overlapping commonalities.

Will the new media primarily bring us together, or will they tear us further apart? This is a question about the future of the public sphere. The most popular answer to this question emphasizes fragmentation as well. The reasons are evident. At first sight, three conditions of the modern public sphere, as we came to know it in the 20th century, disappear in the new media environment:

Future of the public sphere

1   the alliance of the public sphere with a particular place or territory;
2   the presumed unitary character of the public sphere that is transforming into a patchwork of different and partial public spheres;
3   a public–private distinction that is becoming blurred.

A short explanation will be sufficient here. As to the first condition, members of a particular organic community or a nation are no longer tied to a given territory to meet each other and build collectivities. They might use old media such as the press, the telephone or satellite broadcasting, and new media such as the Internet in particular, to (re)construct their own public sphere and form imagined communities (Anderson, 1983) or virtual communities. The pattern of the Jewish and the Armenian public spheres, for instance, which was not confined to Israel and Armenia long before the advent of the Internet, will be multiplied.

Second, what binds people in a contemporary public sphere is not a fixed number of common situations, views, habits and other social, cultural and political characteristics. It is an extremely diversified and shifting complex of overlapping similarities and differences, particularly in the growing number of multicultural societies. The 'common ground' of the unitary nation or mass society is an idea from the age of national broadcasting through a few channels. It is still rooted in the minds of the intellectual political and media elite of the nations concerned, though it was never firmly based in reality (Keane, 1995; Meyrowitz and Maguire, 1993).

Finally, the imagined borders of every public sphere in modern society become blurred, as has been demonstrated in many earlier sections. Public affairs become private in home television viewing, radio listening and surfing the Internet. The private becomes public in the numerous invasions of privacy by computer registration, in the pouring out of intimate affairs in talk shows and reality TV, and in the personalization of politics. The new media, the Internet in particular, add a new dimension to the blurring public–private distinction as new kinds of association and communication appear between interpersonal and mass communication.

Does this mean that the three conditions of the modern public sphere will disappear completely and that all common ground for societies at large will dissolve? No, it just means that the conventional idea of a single, unified

Reconstruction of the public sphere

public sphere, and the accompanying ideas of a distinctive public opinion, a common public good and a particular public–private distinction, are obsolete (see Keane, 1995). Instead we get a 'complex mosaic of differently sized overlapping and interconnected public spheres' (1995: 8). The Internet itself, with its hyperlink structure of connections and its numerous overlapping discussion fora, is a perfect model of this mosaic. It is complemented by the increasing number of cross-references and cross-fertilizations between new and old media, such as newspapers and television programmes referring to web sites and vice versa.

So, the three conditions mentioned will reappear in different forms. We will get a new type of social cohesion and public sphere with contours we cannot exactly anticipate yet. What we do know, however, is that the imagined unity of modern public spheres will transform into much more complex and differentiated unities. The public–private distinction may blur, but it will not vanish. New distinctions will be negotiated in struggles for privacy and personal autonomy, for more public or more private, market-based information supply, and for the soul of the family and spheres of living and working. Finally, public communication will be less tied to the parameters of time, place and territory than ever before. But this does not mean that the physical, social and mental make-up of the people engaged and the material environment of the resources used in this type of communication will no longer matter. Chapter 9 (on psychology) explains that this popular idea is wrong.

NETWORKS AND SOCIAL (IN)EQUALITY

Uneven and combined global development

Contemporary globalization of production, distribution and consumption is a process of uneven and combined development. From the command centres of transnational corporations and developed states, the division of labour is becoming more selective and more encompassing than ever before (see Barnett et al., 1998). Media networks are the most important infrastructure for this process (see Chapters 2 and 4). Nowadays, information processing is spread globally. Philippine programmers produce online software ordered by American companies: they may be paid only a third of what programmers in the United States demand as a salary. Irish data typists process the claims of a New York insurance company at wages about 20 percent below those in the United States.

At first sight, these examples appear to add to the diffusion of employment and therefore to social equality worldwide. In fact, the positive effects of this transfer of employment to less developed countries are disappointing, since this kind of employment is highly selective and limited. The tasks are designed from the perspective of the needs and interests of the centre and not from the perspective of a better organic development of the region concerned. Therefore, we might observe increasing differences in the number of telephone and Internet connections between rich and poor countries, while at the same time the latter are being connected to ultramodern international networks.

The negative effects of this transfer of employment for the developed countries, on the other hand, may be greater than expected because simple administrative and programming work is disappearing rapidly. Moreover, it could add to a further segmentation of the labour market in western countries. This process is sometimes referred to as First World countries partly resembling the Third World or a Fourth World (Castells, 1998): in developed countries, there are enclaves of economic activity with conditions close to those of developing countries. The employment structure created is characterized by high-quality jobs at the centre, usually in a western capital, carefully selected according to criteria of logistics and management. Simultaneously, it is marked by relatively low-skilled jobs at the periphery of the system, selected just as carefully and located all over the world. The economic effects on the immediate environment of both the centre and the periphery are much less important than the emanation of the traditional infrastructure of production (factories, offices) and transportation (stations, harbours, airports).

This network economy stands alone as a system within traditional economic environments. Streams of products, goods, services and information initially flow *inside* (inter)national networks. This observation is of crucial importance to any regional or national economic policy and to every local geographic plan (see Harrison, 1994). The importance of spatial frontiers and proximate areas decreases in a global network economy, though the selectivity of space increases for the structure as a whole. This structure does not seem to 'care' that millions of unemployed Indians live around Bangalore, as long as this region provides sufficient cheap software programmers with direct connections to the global communication networks. Actually, it would 'prefer' such unemployment because it keeps the wages of the programmers low.

The result of this global network structure is a diffusion and division of jobs all over the world (combined development). These days there are computer programmers almost everywhere, and even the poorest country is connected to the Internet. At the same time, the quantity and quality of jobs in the global economy across countries and regions is becoming more unequal (unequal development). Without measures that help to increase the spill-over of wealth created in the enclaves of the global economy into their local environment, these inequalities will increase. Moreover, the spatial distance between the poor and rich parts of the global networked economy is decreasing. For example, top executives, high-tech specialists and financial experts, when coming home from work, run into beggars on the street and people working in sweatshops. This might have great consequences for social cohesion in a particular area.

Regarding the subject of social inequality, the *type* of employment being created or disappearing is even more important than the extent. In the broadest sense, we will have to deal with the question of the influence of networks on *class structure*. This question first appeared in this book in Chapter 5, when the future of middle management in organizations was discussed. Following Erik Olin Wright (1985), I want to define social classes with

Influence on class structure

the dimensions of (a) ownership of means of production; (b) control of organization; and (c) ownership of skills and qualifications.

Ownership of means of production

The decentralization of production will lead to an increase in the number of formally independent companies or agencies. In the ICT sector, these corporations relatively often consist of one or a few persons. Many independent companies are created in service provision. This mainly concerns professionals running all sorts of agencies. There is no great barrier preventing people from entering the market, since a single network connection already gives access to large-scale means of production (such as the Internet) and only a small amount of starting capital is needed. Providing services on the Internet is fairly simple. However, the increase in the number of independent businesses resulting from this situation is compensated by the fact that successful projects are partially or completely taken over by larger companies within a short period. Concentration in the media sector continues to grow.

Control of organization

In Chapter 5, we saw how the use of networks is able to change the ways organizations are controlled. Traditional middle management and supervision are replaced by top executives and technical staff controlling the organization with information systems on the one hand, and executive personnel working with the same systems on the other hand. A polarization between top management and technical staff with increased power to control, and executive staff working with a selective, electronically controlled set of tasks and under flexible conditions, is the most likely development. Other possibilities were described in the same chapter, but this one is the most likely. However, in all cases, supervisors and middle managers are replaced by technicians and information staff managing and maintaining networks. If this observation is correct, the use of networks will increase the almost unbridgeable gap between groups of employees with different skills and qualifications that is starting to appear in larger organizations. Promotion within the organization, from the bottom of the shop floor to top management via supervisory work and middle management, will become nearly impossible.

Ownership of skills and qualifications

So, acquiring skills and qualifications will be even more important than it used to be. In any case, having many digital skills offers a skill premium in the level of wages (Nahuis and de Groot, 2003). Differences of digital skills possessed will create more inequality, among others on the labour market. At first sight, ICTs seem to create a lot of high-skilled jobs and make redundant low-skilled ones, particularly in transportation and administration. Generally speaking, the complexity and autonomy of labour in the information society are increasing with a rising use of ICTs, according to empirical research in the Netherlands (Steijn, 2001). The more one uses ICT on the job, the higher the complexity and autonomy of the job with the exception of data entry and the like (2001: 105).

However, the last observation points at something particularly important: polarization. When considering individual positions, one also is able to observe a polarization of the consequences of ICT for the different types of labour.

> With regard to autonomy on the job, it is primarily managers and professionals who produce a high score; service personnel and semi-professionals show relatively low scores. Concerning complexity, the scores of (chiefly) managers,

professionals, and semi-professionals are high, and the scores of commercial and service personnel and manual labourers are low. (Steijn, 2001: 108, my translation)

We can draw two conclusions from these findings. The first conclusion is that not having access to ICTs on the job, or using them less, provides fewer opportunities for increasing the quality of labour (complexity, autonomy, acquisition of skills) for the employees concerned. The second conclusion is that having access to ICTs on the job and using them more extensively can have very divergent consequences for a user's labour position and content, depending on the type of labour organization and labour function. Entering data all day and working with spreadsheets and databases is a type of ICT labour that is completely different from working with advanced search systems and decision support systems, designing programs, or programming software.

It is well known that the number of women is lower in the first segment (i.e. the high quality jobs at the centre) than in the second. An important part of 'female' employment, in administrative and partly in low-skilled commercial work, may even disappear from the second segment. But apart from this, female employment is not particularly threatened by the introduction of networks. Other sectors employing mainly women, such as care and education, cannot easily be fully automated and transferred to self-service. We would probably expect an increase in employment for women in these sectors. Much more important for the future of 'female' employment, and from an emancipatory point of view, is the estimation that network society will increasingly require a lot of communicative, didactic and commercial skills. These capabilities, for which women have a particular affinity according to the current divisions of labour, gender roles and gender identity, will gain importance in all segments of the job market in the network society. So, the position of women on the labour market of the future might be much better than it was in the 20th century. *Position of women*

The future is considerably less bright for migrants and ethnic minorities with low education in a network society dominated by natives and ethnic majorities. Usually they lack digital skills and, what is worse, they do not speak or command the native or dominant language sufficiently. So, they run the risk of missing out on the technical and communicative skills required in a network society. The major handicap is having insufficient command of the dominant language. The only exception is to be able to speak and write in English. Without the command of either the dominant or the English language in a particular country, one is not even able to do simple terminal work at the level of data entry. If this situation is not improved, ethnic minorities will undoubtedly be among the 'misfits' of the network society in every respect, both in work and in social communications. *Position of ethnic minorities*

THE DIGITAL DIVIDE

This section summarizes the main themes of a book I published recently: *The Deepening Divide, Inequality in the Information Society* (van Dijk, 2005). At the end of the 1990s, a new term appeared in the discussion about the *Conceptual framework* consequences of the new media for society: the digital divide. Commonly, the digital divide is defined as the gap between those who do and do not have access to computers and the Internet. While the focus in the previous section was on social classes and groups, here the attention shifts to individuals, including their relationships with other individuals.

My research and analysis of the digital divide has the following characteristics. First, a distinction is made between four successive kinds of access to the new media or ICTs. These are: motivational access; material or physical access; skills access; and usage access, a distinction to be explained below. Second, the causes and consequences of inequalities to be observed with these kinds of access are made explicit in a theory of inequality in the information and network society. I start with the second characteristic.

Causes of the digital divide

The direct cause of unequal access to digital technology in society is the distribution of a large number of resources. These are not only material resources, such as income and the possession of equipment, but also temporal resources (having the time to use the new media), mental resources (sufficient technical knowledge), social resources (networks and ties that help to attain access) and cultural resources (the status and other cultural rewards that motivate people to get access). The way these resources are distributed among people can be explained by a large number of personal and positional inequalities in society. Personal inequalities are age, sex, ethnicity, intelligence, personality and health or disability. Positional inequalities are defined by a particular job or occupation, a specific level of education and a life in a poor or affluent country and region and in a particular household role (parent or child, husband or wife). All these inequalities appear to be related to the amount of access different people have to the new media (van Dijk, 2005).

The potential of access to a particular medium is also shaped by the technological characteristics of the medium concerned. Access to TV sets and telephones is not the same as access to computers and networks. All media have characteristics supporting and impeding access. Computers and their networks support access because they are multipurpose or multifunctional technologies enabling all kinds of information, communication, transaction, work, education and entertainment. So, there are useful applications for everybody. Moreover, the extension of networks produces network effects: the more people gain access, the more valuable a connection becomes. However, multifunctionality also results in extremely different applications, both advanced, with many opportunities to learn and build a career, and simple, mainly focused on entertainment. Other characteristics decreasing equality of access are the complexity, expensiveness and lack of user-friendliness of many contemporary new media.

Consequences of the digital divide

The consequences of unequal access to ICTs can be conceived as more or less participation in the most important fields of society (van Dijk, 2005). It can be shown that new media access is necessary for an increasing number of jobs, for making progress in almost every career on the labour market and to start one's own business. In social networking, access is required to create new ties and to maintain old ties in modern society, as explained earlier in this chapter. Those without access will be isolated in future society. In

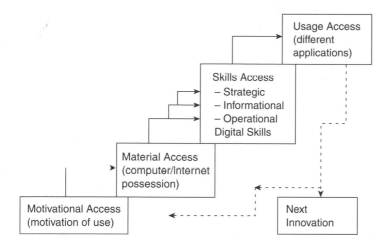

FIGURE 7.2   Four stages of access to digital technology

spatial terms, they will stick to local opportunities for jobs and social and sexual relationships, and leave the most promising opportunities to mobile people conversant with digital media. In the cultural field, those without access will not be able to benefit from the many new applications and types of expression offered by digital culture (see Chapter 8). In politics, citizens who have access are participating relatively more in government, political organizations and all other bodies of public decision-making in society. Finally, even the institutional participation of citizens in society (equal access to social benefits, scarce public resources and future electronic polls) may be affected by new media access.

Unequal participation in all these fields of society reinforces the existing personal and positional inequalities and unequal distribution of resources. The new media are important new tools (resources) that help people to obtain better positions in society and to improve their personal characteristics in relation to others, particularly in relationships of power.

In the early years of the discussion and investigation of the digital divide, the concept of access was confined to physical access to computers, the Internet and other digital media. Most people thought that the digital divide would be closed as soon as everyone had a computer and Internet connection at home or was able to use them at a public place. After a while, a number of critics appealed for going beyond access and emphasizing the use and the skills needed to apply digital media. In fact, the digital divide and the question of differential media access are even more complicated than these critics have suggested. In a series of publications (van Dijk, 1997b, 2000b, 2004; van Dijk and Hacker, 2003) I distinguish four successive kinds of new media access as portrayed in Figure 7.2, which is explained in the following paragraphs.

The process of appropriating the new technology starts with motivational access. Motivation influences the decision to purchase a computer and network

Motivational access

connection, to learn the requisite skills, and to use the interesting applications. Some people are not sufficiently motivated. They may be people who do not want to use computers because they do not like them or even fear them (suffering so-called computer anxiety or 'technophobia'). Others have used computers and the Internet in the past, but have stopped using them, or they have only temporarily used them. Finally, there are people who have no real choice or opportunity to obtain access to computers and the Internet because they lack the material means or the mental and educational capacities. They are the truly unconnected. The dividing line between the 'want-nots' and the 'have-nots' is not sharp and it is ever shifting.

The direct causes of this lack of motivation may be insufficient temporal, mental, material, social and cultural resources. They are a lack of time, of technical knowledge and affinity, of money, of social relations that inspire and help people to appropriate new technologies and of cultural lifestyles and identities that fit to computer and Internet use. In their turn, the lack or the availability of these resources are explained by personal inequalities first of all. It is well known that, on average, young people and males are more motivated to adopt and use computers and the Internet than elderly people and females. Intelligence and personality also count (Finn and Korukonda, 2004; Hudiburg et al., 1999). Positional inequalities are less important for motivation. Nevertheless, having or wanting a particular job or education urges people to obtain access. The same goes for inhabitants of high-tech countries where it is becoming obligatory to have a computer and Internet connection.

Material and physical access

After acquiring the motivation to get access, the challenge for new users is to act on it. They may purchase a computer and Internet connection themselves, or they may use those of others. This may be done privately at work or at school, or with family and friends, or in public places at a particular access point. Public opinion, public policy, and all kinds of research are strongly preoccupied with this second kind of access that I call material or physical access. Many people think the digital divide will be closed as soon as everyone has a computer and a connection to the Internet. This is wrong because inequalities in other types of access will come to the fore. However, material or physical access remains a necessary condition for the other types of access: the requisite skills and the actual use of the technology. Material access is broader than physical access: it not only refers to the opportunity to use computers and the Internet at a particular place, but also to access particular channels, programs or sources of information. Increasingly, this is limited by conditional access when subscriptions have to be paid for always-on facilities and when the familiar screens of username and password appear.

It can be shown that in the period between 1985 and 2000, all divides of physical access to computers and the Internet increased in both the developed and developing countries (van Dijk, 2005), except for the gender gap and the gap between people with and without disability. However, at the turn of the century in some developed countries, the categories with relatively high physical access entered a phase of saturation, while the categories with low physical access, which had started later, were still catching up. This means that the physical access divide concerning basic computer and Internet technology is narrowing in developed countries. Conversely, this divide keeps widening in the developing countries (ibid.).

The most important resources enabling material or physical access are material resources (household income), temporal resources (sufficient time to work with computers) and social resources (a social network that inspires and helps people to obtain access). Decisive positional categories appear to be the labour market and educational positions (having a particular job or schooling), followed by the contextual positions of being part of a particular type of household (for example with school-going children) and a developed country or region. The most significant personal category appears to be age, followed by gender and disability (all data published in van Dijk, 2005).

After having acquired the motivation to use computers and some kind of physical access to them, one has to learn to manage the hardware and software. For this purpose, at least three types of digital skills are needed, in order: operational skills, information skills, and strategic skills. My definition of *digital skills* is the collection of skills needed to operate computers and their networks, to search and select information in them, and to use them for one's own purposes. Within the category of digital skills, *operational skills* are the skills used to operate computer and network hardware and software. *Information skills* are the skills needed to search, select, and process information in computer and network sources. Finally, *strategic skills* are the capacities to use these sources as the means for specific goals and for the general goal of improving one's position in society (in the labour market, in education, in households, and in social relationships).

Skills access

These three types of digital skills expose an increasing level of inequality. Information and strategic skills are extremely unevenly divided among the populations of both developing and developed societies. Information skills consist of formal skills such as getting to know and control the special computer and Internet file and hyperlink structures, the perception and elaboration of multimedia screens and the ability to work with the continually changing content and fragmented nature of the Internet. Information skills also contain substantial skills such as the selection of information, editing information oneself, assessing the quality of information and combining information from an increasing number of sources.

Obviously, this type of inequality rests more on the distribution of mental than of material resources. Increasingly, the inequality is in the intellectual information skills and the positional strategic skills. Those having a high level of traditional literacy also possess a high level of information skills. The second most important type of resource for digital skills is social and cultural resources. The social context of computer and Internet users is a decisive factor in the opportunities they have for learning digital skills. They learn more from practice and their everyday social environment than from formal computer education and guidance.

Both positional and personal categorical inequalities are responsible for the unequal distribution of these resources. The positional categories of having a particular education and employment define the social contexts that enable computer and Internet users to learn digital skills in practice. The personal categories of age and intelligence appear to be the strongest individual determinants of digital skills, followed by sex or gender (all data in van Dijk, 2005).

Usage access   The fourth kind of access may be called usage access. This is the ultimate aim of the appropriation of any new technology. The kinds of access described above are necessary, but not sufficient conditions of usage. A user may be motivated to use computers and the Internet, have access to them physically, and command the digital skills necessary to use them, but nevertheless have no need, occasion, obligation, time, or effort to actually use them. Usage data indicate that many skilful users only use their computers and Internet connections once or twice a week. Usage access has its own grounds, although the resources and positional or personal categories concerned overlap with those determining the other kinds of access. Candidates for explanation might be a particular job or school training, a certain level of education, age, gender, culture, and the time and opportunity to practice computer use.

Usage access can be measured in a number of ways. First, actual use can be observed, because having a computer and an Internet connection does not have to mean that they are used. Secondly, usage time can be observed in time-diary studies or surveys. Thirdly, the diversity or the type of applications used on computers and the Internet can be listed. The final ways to investigate usage are to look for more advanced types of computer and Internet use in broadband channels and in creative use (not only consuming information content, but also producing content for computer files and (personal or other) web sites, discussion lists and chat boxes.

My extended survey of computer and Internet use has shown that the differences in actual use, usage time, diversity of use, broadband use and creative use generally are bigger than the gaps in motivational and physical access (van Dijk, 2005). To give just one example: in the last ten years, the physical access gap of gender has almost closed in the developed countries; however, the skills access gap has remained and the differences of usage also remain very pronounced. In the Netherlands, the usage time for computers and the Internet at home for males in the year 2000 was still 2.5 times longer than that of females. Use is very much gendered. Women use computers more at work than their male colleagues do, but they do so with a far more limited number and level of applications. Most applications are used for administrative and secretarial work and for purposes of teaching, health care, and selling (retail): word processing (including email), billing, filing, and entering data into databases and spreadsheets. Male employees use computer and Internet applications more for purposes of searching and creating information in the context of their relatively more technical jobs or for business and finance.

At home, females use email more often and for longer periods than males (Boneva and Kraut, 2002; Howard et al., 2002). The perhaps surprising fact that females like Internet chatting less (Howard et al., 2002) might also reflect particular gender preferences in electronic communication. The same goes for information: searching for health information is very popular among (at least American) women, but getting the news or political information and checking sport scores are quite unpopular. Finally, the use of electronic business and shopping appears to be gendered. These applications are significantly less used by (American) females. This even goes for shopping (Howard et al., 2002). Perhaps here, as with chatting, the physical mode is preferred, as compared to the virtual mode.

The material and mental resources that are decisive for physical and skills access are less important for usage access. Here, temporal, social, and cultural resources, lifestyles included, come to the fore. The personal categories of age, sex, race, intelligence, personality, and health or ability primarily account for these resources of new media usage. They determine the interests people have in using particular applications of the new media. As compared to social and cultural resources, the temporal resources accounting for the extent and level of new media use are primarily explained by the positional categories of labour, education, household, and being an inhabitant of a nation or region (van Dijk, 2005).

One of the most revealing facts about inequalities of usage access is the diversity of computer and Internet use by all positional and personal categories of people. Here, all inequalities in the other kinds of access discussed above come together. Subsequently, they are mixed with all existing economic, social, cultural, and political inequalities in society. I have analysed data about the diversity of computer and Internet use from the United States and the Netherlands in previous publications (van Dijk, 2000b, 2004; van Dijk and Hacker, 2003). These data indicated that people with high levels of education and income tend to use database, spreadsheet, bookkeeping, and presentation applications significantly more than people with low levels of education and income, who favour simple consultations, games, and other entertainment. Han Park (2002) replicated these statistics for South Korea, revealing the same distribution between Koreans with high and low levels of education. Using the same Pew Internet and American Life Project 2000 data as Howard et al. (2002), Cho et al. (2003) claimed that US Internet users who are young and have high socio-economic status used this medium in a very specific goal-oriented way; that is, to strategically satisfy their motivations and gratifications of connection, learning, and acquisition of products and services.

Usage gaps

At first sight the usage gap looks similar to the classic *knowledge gap* (Tichenor et al., 1970): 'As the diffusion of mass media information into a social system increases, segments of the population with a higher socio-economic status tend to acquire this information at a faster rate than the lower status segments' (p. 159). However, the knowledge gap is only about the differential diffusion and development of knowledge or information. The usage gap is broader, as it is about unequal practices and applications; that is, action or behaviour in particular contexts. This includes knowledge and information.

It appears that those who already have a large amount of resources at their disposal benefit first and most from the capacities and opportunities of the new media. This phenomenon has been called the 'Matthew effect' by the sociologist Robert Merton (1968), because according to the Gospel of Matthew: 'For to everyone who has, more shall be given' (Matt. 25:29, New American). A popular version of this might be: 'The rich get richer.'

The Matthew effect

This rich-get-richer phenomenon has recently also been observed by a number of network analysts as a conspicuous property of all so-called scale-free networks. It calls attention to the relationship between networks and inequality in the network society, so it should be discussed in this section. Scale-free networks have no inherent scale for the number of links, such as random networks, that connect everybody in principle. This means that not all actors are linked or that they are not connected in the same way and with the same intensity. Scale-free networks are highly clustered, with large hubs attracting many links and with connectors linking actors and clusters far apart, although most actors maintain only a few links. Buchanan (2002) calls the so-called random networks, where everybody has the same chance of being linked, 'egalitarian' and the scale-free networks 'aristocratic' (p. 119). Scale-free networks are more similar to real-life social and media networks, such as the Internet, than random networks. The rich-get-richer phenomenon appears with the growth of these scale-free networks and with the preferential attachment of all actors concerned. This means that the best connected and most central actors or hubs tend to attract more and more links. For example, this is the result of the way search engines such as Google proceed and present their findings. They first list the most popular links. In this way they make them even more popular.

So, although social and media networks have the characteristic of diffusing and spreading information, knowledge and power among everyone connected, they also have an inherent quality of centralizing information, knowledge and power. They draw resources to the already more powerful. This is the meaning of the 'Matthew effect' and the rise of usage gaps.

Structural inequality The important point is that usage gaps are likely to grow, instead of decline, with the larger distribution of computers and networks among the population. If this turns out to be true, the difference between advanced and simple uses will increase. The consequences of this systematic pattern of unequal use will be more or less participation in all relevant fields of contemporary and future society (see van Dijk, 2005 for more arguments and data). This happens faster and more definitely as the new media pervade society. Increasingly, the old media and face-to-face communications will become inadequate means of full participation in society. Progressively, more people will even be completely excluded from particular fields of society. The result will be first-, second-, and third-class citizens, consumers, workers, students, and community members.

This division would mean structural inequality. What exactly is *structural*? Absolute exclusion from the network society and new media use is a clear case of structural inequality that can be demonstrated empirically. It can be shown that people who have no ICT access whatsoever have less chance on the labour market and lesser educational opportunities (van Dijk, 2005). It can be demonstrated that a complete lack of ICT access will lead to shrinking social networks and cultural resources. This lack will also give them less chances of participation in politics and citizenship entitlements such as public benefits and healthcare (van Dijk, 2005).

Relative exclusion, which means having less motivational, material, skills and usage access than other parts of the population, is more difficult to demonstrate, as it requires detailed investigation into the amount of participation in particular fields of society and its consequences for specific positions of affluence and influence. However, in the long run, relative exclusion can also lead to clearly perceptible structural inequalities.

Structural inequality appears when, on the one hand, an 'information elite' strengthens its position, while, on the other hand, those groups already living on the margins of society become excluded from communications in society because these are practised in media they do not possess or control. The differences become structural when the positions people occupy in networks and other media determine whether they have any influence on decisions made in several fields of society. Here we can refer to Chapter 5, which explains the importance of positions in networks for the exercise of power.

The tripartite network society

So, the picture is not the usual simple one of a two-tiered society, or of a gap between information 'haves' and 'have-nots' as two clearly separate groups of the population. On the contrary, the pattern described is increasingly complex social, economic and cultural differentiation. A better representation would be a continuum or spectrum of differentiated positions across the population, with the 'information elite' at the top, a more or less participating majority of the population in the middle, and a group of 'excluded people' at the bottom.

The digital divide amplifies such a situation of structural inequality that was already growing before (van Dijk, 2005). It can be portrayed in a simplified picture of a tripartite, instead of a two-tiered, network society (see Figure 7.3). This diagram sketches a (developed) society with an information elite of about 15 percent of the population; a majority of 50 percent to 65 percent that participates to a certain extent in all relevant fields of society, with both social and media networks; and a class of outsiders that is excluded from the new media networks and has a relatively small social network. The information elite, in the first ring, consists of people with high levels of education and income, the best jobs and societal positions, and a nearly 100 percent access to ICTs. This elite in fact makes all important decisions in society. The elite lives in dense social networks that extend to a large number of strategically important ties at a distance. Most people belonging to this elite are heavy users of computers and the Internet. Some of them form a 'broadband elite' that works with these media all day.

In a second ring we find the majority of the population, which participates significantly less. It contains a large part of the middle class and the working class. This majority does have access to computers and the Internet, but also possesses fewer digital skills than the elite, information and strategic skills in particular. Moreover, it uses fewer and less diverse applications. These applications are less focused on a career, a job, study, or other ambition and more on recreational and entertainment uses. The majority has a smaller social network and fewer weak ties spanning large distances.

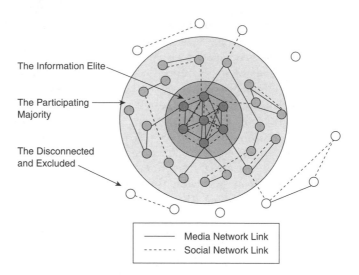

The Information Elite

The Participating Majority

The Disconnected and Excluded

——— Media Network Link
- - - - - Social Network Link

FIGURE 7.3   Tripartite participation in the network society

Largely excluded from participation in several fields of society and having no access to computers and the Internet, voluntarily or not, we find the unconnected and excluded outside the rings of the drawing. They comprise a quarter to a third of the populations of (even) the most advanced high-tech societies. Increasingly, they become equal to the lowest social classes, particular ethnic minorities, and a majority of (new) immigrants. At this stage of new media diffusion, the unconnected still contain a large proportion of elderly people, some of higher social class, but isolated socially and without access to computers and the Internet.

THE INSTABILITY OF THE NETWORK SOCIETY

Opposing tendencies Reading the previous sections, it becomes obvious that the structure of the network society is full of opposing tendencies. Space and time become both less and more important. Moreover, global and local spaces and times are both merging and clashing. The traditional distinction between public and private spheres is both dissolving and reconstructed in new ways. Traditional communities are falling apart and they are rebuilt in online communities and communities online. Networks are both spreading messages, information and resources and they reinforce old inequalities adding new ones.

As a general tendency, networks combine scale extensions and scale reductions. While this happens, they move existing structures, articulate these structures and intensify or even polarize them. This puts unknown pressures on the social system as a whole. By nature, the network society is an unstable social system. The reason for this instability is not only the speed of technological development and the technological vulnerability of media networks as explained in Chapter 6. It is also caused by the nature of social networks as infrastructures that organize society. Before this is explained in a more abstract way, I want to list a number of apparent instabilities of contemporary societies that are reinforced by networks.

In the economy, we cannot escape the increasing volatility of the stock and currency markets, with sharply rising and falling prices, which puts a continuous pressure on the economy. The exchange of monetary values has surpassed the exchange of goods many times. Electronic networks run this exchange and they reinforce the speeds of prices going upwards and downwards. They have inspired numerous speculative bubbles in stocks and currencies. Crashes in stock markets, currencies and stakes of individual companies are always imminent and they happen increasingly often. They aggravate the periodic recessions and upturns of the capitalist economy and they multiply financial crises.

Contagion and volatility

In politics, we can observe the drifting of voters that are less faithful than ever to their favourite parties and political leaders. With the help of the media system, TV in particular, voters jump from one candidate with a strong media appeal to another. Populism is on the rise. Voter drift is not only supported by broadcast networks but also by computer networks, such as the Internet, that serve grass-root or central mobilizing agencies and electronic pressure groups. The image of a political leader can be broken in a few hours when accusations, with or without good reason, spread on TV and the Internet. Other, more basic examples of instability of the political system reinforced by networks have been discussed in Chapter 5.

In culture, we can witness an increasing scale and number of confrontations between cultures globally and locally. They increase tensions in cultural systems previously dominated by a single culture. Cultural conflicts between ethnic and other social categories that mainly communicate among themselves may be the result, just like the open exchange and mixture of cultural expressions. Computer networks enable both possibilities. However, cultural adaptation needs time and the capacity of a computer network such as the Internet is likely to provoke confrontation such as the contemporary one between Islamic fundamentalism and Christian and Jewish fundamentalism, or between eastern and western cultures in general.

In the media, all kinds of rumours, fads, fashions, hypes and innovations are spreading faster than ever before. The diffusion power of broadcasting, telephony and computer networks multiplies the speed of the age-old transmission of gossip and local news in social networks. It leads to all kinds of message cascades. The lifecycle of fashions, hypes and innovations is shorter than ever before. Still, their impact on society rises accordingly.

In ecosystems, various kinds of human and animal diseases are spreading across the world in a few days via air networks. The same happens, with even greater speed, to viruses and worms in computer systems. The instability of both kinds of systems has increased substantially with their internal transportation speeds and their vulnerability to contagion.

At first sight, these instabilities of the network society can simply be ascribed to its increasing connectivity. Unfortunately, the situation is far more complicated. In Chapter 2, it was argued that networks increase the adaptive capacity of systems, in this way continually restoring broken stabilities. This would

Too much connectivity

mean that rising connectivity increases adaptive capacity and stability. However, we have just seen a number of examples that seem to indicate too much connectivity. This happens to be in agreement with the contemporary theory of networks and complex adaptive systems. Stuart Kauffman (1993) has shown that while too few connections may result in insufficient change and adaptation of systems, beyond a particular level too much connectivity decreases adaptability. Large networks with thousands of members adapt best with less than ten connections per member. Mulgan (1997: 162) explains that with increasing connectivity 'too much time and energy is spent on them. Conformity spreads too fast and dampens innovations.' Watts (2003: 241) adds that 'networks that are not connected enough prohibit global cascades because the cascade has no way of jumping from one vulnerable cluster to another. And networks that are too highly connected prohibit cascades also, but for a different reason: they are locked into a kind of stasis, each node constraining the influence of any other and being constrained itself'.

Conformity may spread too fast because the social contagion of ideas spreads faster than the biological contagion of diseases. Every single disease contagion is independent from the other and has the same chance of occurring, while social contagion is strongly dependent on the number of others infected by the new idea (Watts, 2003: 223). Traditional hypes or fashions ran harder and harder in the past, but their speed is multiplied many times in contemporary media networks. In Chapter 8, it will be observed that they may lead to the phenomena of information overload and overcommunication increasing noise and instability in social systems.

CONCLUSIONS

- Space and time are becoming not less, but more important in the network society. There is no 'death of distance' and no 'timeless time'. Media networks enable more selectivity to choose the right times and places. In social terms, space and time are both expanded and compressed in the most abstract characteristics of contemporary social structure: network socialization (the expansion of society in private lives by means of social and media networks) and network individualization (the compression of society in the individual as its core unit that is linked by social and media networks).
- Social and media networks blur all spheres of living and they connect all levels of the social (individual, group, organization and society). However, these spheres and levels continue to exist. Networks only link them more directly than before and this enables more activities in particular places and all activities in mobile spaces. Tele-activities such as telework and telestudy are added to traditional offline activities at particular places.
- Virtual or online communities will be added to organic or physical communities via communities that have gone online. Perhaps this will recover community-building, albeit in altogether different shapes than

traditional community life, as it will be based on a combination of network individualization and socialization. Computer networks such as the Internet are able to reduce and to enhance sociability with chances for both 'nerds' or the socially isolated and the hyper-socially active.

- The network society will create all kinds of new communication groups between mass and interpersonal communication that are characterized by a mixture of public and private aspects, as can be observed with online chatting, web-logging, web-camming and gaming.

- Public networking on the Internet will not bring us together, neither will it tear us apart. The public sphere will be reconstructed as a complex mosaic of distant, but overlapping and interconnected public spheres. A public sphere and the idea of a society will continue to exist, albeit in much more differentiated forms.

- The network society tends to become more unequal than the mass society. In principle, networks are more appropriate to exchange (im)material goods than other communication structures. In practice, they concentrate them in a few powerful hubs, clusters or portals and they have a polarizing effect on class and power divisions and job hierarchies. The 'Matthew effect', which can be observed in networks, means that the rich are getting richer. A tripartite division is appearing: the information elite, the more or less participating majority and the excluded.

- The digital divide in terms of physical access to computers and the Internet is closing in developed societies; in developing societies it is still growing. However, the divide in terms of digital skills and new media usage is both widening and deepening. With regard to usage, a gap is appearing between those who benefit from the advanced applications to be used in job or school careers and in relationships of politics and power, and those who use the simple applications for entertainment, e-commerce and basic communications.

- The network society is an unstable type of society. This is for the paradoxical reason that it is both too connected and too divided.

CULTURE

A culture is a particular way of life of people in a certain period in history that produces all kinds of signs and artefacts that can be transmitted to following generations via information products and communication channels. According to Charlie Gere, digitalization can be seen as 'a marker of culture because it encompasses the artefacts and the systems of signification and communication that most clearly demarcate our way of life from others' (Gere, 2002: 12). He thinks digital culture is not as new as it might appear, and that its development ultimately is not determined by technological advances. Digital culture refers to ways of thinking and doing that are embodied within technology (p. 13).

In this chapter, I try to extract these ways of thinking and doing from the technology. The first question I discuss is what influence digitalization has on cultural expressions. Does digitalization only change the form of these expressions or does it also produce substantial changes? For example, are signs and artefacts becoming increasingly similar because the same digital code applies to all of them, or does differentiation occur?

A first look at digital culture shows that the quantity of expressions rises exponentially. The same goes for the speed of production, transmission and exchange. What are the consequences of a culture that explodes in this way? I discuss the phenomena of information overload and communication overload. To what extent are they a problem? Research indicates that in the 20th and early 21st centuries the quantity of data and sources of information has multiplied. What is the matter with the quality of information? Does it enable more knowledge and better understanding of the increasing complexity of our society?

Another first impression is that most digital culture appears on screens. Currently, people in the developed countries spend on average 5 to 8 hours a day watching television, video, computer, cinema, presentation and telephony screens. What will be the consequences of this visual culture?

Digital culture is clearly changing daily media use. A print media culture is transforming into an electronic culture of audiovisual and computer media. Are radio and television the next media to be replaced by computers and the Internet? In the multimedia environment, media use seems to diversify. Is this really happening and, when it does, is it equally valid for everybody? Another topic covered at the end of this chapter is the transition from linear to hyper-link media. This is one of the most important cultural effects of the rise of computer networks that might completely change future media use. Another consequence is the rise of interactivity and the presumed active user who no longer needs the intermediation of editors and retailers in the network. Are the users of digital media really that (inter)active and autonomous?

LIVING IN A DIGITAL CULTURE

The meaning of being digital

Views differ as to which technical part of the new media has the greatest cultural impact. Many think it is the fact that they are **digital**. At least, this word is very popular in all kinds of prefixes: digital revolution, digital city and even digital being (Negroponte, 1995). Used in this way, the word suggests more than it says. Chapter 1 explained that digitalization is only one of the technical characteristics of the new media. What effects could it have on culture? To answer this question we will have to dig deeper than is usual in popular accounts of digitalization.

Digitalization means that every item can be translated into separate bytes consisting of strings of ones and zeros (called **bits**). This applies to images, sounds, texts and data. They can be produced and consumed in separate pieces and combined in every manner imaginable. From now on, every item can be presented on screens and accompanied by sound. All items can be stored on digital data carriers and retrieved from them in virtually unlimited amounts and at virtually unlimited speed. In the preceding sentences, digital technology and cultural impact have already been linked. Thus, at this point in the discussion, the reader can gather that digitalization increases the *chances* of:

- a standardization and differentiation of culture;
- a fragmentation of culture;
- a collage of culture;
- an acceleration of culture;
- a visualization of culture;
- a larger quantity of culture.

Pre-programming and creativity

Unlimited Choice?

In popular literature on the new media, the suggestion is made that these media will create unlimited choice from our sizeable cultural heritages and a new creative potential among the population, as people are enabled to create their own works of art and other products with multimedia. In *The Road Ahead* (1995), Bill Gates claimed ICT will offer new ways for people to express themselves. Apparently, ICT offers 'unprecedented artistic and scientific opportunities to a new generation of geniuses' (p. 154). Indeed, these opportunities do exist for people with the means and the skills to use them. However, the chances that we are dealing with a 'new and original type of work', in the terms of Dutch copyright law, are decreasing. More and more often we will be processing, reworking or adapting things other people have created. This is just the next phase in the evolution of art. In the course of (modern) history, the work of art has been taken away from the artist step by step and put into the hands of consumers. After the era of large-scale technical reproducibility of art (Benjamin, 1968), we are now entering an era enabling people to create their 'own' works of art consisting of all the bits and pieces of the cultural heritage. Multimedia encourage users to make all sorts of video collages and images, to sample and compose pieces of music from a CD, to decide the ending of a film by picking one from several scripts, and to create their own abstract Mondrian-style painting from red, yellow and blue squares. Of course, professional and popular art have always been a matter of reworking and adapting the cultural heritage. But now we are taking one essential step further. Qualitatively more means are inserted between source and result. There is more than pencil, pen and ink on paper and paint on canvas. The means of production offered by digital media are (pre-)programmed themselves and they partly work automatically. They only have to be adapted by the user to gain some craft. The material worked upon is not empty, but it is filled with existing cultural content. In this way, creativity is put in an entirely different perspective.

Preprogrammed creativity The same can be said of the presumed infinite options in digital media. In fact, the whole thing is about options from a menu, in other words entirely pre-programmed. Usually, the user is able to make general choices only. Allowing users to choose from details would require too much pre-programming work.

Anyway, these options do lead to both a differentiation and a standardization of culture. The amount of content from which one can choose is increasing. At the same time, however, the elements of this content increasingly resemble one another. Everything is arranged in similar (menu) structures. Sources of information that used to be separate are combined in multimedia. Under certain circumstances, this may lead to diluting sources of information and eroding contents (see below).

Fragmentation and collage

Effects of fragmentation on cultural contents Digitalization causes a technical division of analogue sources into bits and bytes. This enables an unrestricted division of the content of these sources. Digitalization and processing of analogue sources by multimedia equipment have already had a fragmenting effect on our culture. Michael Heim (1987) pointed out this trend some years ago by analysing changes in text caused by word processing. Text is provided with a pointed structure. The argument is structured in advance and divided into separate subjects, items and paragraphs.

Items can easily be added or deleted later on – which may result in some loss of the course of the argument. Another example is the structure of the Internet. The content of web sites is spread over several pages and images which can all be accessed in one click. In this way, the traditional linear processing of content is replaced by the making of links, jumps and associations.

Finally, we come to the content of pieces of music and films processed by using interactive programs. Interactive music CDs are composed of separate, accumulated layers and fragments that may be easily isolated, manipulated, sampled and (re)combined. This *modularization* quickly causes the unity of a creative work to be lost. For the idea is to give listeners the opportunity to create their own collages. Many traditional artists, designers and producers find this anathema. They think the unique construction and coherence they have made is the essence of their creation. They dissociate themselves from the results obtained by the consumer, or accept them only because it pays to do so.

Acceleration

Digitalization allows a considerable increase in the production, dispersion and consumption of information and the signals of communication. In hardware, 'fast' has become the key word: fast computers, fast modems, fast lines, fast programs. The hunger for speed is never appeased. This gives all the more reason to believe that the popular assumption of the irrelevance of time in the new media is wrong. On the contrary, the importance of time is radicalizing (see Chapter 7). Saving time is immediately followed by new needs to be filled and created.

The need for speed is determined by motives in the economy (maximization of profits on the surplus value of working time in capitalism), the organization (efficiency) and consumption (immediate fulfilment of needs). Driven by a swift increase in technical capacities, these motives call into existence a *culture of speed*, (Miller and Schwarz, 1998; Virilio, 1988). This means our culture changes substantially as well. The following examples may be useful. First, expressions of culture date quickly. Trends follow each other at high speed. In the modern world, various trends exist side by side, competing for popularity. Second, information is sent in increasing amounts, ever more frequently and at ever higher speed just to attract attention. This phenomenon is called information and communication overload (see below). The result is shallowness in the perception of cultural expressions, a fact producers are anticipating and reinforcing. Furthermore, communication and language have increased to such a speed that we cannot sit down to think about a message, such as writing a letter or starting a conversation. Instead, we immediately pick up the phone and give ad hoc answers by telephone, or by email. Language also changes under the influence of the new media. This will be discussed in the next chapter. It acquires an abrupt style (like staccato) and contains increasing amounts of jargon with innumerable abbreviations. The final example is the rising importance of images in our culture, a type of data that

A culture of speed

is presented and consumed much more quickly than the others (speech, text and numbers).

Visualization

The centrality of screens The fact that monitors are increasingly being used for the *presentation* of cultural content has the most visible and direct effect on human perception and understanding. The monitor is everywhere in the network society. It is not merely a medium for reproduction that increasingly dominates mass communication, thanks to the rise of audiovisual media; it already characterizes data communication as well, and in the near future it will also symbolize telecommunications (by means of the videophone and video conferencing). Monitors in data and telecommunications will have the quality of current and future (HDTV) television screens. They will be able to contain several images at once and they will serve as touch screens. This means a single monitor can be used for tele- as well as data and mass communications. Screens will be not only the *window* to our world, but also our *second front door* – a most important, perhaps even *the* most important entrance to, and exit from, our homes. This will give the monitor a position in society important enough to have profound effects on our culture. There is no way to predict what the consequences will be, because monitors and terminals may change considerably in the next few decades. Yet, it seems worthwhile to make an inventory of a number of probable and lasting consequences of the dominance of the screen.

From active reading to passive viewing? The rise of the screen as a means of communication will lead to a partial replacement of text on paper, of separate audio and of direct physical transmission of signs in face-to-face communication. The last replacement is a much more basic development than the other two. That is why it is one of the central themes of this book. The current replacement of reading printed texts by watching television or looking at images in other media, together with the transformation of listening to the radio and to audio as a main activity into using them as a background, have been judged far too easily by intellectuals and culture pessimists as signs of blunted culture and losses of creativity and imagination. The Flemish expert in audiovisual semiotics Jean-Marie Peters (1989, 1996), has convincingly challenged these opinions. Peters (1989) opposes the popular assumption that watching and understanding images takes only a small mental effort, claiming that all sorts of imaginative thinking are required. Even the simplest image is very complex: it contains a large amount of symbols to be perceived and interpreted simultaneously. Comparing reading and listening on the one hand and watching on the other, one has to realize that all three can be performed with full or partial attention. Peters opposes the idea that an image cannot have any depth, given that readers and listeners are themselves urged to employ abstraction and creativity by calling images to mind. He argues that images have not only the capacity of reproduction and representation, but also symbolic and creative values. Viewers are able to discover and shape these symbolic and creative values themselves (Peters, 1989). From this line of argument, he also challenges the assumption of a culture of images smothering creativity and imagination. Perhaps people who have been raised in a culture of reading have forgotten how to look properly?

Extending Peters' argument, we may say that the most important problem concerning the replacement of text on paper with audiovisual display is *complication, not simplification!* Screens will contain large amounts of information. They are able to present image, text, numbers, graphics and visual augmentations of sounds, close to each other and in extremely complex shapes. In audiovisual entertainment, we have already become acquainted with the rise of a 'staccato culture' containing a bombardment of stimuli growing stronger and stronger: brief, flashing, swift and full of action.

Simplification or complication?

Intellectuals or culture pessimists should worry less about the decline of reading and listening (even in a culture of images, these activities will quantitatively increase rather than decrease) than about *writing and speaking* and about the extent of *activity and initiative* required. With the rise of the new media, the pattern of allocation shifts to consultation, registration and conversation. This seems to indicate an increase in the extent of local activities and initiatives, but this does not have to happen. Even though receivers of messages of allocation are able to reshape them in their minds, they are and always will be transferred messages. Consultation also means choosing from an offer, and registration includes answering questions. Conversation is the only pattern requiring active multilateral communication. Yet, this pattern has advanced the least in the new media until fairly recently. Videophony has not yet been introduced on a large scale. Email is becoming the most important new media application. Still, it remains a rather limited mode of expression (see Chapter 9). The exchange of more advanced types of expression, such as self-made audio, video, software and all kinds of graphical designs, is still an activity for a small elite.

The increasing presence of screens in all spheres of living leads to an accumulation of similar activities. And this will apply even more when the accompanying, omnipresent use of push buttons is taken into account. It is conceivable that, in the near future, many people will spend 8 to 10 hours a day in front of screens of all kinds. For example, people in the United States watch television or video for about 5 hours a day. The acceptable amount of working time spent in front of a computer screen is 5 hours a day, but this is often exceeded in practice. The use of mobile equipment with displays will perhaps add an hour to the daily total. An excessive use of screens can have negative consequences in terms of the physical and mental pressure it causes.

Excessive use of screens

The influence of universal screens will increase even further when opportunities to relax in other environments and in face-to-face communication are reduced. In their leisure time, screen workers are confronted with similar activities. Verbal and nonverbal behaviour in face-to-face communication, with the physical exercise accompanying it, still have important functions of relaxation for human beings – functions left largely unfulfilled in mediated communication. Thus, an excessive amount of time spent in front of screens will restrict physical and mental development.

Adaptation of communication contents

Mediated communication is always marked by some kind of adaptation to the technical characteristics of the medium concerned. Obviously this has consequences for the content of communication. The screen as a medium of reproduction has both possibilities and limitations. They differ according to the target and the type of communication desired in tele-, data and mass communication. However, there are also substantial similarities.

The power of screens is the attraction of human attention. The biggest problem in mass communication nowadays is that attention is slackening fast. The stimuli offered become ever shorter and more powerful in an attempt to prevent the slackening of attention. Short and impressive news-flashes, fast shots full of action in films or video clips and sparkling shows tend to fragment contents. Background information and reflection disappear or are pushed to the sidelines. According to many media critics, this will result in shallower mass media content, although we have seen that the form of images is becoming more complicated.

In data communication, one may expect the partner in communication to have enough self-discipline to continue following the contents of the screen. Here communication has been disciplined by the general characteristics of computer language: formalized, standardized and programmed in algorithms. It is a well-known fact that this will lead to the accentuation of one type of content and the limitation of another type. Signs of qualitative information are replaced by quantitative ones. In data communication, compressed data, tables, graphs and the like are the most favoured signs presented on the screen, for understandable reasons. This is done in a pre-programmed order. Take, for example, someone who consults data in videotex or in a databank. The information is compressed in short chunks fitting (part of) a screen. Long text, for instance background information, is not feasible. Main points or abstracts are preferred. Chunks of information are ordered in entirely pre-programmed search structures. Consulting such information is a completely different cognitive activity from reading a newspaper. In the latter, the reader has much more freedom to decide on the speed and intensity of reading, on stopping, skipping and starting to read again. Furthermore, no knowledge of search structures and operations is required.

Early experiences with telecommunications consisting of conversation that was not only sounds but also texts and/or images seem to reveal a selective limitation and articulation of particular content. In Chapter 9, the abrupt and ad hoc manner of communication in email is discussed, for example. Many sentences are either shortened or left unfinished. Many stopgaps and abbreviations are used.

Disappearing contexts

As communication media integrate further, more types of senders and messages are presented on the same screen. In theory, allocution, consultation, registration and conversation can all use the same screen as a medium of presentation. As a result, receivers may have problems distinguishing between these patterns and the various senders and messages they are getting. Well-known specific contexts disappear. This can be explained with a few examples.

First, people tend to look at the source of a message to determine its plausibility and reliability. Many investigations in mass communications have shown that reception of messages on television is considered to be more trustworthy than messages from newspapers and magazines. Audiovisual media are trusted more than printed ones.

Second, in the separate mass media of the late 1990s, receivers were still able to make a clear distinction between allocution, consultation, registration and conversation. This is evidently more difficult when working with integrated media. The situation has already changed with the advent of tele-text. This medium is considered by some to be allocution (as it is linked to television), whereas others say it is consultation (it looks like an electronic paper). The fact that new media can be 'interactive' in several ways may also lead to misunderstandings. The choice from extensive menus in allocution may be viewed as free consultation, whereas consultation in a medium in turn, may be considered a kind of conversation with this medium. Consultation and registration (for instance addressing an electronic mail order catalogue) can be veiled types of advertising (that is, allocution).

The final example is of people thinking they are taking part in allocution, consultation or conversation, whereas actually they are also being registered without knowing and wanting that.

Increasing presentations of information and communication on screens may also lead to blurring the distinctions between types of information and communication *within patterns*. We already know this phenomenon from allocution by TV. News, current affairs, entertainment, information programmes and advertising increasingly resemble one another. They are combined in overall programmes or presented in a similar manner. Advertisements are inserted in and between programmes as commercials or as hidden and clandestine advertising. In the future, forms of allocution and consultation, sources of information, propaganda and advertising will be hard to tell apart. In newspapers or magazines, one glimpse usually suffices to know whether you are dealing with an advertisement. On a screen this can be veiled much more easily. Take, for example, the ingenious ways of advertising on Internet pages and on the screens of commercial television.

> The fact that *all* of these cultural expressions have to be communicated through the screen transforms the culture into spectacle. Our civilization tends to substitute images for experience: journeys become window viewing and slides become souvenirs; gymnastics a TV program; music a video-tape. The old media of culture based on a process of symbolic exchange do not work any more in the new media. (Sabbah, 1985: 221)

Artifical reality

The most fundamental result of the universal presence of screens is undoubtedly the gradual replacement of a person's direct personal experience and direct interaction by observation through glass and camera lenses, usually someone else's, and by mediated interaction. This is one of the first psychological aspects to be dealt with in Chapter 9. There is a danger that people will start living in an artificial reality offering less room for personal experience and experiences shared directly with others. People become dependent on the nature and quality of images produced by the various media with their more or less limited communication capacities. Debord (1996) speaks about a *society of the spectacle*. However, attending a football match is a completely different experience from watching that same match on television. Going out shopping cannot be compared with teleshopping. Meeting a friend will always be different from communicating over the best videophone imaginable.

Individual perception

Replacing direct personal experiences with produced images will have more social impact as the process of individualization continues. The *individual* is increasingly confronted with a world made up of images. Conversations about the images offered are decreasing, both at work and in one's leisure time. People travel home, perhaps listening to a personal stereo, from their more or less isolated work behind a monitor, to watch their own favourite programme on TV. Watching TV all night as an entire family is becoming history. The number of individual options has increased so much that it has become almost impossible to talk to others about one's own observations. This is the main reason why some social scientists fear a culture of images, as they fear social cohesion will be undermined through a combination of this culture with social segmentation and individualization.

Watching a screen is not only fascinating, but also compelling. As said before, screens are exceptionally powerful in attracting attention. Even during interpersonal conversations, we are easily distracted by nearby screens. People can also be 'glued' to a screen. When immobile equipment is used, people are bound to their workplaces too. However, the latter trend will be reversed when mobile equipment makes a breakthrough.

Manipulative impact?

The fascinating and binding effects of screens can be a threat to human freedom in several ways. In the past, the manipulative impact of the television and other visual media has been overestimated. Today, a more modest role is ascribed to these media, namely that of setter of the agenda and the topics of conversation. To a large extent they help to determine what people talk about and what (they say) they think is important. The universal presence of screens and the selective articulation of their content are able to reinforce the agenda-setting capacities of visual media.

Qualifications

The aspects of the culture of images described will mainly be considered negative. This impression has to be corrected, for several reasons. In Chapter 9, on psychology, we will stress that visual perception and visualization are the most important perceptual and cognitive mental capacities of humans. Perhaps these capacities have been underused in the history of linguistic media. In that case, a further visualization of culture might mean progress.

This description has to be refined in two other ways. In the first place, the results discussed only apply to the extent to which screens will *dominate* all media of presentation and the extent to which they will *push aside* other types of mediated communication as the most visible type. In the second place, we have not taken into account the educational and cultural policies trying to confront the negative effects. Their first priority might be an adjustment of teaching courses in language(s), information and computer science, social studies and the humanities. These subjects should be used to teach students an active and conscious engagement with our visual culture and to give them (some) insight into the shape, the content and the selection processes of visual communication. Cultural pessimists might better use their energy in these ways than in futile attempts to restore the reading of printed texts as the presumed most important type of intellectual activity.

THE QUANTITY AND QUALITY OF NEW MEDIA CONTENT

Seemingly, the new media enrich our culture with a huge increase of information and communication. We might get the impression this is true in both a quantitative and a qualitative sense. But is this impression correct? On second thoughts, many critical comments can be made here. First, we will have to explain the distinction between information and communication. Information* consists of data or signals that have been interpreted by people. Here, the process of interpretation by the receiver is emphasized. Communication*, however, is a transfer of information from a sender to a receiver, the former being aware of the existence of the latter. Here, the emphasis is on transfer: the social processes of transmitting (allocution) and exchanging (consultation, registration and conversation) information. Communication presupposes information, as the transfer of signals should not be represented as some kind of delivery of post parcels or the exchange of data in a pipeline between senders and receivers, but as the construction of a shared meaning by people interpreting the signals in their social context (Mantovani, 1996).

Definitions of information and communication

The supply of *information* in our society is increasing rapidly, perhaps even exponentially. Pool et al. (1984) have assembled a large amount of data and research indicating an increase in information supply of some 8 to 10 percent each year since 1950, while demand lags behind with about only 3 percent. The increase in the amount of *knowledge* our society extracts from this information is much more moderate. Information supply overlaps and repeats itself many times, and in receiving information we have to deal with selective attention, selective perception and a surplus of information. The most astonishing and dramatic conclusion, however, is about the consequences of information. The impact of information in *affecting behaviour* (pragmatics) appears to be marginal: the activities of individuals and organizations are highly insensitive to information once a particular stage has been reached. Compared with 30 years ago, public institutions and companies turn out to be using more information to reach the same kind of decisions (van Cuilenburg and Noomen, 1984: 51). According to these Dutch communication scientists, decision quality has not improved very much. Similarly, Dordick and Wang (1993) have referred to the well-known 'productivity paradox': information technology produces fewer productivity gains than expected, especially in the service sectors.

Information use lagging behind supply

How should one explain these daring and disturbing conclusions? They certainly do not mean that information technology is not working. On the contrary, they may indicate that the level of complexity of our societies, organizations and personal lives has grown so dramatically that we would no longer be able to handle that complexity without this technology. Imagine a present-day corporation or government department without it. They would get stuck in old types of bureaucracy. The best explanation might be the conjecture that ICTs are barely able to keep up with the complexity of social, economic and cultural life we have produced.

Information overload

Anyway, the difference between the increase of information and knowledge on the one hand and their application on the other produces *overinformation*: too much information is produced in relation to its use. Furthermore, it points to a phenomenon Van Cuilenburg and Noomen have called 'information dud' (1984: 52): an increasing amount of information does not offer answers to questions asked, but produces answers to questions that still have to be posed. Indeed, the production of information has partly become an autonomous, self-augmenting process. David Schenk (1997) calls these phenomena simply *data smog*. He claims our information supply is so contaminated with useless and redundant data that information is no longer valuable or empowering, but is overly abundant and is making us helpless. 'At a certain level of input, the law of diminishing returns takes effect; the glut of information no longer adds to our quality of life, but instead begins to cultivate stress, confusion and even ignorance' (p. 15). For human minds, information overload is not a problem until we are forced by our environment to select information and knowledge from an overwhelming amount of data, for instance at school, at work or in an overfull leisure time programme. In all of these cases, information overload leads to stress. However, outside of situations of this kind, people simply do not perceive the surplus of signals. Humans have several mental mechanisms to prevent signals coming into their minds, and these mechanisms will work even more strongly in times of stress until they break down and nothing at all is recorded any more (see Milgram, 1970). Under normal circumstances, our cognition has all the filters necessary for perceiving and processing signals. They are intensified when there are too many signals to record. Another reaction is to spend less time on each input. Low-priority signals are ignored. In social exchange, the problem is transferred to others: 'ask someone else', 'let others find out'. Signals are also rejected, by the recipient not responding or by putting on an unfriendly face. Finally, the things causing the damage – sources such as documents, tapes, files or programs – are simply ignored and not used any more.

Over-communication?

Another question is whether we are also dealing with *overcommunication* and *communication duds*. After all, the quantity of mediated communication is increasing fast. This is most obvious in the case of mass communication (referring to the overabundance of broadcasting channels, for instance). Over the past decades, the amount of data communication and telecommunication has also increased strongly. Here the situation is different from mass communication, as supply is not able to exceed demand so easily. After all, telecommunication is a two-way process. Its capacities may increase, but this does not mean they will be used. Large corporations, for example, make extensive use of data communication, but households use it very little, compared with telephony. This fundamental difference between information and communication relieves the potential discrepancy between the growth of communication, the amount of knowledge derived and the effects on behaviour as compared with information. We might say that by the late 1990s, only the communication supply in particular mass media had reached a point of overcommunication. An increasing number of radio and television channels offering the same (kind of) programmes has been accompanied by decreasing average numbers of viewers and listeners for each of them. The results are fragmentation and redistribution of the market. Supply continues to expand, driven by the revenues from commercials. Here 'communication duds' may arise: general interest channels with broadly the same content are created, but with few viewers and listeners.

Demand for data communication and telecommunication in the late 1990s was still exceeding supply. There is no question of overabundance here. However, here we are also confronted with 'data smog'. It is getting harder to extract relevant data from an ever growing supply. The Internet, for instance, has a problem of abundance, supplying innumerable sites and pages and offering an unmanageable number of sources as a result of using search engines. In the use of email, fax and answering machines, we are dealing with phenomena like 'junk mail' or 'spam' (unsolicited email) and simply too many messages in general.

Another phenomenon, which might become very important in the future, is much harder to call a general problem. There is a problem of 'communication overload' for those people trying to protect themselves from being reachable at any time and place as a result of digital and cellular telephony. In general, these new kinds of telephony provoke a huge number of messages that subsequently appear redundant or valueless.

Technical solutions to both information and communication overabundance are being developed and introduced rapidly. All kinds of personal or information agents, systems to filter all incoming information and messages, and search engines are offered. These techniques will become essential in the information and network society. A matter of decisive importance, however, will be the extent to which we use these means. We should not rely on them completely, as three great risks with fundamental consequences are associated with them.

Information agents as a solution

The first of these risks is to *rely too much on their intelligence* and to allow one's own ability to judge to remain weak. Systems do get smarter, but their users might become stupider. In fact, these systems possess all the pros and cons of artificial intelligence (see Chapter 9). Intelligent systems are able to adapt to changing user preferences. However, people's standards, values and emotions are changing much faster. And what is more, they differ depending on innumerable contexts. They cannot be entirely (pre-)programmed.

Risks

A second threat is that by continuously using these information devices, people might cut themselves off from new and surprising impressions and contacts. People may even lock themselves up in a personal 'information prison' (Schenk, 1997: 120). We may settle down in environments that are as safe and controllable as they are limited. We may create a personal subculture locked away from the rest of the world or society, perhaps not in principle but very often in reality.

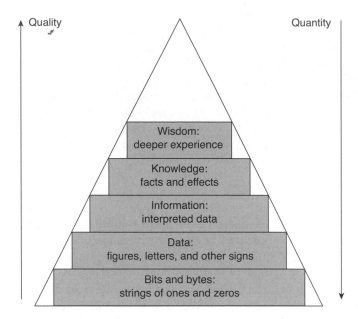

FIGURE 8.1   The pyramid of information processing

The final risk is a threat to the *privacy* of users who increasingly entrust their personal preferences and characteristics to systems of registration. In the 21st century, your information agent will inform your contacts who you are. Authorities and corporations will be very interested, without doubt.

So, it is necessary to use these systems critically and in a selective manner and to retain control over all important steps and judgements.

Substantial quality To a certain extent, the appreciation of information and communication quality is an arbitrary affair. Therefore, we need to develop particular criteria for the quality of information and communication. This last section will consider quality criteria in terms of the substance and pragmatics of new media content.

According to standards concerning the substance of information and communication, the huge quantities supplied in the new media do not necessarily lead to better quality. The so-called pyramid of knowledge is often presented to clarify this statement. A better term would be the *pyramid of information processing*, for knowledge is only one of the results of processing information mentally and technically (see Figure 8.1).

In the process of digitalization, at the base of the pyramid, endless amounts of *bits and bytes* are produced. Subsequently, every digital zero and one can be translated technically into certain *data* by means of computer machine language. These data can be letters, images or other tokens. Then humans are able to mentally translate these data into *information*, for information merely consists of data being interpreted: they are tokens bearing a particular meaning. Data are not interpreted when humans do not consider them relevant. In turn, information is often only temporarily important, or is even trivial.

A relatively small amount of information has a lasting importance: this is what we call *knowledge*. Knowledge consists of facts (describing reality) and relations of cause and effect that explain how things work and how we can use them. A specific type of knowledge is called scientific knowledge. Finally, the top of the pyramid contains the most rare result of human information processing: *wisdom*. This rather vague term represents the deeper experience to be gained by associating specific types of knowledge over time, putting them in a context, offering explanations about backgrounds, and connecting them with the values and standards important to humans.

So, information processing using ICT increases the quantity of information as one descends the pyramid toward the base of bits and bytes, while decreasing its quality. In the opposite direction, as one ascends the pyramid towards wisdom, using ICT will improve quality. However, ascending the pyramid gets harder and harder as one approaches the top. More and more data smog or information overload has to be disposed of to reach the next step. So, the use of ICT as such is no guarantee of higher information quality. It does provide us with more opportunities, but we can only use them by making more and better selections simultaneously.

A similar balance can be drawn up for the quality of *communication* content. The new media are a considerable improvement for fast communication over long distances. More, better and faster channels for communication are being constructed. This does not mean an improvement of communication in all respects. Kubicek and Rolf (1985: 367) once said that modern relations of communication are spatially global but limited in content, while traditional relations are spatially limited but comprehensive in content. In this chapter, we have noted the selective enhancement *and* limitation of communication content. The improvement of channels of communication might mean they are used for shallower and more ephemeral types of communication. Think about most 'chatting' on the Internet and about many conversations on the mobile phone: the simplicity of the connection promotes 'small talk'. And communication might be limited by the capacities of the new channels, as will be explained in the social-psychological section of Chapter 9.

An assessment of the *pragmatic* quality of information and communication implies, among other things, questions about their efficiency. What is the relationship between costs and yields? Van Cuilenburg and Noomen (1984: 49ff.) state that information involves diminishing returns. At a particular moment, the point of satiation is reached: then human actions become highly insensitive to more information. Does such a relation exist in connection with increasing communication? Yes – and no. The essential difference with information is that the initial costs of mediated communication are much higher than the returns, because a costly infrastructure has to be constructed. After some period, the costs of the investment are recovered. Then the marginal returns increase strongly. So, efficiency would seem to be the most important characteristic of improved communication facilities.

Pragmatic quality

However, it would be wrong to think that time and capacity are no longer important. On the contrary, they become more important, particularly in economic transactions. The construction of an online connection between international stock markets, for instance, was a great improvement. However, once these were introduced, transmission times between these markets could never be fast enough. Fractions of a second are vital. Huge investments have had to be made to increase transmission speed, while the size of financial transfers grows simultaneously. The same applies to connection and processing times in data communication between companies. After some period, the law of diminishing returns applies to communication connections as well. This phenomenon will also appear in the content of communications. The need to be 'within reach at any time and place' will lead to various forms of 'overcommunication' (see earlier): the telephone or a similar device is picked up too readily, and too much talking takes place. No one saves on messages. Subsequently, a lot of communication turns out to have served no purpose, or could have been much shorter. In these cases, communication appears to be inefficient, though it may have served an important emotional and informal need.

CHANGING MEDIA USE

Sources of change In the previous sections, the substantial characteristics of digital culture were emphasized. In this section, the media forms and media uses in the network society will have the focus of our attention. The characteristics and communication capacities of the new media discussed in Chapter 1 enable profound changes in people's daily use of media. The characteristic of integration or convergence creates multimedia practices unknown before. Moreover, it causes a shift from analogue, separately used print and audiovisual media to digitally integrated electronic media. The characteristic of interactivity allows a much more active or productive media use than previously. The technical infrastructure of computer networks and digital code facilitates altogether new links between media, such as hypermedia and the transmission of media content by users themselves exchanging music files, pictures and videos. All these characteristics taken together will drastically change the face of future media use and digital culture as a whole. In this section, I unravel and summarize these changes through examining a number of trends.

Convergence The first trend is the process of convergence that was a pivotal theme in the early chapters of this book. The integration of tele-, data and mass communication inspires ideas of a complete mixture of digital media in a single medium (e.g. a broadband Internet) and ideas of the disappearance of the separate old media. I think both ideas are wrong. They wrongly assume that technical convergence will automatically lead to convergences in social practices and daily media use and they neglect the trend of media differentiation also present in contemporary society. It is possible to show web-pages and email messages on television and mobile telephone screens. One is able to make a phone call on the Internet using Voice over IP. But do these applications meet the needs of users in their familiar environments? Chapter 4 explained that TV use is a matter of (often) collectively viewing large screens in a living room or bedroom, mainly for purposes of entertainment. Computer and Internet use is a practice of individuals operating keyboards right in front of a relatively small screen for purposes of information, communication and work or study in rooms suitable for these activities. The rise of cellular telephony proves that it requires mobility and not fixed web-cams.

Contemporary society is in a process of social and cultural differentiation that does not fit with a unitary media environment. A single all-embracing medium that serves all applications and usage contexts is not a realistic prospect. In fact, different social classes, age groups and cultures keep using different media or advanced and simple types of the same medium. Diversity even is increasing, as I argue below.

Another popular view is that the new media will replace the old media. This has appeared to be erroneous many times in media history. The most famous example is the TV which was expected to replace the cinema. This time many people think the digital media of computers and the Internet will replace print media, TV and radio.

Old media replacement?

Recent findings indicate that the use of the Internet and computers does not, or only partially and very gradually, displace print media or the use of broadcasting (Adoni and Nossek, 2001; Ferguson and Perse, 2000; Huysmans et al., 2004). This is no surprise, because using the Internet with its relatively active ways of information seeking and message exchange is not functionally equivalent to watching television or listening to the radio as a consumption of information and a relaxing pastime. Neither is it equivalent to reading printed material in a comfortable environment. In the second part of the 20th century there was a shift from reading to TV viewing. However, up to now, a shift from TV viewing to computer and Internet use is occurring only among young people (Ferguson and Perse, 2000; SCP, 2001). Table 8.1 reveals a number of long-term shifts in the Netherlands between 1975 and 2000. As far as I know, they are fairly representative for all contemporary developed countries. The table shows a dramatic decline in time spent on print media, radio and face-to-face communication. Simultaneously, but not necessarily serving as a replacement, time spent on TV, video, telephony, computers and the Internet was rising fast. More recent figures indicate that between 2000 and 2005 these trends have persevered with a steep incline in computer, Internet and (mobile) telephony use and a small increase in television viewing, while the use of print media and radio as main activities continues to drop. Nevertheless, Huysmans et al. conclude that there is only a gradual and partial replacement of old media by new media (2004: 229).

One of the reasons for this limited extent of replacement is the growing multifunctional use of all media. Until fairly recently, media were used for a particular main purpose: TV for entertainment, papers and magazines for the news, books for education, telephony for conversation and computers to process data. The rise of electronic, digital and multimedia technologies enables all these media to become more multifunctional. Television becomes more of an information medium with teletext, continuous news and current affairs programs and all kinds of banners, boxes and subtitles on the screen.

Multi-functionality

TABLE 8.1   Time spent on communication as main activity among the Dutch population 12 years and older between 1975 and 2000 in hours per week.

	1975	1980	1985	1990	1995	2000
All Communication	32.2	31.2	31.4	31.1	30.6	29.7
Mass Media	18.5	17.8	19.0	18.8	18.8	18.7
Radio and Audio	2.2	1.8	1.4	1.2	0.8	0.7
TV and Video	10.2	10.3	12.1	12.0	12.4	12.4
Print Media	6.1	5.7	5.3	5.1	4.6	3.9
PC and Internet			0.1	0.5	0.9	1.8
Interpersonal	13.7	13.4	12.4	12.3	11.9	11.0
Telephony		0.4	0.5	0.6	0.7	0.7
Face-to-Face	13.7	13.0	11.9	11.7	11.1	10.3

Source: Huysmans et al., 2004, p. 195.

Radio has become a background medium without losing popularity. Papers, magazines and books have increased their entertainment value with more pictures, short stories, lifestyle information and more fiction in cheap paperbacks. Current telephony offers mobile information, games, pictures and even video or TV. The computer has turned from a number-crunching machine into a multipurpose information device. The Internet has even become the most multifunctional medium in history.

Increasingly, both old and new media integrate the following functions: information, communication, transaction, entertainment, sociability, education and identity building. To a certain extent, they become functionally equivalent. In the network society, these media are interconnected more and more, and when they cannot be connected they refer to each other inside programs and services.

Context and diversity

This does not mean that the differences between media disappear. On the contrary, their special communication capacities (Chapter 1) become even more crucial. People's selectivity in choosing media is increasing. This choice is increasingly context dependent. In the near future, information and a multitude of media will be almost everywhere. Only the most appropriate medium for a particular need in a specific context will draw our attention and invite our use. Here are a few examples. In the living room we want the home cinema, in the bedroom a book, magazine or small TV set. In the kitchen and the car we prefer the less disturbing radio or audio set. While we are on the move, we want to communicate and receive or carry all necessary information. When we are working we need the most advanced information and communication machines: computers and the Internet. However, rarely are these media exclusively used in these contexts; most often other media and connections are available. Multitasking in media use is on the rise, especially among young people.

Across the population as a whole, the diversity of media use has not increased, at least not among the Dutch population that is chosen as an example here (Huysmans et al., 2004: 192). Media use is spread among more media (the media differentiation discussed previously), but total communication time has not increased (see Table 8.1). This may sound surprising, but the explanation is that not all the functions mentioned above are used by everybody to the same extent. Within the total amount of diversity that remains equal a very conspicuous trend has appeared between 1975 and 2000: people of higher social class are increasing the diversity of media use functions, while people of lower social class are reducing them (Huysmans et al., 2004: 192–194). To use the most familiar stereotype: the people of lower social class watch television all day for entertainment, and have done away with the newspaper. This trend refers to the knowledge gap and the usage gap that were discussed in Chapter 7.

The transition to electronic media and a digital culture implies that the forms of the data types distinguished in this book (sound, text, images and numerical data) and the way they are integrated in multimedia are changing. It does not *necessarily* mean that there is a transformation in their content, with the exception of the characteristics of digital culture discussed in this chapter. In the recent past, we have seen many occurrences of printed content that was simply reframed in an electronic format. Of course, this requires new literacies that are called digital skills in this book. But, what I want to emphasize is that the decline of print media, for instance, does not mean that people are reading less. Perhaps they read even more when all the media sources they use these days are taken together. They read from screens and from sources that contain not only words but also images and numbers. In Chapter 9, I argue that there is no decisive reason to deplore the demise of print media. The same goes for the partial replacement of face-to-face by mediated communication. This transition has both advantages and disadvantages.

Changing forms, changing contents?

An instance of changing media forms that are transforming media content is the rise of hypermediation. Hyperlinks and hypermedia in general will cause a revolution in media use. We are just beginning to realize their importance. Until now, media were offered as separate *products*: devices, pieces or bundles of content (books, papers), services and programs. In hypermedia, they become *processes* of information retrieval, communication and entertainment as people jump from one source to another via the links of media networks. Many visible distinctions between media will disappear. We will go less to a library to borrow a pile of books but increasingly consult an electronic library and roam through a large number of sources to collect what we are looking for, just like we have started to do with search engines on the Internet.

Hypermediation

Hyperlinks do not interconnect people but content. They will diminish the linear perception and processing of content (reading and watching from the beginning to the end) and turn them into associative modes of perception, processing, memory and learning. In Chapter 9, I argue that this is able to support learning considerably. However, there is another side to this opportunity. Hypermedia support the selectivity capacity of the new media to the extreme. They offer many wonderful new features for searching, processing and recording content. A necessary condition is that users know exactly what they are looking for so that they do not get lost in an overload of sources and information. This requires a high level of information skills that is simply not available among a large part of the worldwide population, even in societies with high literacy (see Chapter 7 and van Dijk, 2005).

With digitalization, the number of interactive media among the total class of available media increases. This means that the **interactivity** in media use is

Interactivity and creativity

also likely to grow. Perhaps the levels of interactivity distinguished in Chapter 1 will be enhanced as well. The bandwidth of two-way channels grows. Interactive media are becoming more synchronous. Choice opportunities in menus multiply. Users are able to contribute more to central exchanges, from chat boxes to interactive TV programmes. When they are able to hold conversations with each other in videoconferences and the like, even the level of understanding may grow.

However, it is by no means certain that people take advantage of these opportunities. Many developers of interactive media and programs doubt whether there is sufficient need for interactivity among users. Many media users prefer *relatively* passive viewing, reading and listening, and do not want to make their own contributions. Choosing from (not too) extensive menus serves their needs. For instance, only a minority of Internet users have their own web site, post contributions to discussion lists, regularly exchange music files and videos or produce a personal web log. Probably, interactivity in media use is a phenomenon that needs time to grow among audiences that have been raised in a culture of relatively passive media consumption (Stewart, 1998–99; van Dijk and de Vos, 2001).

In the first section of this chapter it was argued that the thesis of higher creativity in digital culture should also be qualified. As compared to analogue media, it assumes more the character of a collage, reframing, reworking of, and change to, already existing content.

From broadcasting to narrowcasting
A related popular idea is that in the digital media, intermediation of publishers, editors and service providers is no longer needed or needed less. Users are supposed to make their own choices and carry out their own editing. This idea is incorrect as well. In the overly extensive and complicated new media environment, assistance to users is required more than ever before. The rise of portals, information agents, communication services, auctions and exchange servers for peer-to-peer networking on the Internet confirms this need.

What is actually happening is a transition from broadcasting to narrowcasting and from the mass marketing of homogeneous audiences, via the segmentation and tailoring of parts of audiences, to the customization of media content and the personalization of users or consumers to be reached. After the era of segmentation that has created a multitude of channels and media products for special target groups, we now enter a time of attempts at a one-to-one approach in personalized media forms and content (on demand). However, this is not the end of intermediation, but the start of a host of new services assisting users with making selections.

CONCLUSIONS

- Digitalization has a significant, but hardly noticed, creeping influence on all cultural expressions concerned. The division and recombination of every item of culture, be it images, sounds, text or data, creates a culture that is both more differentiated and more standardized because the basic items are pre-programmed chunks and operations.

- Digital cultural expressions appear in fragmented and recombined collated forms. Digitalization also produces a culture of speed because creative production is assisted by the power of accelerated processing and distribution in computers and networks.
- However, the most important effect is the rise of images and screens in multimedia expressions. This has both positive outcomes (the importance of vision for human perception, the support of ways of visual thinking and new opportunities for creativity) and negative ones. Among the negative outcomes are spending too much time looking at a screen, the temptation for shallow instead of insightful viewing, and the loss of context and of the original sources of the images presented on multimedia screens which are filled with heterogeneous contents (e.g. both advertisement and neutral information).
- Digital culture tends to produce information and communication overload that ruins the opportunities for higher quality. Huge quantities of bits and bytes, data and, to a lesser extent, irrelevant information are created while the valuable information, knowledge and wisdom to be extracted are scarcely sufficient to keep up with the rising complexity of society.
- Media use in digital culture will significantly change. Old media will partially and gradually be replaced by new media. For example, printed media are giving way to electronic media. The rise of multimedia entails a growing multifunctionality of media increasingly linked in networks. The diversity of media use among different social classes and cultural contexts is increasing. Hypermediation transforms traditional linear media use into associative use driven by high selectivity. The interactivity of media use is enhanced. Broadcasting changes into personalized narrowcasting. However, change is not as revolutionary as it often seems. The daily media needs and functions of users do not change that quickly. Often only the forms and modes of service of the media change, while content offered still addresses the same basic human needs: information, communication, transaction, entertainment, education, sociability and identity building. It has to be stressed that these forms and modes of service require new, digital skills.

PSYCHOLOGY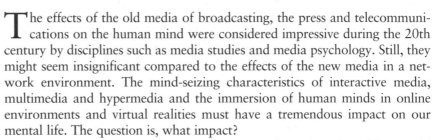

The effects of the old media of broadcasting, the press and telecommunications on the human mind were considered impressive during the 20th century by disciplines such as media studies and media psychology. Still, they might seem insignificant compared to the effects of the new media in a network environment. The mind-seizing characteristics of interactive media, multimedia and hypermedia and the immersion of human minds in online environments and virtual realities must have a tremendous impact on our mental life. The question is, what impact?

It is easy to see that we live in an increasingly mediated world. Age-old direct experience and physical interaction with the environment have been gradually replaced by mediated experience and environments. The new media accelerate this development. What will the effects on our perception and modes of communication be? Will direct interaction with a physical environment be replaced by interfaces with a world of images and by artificial models and simulations? Will oral, textual and nonverbal modes of communication be substituted by audiovisual or graphic modes and by computer language?

What effects will the new media have on our cognitions and emotions? Humans and the computer, a technology steering all new media, have so many similarities as information processing actors that the science of artificial intelligence and some psychologists argue that there are no fundamental differences between the two, and that the appearance of intelligent machines equal to human beings is just a matter of time. The opposing view says that current frictions in human–computer interaction can only be explained by fundamental differences between humans and computers. Which view is right?

CMC has been accused of being asocial (i.e. cold and unfriendly) and even antisocial (diminishing face-to-face interaction). There were fears that CMC would reinforce loneliness and stimulate Internet and computer addiction. However, in the past couple of decades, we have seen people using computer networks for very personal and intimate affairs, such as online dating, and to build and maintain social relationships and identities. Is CMC really inferior to face-to-face communication in terms of communication richness?

What effects do the use of computers and other new media have on our personalities in the long run? There is much speculation about this. We might become some kind of *cyborg*, half computer and half human. Sherry Turkle (1984) claimed a long time ago that computers are able to serve as a 'second self'. It is certain that our relationship with the media has been personalized: we treat media like human beings (Reeves and Nass, 1996). Is this even more the case for the new media, or are we able to keep a distance?

In the sections that follow, I first deal with the influence of the new media on perception, followed by their impact on human cognition and learning. Then the focus shifts from human–computer interaction to CMC. Finally, issues of personality and identity are discussed.

PERCEPTION AND THE NEW MEDIA

From direct experience to mediated perception

In all mediated communication, some kind of entity is present between human beings and their experience of reality. In allocution we are dealing with a medium–human monologue. In consultation and registration, the patterns shift to a medium–human dialogue. In the pattern of conversation, this is turned into a human–medium–human dialogue or polylogue. In all of these cases, direct *experience* is replaced by mediated and technically supported or affected *perception*. Direct human experience has always been an observation of reality involving all the senses *simultaneously*. This consists not only of *knowledge*, but also of *skills* (for instance mental, social and communicative skills), *values*, *feelings* and *abstractions*. Compared with this, mediated communications always involve *particular restrictions*. Here the use of all senses is impossible. Some types of knowledge can be gained, others cannot. Specific skills are used. One medium is suitable for a transfer of feelings, values or abstractions, while another is absolutely incapable of doing this.

Restrictions of mediated communication

In opposition to all the restrictions of the old and new media in relation to direct experience, these media also offer *additions* to experience, of course. Media are the extensions of man, according to a famous expression of McLuhan (1966). To an increasing extent, they help us to overcome the limitations of space, time and lack of information. These forms of help cannot compensate for all limitations, but for many purposes, for instance formal and business communication, this does not have to be a problem. Moreover, the creative human mind is able to fill the gaps, as is argued below.

A second aspect of the transition from direct experience to mediated perception is a partial *pre-programming* of perception and experience in using media. With respect to allocution, this is obvious. It explains the large number of studies about the influence of TV. In consultation and registration, perception is also pre-programmed to some extent. In mediated conversation, it

Pre-programming

is either restricted or enhanced by the communication capacities and the practical applications of the medium concerned.

Therefore, aspects of comprehensiveness, freedom and the individual's own initiative are at stake in the shift to mediated perception.

From learning by action to learning by symbol systems and visual models

Bruner and Olson (1973: 213ff.) hold that three *modes of experience* fit three *types of learning*:

- the *enactive* mode fits learning by direct action;
- the *iconic* mode fits learning by the observation of visual models;
- the *symbolic* mode fits learning through symbol systems (for instance languages).

With the transition from direct experience to mediated perception, the first of these automatically shifts to the other two types of learning. On the one hand, we could say this does not make any difference. All these types of learning are able to provide the same basic structure of knowledge (1973: 220). On the other hand, knowledge gained in a particular mode cannot be gained in another mode. Symbol systems (such as languages) merely enable us to process knowledge we have gained in other modes: 'Instruction through language is limited to rearranging, ordering and differentiating knowledge or information that the listener already has available from other sources such as modeling or through his own direct experiences' (p. 220). A similar point applies to learning through visual models: 'Complex acts cannot be simply imitated unless the performer already knows how to carry out the act' (p. 218). A person cannot imitate completely unknown behaviour. In the end, knowledge is always tied to personal experience (p. 225). Furthermore, learning through language and models always requires particular skills to be acquired first.

The new media offer new possibilities for all three modes of experience and types of learning, but this applies much more to the iconic and symbolic modes than to the enactive mode. The former modes are aided by all kinds of facilities such as slow motion, rewind, fast forward or searching, and by new ways of presenting information using menus, windows, hyperlinks, graphs, figures and other images. Furthermore, the combination of images, sounds, text and data enables easier usage of several languages/codes at the same time. In this way, new media will only support learning by action in an artificial way, leaning on the other two modes of experience (iconic and symbolic). This is done in simulations or pre-programmed instruction and practice.

Reduction in learning by direct action

On the whole, however, the use of new media will reduce learning by direct action even more than the old media did. As direct action remains the basis of human experience, heavy use of the new media could lead to a decay of this type of learning. Some examples will help to explain this statement. Testing a product in a shop will give you a better impression of the product than reading about its specifications on the Internet. For a long time to come, physical examinations by a doctor will not be replaced in a satisfactory way by medical diagnostic systems. In general, iconic and symbolic modes of experience do not stimulate *active* engagement with the media concerned. A *comparably* passive mode of perception will prevail: far more is read than written, more is listened to than spoken, more is viewed than depicted, and more use is made of a device/program than of calculation or measurement. The new media will continue this development, which had already been started by the old media. Even though the interactive new media offer more opportunities for active inputs and choices by local units, they start with enlarging the 'weight' and complexity of the medium itself. A lot of viewing, reading, listening and operating has to be done before any active input can be realized. When an overload of information and instructions occurs, this does not stimulate such input either.

Shifts in the modes of symbolic communication and mental skills required

---

Gross (1973) has made a distinction between the *linguistic*, the *social-gestural* (nonverbal), the *iconic*, the *logico-mathematical* and the *musical* modes of symbolic communication. In the course of human history, many alterations have occurred in these general modes of communication and their specifications. The linguistic mode, for instance, has an oral, a written and an audiovisual variant. They were the dominant ones in this sequential order. Several modes of communication, or their variants, have become more important in the first and in the second communications revolutions, and others have become less important. The relative importance of the oral-linguistic and the social-gestural modes of communication, which every human being learns as a child, have decreased in western cultures. The written-linguistic mode and subsequently the audiovisual-linguistic, the logico-mathematical and the iconic modes (photography, film and all sorts of visual signs and designs) have come to the fore.

In the new media, shifts occur once again. Within the linguistic mode, the audiovisual variant (texts accompanied by images and sounds) is gaining importance at the expense of the oral and written variants. This includes the rise of the iconic mode in the shape of film, photographs, figures, graphs, windows and other pictures and images. This reveals the central position of the screen and the rise of a culture of images. The logico-mathematical mode is also becoming more important. Computer operations dominate not only data processing, but all kinds of software and operating instructions to be used in CMC. In the new media, the role of the musical mode is not decreasing, but it no longer operates on its own. Increasingly, music is accompanied by images. And radio music is downgraded to serve as a background for other activities.

The nonverbal (social-gestural) mode is receiving the least attention in the new media. It has disappeared where mediated communication using only speech, text or data has replaced face-to-face communication. Although the nonverbal mode returns in a limited way when video starts to transmit faces and gestures of bodies in the new media, all expressions and transmissions taken together, this mode has lost space to the verbal or linguistic modes of communication. The intelligentsia's ceaseless mourning of the decline of printed text should not conceal the fact that in the new media one has to read more and more and that the verbal modes continue to gain importance, even where multimedia are concerned. The misunderstanding that reading is getting less important is inspired by the fact that in the new media spoken and printed words have growing audiovisual and iconic support. This enables some people to concentrate on this support and overlook the words (see below).

Integration of modes of communication

The most basic trend in the modes of communication used in the new media is their advancing *integration*. With the combination of images, sounds, texts and data in a single medium, the modes of communication are also integrating. The resultant multimedia combinations acquire a power of communication unprecedented in human history. They will have a largely unpredictable influence on human perception and cognition. However, a number of assumptions can be derived from known psychological implications of the use of communication modes in older media.

Symbol systems

In his classic book *Interaction of Media, Cognition and Learning*, Gavriel Salomon (1979) has explained the psychological differences between 'symbol systems'. This term is comparable to the concept of modes of (symbolic) communication used above. It is taken from the work of Goodman (1968). (Others prefer the term 'sign systems', since some signals in communications are not symbols, for instance realistic images.) Salomon distinguishes the following four differences to be related to the mental effects of new media use.

Differences of content and complexity of processing

Each symbol system or mode of communication is particularly suitable for the transfer of a specific type of content. For instance, the linguistic mode is used for explanations, the iconic mode for portrayals or expressions and the nonverbal mode for emotions. Abstract notions, arguments and all the things important in a dialogue can be best explained in words. Mediated images are preeminently suitable for giving a direct view of reality or for clarifying things usually not visible to the human eye with the aid of a particular visual language.

Notational and non-notational systems

Symbol systems or modes of communication are either *notational* or *non-notational*. They contain a set of notations for the clearly identifiable, specific matters they are referring to, or they contain signs not unambiguously referring to a particular thing or matter, for instance all kinds of images with their varied and mostly ambiguous contents (Salomon, 1979: 33). The logico-mathematical mode and the musical mode (represented by stave notation) are notational systems, while the iconic and nonverbal modes are non-notational. The linguistic mode is partly notational, since several interpretations of spoken and written words are possible. In the new media, especially multimedia, the linguistic mode becomes less ambiguous under the influence of strict notational computer language and the advancing integration of texts, images, sounds and data. In multimedia, the iconic mode is joined with the audiovisual linguistic mode. *All in all, the notational symbol systems or modes appear to be intensified in the new media.* This will have important consequences. Mental processing in notational systems is known to be more complex than in non-notational ones. The appropriate codes have to be learned and subsequently applied over and over again. In non-notational systems, the distance between symbols and representations (for instance images) in a person's mind is shorter (1979: 73–4).

The notational linguistic, logico-mathematical and musical-written modes of communication are primarily processed mentally in the left half of the brain, and the non-notational nonverbal, iconic and musical-auditive modes are primarily but not exclusively processed in the right half of the brain (Ivry and Robertson, 1998). So, in general the new media will appeal relatively more to the left half of the brain. However, the expectation of a much stronger simultaneous appeal of integrated new media (multimedia) to both halves of the brain is far more important. An intense dialogue between both halves through their cross-connections is required. This requires all-round mental development. *The ability to benefit fully from all the opportunities of the new media demands a full-grown visual, auditive, verbal, logical and analytical mental development.* Of course, this will increase the complexity of the mental activities required. But the level of this complexity depends on three other crucial factors (Salomon, 1979: 71–2):

Mental skills required

- the cognitive development of individuals, being related to age, education and experience;
- individual cognitive preferences in perceiving texts, images, sounds or data;
- the tasks to be performed being more or less demanding: study, information retrieval, conversation or amusement.

In conclusion: an *optimum* use of the new media requires full-grown and versatile mental development and a multifunctional use of their capacities.

Various (types of) modes of communication can cause different meanings to be ascribed to one and the same content. Listening to a sound recording of a speech will result in meanings other than those obtained by reading its literal transcription (Salomon, 1979: 78). This is caused not by the contents themselves, for they are (almost) entirely the same, but by the skills of the receiver. In their turn, these depend upon two factors: the basic knowledge of the receiver and the novelty of the information.

Differences in the construction of meaning

The broader the basic knowledge of the receiver, the less sensitive this person will be to the (type of) mode of communication offered (1979: 79ff.). This means that less educated people depend more on the mode of communication concerned than better educated people do. This must be very relevant to any introduction of the new media because, in theory, the range of options in choosing modes of communication is increased.

In spite of all the myths about the stultifying impact of modern visual culture, almost all psychological research shows that reading in general has a more *compelling* but not necessarily greater appeal to our mental efforts than perceiving audiovisual messages. Conceptual thinking, required by reading, goes beyond perceptual thinking (Peters, 1989). On the basis of these statements we might expect (new) media containing audiovisual presentations to be more easily accessible to less educated people than the (new) media mainly using text and data. At the same time, (new) media would be less instructive for them than they are for better educated people, for the latter are less dependent upon the particular mode of communication offered and they profit more from the increasing elements of text and data.

Differential cultivation of mental skills

The (types of) modes of communication not only appeal differently to mental skills, but also help to develop them differently. In order to do so, they have to be demanding and they must force receivers to develop their skills (Salomon, 1979: 82). However, there are several modes of communication, particularly the non-notational types, that allow the receiver to choose the line of least resistance. 'The pictorial system of television *allows* (but does not require) shallower processing than a written story or a verbally told one. To generalize, some symbol systems may *allow* shallower mental processing and others may *demand* deeper mental elaboration' (1979: 223, final italic added). 'Notational symbol systems require crystallized ability, based on verbal skills, and non-notational symbol systems require mainly fluid ability, based on spatial and perceptual skills' (1979: 224).

All this has relevance to the new media. In theory, they can help to develop mental skills better than most old media, as they integrate a multitude of modes of communication. In practice they require full-grown mental capacities and a multifunctional usage. The problem is they do not have to be used optimally. The integration of modes of communication in the new media can also be accessed separately and enable a much shallower use. The strength of the audiovisual and the iconic modes offers potential uses that do not stimulate the mental skills required for notational symbol systems. 'The employment of charts, graphs or pictures could save mental effort and make the acquisition of knowledge more effective, but it will impede skill development' (1979: 83). The transition from the (audio)phone to the videophone is a good example. The latter gives more cues and therefore requires less mental skill to understand the conversation (see later in this chapter). People who have to rely on one or two modes of communication must develop the appropriate skills, no matter how one-sided these skills may be. The best case of this until now has been the written linguistic mode.

So, a paradoxical situation arises. On the one hand, the new media (can) make human perception and cognition more complicated and, on the other hand, they (can) facilitate and simplify them. Therefore, the goal and the task of the user determines what happens. Experiments have shown that children learn more from watching television, for instance *Sesame Street* (1979: 225), when they are guided by their parents or by courses for achieving educational goals. Since people with high education in general will be willing to 'do' more with the new media than people with low education, the former will benefit more and will increase their mental advantage. This is the most fundamental psychological cause of the usage gap described in Chapter 7.

In this section, I am mainly concerned with the fact that the new media require the mental combination of an ever growing quantity and heterogeneity of information and that they call for the mental integration of mediated and face-to-face communications. People are faced with an unprecedented mixture of old and new media. There are no fixed limits to the human capacity to handle information (Neisser, 1976: 97ff.); it is very 'elastic'. For this reason, the effect of phenomena like information overload and 'overcommunication' should not be exaggerated. However, problems arise whenever we begin to combine tasks that have no natural relationship to each other (1976: 101). In the new media, human communication and the handling of data are more and more accompanied by and sometimes even taken over by technical communication and data processing. The key questions then become whether these forms of communication and processing look alike and whether they are able to develop a natural relationship to each other. If the answers to these two questions are primarily positive, there is no reason to worry about any special problems in mentally dealing with the new media. These media will become very useful tools. When, on the other hand, the answer is primarily negative, problems are bound to arise. In the latter case, communication between human beings and media/computers will meet limitations and complications.

Mental combination and integration

The *similarities* and possible relationships between processing and communication performed by human beings on the one hand and by media/computers on the other are evident. Computers are used as a metaphor (image) for the description of the human mind, and for good reasons. Terms derived from this source, such as information, processor and memory, play a key role in computer jargon. The same goes for terms derived from communication between human beings, like interaction, interface, dialogue, sign and command. In media technology jargon, terms derived from human perception, symbolization and representation of reality, prevail. Media and computers may be considered an extension of or even a substitute for human perception, cognition and communication. They span time and space and they decrease the effects of the limits our body and mind impose upon us.

Human–computer similarities

In answering the two questions posed earlier, a discussion of the *differences* and the possible malfunctions in processing and communication by humans and by media/computers is important. Critics of the new technologies and the accompanying computer culture and visual culture often phrase these differences in philosophic, humanistic and romantic terms. Human beings, they claim, differ from computers, because they have a broader range of experience, associations, intuition, feelings and emotions at their disposal. Well-known critics in the 1980s and 1990s were J. Weizenbaum, Th. Roszak, J. Searle and H. Dreyfus. Usually, their reactions were much too defensive. This has left them no option other than to stand by and watch how the fifth, sixth and later generations of computers seem to be clearing one difference after

Human–computer differences

TABLE 9.1   Basic differences between human and computer/medium processing

Human processing (cognition)	Computer/medium processing
Situation-bound	Context-free
Total experience	Separate and successive perception and cognition
Flexible schemata	Fixed schemata
Operant and intelligent learning	'Intelligent' learning
Processing through social communication	Processing through technical communication

another. Devoting oneself to modern psychology, and even to so-called cognitive psychology, which actually uses the computer as the most important model of the human mind, would be a wiser thing to do. Additionally, one should take note of empirical studies about the ways humans really use computer hardware and software and one should observe attempts to make designs that take into account the psychology of the user. After all these efforts, at least five differences will continue to exist (see Table 9.1).

Situation-bound versus context-free processing   The most basic difference can be attributed to the fact that human perception and cognition are *situated physically* in a tangible world. A human being has an active and autonomous relationship to its environment. This is of crucial importance to the versatile perception and cognition in the so-called 'perceptual cycle' (Neisser, 1976). The basic principles of this perceptual cycle are perceptual activities that are controlled by continuously changing mental schemata. This is caused by the *direct intentionality* of the human mind. Intentionality is inspired by the needs and values of human beings as biological and social beings in a particular environment.

This is the basic principle used by neurobiologist Gerald Edelman and his Neurosciences Institute. Edelman's work, summarized and popularized in his books *Bright Air, Brilliant Fire: On the Matter of the Mind* (1991) and *A Universe of Consciousness* (Edelman and Tononi, 2000), firmly supports the five differences dealt with in this section. Edelman rejects the principle of most cognitive psychologists that the human brain can be compared to a computer or to a power plant of neurones. He claims it is more like an organic jungle of continuously changing groups and connections of neurons that are unique for every human being. They are only partly specified by genes. The needs every human being appears to have in their ongoing interaction with the environment cause a continuous *selection* of neurons in the Darwinian sense, changing the human brain ceaselessly. A process of *trial and error* produced by these needs shapes the brain. The workings of the human brain should not be separated into the functioning of hardware (brain) and software (mind), as most cognitive psychologists do. According to Edelman, the complete human brain/mind, but obviously not particular thoughts, can be explained by neurobiology.

Perception and processing in computers or other media, on the other hand, can only start with some kind of *derived intentionality*. Computers are programmed by others and only reproduce or present programs. 'For a computer to have intentional states, it would have to be a robot of some kind', is how one of today's most important cognitive psychologists, Jerry Fodor (1986: 103) phrased the prime difference between man and computer in an interview. The principle of computer processing is programmed *instruction* following algorithms, not neural *selection* as in mental processing (Edelman, 1991).

Computers and media are programmed for various purposes and environments. So to some extent they are *context-free and abstract*. They are intended (instructed by a command) and they follow a rational planning model of the human mind. In her book *Plans and Situated Actions*, Lucy Suchman (1987) has severely criticized this model. In her empirical, anthropological study of the ways people use modern electronic equipment in everyday life, Suchman came to the conclusion that people do not use this equipment according to a certain plan, the way developers of this equipment expect them to do. Planning models of human action and thinking do not match the reality of 'situated action', which Edelman claims is inspired by neural selection following needs. Suchman feels plans are merely an anticipation and a reconstruction of action. They are a way of thinking, not a real-life representation of action. 'Situated action is an emergent property of moment-by-moment interactions between actors and between actors and the environments of their action' (1987: 179). This interaction has four features that go substantially beyond the three levels of interactivity that computers and media have been capable of supporting so far (two-way communications, synchronicity and, to some extent, control from both sides: see Chapter 1). In fact, these features are an interpretation of the fourth and highest level of interactivity distinguished in Chapter 1 (1987: 180):

Situated action

- Ordinary interaction between people presupposes *mutual intelligibility* of the parties involved. This understanding is effected during intense cooperation and communication in *fully fledged environments*.
- General communicative practices that people have learned in these environments are designed to *maximize sensitivity to particular partners and occasions of interaction*.
- The use of face-to-face communication includes *resources for detecting and remedying difficulties in understanding*.
- Human communication is embedded in, and makes use of, *a background of experiences and circumstances*.

Opposed to this, interaction between humans and computers/media is characterized by the following problems. A human being usually understands only partially what the equipment/software 'intends' (its derived intentionality) and why this is the case. Equipment and software 'understand' even less of the user's motives (his/her direct intentionality). Equipment/software works according to general schemata that are relatively insensitive to special users and circumstances. Communication malfunctioning will often not be noticed by equipment, let alone solved. Ultimately, the background knowledge programmed in computers/media is not broad and profound enough to fully support the broad range of potential situated (inter)actions.

Human–computer interaction

Of course, developers of software and pioneers in artificial intelligence have been trying to solve these problems for many years now. Some try to make hardware and software more transparent for users (see Norman, 1991, 1993, 1999; Norman and Draper, 1986). Others want to give users the means to involve their social environment, for instance colleagues, in solving problems of human–computer/medium interaction (see for instance Bannon, 1986: 433ff.). Furthermore, all sorts of 'intelligent' tutor systems and user models are available that are built through 'observation' of the users' successive input. With these systems, the computer should be able to derive the user's knowledge and misconceptions to a certain extent (see Suchman, 1987: 181ff.). Finally, computers are increasingly equipped with 'scripts' of concrete situations of a standard appearance that enable them to 'interpret' specific situations. In hardware, developers try to offer human cognition more context as well. The integration of types of data and modes of communication in multimedia creates (virtual) environments that are harder to distinguish from reality than in the old media, for instance TV (Bryant and Zillman, 1991; Kubey and Csikszentmihalyi, 1990). This applies in particular to the media of virtual reality created to simulate artificial environments, immersing users (almost) completely. The huge problems met by these advanced designs perfectly reflect the essential differences between human interaction and interaction between humans and computers or other media (Biocca, 1992; Norman, 1991).

'Total' experience versus separate perception and cognition

Being physically present in a tangible reality is largely responsible for human experience as well. In a way this can be called 'holistic'. From a varied and active relationship with their environment, from the use of many senses simultaneously and from a whole series of special mental schemata and general conceptual models (among them representations of space and time), people develop a comprehensive view of reality. When we take into account the associations between these schemata or models and the needs, drives and emotions also affecting them, because their neural selection processes all contribute to shaping this comprehensive view, we get the 'total' experience of human beings. Of course this experience is selective, but this is how human beings observe and process objects all at once. Human perception and processing is not a step-by-step process and does not happen linearly. 'Because of their physical condition, human beings first observe the whole with all its internal relations before getting to the specification of aspects. ... That is how we recognize the face of an acquaintance before noticing certain details in the person's countenance, such as the eyes' (Coolen, 1986: 144, my translation from the Dutch).

Instructional processing

Computers and other digital media operate the other way around, namely according to the principle of instruction. They work with an atomizing perception of one piece of information after another (in the shape of digital bits). Then a piecemeal transmission of these data will lead to step-by-step processing by means of algorithms. So, perception and cognition are separated. It is a sequential and linear process unhindered by indefinite associations, drives and emotions that one cannot program. These fundamental differences in perception and cognition are responsible for the innumerable problems in the interaction between humans and computers or other media and in the attempts to let computers handle human language. For the time being, they will be solved only partially. This even applies to computers working with numerous parallel processors (the so-called fifth generation) and to present neural networks and future neural computers superficially resembling the workings of the human brain.

'Total' experience also means perception, interpretation and interaction in continually changing *contexts* (see above). Most attempts by software developers and artificial intelligence experts to solve the problems just described are aimed at creating some sort of context in the programs and the presentation on a screen. Traditional languages using only commands have been partly replaced by visual overviews – menus from which to choose with the click of a mouse button. The second step was to display several windows on a single screen. Each window is a separate context. It may connect to another window, integrate another window or (partly) overlap. As a result, interaction with computers and other media using screens could be improved (Reichman, 1986). However, it will be far more difficult to create contexts by trying to make devices and software that fit or connect better to natural human language and senses. There has been considerable progress in speech recognition (using the human voice as an input and output medium), in visual presentation techniques and in pre-programmed scripts describing contexts for the interpretation of human language.

Changing contexts

All these means are useful, but they will not help to overcome the difficulties completely. For example, voice recognition only simplifies human–computer interaction by replacing logico-mathematical and written linguistic communication modes with an oral linguistic communication mode. A second example are contemporary window systems with independently operating windows that still insufficiently contextualize the perception and cognition of users. Another solution mentioned, programming contexts in scripts, will always prove to be incomplete: 'The number of relevant facts needed to completely define a context in theory is unlimited. … On the one hand, you always need a broader context, or you will never be able to distinguish relevant from irrelevant data. On the other hand, you need a final context that needs no further interpretation, otherwise an infinite regression of contexts will occur and you would never be able to start formalizing relevant data' (Coolen, 1986: 137–8, translation from Dutch by the author). In some fields, computers and other media considerably exceed the performance of human perception and cognition. (For instance, a camera can see/ show much more than the human eye is able to do.) But these devices will never be able to replace fully the 'total' experience of humans and their face-to-face communications. The basic reason is that human experience and consciousness are grounded in physical and mental feelings of what happens inside and outside the body according to recent neuropsychological theories (Damasio, 1999, 2003; Edelman and Tononi, 2000).

Human cognition is controlled by a series of *continuously* changing schemata referred to as mental maps by Edelman (1991). 'The schema accepts information as it becomes available at sensory surfaces and is changed by that information; it directs movements and exploratory activities that make more information available, by which it is further modified' (Neisser, 1976: 54).

Flexible versus fixed schemata

So, schemata are stable to a certain extent without being fixed. This is what makes humans capable of learning and of creative thinking. (See Neisser, 1976 for the schemata and Edelman, 1991 for the concrete neural processes involved.) On the other hand, computer programs, and to some extent other media programs, are relatively fixed. The number of states that the human nervous system is able to adopt is almost infinite, whereas the number in computers is by definition limited (Edelman, 1991). The basis of computer programs is the idea that all human knowledge can be formalized. 'Everything ... can be presented in a structure consisting of unambiguous terms linked by formal-logical or mathematical relations' (Coolen, 1986: 134). Fixed forms are the basis. Subsequently they have to be turned into more or less flexible programs. However, formalization, standardization and all sorts of automatization remain present in a prominent way. This is what causes the inevitable communication breakdowns in human–computer/ medium interaction. 'The process of achieving mutual intelligibility in face-to-face human communication rests on detection and repair of misunderstandings through the use of a variety of linguistic, contextual and cognitive resources – a capability that current interactive systems crucially lack' (Brown, 1986: 476). This 20-year-old quote can easily be repeated today.

Compensating for inflexibility

Developers of software and artificial intelligence experts try to compensate for this inflexibility by creating programs able to 'learn' from communication breakdowns and (user) errors (Brown, 1986: 464ff.; Norman, 1991, 1993; Suchman, 1987: 181ff.). These 'intelligent' programs are not designed for a more flexible communication between computer/medium and users or for avoiding errors, but for mutual 'learning' from mistakes and problems deemed to be inevitable.

Another way of compensating for inflexibility is to enlarge the learning capability of the user by increasing the levels of interaction and integration typical of the new media. Extensive psychological research shows how people can learn better and more quickly by using interactive (multi)media and programs. (The next section is dedicated to this issue.) However, these programs will never be as flexible as the schemata of the human mind, for the reasons explained earlier in this section.

Operant and intelligent learning versus 'intelligent' learning

One of the reasons for the difference in flexibility is the structure of the human brain. According to several psychological theorists (for example see Koestler, 1967; Maclean, 1978; Ornstein, 1986), the 'triune' human brain is a not fully integrated whole of three parts accumulated in a long evolutionary process. These parts are the brainstem with its instincts and reflexes ('the reptile brain'), the limbic system as the source of emotions ('the mammal brain') and the neocortex as the source of intelligence ('the typical human brain'). Computers are designed to come close to the last of these three parts only. In these devices, developers try to simulate intelligent learning. The previous exposition of the differences has shown they have succeeded only partially. All human learning is based on neural processes of *selection* driven by concrete needs and values. Simulation of intelligent learning by computers, however, results from abstract, programmed *instruction*. Furthermore, the human brain is not entirely driven by intelligent learning. Instincts and emotions are essential. Recently, neurobiologists have demonstrated that humans cannot even think without emotions. The classical Cartesian dividing line between reason and emotion is based on a misconception (see Damasio, 1995). Operant learning*, a capability of all mammals, in practice often dominates intelligent learning by humans. Operant learning happens when rewarded behaviour is repeated, and punished behaviour is not displayed again. It concerns direct consequences and immediate reactions. It is short-term learning. Intelligent learning, on the other hand, is drawing conclusions from consequences in the long run. This is the basis for planning. Intelligent learning by humans is often influenced by, is competing with, and is often even defeated by much more direct types of operant learning and by the remains of ancient instincts and reflexes. And most of the time this is not a disadvantage. It enables human beings to respond rapidly (to danger for instance) and yet adequately as seen from the person's needs.

Obviously, classical commentary on computer culture (claiming humans are capable of having emotions, contrary to computers and the like) is related to this fourth difference, although it is not based on the psychology concerned. From neuropsychology, neurobiology and the ethnography of human–computer interaction, better explanations can be derived for a large number of phenomena in contacts between humans and computers/media. An instance is Suchman's finding that humans do not use this equipment in a planned way. Furthermore, all kinds of ergonomic observations in psychology become clear: physical signs of stress and even panic if there is a problem, reflexes in the operation of a keyboard, energy-consuming response times, physical aggression towards computer equipment and so forth. In addition, numerous social-psychological phenomena in the contacts of humans with media and networks – see 'The Social Psychology of CMC' later – can be explained by the theories developed by Koestler, Maclean and others: for instance, the uninhibited nature of CMC resulting from the absence of non-verbal cues and immediate sanctions.

Of course, software developers have taken this fourth difference into consideration. Interactive programs are pre-eminently capable of incorporating elements of operant learning. They provide direct output after a particular input, such as error messages. However, this important didactic principle does not help to remove the ergonomic phenomena mentioned above (such as stress in case of malfunctions or error messages) and the problems occurring in the integration of intelligent and operant learning (the problem of not understanding an error message, for instance).

Human cognition requires communication with other people by using language. Without it, mutual understanding would be hard to accomplish. It makes a great difference, however, whether natural language is used or a (partly) artificial, technically mediated language programmed and transferred by computers and other media. Developers have still not been able to relate artificial languages to natural languages adequately and satisfactorily. The fundamental reasons were explained earlier in this section. In fact, it is wrong to speak of 'communication' and 'dialogue' in human–computer/medium interaction. However, humans have tried to improve the conditions

Social communication versus technically mediated communication

of their natural social communication by using media. In the course of human history, natural types of social communication have been supplemented with, and partially or completely replaced by, technically mediated communication. This means that one or more parts of the communication process are shaped technically. This can be the sender, the message, the medium, the channel and the receiver. This technical *design* can have great influence on the *content* of the communication process and on the mental processing of information produced in it. The number of cues for mental processing can not only increase but also decrease. When using face-to-face communication as a normative reference point, this will be the case almost by definition. However, this may be called the bias of face-to-face communication, as the comparisons made are not fair. In fact, this kind of communication has many disadvantages as well, which may be removed in technically mediated communication. A fair comparison means a study of the decrease *and* increase of cues that the technical parts of a communication process bring about.

LEARNING WITH THE NEW MEDIA

An increase of cues is partly responsible for new potentialities of learning with the help of new media. They can make a great contribution to the improvement of education in general and didactics in particular. These opportunities are derived from the two distinguishing characteristics of the new media: interactivity and integration. The following summary shows a sizeable potential (see Issing and Strebkowsi, 1995 for elaborations).

Interactivity of new media: independent studying   The *interactivity* of the new media enables a more active and more independent way of learning than we are used to. Interacting with and through these media, the superior type of enactive learning (see the first section in this chapter) is *simulated*, not equalled. In this way, the three modes of learning – enactive, iconic and symbolic – can be combined, as all three of them now use media. With these means, students are enabled to study independently and teachers are gaining another role. Until now, teachers have mainly passed on large amounts of information (allocution). In the future they will mainly be tutors of students studying independently and sitting in front of a terminal in a computer classroom or at home using the means developed for distance education. This will result in a complete, unprecedented transformation of our educational system. This transformation will take at least one and probably two or three generations to complete. The following five opportunities of interactive learning can be summarized:

- Students will be able to *manipulate subject matter themselves*. The order, the speed and even the complete contents do not have to be determined in advance. Thus, with enough additional and stimulating guidance from their tutors, they will be able to determine their own course, style and speed of studying.

- Making use of the many choices available in multimedia course material, students are able to *learn by exploring and experimenting* in open environments. Extensive research in education and psychology proves that self-directed and exploratory learning can be highly motivating.
- Students may *choose from several types of presentation*, each with the same content. This content may take the form of text, data (such as figures, graphs and models), (moving) images and sounds. Thus, students with special preferences for reading text or with special capacities for auditive and visual learning may all be served according to their abilities.
- Course material used in multimedia education is extremely suitable for *visualizing, modelling and simulating* information. 'Playing' with this material proves to be a very valuable experience. It helps to clarify and understand abstract matters.
- Finally, interactivity enables the student to start a *direct dialogue* with a program in a device. This combination of hardware and software is called 'intelligent'. Students receive direct feedback and immediately know what they are doing wrong.

The *integration* offered by the new media, particularly multimedia, mainly has consequences for the perception and cognition of students, as discussed in the previous two sections. Three of those consequences can be repeated and renamed in the following way.

Integration in studying

- The *addition of new data types*, such as images and speech, to the traditional ones of text and numbers increases the chances of more attention being paid to the subject, more intensive processing and better remembering. The same applies to the addition of audiovisual linguistic, iconic and logico-mathematical modes of communication.
- These chances can be improved even more when the types and modes mentioned are combined in a didactically appropriate way to allow them to be *integrated cognitively* by students.
- This integration enables perhaps the most basic transformation in education. This is the transition from *linear learning to learning by association*. Traditional memorizing of a string of words, facts or figures is an expression of linear learning: trying to bang knowledge into the student's head in bits and pieces. This is an extremely poor and ineffective way of learning. It achieves only some result with young people but not much. The larger part of our brain capacity is not used in this process. Associative learning is a quite different mental activity. (Inter)actively dealing with parts of the course material, which can be not only chopped into pieces but also recombined, has much more effect. Neuro-psychological research shows that the right half of the brain is used more and interacts better with the left half in associative learning, among other things with the help of visual cognition.

  Learning by association is considerably supported by the rise of hypertext and hypermedia. Learners are no longer confined to the content of a particular book or other source. Provided that they know exactly what they are looking for – a condition unfortunately not often met – the Internet offers an abundance of sources for associative learning.

Shortcomings in education At the time of writing (2005), these opportunities are barely used in educational systems, not even when a school has sufficient new media and computers at its disposal. A lot of preliminary work has to be done first. New course material will have to be made and adapted to the didactical concepts outlined above. Furthermore, a lot of didactical and psychological research will have to be conducted. Only good new course material and an improvement in teaching methods will convince teachers of the potential benefits of multimedia education and motivate them to learn and explore it. Large-scale retraining will be necessary. These are merely the most important conditions. Chapter 10 contains more policy perspectives.

THE SOCIAL PSYCHOLOGY OF CMC

Approaches in CMC research Next to human–computer interaction, CMC is the most intensively investigated field of new media research in psychology and communication science. This field immediately drew the attention of many researchers, as CMC was accused of being *asocial* (i.e. cold and unfriendly) and even *antisocial* (diminishing face-to-face interaction). Thurlow et al. (2004: 47) summarize that it was held to be 'impoverished, impersonal, ineffectual and emotionally cold'. In the first period of CMC research, the 1970s and 1980s, the so-called *deficit approaches* to CMC (2004: 48) were the most popular. The accompanying theories have already been introduced in Chapter 1: social presence theory, reduced social context cues theory and information or media richness theory. These theories emphasized the objective defects of CMC as compared to face-to-face communication, which was considered to be the norm and the best quality of communication.

In the 1990s, the deficit approach was severely criticized by the so-called *social information approach*. The theories concerned were also discussed in Chapter 1: the social information processing model, the relational perspective and social identity theory. They stressed that users of CMC compensate for potential technical limitations in actual, information-rich social environments. They accomplish this by great subjective creativity in human communication elaborating all existing CMC cues and adding other cues. According to the social information approach CMC is all but asocial and antisocial: It might be very personal, even hyper-personal, and it helps to build social relationships online and offline.

I want to summarize some of the main results of both approaches of CMC research under the labels of the following five characteristics:

1 technological dependence;
2 assets and deficits for interpersonal communication;
3 group dynamics;
4 participation and decision-making;
5 standards and netiquette.

CMC is very much dependent on technology. This applies even more to CMC than to the old media of telecommunication and surface mail. In Chapter 5, I discussed the vulnerability of networks in great detail. Computer meetings, video conferencing, email and videophony are obviously more vulnerable than traditional surface mail and telephony. The more use is made of computers, complicated switches and video media, the greater the chances of a partial or even complete technical failure of the conversation. It only takes a defective microphone or camera, a wrong communication protocol or a slow switching/processing unit to cause great damage to the entire conversation process. Although such malfunctions do not occur very often, they are always unexpected and hard to repair.

Vulnerability of networks

A second aspect of technical pressure on all mediated conversation is a lower capacity of adaptation to the environment. In traditional meetings, participants are able to repair bad conditions for conversation immediately, for instance by altering the pitch of the conversation and by repositioning furniture, changing seats, closing doors or windows, and so forth. In electronic meetings, most conditions are fixed. Participants are tied to their equipment in all sorts of ways (see Johansen et al., 1979: 24). A third aspect is the pressure of 'having to be available at any given place and time', caused by the new conversation media. This causes an increase not only in *time pressure*, but also in the *pressure to communicate* as a matter of course. Although the new media also offer opportunities to block or to not engage in online conversation and to wait with replies in asynchronous communication, their overall effect is to enlarge the pressure of communication at any place and time. The availability of these media also increases everyone's expectations of each other's communication behaviour. In computer meetings, for instance, quick and well-considered answers are expected (Kiesler et al., 1984: 1125). Most often, the people and devices involved cannot meet these expectations.

Lower adaptive ability and pressure of availability

Finally, we can point out the *lower sense of responsibility* of groups for a communication process that is so much determined by technology. The burden of taking the initiative of starting and maintaining the communication is left to the technical medium much more than would happen in face-to-face communication (Johansen et al., 1979: 24).

Reduced responsibility

Assets and deficits for interpersonal communication

Technical mediation of parts of the communication process causes the following *extension* of facilities being perfected in CMC (Weingarten and Fiehler, 1988: 59–60):

Extensions enabled by CMC

1 Communication partners do not have to be present in the same location.
2 They do not have to communicate at the same time (synchronously).
3 Computers or media can partially or completely replace humans as conversation partners.
4 The mental processing required for conversation can be replaced (partially) by information processing devices.

The last facility enables users to involve external sources (knowledge, advice) in the conversation process. Users no longer depend on their communication partners' direct knowledge. Teleconferences can receive the assistance of databanks and knowledge systems.

When the new media turn to broadband transmission for a simultaneous transfer of images, sounds, text and data, they can open up communication channels more widely than ever before.

Limitations of CMC Compared with face-to-face communication, each new medium imposes its own *limitations* on communication channels. As we have seen, some modes of communication are given room, others are not. The nonverbal mode of communication, body language in particular, is restricted most in CMC. This mode is transferred only in video conferencing and in videophony, albeit in a limited and altered form. Here kinetic communication is very limited. It has been known for a long time from experimental research that small images of, for instance, faces in videophony give few more cues than sound telephony; much larger images, on the other hand, will increase cues (Midorikawa et al., 1975). Sign language on a screen comes across differently: it is emphasized and gestures may appear undesirably aggressive (Johansen et al., 1979: 56).

These limitations make it hard to build a good relationship with, and confidence in, conversation partners. Preferably, they already exist when CMC is used. Teleconferences and email are not suitable for getting to know people or for problematic conversations (for instance, in the case of a conflict). They serve best when the participants already know each other and have a good (business or personal) understanding. Computer meetings (synchronous) and email (asynchronous) are suitable for the exchange of information, opinions and orders, for asking questions, maintaining existing contacts and generating ideas (Vallee, 1978). Apart from face-to-face meetings, video conferencing is the most suitable medium for complex communication tasks in interpersonal communication. However, high-quality channels for video conferencing still are very costly and not widely available. Most often only a small number of groups with a limited size can take part, and not all participants can be seen simultaneously. For most business purposes, email, instant messaging and audio meetings are more efficient and cheaper alternatives.

Compensation for limitations The consequences of these limitations need to be qualified in three ways. In the first place, it is remarkable how well people are capable of compensating for missing cues in images, sounds, text and data by using other cues. In a telephone conversation, most people prove capable of compensating for the lack of visual and nonverbal signs by making subtle adaptations to their conversation style (Fielding and Hartley, 1987). Fielding and Hartley draw the conclusion that ordinary human communication is much more flexible and robust than is expected by most people. It can cope with considerable decline in quality before normal patterns of communication break down (1987: 121). After all, we are dealing with the *totality* of cues people derive from information, even when it is only partial.

Similar effects occur in CMC. Compared to face-to-face communication it often does not perform worse in formal task performance, quality of decisions and social or group influence and social or personal attraction attained (Chun and Park, 1990; Dennis and Kinney, 1998; Postmes and Spears, 1998; Spears et al., 2001; Walther, 1996, 1997). Performance strongly depends on contextual factors that work in both types of communication: how much the participants know each other and have already used other media reaching each other, the type of group and the task or activity concerned and the whole social and organizational context.

The second qualification is connected to the first. In their comment on the social presence and reduced social context cues approaches, Spears and Lea (1992) have claimed that users involve all of their social, cultural and personal identities when participating in computer-mediated communication. Mantovani has put it this way: 'The social world is not only outside but also inside people, as part of their individuality, and functions even when they sit – physically alone – in front of their computer screens' (1996: 99). Limitations are to be compensated for by the use and amplification of *available* cues. If this is true, the social identity of individuals and groups is more likely to be stressed than to be reduced in CMC.

A third important qualification is the fact that limitations of communication channels are not by definition a disadvantage. They enable the user to gain more control. (Conversely, a lack of privacy and control is one of the reasons for the failing acceptance of the videophone until now.) A cause of the enormous success of the (audio) telephone is the limitation of this medium. It enables users to have a more or less personal conversation without exposing themselves completely to the other person. Computer conferences and email enable anonymous communication. In these media, business conversation can be carried out without social obligations or distractions. Furthermore, a limitation to one or two types of data enables concentrated mental processing. In computer conferences and email, participants can concentrate fully on the text and the data, and they are able to consider these things for longer when communication runs asynchronously. Moreover, experienced computer users tend to reach full expression, while people in meetings keep many things to themselves.

Group dynamics

In comparison with face-to-face meetings, conversation in the new media is usually at a disadvantage when it comes to coordinating communication.

Coordinating communication

In the first place, participants contribute much more as they can 'talk' simultaneously. A second reason is the lack of nonverbal cues. The communication process is extremely vulnerable in its technical mediation.

> Electronic communication can be inefficient when it comes to solving problems concerning coordination, such as letting someone who is explaining something to you, know you already have this information. ... Terminals and electronic signals offer less historic, contextual and non-verbal cues. Electronic media do not effectively transfer nuances concerning meanings and frames of reference. (Kiesler et al., 1984: 1125–6)

Coordination problems apply in particular to computer conferencing and email, especially when they are used asynchronously. Direct feedback is greatly missed. In audio or video conferencing or in a conversation by telephone, these deficiencies are partly overcome spontaneously. Ending the contribution and taking turns is accomplished in extremely subtle ways.

Leadership   Coordination problems are different for each medium of CMC, but they do have some general consequences. People need more time to build and maintain group organization (Weston et al., 1975). Natural leadership is created far less easily in CMC group sessions (Kiesler et al., 1984). This is one of the reasons why much more time is needed to reach mutual understanding (see below). In CMC, coordination and leadership have to be introduced artificially. The chairmanship and technical organization of teleconferences have to meet many more demands than in face-to-face meetings. Moreover, many teleconferences are controlled by programs, otherwise all sorts of subjects and lines of discussion get mixed up.

Order   For all these reasons, communication sessions in CMC, with the exception of more individual CMC media such as email or billboards and completely informal CMC media such as electronic chatting, are more orderly than in face-to-face meetings, as was observed a long time ago by Johansen et al. (1979: 23). Even so, contributions made in electronic groups and forums are less inhibited (McLaughlin et al., 1995; Joinson, 1998; Joinson, 2001). This might lead to more self-disclosure (Joinson, 2001). However, uncontrolled outbursts also occur regularly. This is called *flaming* (Joinson, 1998; O'Sullivan and Flanagin, 2003; Wallace, 1999). It runs the risk of prematurely ending the conversation by argument or by participant drop-out.

Another striking phenomenon in CMC groups discussing a particular issue is *group polarization* (Spears and Lea, 1992; Wallace, 1999). This occurs when the members of the group feel some sense of group identity. While the drive to come together regularly prevails in face-to-face groups with common identity, individual leanings towards one of the extreme group views intensify in CMC groups. When people participate in CMC discussion groups without identification with the group, for example in large-scale Internet discussions, 'the isolation, deindividuation, and physical distance typical of the Internet make them ignore the group's views and go their own way' (Wallace, 1999: 78). In both conditions, with or without group identification, general conclusions, from consensus to majority decisions, are difficult to reach.

Participation and decision-making

Until the 1990s, most social psychologists were convinced that status, power and prestige had a smaller chance of affecting CMC than traditional communication. The more limited a communication channel, the more the necessary context cues and nonverbal behaviour cues are lost (Edinger and Patterson, 1983) and the more the remaining cues become important (Lea, 1992). Taking this into account, it is no surprise that participation in well-organized mediated group conversations appeared to be more equal than in (similar) face-to-face conversations in laboratory contexts. This opinion was backed by extensive experimentation (see for instance Finholt and Sproull, 1987; Johansen et al., 1979; Kiesler et al., 1984; Vallee et al., 1975).

It is well known that face-to-face meetings with a particular task in organizational contexts are often dominated by one person or a few people. In contrast, it turned out that people who usually keep quiet contributed more to electronic group conversations (see Finholt and Sproull, 1987: 221 for instance). And research also indicated that women were more forthcoming in electronic meetings, particularly in meetings mediated by computers (Turoff, 1989: 115). The result of this removal of traditional barriers in electronic conversation was held to represent an equalization of participation and influence in discussions. The presumed key for it was the *emphasis on content*, as the lack of cues prevents all kinds of (status) distractions.

This common view among psychologists in the 1970s and 1980s was countered by a clearly different situation outside the laboratory in less organized large-scale Internet conversations. In discussion lists or electronic chatting groups on the Internet, everyone could observe a lack of participation and equality among the unlimited number of potential members addressed and a lack of central moderation of discussion, leading to anarchy and the rule of the hard core instead of democracy. The dominant practice is that a relatively small core of people dominate the discussion, while the majority contribute only once in a while or just read the contributions of others (e.g. Rojo and Ragsdale, 1997).

The practice of Internet discussions and email, collaboration and discussion in real organizational settings outside the laboratory has cast doubt on the presumed equalizing effects of electronic conversation. Bikson et al. (1989) tried to show that CMC generally tends to strengthen existing patterns of hierarchy, status and interaction in organizations instead of creating new ones. Rice (1998) even expressed the view that CMC increased rather than decreased status differences in real organizational contexts. Research by Saunders et al. (1994) on the use of teleconferences in health care and research by Scott and Easton (1996) on the equality of participation in group decision support systems revealed a persistence and even a reinforcement of status barriers. Smith et al. (1988) showed that the vast majority of email messages in the organization they investigated were addressed within the same divisions and hierarchical levels. The same conclusion was reached by Lux Wigand (1998) ten years later when email had become a widespread medium inside organizations.

Reduced status marks and equalization

A counter view

Doubts on equalization

The most important reasons given for these remaining or increasing status barriers are the lack of accessibility and usability of computer networking and the organizational rules and authorities reinforced by the control of computer programming. Spears (1994) even expressed the view that the apparent freedom of CMC conceals the hidden power of management opposing the privacy and autonomy of employees.

Power is internalized

Mantovani (1996) reaches the conclusion that on most occasions, electronic democracy in organizations is a myth and that the actual use of CMC is determined by decisive social and organizational contexts. He questions the validity of the laboratory experiments, mainly on American students, of Sproull, Kiesler and others. Spears and Lea (1992) cast doubt on the individualistic assumptions behind their approach. According to Spears and Lea, social power not only comes from outside the individual. Individuals will not be released from group and organizational power in electronic environments. Power is a relational affair and it is internalized in the self- and the group-identities of individuals. When status cues are lacking, people will attach more importance to the remaining cues and to the identities they bring with them in electronic conversations (Postmes and Spears, 1998; Spears and Lea, 1992).

We may conclude that the evidence of more equal participation and influence in electronic conversations is contradictory. Actual social and organizational contexts and the use of particular conversation media (from closed and regulated organizational networks to open and free Internet discussions) appear to be decisive.

Standards and netiquette

Undeveloped standards

Conversation in the new media has not yet developed accepted standards. No socially accepted codes of conduct apply. So, we must be very cautious in generalizing the findings discussed in this section. The limitations of conversation in the new media are not conducive to the creation of group structures with clearly defined standards of behaviour. In computer meetings and in email, formal and informal, public and intimate messages run side by side. People do not yet know how to exchange greetings and other courtesies. The right mixture of politeness and efficiency (speed) is not easily achieved.

Groups not having a close mutual understanding prior to the mediated exchange run the risk of adopting an apparently conflictive and aggressive style. So, one should always ask oneself whether an electronic meeting really is the most effective means. 'In order to be effective, instead of objective, groups may need personal relations, a division in status which helps in choosing between several targets, and a hierarchy which determines possible influence, even if this behaviour obstructs "good" decision-making' (Kiesler et al., 1984: 1127).

Netiquette and identity formation

This does not mean that there are no standards in electronic conversations. They are not widely known and accepted, however, and they are always strongly determined by specific contexts (Spears and Lea, 1992). After some time, groups develop their own standards and language systems, such as so-called *netiquette* for behaviour on the net and *smileys** or *emoticons** as a paralanguage – certain key combinations indicating emotions, such as ☺. Group identity and personalities are able to grow in electronic meetings (Walther, 1992, 1996). CMC may even become 'hyperpersonal' (Walther, 1996); it can become more personal, intimate and friendly than face-to-face communication when people feel closer to the people at the other side of the screen than they usually do in meetings. Sometimes people fight over identities in online environments (Finholt and Sproull, 1987: 18). This is a part of online impression management.

In organizations, new media are also often used for less formal communication. They seem to serve as a safety valve for emotions (Finholt and Sproull, 1987). Paradoxically, in these cases it is the presumed 'impersonality' of the medium that enables intimate communication (see Rice and Love, 1987) – a phenomenon with which we are already familiar in sex lines, electronic personal adverts and the like. In the next section, I try to resolve this apparent contradiction.

CHANGES IN THE HUMAN PERSONALITY?

Several authors expect interaction with computers and other media to change human personality in the long run. They might be right. Still, their expectations are extremely speculative, although they are supported by some empirical research. The oldest examples are the interviews Sherry Turkle (1984) conducted with 400 computer users, 50 percent of them adults, the other 50 percent children. The results were used for her book *The Second Self: Computers and the Human Spirit*. More recent examples can be found in contemporary social-psychological research. Such research shows, for instance, how people with certain personality characteristics are attracted to mediated communication (see below). Finally, we can refer to research on mass communication, which has always been engaged in establishing the influence of media on the human spirit.

The main starting point in this section is the universal approach of ICT in using names derived from the human mind and human communication. This anthropomorphization (humanization) of technology can easily lead to technical influences on humans and their personalities. It is well known that people tend to approach computers as if they are partners instead of devices. Reeves and Nass (1996) have published a large number of experimental cases indicating the *media equation* that media experience equals real life, as people treat media like real people and places. People consider contact with a computer to be a dialogue, and technically mediated interaction with and through other media to be full human communication. This anthropomorphization of computers and media is very understandable. At least three fundamental reasons can be given (Brown, 1986: 459ff.; Suchman, 1987: 10ff.; Turkle, 1984: 281ff.):

Anthropomorphosis of technology

- The technologies concerned are *non-transparent*. Computers are like closed black boxes. Large-scale networks are opaque to most people. Even if one sees through the structure of these technical complexes (something far more difficult in micro-electronic devices than in mechanical ones), this still does not clarify their functions, for computers and other new media are reprogrammable and multifunctional. So, these new technologies cannot be compared with the old ones to serve as a basis for insight.
- These technologies appear as *autonomous units responding to questions and commands*. The tendency to talk about devices and even to devices (such as cars and cameras) using terms derived from communication with humans is intensified.
- These technologies respond as *intelligent equipment/software*. They are *logical* units operating with a *linguistic* mode of communication. They work with languages themselves, and interact with humans. It is no surprise that humans get the impression they are dealing with units similar to the human mind. This impression will be strongly reinforced as soon as speech recognition, spoken output and biometrics (enabling recognition of the user by a computer) enter the world of computer technology on a mass scale.

Humanization of human–computer relations

The result is a humanization of the *relationship* between humans and computers or other new media. Three phenomena are observed over and over again (see Reeves and Nass, 1996; Turkle, 1984):

1 The relationship is *personalized*. People handle computers as if they are other humans. Consulting help utilities or information services gives the impression of a dialogue with a human service provider. During an electronic conversation, people unconsciously compensate for the limitations and impersonality of communication taking place.

2 The relation becomes *binding, fascinating or even addictive* to humans, because they have far greater *control* over these relations than over relationships with other humans. A whole series of psychological needs can be fulfilled (to be discussed later). The binding and sometimes even addictive relationships of humans with computers and existing mass media are well-known phenomena.

3 A *partnership* develops between humans and computer/media. People consider computers to be partners fulfilling several psychological and social needs. A computer is a powerful projective medium (cf. Turkle, 1984): it is a second self, it can be used by humans to project a (desirable) other identity onto it. Subsequently they are able to communicate with this safe environment created by themselves. A related characteristic of computers and other media such as radio and TV is their well-known social function of serving as a substitute for company.

Changes in language

In humanizing their relationships with ICTs, humans submit themselves to technology without knowing it. This is most obvious in *language*. We are referring not only to the increasing use of technical jargon, but also to changes in 'normal' language. In human–computer interaction and in email and computer conference conversations, the number of words used decreases, the sentence structure becomes more rigid, the number of abbreviations, stopgaps and half-finished sentences increases, and the expressions of emotions become less rich and varied (see Wallace, 1999: 9–12). Other examples are to be found in word processing, which appeared to have a fragmenting effect on messages right from the start (Heim, 1987).

The consequences are most severe in processes of making *social contacts*. Technology allows strong control in making contacts and turn-taking in ensuing communication. These processes can be planned more than ever before. A likely consequence is a reduction in the number of chance meetings in and by the media of the network society. Of course, surfing on the Internet and clicking or responding to hyperlinks and addresses still offer opportunities for surprise, chance and adventure, in the same way that people previously ran into unexpected programmes and content in the overwhelming supply in the old media of allocution and consultation. However, one is not forced to pay attention. The supply is overabundant and there is absolutely no social pressure prompting people to pay attention. Therefore, future uses of personal information agents will block unexpected and unselected contacts and content. The most likely result will be that social relations will become more pragmatic, businesslike and rationalized. Another effect might be a decay of traditional social skills, such as responding flexibly to chance meetings in the public sphere.

Social contacts

A similar phenomenon is the booming popularity of *online dating*. This is a good example of the increasing selectivity and control potential of online social contact. Here the fancy romantic ideal of finding 'the only one' by chance is replaced by a more businesslike search for potential partners with particular characteristics. Of course, chance meetings also occur in online dating, as the number of potential contacts is much bigger than in the offline world, but the online dating software immediately reduces this number to manageable proportions. It appears that partners with similar characteristics, attitudes and ideas are (even) more attractive in online than in offline dating (Wallace, 1999: 141–2). Online dating makes things easier for finding someone attractive (Thurlow et al., 2004: 140); it stimulates efforts to be attentive to partners and to disclose oneself. However, it also is easy to drop out of an online relationship and immediately or simultaneously start another. In the long run this may shorten the life span of romantic and sexual relationships. After some time, the traditional skills of courting and flirting may be lost and replaced by skills of online impression management.

Online dating

John Naisbitt (1982) once stated that human needs and opportunities for social contact will increase as technology develops further. He used the expression 'high tech, high touch'. The problem is, however, that communication technology can serve not only as a mediator, but also as a substitute for social contact. Apparently, this technology relieves loneliness. How can loneliness survive 'in a world where the choice of media contacts with another person is always possible' (Gumpert, 1987: 189)? In order to answer

Loneliness

such a big question, one must realize that the initiative in making contacts is placed increasingly on the individual in the network individualization characterizing the network society. The individual will have to negotiate continuing communication. Some will succeed; others will fail. Perhaps this (partly) explains the astonishing fact of increasing loneliness in modern western society, according to countless social surveys, while the number of media at the disposal of this society grows and grows. Mediated communication with familiar people and with strangers is often no satisfactory substitute, as to some it produces a gnawing feeling of remoteness and asynchronicity of communication (1987: 186). For others, it may be intimate, personal and even hyper-personal (see above). However, in spite of the advantages of online personal relationship building and maintenance at large distances, many modern people continue to long for small-scale face-to-face communication in dense social networks and close-knit communities (1987: 167ff.).

Personality changes The impact of technology on human language and communication may lead to personality changes in the long term. At best, the increase of opportunities for information and communication will contribute to *a universally developed personality*. In the worst case, these changes may lead to the four related personality types described below.

Rigid personality The first could be called the *rigid or formalistic personality*. People working frequently with computers or other media and, in doing so, being constantly confronted with the changes in language and (coarsening) manners described above, may start to make the same demands on natural communication with their fellow humans as they do on technically mediated communication. For instance, they might get annoyed with vague, ambiguous and incomplete, in other words normal, human language. They could become irritated by chatter and communication with no clear direction or goal except in places that are explicitly designed for this type of communication such as online chatting and instant messaging. In the end, they might only be satisfied by the quick and clear answers they are used to receiving from their computers or information services (see Kubicek and Rolf, 1985: 259 for these speculations). In interpersonal communications, these people might desire the same extent of control they have gained over their relationship with computers/media. If the other person does not wish to meet the demands made, the rigid personality will withdraw and return to the safe, self-created environment of his/her 'second self':

> But if the sense of self becomes defined in terms of those things over which one can exert perfect control, the world of safe things becomes severely limited because those things tend to be things, not people. Mastery can cease to be a growing force in individual development and take on another face. It becomes a way of masking fears about the self and the complexities of the world beyond. People can become trapped. (Turkle, 1984: 124)

Computerized personality A second type, often combined with the first, could be called the *computerized personality*. When the popular comparison between the human brain and the computer is taken too literally, some people may start considering the human brain to be a series of parallel connected processors and the personality to be programmed and reprogrammable software. In her research among the first generation of computer users, Sherry Turkle found several indications pointing in this direction. Users defined their personalities in terms of the differences and similarities with computers (and computer programs).

A third type could be called *the unsocial personality*. Computers and other media serve as a safe substitute for direct human company. This applies in particular to all those people who, for some reason or other, are afraid of intimacy, or rather, who want to gain more control over it.

Unsocial personality

> Terrified of being alone, yet afraid of intimacy, we experience widespread feelings of emptiness, of disconnection, of the unreality of self. And here the computer, a companion without emotional demands, offers a compromise. You can be a loner, but never alone. You can interact, but never feel vulnerable to another person. (Turkle, 1984: 320)

Turkle (1984: 216–17) also observed computer hackers, particularly male hackers, fleeing from direct contact with other humans. In email and during computer conferences, the more silent, introverted participants have appeared to come out very well (Kiesler et al., 1984; Turoff, 1989). One can only guess at the types of personality among people calling sex lines or practising some kind of erotic conversation using web-cams. In any case, the new media offer a lot of opportunities for 'intimate strangers'.

Our final speculative type is the *multiple personality*. The Internet and many computer games enable us to play several roles and to assume several other identities by taking on pseudonyms. A game or simulation, such as a multi-user dungeon or domain (MUD) is based on these opportunities. Seriously playing with identities is a typical activity of modern society. Here, for the first time in history, people are not simply offered a fixed personality, but have to partly shape their own personalities (Giddens, 1991b). Coolen (1997) claims the use of several identities on the Internet holds a mirror to our eyes. In this mirror, a modern view of people and the world is projected. This reality is not merely counterfeit, for modern identities are not fixed in advance. In modernity, personalities become more multiple as some parts of our identities are revealed in some social contexts and other parts in others.

Multiple personality

Sherry Turkle (1995; 1996a; 1996b) believes the positive side of MUDs and all kinds of role-playing on the Internet is the chance to experiment with our identities, as much as we like, and to find an answer to the question: who am I? Adolescents, in particular, could benefit from this. The negative side of this play for the construction of even more identities is the fact that it does not help us very much in real life. Habitual searching for one's actual multiple identity already causes existential doubt (Giddens, 1991b). The problem with these Internet creations and games lies in the fact that *this reality does not offer any resistance* (Coolen, 1997). It offers safe environments (see above). Users are not corrected and they can assume another identity when they want to.

A continuing development of these personality types and the advance of the technical capabilities of ICT and biotechnology may turn humans into some sort of *cyborgs*. This term links *cyber*netics with the human *org*anism.

Cyborgs

This combination results in a system of human and technical components increasingly regulating itself within the environment and constituting a new whole. Little by little this technology is taken out of the sphere of science fiction and films such as *Robocop* and *Blade Runner* and adopted in reality (see Featherstone and Burrows, 1996; Thomas, 1996). Cyborgs are humans integrated in technology and technologies integrated in humans. It is a fact that people are more and more often equipped with artificial limbs and other technical devices, carrying them around everywhere and even inside their bodies. On the previous pages, the potential consequences of humanizing technology and of technology taking over more and more functions from humans have been described. The influence of ICT on humans must be greater than that of any other instrument. After all, it is an 'intelligent' technology having a direct impact on the human mind. Thus the means of ICT come closer and closer to the human brain. In the future, ICT devices will be located not only in front of us, but also on and even inside our heads or bodies. Try to imagine what the mental consequences might be if, in 50 years' time, humans carry around a miniature but extremely powerful multimedia computer in the shape of a head installation for 24 hours a day. A simple oral command processed by voice recognition would suffice to literally see each image or piece of information desired projected in front of their eyes (through glasses) or perhaps even directly on the retina through an implant chip. This extremely personal computer would serve not only as a second self, but also become a part of our 'first self', increasingly entering our deepest and most intimate personalities. When this time comes, we humans have to know who we are, what makes us different from machines such as computers, and, even more importantly, who we want to be. Otherwise one of our strongest capabilities, the ability to adapt quickly to our environment, will turn into a submission to a technology we would at present call inhuman.

CONCLUSIONS

- In the new media, the historical transition from direct experience to mediated perception is continued. Learning by action is gradually replaced by learning through symbol systems and visual models. This produces shifts in our modes of symbolic communication and the mental skills we need. Within the linguistic mode, the audiovisual variant is gaining importance at the expense of the oral and written variants. The growing use of graphics emphasizes the iconic mode and the use of computer language the logico-mathematical mode of symbolic communication. The nonverbal mode has become less important, at least in new media without high-quality moving images. However, the most basic trend is the integration of modes in the multimedia.
- The ability to benefit fully from all the opportunities of the new media demands a full-grown visual, auditive, verbal, logical and analytical mental development. The problem is that the new media do not have to

be used optimally. The integration of modes of communication also enables a much shallower use. In this case, there is less development of digital skills and knowledge gaps or usage gaps appear.

- To evaluate the meaning of the new media for human cognition we have to know that there are human–computer similarities and differences because the new media work on the basis of digital computer technologies. The similarities intensify the phenomenon of humanization of our interaction with computers and the differences explain the numerous frictions in human–computer interaction. A similarity is that both humans and computers are information processing creatures. Differences are that computers apply a context-free and fragmentary perception and cognition that are completely pre-programmed. Computers use fixed schemata and they only achieve artificial 'intelligent' learning, without willpower, drive or emotion. Computers follow instructions, while humans make selections according to their needs. Evidently, computers are not biological and social creatures.

- The new media characteristics of interactivity and integration (multimedia, hyperlinks) enable types of learning far superior to the traditional ones. For instance, linear types of learning things by heart are partly replaced by associative types of learning.

- CMC has been accused of being asocial (i.e. cold and unfriendly) and even antisocial (diminishing face-to-face interaction). In the 1980s, the so-called deficit approaches of CMC prevailed: it was supposed to be poor, revealing insufficient cues and social presence compared to face-to-face communication. In the 1990s, deficit approaches were criticized from the point of view of social information processing. Critics stressed that users of CMC are able to compensate for technical limitations to produce actual, information-rich social environments. In this way, CMC might become personal, even hyper-personal, and help to build social relationships online and offline.

- Whether the new media are able to change our personalities is a speculative issue. It is certain that our relationships with these technologies are humanized. They are personalized, they are binding, fascinating or even addictive and they might even become our 'second self' in identity building. When humans are directly connected to computer technology, they come close to being cyborgs and our imprint in these media might even become a first self. Less speculative impressions are that very intensive new media use is able to change our use of language, our social relationships, our view of the world and even our multiple identities in (post)modern society.

CONCLUSIONS AND POLICY PERSPECTIVES

This final chapter starts with the general conclusions of this book. What is the significance of the network society concept? Does it overrule other classifications of society? What is the meaning of the main observation that networks pervade all spheres of contemporary developed societies? Have networks become their basic units? When networks shape such basic (infra)structures: can they be changed by people or should they be considered as some kind of natural laws?

The tenor of the second section is that they are not natural laws, because, here, the more or less conscious design of the information and network society in the most important parts of the world is analysed. A number of models of views of the information society are compared. We will notice many similarities, but we will also see that the differences between these parts of the world are growing with the immersion of ICT in their societies.

The final section of this book deals with a number of general policy perspectives linked to the analysis contained in the book. Seven crucial strategic characteristics of the introduction of networks will be discussed: access, security, design, control, legality, returns and content. This will be done against the background of explicit social values such as freedom, democracy and material or spiritual welfare.

Network society defined

In Chapters 1 and 2, network society was defined as a form of society increasingly organizing its relationships in media networks, which are gradually replacing or complementing the social networks of face-to-face communication. This means that social and media networks are shaping the prime *mode of organization* and the most important *structures* of modern society. They are not the whole *substance* of society, as they are in the exaggerations of Manuel Castells (1996, 1997, 1998; see van Dijk, 1999). Society still consists of individuals, pairs, groups and organizations. Of course, they establish external and internal relations, but these relations do not equal society. The organic and material properties of individuals, pairs, groups and organizations with all their rules and resources cannot be cut out of society in order to return it to a set of essential relationships. Even a totally mediated society where all relations are fully realized by, and substantiated in, media networks, where social and media networks equal each other, would still be based on bodies, minds, rules and resources of all kinds.

The first conclusion of this book is that modern society is *in a process of becoming* a network society, just as it is developing into an information society, a related concept. It is in a transition from mass to network society. In the preceding chapters we were able to identify a network structure in the economy (within and between corporations and on the global electronic market), in politics (the political system) and in society at large (in a combination of unity and fragmentation, inclusion and exclusion, organic and virtual community). A network structure not only pervades these spheres, but increasingly connects them as well: the metaphor of a nervous system of society was seen to be appropriate. For example, global economic networks undermine the central role of the national state in the political system. Virtual communities are a new market in electronic commerce. The selectivity of global electronic networks in the economy aggravates social exclusion.

Transition of mass to network society

Finally, a network structure connects all levels of society, usually called the micro-, meso- and macro-level, or the private and the public spheres. It was noticed that the dividing lines between these abstractions are blurring in reality. On the Internet, interpersonal, organizational and mass communication come together. Using this medium, we bring the 'whole world' into our homes and workplaces. However, the public computer networks used are intruding into our personal privacy here as well. Conversely, the personal autonomy of network users might increase through opportunities of individual choice never previously known in history. The blurring of traditional dividing lines does not result in their disappearance. On the contrary, it means both more integration and more differentiation, as has been observed in several chapters. This is a feature of rising complexity in society.

Network structure pervades society

The second of our main conclusions is that the network structure is a *dual structure*. A combination of scale extension and scale reduction marks all applications of the new media in the economy, politics, culture and personal experience. This combination is the prime advantage and attractiveness of these media. It explains their fast adoption in what was considered to be a communications revolution. A dual structure results in several oppositions explained in the previous chapters: centralization and decentralization, central control and local autonomy, unity and fragmentation, socialization and individualization. To claim that these opposites form a whole and may be observed in both the causes and the effects of new media usage is not the easy assertion of an indecisive author. It is a prime characteristic of network structure itself. Networks both connect and disconnect. They have centres, nodes and relations between them. At these points we find human beings who participate and decide differently and who are central or marginalized, included or excluded.

The dual structure of networks

Network structures are defining and enabling

The dual structure of network use leads to a third main conclusion. This structure should not be reified to the status of an autonomous existence. Structure, action and consciousness or mental states are a dialectic unity, such as that explained in the theory of structuration, for example (see Giddens, 1984). Structures appear in communicative action. This leaves room for agency and consciousness. Dual structures are not natural necessities, but they are both defining and enabling. They offer choices within particular limits. This is the reason why the duality of centralization and decentralization, central control and local autonomy, enables both more and less freedom in using networks and both more and less choice in all kinds of affairs. This is why it is claimed here that the views presented in this book are neither pessimistic nor optimistic. In the context of the huge euphoria accompanying the hypes about the Internet and other new media in the 1990s, they might seem pessimistic, stressing the dark sides of the technology concerned. However, as compared to the voices of disappointment sounding after the collapse of the Internet shares at the stock markets in 2001, they rather are optimistic, proclaiming that the golden age of the 'new economy', the Internet and the network society has yet to come. In fact, a balanced view is needed. In the first decade of the 21st century, new media such as the Internet are gradually appearing to be 'normal media', because they are used by ever larger sections of the population and by those with vested interests in the economy, politics and culture. I hope that a balanced view might be accepted more easily after the upturn and downturn of the Internet in public opinion and with the integration of this medium and other new media in every day life.

The bias of vested interests

There is another reason why those with vested interests should receive major attention anyway. Despite the duality stressed, it must be admitted that there is a certain bias in the uses and effects of ICT. The main actors designing and introducing this advanced and expensive technology are at the top of corporations and governments. They are the investors, the commissioners and the decision-makers. It is to be expected they are using it to strengthen central control, albeit in flexible forms, and to limit personal autonomy and free choices at the bottom of the organization that do not match their interests. It would not be the first time in history that a new medium with radical potential approaches normalcy when it is incorporated in society with its vested interests (see below). In this book, it has been noted several times that ICT is more advantageous for advanced and intelligent forms of central control than old technologies. It is a matter of social and organizational struggle whether the (other) opportunities of ICT to spread decision-making will be utilized.

Media networks as new social environments

The pervasiveness of network structures in modern society is enforced by combinations of social and media networks. Media networks are not simply channels or conduits of communication: they are becoming social environments themselves (Meyrowitz, 1985, 1997). They are settings for social interaction, bridging the individual settings or environments of numerous people acting at their nodes and terminals. Media have their own particular characteristics, which are called communication capacities in this book, but we cannot understand how they work out in practice if we do not learn about the social context of their use and their users. This contextual approach explains the attention to the relationship between mediated and face-to-face communication in this book. The central conclusion is that media networks and mediated communication do not replace social networks and face-to-face communication, but are added to them. They become interwoven, and both will benefit if their strong characteristics are utilized.

The emphasis on context, environment or embeddedness in the analysis of network use has yet another consequence. Popular views about the irrelevance of fundamental dimensions of existence such as time and place in new media networks are not taken for granted. On the contrary, the physical, biological, mental and material conditions of their users and usage are expected to retain their causal effects. Their relevance will even grow, as the new media offer better chances to select and confront directly the different conditions, needs and opinions of their users. Organic, or physical and virtual reality will link up to each other, hopefully to the benefit of both.

Organic and virtual reality are linked

A last conclusion concerns the overall effect of the new media on modern society. Will they have revolutionary implications for society, will they transform society only gradually, or will they have no substantial effect? To put it another way: will the network society be an altogether different type of society? The answers to these questions in this book are that changes will be evolutionary rather than revolutionary and that the network society will not be an altogether different type of society. This does not rule out that current changes are very fast, faster than ever before. In Chapter 7, I argued that the network society is an unstable type of society. In social, economic and media networks, goods, ideas, monetary values, diseases and all kinds of crises are diffused and exchanged quicker than ever.

Evolutionary change

These answers do not oppose the acceptance of the concept of the communications revolution discussed in Chapters 1 and 3. This is a revolution at the level of media development itself. It is not a concept of the revolutionary effects of media on society. On the contrary, the first communications revolution at the turn of the 19th to 20th century, as described by Beniger, was a *consequence* of a revolution – the industrial revolution. In this book, we have frequently observed that the new media intensify trends that have already appeared and reinforce existing social relationships in modern society. The new media are *trend amplifiers*. This comes close to the picture presented by Brian Winston in his *Media Technology and Society* (1998). In a detailed overview of media history from the telegraph to the Internet, he contends that modern media's most important contribution is the so-called 'law of the suppression of radical potential'. New media technologies, which have a revolutionary promise at first, are later moulded to existing social processes. According to Winston, we should not forget that these processes both promote and hinder the adoption of new technologies. It would be interesting to test this 'law' in the development of the Internet from its revolutionary promise in the 1990s to its 'normalization' in the first part of the 21st century.

New media are trend-amplifiers

However impressive and wide-ranging the potential social consequences of the new media, as described in this book, they will not change the foundation of present developed societies, let alone developing societies. Perhaps

ICT has made a contribution to the collapse of the Soviet Union and other communist states, as this technology does not fit traditional bureaucratic authority and planning (see Castells, 1998). However, capitalism is here to stay. It is likely to be reinforced or reinvigorated by the new media in a more effective, flexible and socially harsher shape. Patriarchy may be in crisis in large parts of the world (Castells, 1997), but it will take a very long time before it withers away, and the new media will have only a small, if any, part in that process. Nor will ecological destruction be halted by the new media. At the most, these media contribute to a dematerialization of the economy and to higher efficiency and effectiveness in helping to save natural resources. The globalization of the economy is not caused by, but is intensified by, ICT. It is to be observed that the national state and sovereignty are undermined by the new media, but they will not disappear. Moreover, a concentration of politics in a surveillance state, party state or infocratic state is a possibility as well (see Chapter 5). Rising social and information inequalities are not caused by ICT, but they might be increased by an exclusive appropriation of its opportunities by a relatively minor part of the population. We could carry on in this vein. It seems wiser to continue describing the diverging ways modern societies have tried to fit the advent of this new technology to their existing policies.

THE INFORMATION AND NETWORK SOCIETY IN NORTH AMERICA, EUROPE, EAST ASIA AND THE THIRD WORLD

Design of the information and network society

Is the information and network society created by policy in a conscious way? This appears to be only partly true. The characteristics of this type of society, as described in this book, are rather abstract. They are not clearly visible and proceed in a creeping way. They change the basic structures (networks) and substances (information) of society. So, it is doubtful whether policy makers of all kinds (governments, businesses, community organizations and households) are able to develop the visions required to influence the information or network society. Nevertheless, the more or less conscious and autonomous actions of these kinds of policy makers are really creating the information and network society we are able to observe.

On the other hand, the information and network society lends itself to conscious policy more than previous classifications of society. Information, at least partially, is a conscious activity that leads to other conscious activities such as education policies. Networks are infrastructures that can be built just like roads. So, in theory the information and network society can be designed before it is put into practice. Such designs are actually made in a number of policy perspectives or models for building the information society, the information superhighway, the global information infrastructure or whatever they are called.

In the many designs that have been proposed worldwide in the last 20 years, a number of similarities have appeared. In addition, a number of diverging information society designs have emerged that characterize policies in different parts of the world. I first summarize the similarities and then examine the differences by describing the information and network society policies in North America, Europe, East Asia and the Third World. For the latter, I gratefully adopt the classification of information society models that Shalini Venturelli (1998, 2002) has made in a similar international comparison.

The most important similarity for its real and lasting impact is the historic decision made in most parts of the world to invite *market forces to take the lead* and construct the nervous system of our future societies. In this age of liberalization and privatization, governments have acquired the role of catalyst and protector of social and legal conditions. Building the (infra)structure and providing the content of the information and network society itself and defining all its opportunities and effects has largely been left to business enterprise. This applies to the policy of every country, from the complete dominance of corporate interests in the United States, through the somewhat stronger public–private partnership in Europe, to the strong stimulus of the developmental states in East Asia (to be explained below).

Similarities in policy perspectives

In this time of cuts in public expenditure, the level of economic investment by governments themselves is low. Most often they do not even have a plan or vision about the shape and nature of a coherent information infrastructure. Therefore business corporations construct this infrastructure according to their own interests and expectations (see Brown, 1997). The governments, perhaps, make corrections afterwards by enforcing competition, interconnection and common standards.

A second similarity is the nature of national policy initiatives and action plans: they are essentially *economic projects*. The predominant intention is to improve nations' positions on the global markets of the future. Clearly, this is a part of the economic race between North America, western Europe and East Asia. This means that the economic aspects always come first and the social aspects second or nowhere at all.

A related point of agreement is the *technological determinist nature* of most perspectives and the *supply-side orientation* of the economics concerned. The focus is on infrastructure rather than on the content and the services that the new media are supposed to deliver. The fast diffusion of ICT, and in its wake the information society, are seen as inevitable. The opportunities are simply too attractive to be refused by corporate and household consumers. They just have to adopt the new media. These expectations have been backed by a series of hypes following one after another: first the Internet in general, then e-commerce and finally broadband and wireless communications.

All policy perspectives adopted by national governments and international bodies and conferences after 1993 clearly are a matter of *promotional action*. The technology concerned was developing for decades and nothing special happened at the beginning of the 1990s. In fact, the Internet and other new media meant nothing to the vast majority of Americans, Europeans and other populations at that time. Launching the so-called information superhighway or national information infrastructure was a matter of raising awareness among corporations and citizens about things to come. Almost every developed country in the world adopted an action plan to support the construction, regulation and promotion of this new infrastructure.

In the 1990s, the things to come were presented in *grand visions* of the immense potential benefits of this technology to the societies and economies concerned. The opportunities were emphasized rather than the risks. The information revolution would produce economic growth, new jobs, better education, a higher quality of life, environmental protection by savings on travelling and energy and a boost to more direct types of democracy. Approaching the risks was a matter of courage and of regulatory protection of universal access, safety, privacy and intellectual property rights.

At the end of the 1990s, propaganda and wild expectations gradually gave way to a more sober view of the information society. In these years, the new media slowly entered social and economic life, producing real problems requiring solutions that were different from the early expectations. After the turn of the century and the collapse of the Internet hype, this trend intensified. Eventually, age-old differences between countries with regard to their economic, social and political systems and cultures drifted to the surface again.

United States The United States reveals the similarities just described in the clearest way. It is the guiding country in the design of information highway plans, products and services. Presumably, it will be the first to be a full-grown information and network society. The country is the main centre of ICT on the global market and it still dominated the Internet with the largest proportion of hosts and connections in 2005. It is leading the market in software and services and, to a lesser extent, (network) hardware.

So, it is no surprise that the centrality of business interest and private initiative with regard to the new media is strongest in the United States. However, according to Venturelli (1998, 2002) this focus manifests itself through three rather different, competing American information society models or 'socio-political frameworks': the libertarian model, the liberal market model and the public interest model.

US libertarian model The libertarian tradition in the US has been dominant among the designers and early adopters of the Internet right from the start – (see the discussion of the libertarian view of democracy in Chapter 5). Its point of departure is the concept of minimal state influence and a maximum of initiative and regulation by citizens, consumers and businesses using ICT themselves. In this view, 'the information networks of a society should be open and non-proprietary, with strict constraints placed upon state intervention' (Venturelli, 2002: 71). It is averse to control, regulation or monopolization of the information society from above. Conflicts should be resolved by consensus or agreement by the network users themselves in self-regulation. The roots of this tradition can be found in the typical American perspective of the perpetual New Frontier, the continuous conquest of new space, in this instance 'cyberspace'.

Although the early days of the Internet are over, the libertarian model persists in the continuous struggle by many Internet business advocates, academics and electronic pressure groups in the United States for open architectures and open source software, for the preservation of fair use rights for intellectual property and for new business models in the Internet economy.

Far more influential, and in fact dominating the American information and network society policy is the US liberal market model. This is backed by all large business interests and their representatives in the US government, who also argue for a minimum of state intervention, but they simultaneously ask for a 'powerful legal regime guaranteeing contractual and proprietary rights in the market place' (Venturelli, 2002: 73). In this respect, the liberal market model opposes the libertarian model, which advocates open sources and fair use rights. Another basic difference is an emphasis on legal and market business regulation, while the libertarians propose self-regulation. **US liberal market model**

So, in the liberal market model, the law should protect contracts and property rights. However, anti-trust law is accepted with reluctance, but general laws to protect privacy and consumer interests are rejected. This is the reason why these are so weak in the United States. According to Yao (2003: 433), the prevailing US perspective is to give the market the time to sort out these types of problem themselves and to develop self-corrections. In the long term this would lead to cheaper, better and safer products that would be in the interest of consumers.

The public interest tradition in the United States aims to balance the interests of consumers with those of industry. The markets in the communication sector are not perfect, but they can be improved by regulation covering competition law, fair trade, consumer protection, universal access, educational investment, government investment in innovation, the protection of privacy and of minors, the interconnection of networks and the maintenance of fair use rights, to mention the most important ones (Venturelli, 2002: 72). **US public interest model**

The public interest model is supported by a minority that includes consumer organizations, civil rights organizations, trade unions, people working in the public media, many intellectuals and those who are called 'liberals' in the United States. This model has lost ground in the last 20 years. Most attempts at the regulation described above have not been successful. The universal access obligations in telecommunications are almost the only achievement. These have funded many computer access points in schools, libraries, hospitals, community centres and other public buildings.

The result of the competition between these models is a clear victory for the liberal market model. This has made the United States the most competitive economy in the world in the information and communication sector. However, this has happened at the expense of many public interests and the basis of support for future innovation, because many Americans do not have access to the information infrastructure and lack the digital skills required (van Dijk, 2005; Wilhelm, 2004). Private law and contract law are strongly emphasized but public law has been neglected (Venturelli, 2002: 73). **Market regulation instead of public law**

In the US market, economic freedom in relation to ICT is not matched by comparable cultural, economic and political freedoms for its users. On the contrary, the US record of restricting this freedom in the name of national security and the fight against crime and terrorism is impressive: the Communications Decency Act, the discouragement or ban of encryption, the proposals of key escrow, a clipper chip and a violence chip, the infringement of fair use rights as compared to copyright and the Patriot Act are clear examples that were discussed in Chapter 6.

People claiming civil and public rights often lose their case in the courts against business interests and government security (Catinat, 1997; Miller, 1996). This is mainly due to legal shortcomings: one has to make an appeal either to one of the many specific acts or to the very general constitution (see Chapter 6). A fragmentary legislation full of holes benefits parties with the best lawyers or well-organized interest and pressure groups.

Canada Compared with the United States, the other North American state, Canada, has produced more safeguards against the effects of corporate dominance, for instance in public information supply and privacy legislation (Magder, 1996). In Canada, the public interest model is much stronger. In this way, Canada reveals more the models prevailing in Europe.

Europe In Europe, we have to make a distinction between the EU of 15 member states in the north, west and south of the continent, the 10 (mainly) Eastern European countries that have been added to the EU in 2004 and the rest of formerly communist Eastern Europe. For the EU, the development of the information society is a matter of the highest priority. The EU risks losing the battle of competition on the global information market with North America and East Asia. It lags behind in hardware production, except for telecommunication equipment, in software and in audiovisual productions. It takes a prime position only in the production of local services and so-called multimedia content because of its allegedly rich cultural heritage.

The biggest difference between the United States and Europe is the European tendency towards government intervention to promote and regulate the information society. This tendency considerably declined in the 1990s. However, according to Venturelli, the EU policy, at least, is still a contest among three principal forms of intervention: the EU liberal market model, the EU public service model and the EU national-cultural model.

EU liberal market model Liberalization and privatization substantially changed the European information and communication sector in the 1990s. However, the liberal market model that promoted these changes is rather different from the US liberal market model. European economic neo-liberalism accepts and even expects public intervention in this sector, both by government stimulation and by public law. The European unification project has served as the main legitimation and mandate to accomplish this. In the EU, every policy is subordinate to the task of creating a common market between member states. Information society projects are excellent opportunities for the European Commission, the Council of Ministers and the central directorates to unify Europe with a new mission, to strengthen Europe's position on the world market and to legitimize their own role as coordinating powers of the EU (see Garnham, 1997).

EU public service model The prime European approach to the information society that opposes the liberal market approach is the public service model (Venturelli, 2002: 76–78). This model derives from the tradition of European countries being welfare states. In this model, the government is needed to guarantee the general welfare of citizens and their access to services that are essential to participate in the information society. This means universal access to telecommunications, high standards of privacy protection, recognition of authors' rights and fair use rights, strong competition rules, standards for the quality of networks and their services and public investment in research and innovation, employment, education and health (2002: 77). The EU public service model should not be confused with the US public interest model. The European model aims to safeguard the constitutional rights of *citizens* in an information society by the distribution of public *services*. In the American model, the only government role is to protect by law the *interests* of *consumers* and *small producers* against unregulated big corporate power.

European policies are complicated by a third model, the EU national-cultural model. This model of the information society emphasizes the content to be distributed and exchanged in networks; this content should safeguard, support and enrich the different national cultures in the EU. The model stresses that the national communities are expressive (cultural) instead of economic or political unities (Venturelli, 2002: 78). For this reason the national media are protected against the threats of the global, read 'American', market as regards audiovisual policy, content regulation and program production of the new media.

EU national-cultural model

The struggle between the EU liberal market, public service and national-cultural models has led to an indefinite project to build the information society since the 1990s. It is no surprise that EU information society policies oscillate between broader social concerns, such as social inclusion for all, national considerations and a more technology- and market-oriented focus (Henten and Kristensen, 2000: 83).

Oscillation between models

The provisional result of this competition is that the liberal market model has reached the most dominant position and that for the EU as a whole the information society has mainly been an economic project. Each year the EU spends several billion euros on information society projects. The legislation of the member states is adapted and harmonized to create a stronger economic position, which is urgently needed from a European perspective. The number of people and enterprises with access to computers and networks in the southern and eastern parts of the EU clearly lags behind North America. With regard to innovation, Europe loses the competition with the United States and East Asia (taking hardware into consideration). The so-called 'Lisbon 2000 agenda', to become the most competitive and innovative economy in the world in ten years, has been a miserable failure.

An achievement of the European public service model is a greater civil rights orientation in the information society policy of the EU compared with the United States and, much more clearly, East Asia. The EU has adopted comprehensive privacy legislation that serves as an example for the rest of the world. It has imposed relatively few restrictions on information and communication freedom; and it is friendly towards encryption and the right to anonymity of communication on the Internet. However, with regard to intellectual property rights, it has adopted roughly the same position as the United States, benefiting the copyright industry and harming the public interests of users, libraries and educational institutions. See Chapter 6 for these differences and similarities.

However, a stronger government role, both European and national, has also enabled the EU to emphasize interconnection and open standards and to confront new monopolistic tendencies on the private market. For example, the EU rather than the United States forced the American company Microsoft to launch a version of Internet Explorer without a media player in 2004.

Eastern Europe

Eastern Europe lags behind the (rest of the) EU in the diffusion and development of ICT, even compared with southern Europe. The Eastern European countries keep large state bureaucracies. To stimulate new media development, they have welcomed a wild type of capitalism that is no longer present in the EU. As the governments in these countries lack the means for investment in new technologies, transnational media and telephone companies have jumped into the gap and offered commercial broadcasting and mobile telephony. The initial results have decreased rather than increased access to information channels for the populations concerned, first of all in Russia (Vartanova, 1998). The cause is rising general inequality. Former state provisions in mass media have been dropped. Although they were censored and their quality was rather low, they at least provided information for everybody. Currently, the distribution of computers and network connections is extremely uneven and the gap between major cities and the countryside has been growing since the 1990s (Konvit, 1998; Vartanova, 1998).

Eastern Asia

East Asia (Japan, China, Taiwan, Hong Kong, South Korea, Malaysia and Singapore) is the second largest actor on the global market of information technology after the United States. It is particularly strong in hardware production. In software and information services it is much weaker. The most conspicuous characteristic of East Asia concerning the information and network society is the large role of the state, which is called a *developmental state* by Castells (1998). In Japan, the powerful MITI ministry introduced the Technopolis programme, trying to imitate Silicon Valley in several regions, and the Teletopia programme to install 63 digital cities. In Malaysia, the government paid for the start of the Multimedia Super Corridor Project; in Singapore the government heavily subsidized Singapore One, a nationwide high-speed multimedia network and in South Korea the same was done in the Korea21 Project.

East Asian development model

The East Asian developmental state is not some kind of socialist planning agency (with the partial exception of China). This kind of state accepts the rules of global capitalism and just aims to transform the economic order in the interest of the nation, neglecting or repressing all other interests like information and communication freedoms in civil society (Castells, 1998: 271). It makes strategic and selective interventions in the economy to promote and sustain development, but it leaves the execution to private enterprise. It guides and coordinates the process of industrialization, sets up the necessary infrastructure, attracts foreign capital and decides on priorities for strategic investment (1998: 256).

This view of stimulating the information society is called the East Asian development model by Venturelli (2002: 80–2). Although hardware production is almost completely privately owned, the telecommunication, broadcasting and other media service sectors have largely remained state-owned public monopolies. However, they have served to support industry and the development of the nation as a whole; but they have not encouraged the civil societies in these countries. These are notoriously weak as compared to the EU and the United States. The public media monopolies have not supported a public sphere with broad participation in debate, there is no large proportion of non-commercial public services in support of the building of communities and associations and no 'educational system that cultivates independent judgment instead of rote learning' (2002: 82). Instead, they have curtailed citizens' information rights with restrictive freedom of information laws and public service obligations for information providers.

This state-led development is combined with a liberalized corporate model that appeared with the global shift toward liberalization and democratization in the 1980s and 1990s. The particular shape this shift adopted in East Asia is a corporatist approach that depends on a close cooperation between the large industrial conglomerates competing on the world market, their workforces and the state.

East Asian liberalized corporate model

This role of the state might be very beneficial to the expansion of information technology hardware industries in these countries. In this market, they are extremely successful. However, the logic of the state and of the international market often collide. In the background are East Asian social and cultural values. Family networks and personal relationships organize business enterprise, the state institutions and the links between them. Personal and state protection prevent unfavourable conditions in industry and bad bank loans from resulting in immediate punishment by the market, or independent control and supervision by financial authorities. The problem is not too much protection by the state and financial supervisors, but the wrong protection, biased by proximate private interests.

The second problem is the growing conflict between the developmental state and the information or network society it has brought to life (Castells, 1998: 236). The emphasis on hardware production and diffusion comes at the expense of innovation in software and services, except for the most generally used in e-commerce and Internet service provision (Wong, 2002). The strategy behind this emphasis is a stage approach to development (van Dijk, 2005: 198). The first phase is to boost the industrial production of ICTs that will subsequently lead to a large-scale adoption of ICT by the population at large. The final phase will be the development of digital information skills, information services and advanced innovation. The problem, however, is that the last phase may never arrive, or arrive much later than in other parts of the world.

Lack of innovation in services and software

The conservative and bureaucratic character of the East Asian developmental state does not fit with the continuous innovation, flexibility and openness (debate to improve things) required in a network society. The lack of openness and innovation capacity in developing computer networks is partly caused by restrictions on communication freedom and even outright censorship of the Internet (Wang, 1998).

Third World   The connection of Third World countries to the global information and communication networks is a clear case of combined and uneven development. It is *combined* because any country in the world has connections to the international telephone system, global broadcasting and data networks such as the Internet. In all countries there is a small elite with new media access and experience. The pronoun 'small' is relative, as the elite may consist of millions of people, as is estimated to be the case in India. This elite is working in the cities and nodes that are connected to global networks. Most of the nodes are business and government research centres, financial markets, branches of transnational corporations, software programming departments and defence or security agencies.

However, the development is *uneven* as well, and increasingly so, because the overwhelming majority of the population does not participate at all. It is lagging behind compared with the diffusion of new media in the nodes of their own countries, and even more as compared with the developed countries. This majority has little access even to old media such as the telephone, radio, TV and the press and to essential services such as electricity. Countries such as India and China have experienced a tremendous rise in the use of computers and connections to the Internet. Their rapidly growing middle classes of hundreds of millions of people are already entering the information and network society. However, India and China typically are dual economies. The majority of their populations lags far behind and remains a poor mass society.

A consequence of this combined and uneven development is a subordination of the organic development required in poor countries to the dynamics of the global economy and its networks. The few computers and network connections in developing countries are barely used for applications in agriculture, health, education, public works, water resources, public transportation, public information, population planning, rural and urban land development or public utilities. Instead, they are used by the military, executive branches of government, transnational corporations, banks, major universities and research centres (Sussman, 1997: 248).

This last paragraph refers to the potential strategies of models to develop an information society in the Third World. Venturelli has not discussed the models proposed in this part of the world. I will add four strategies or models (see van Dijk, 2005).

Stage approach   The first strategy is to adopt some kind of stage approach, as in East Asia. This means, first, rolling out the technical infrastructure and promoting a local industry of ICT production and software development. The second stage is to invest in operational digital skills, first for those who need them most and then for the whole population. The final stage is to develop usage applications for the masses. A consequence of this strategy might be that government policy focuses on business access at the cost of equitable access (Kenny, 2002). This strategy joins with globalization policies and with the liberal market models discussed above.

Leapfrogging strategy   A second strategy is an accelerated version of the stage approach. It is considered possible for a Third World country to leapfrog stages of development and go directly to the production of ICT in enclaves of industrial regions linked directly to the world market, as in some East Asian countries and in Costa Rica (chip production) and India, which focuses on software programming (see Steinmüller, 2001 and Press et al., 1999). A technological infrastructure could be built very quickly using wireless technologies and cheap terminal devices (simple computers and mobile phones). James (2003) suggests this road as one of the solutions for the digital divide in the Third World.

The third strategy takes the opposite view of the stage approach. This version contends that Third World countries are able to evolve only gradually from their current stage of development. The massive introduction of ICTs is not a priority at this stage. Instead, all effort should be spent on the improvement of basic material and human resources. This means electricity, transportation, health, traditional education, and old mass media (the press, broadcasting, and the telephone system).

Organic development strategy

The final strategy is a rejection of all stage approaches by suggesting that investment in technical infrastructure, education and all kinds of usage applications should be made in parallel. Mansell and When (1998) have argued that 'the developing societies will need to find ways of combining their existing social and technical capabilities if they are to benefit from the potential advantages of ICTs' (p. 256). Ideally, they say, investment in both capabilities should be undertaken simultaneously, but when this does not appear to be possible, investment in social capabilities should receive priority.

Combination strategy

POLICY PERSPECTIVES FOR THE NETWORK SOCIETY

This book closes with a number of general policy perspectives that can be linked to the conclusions drawn previously. They are general because some kind of action plan is not intended; it would become out of date too quickly. The introduction of networks as the nervous system of our society has seven crucial strategic characteristics: access, security, design, control, legality, returns and content. They will define the framework for every concrete policy that can be proposed. I now describe these characteristics against the background of a number of *explicit social values* that I have determined to be at stake in this book: material and spiritual welfare, social equality, democracy, safety, personal autonomy, information and communication freedom, the quantity and quality of social relationships and the richness of the human mind.

Strategic characteristics of networks

Access

If it is true that networks are becoming the nervous system of our society, access to networks must be the most vital characteristic. No access, or marginal access, simply means social exclusion. In this book, I have argued that people without (sufficient) access will become second-class citizens, consumers, workers, students and community members. However, access is a multifaceted concept: I have distinguished motivational, material, skills and usage access (Chapter 7). How should each of them be accomplished?

The primary kinds of access are motivation and material access. Influencing the motivation to use computers is a complicated process. It requires the improvement of the accessibility and usability of technology. It also calls for regulation and other measures to remove the repellent practices observed by many people when they start to use computers and the Internet. Physical access is the kind that can be realized by policy most directly. Here we can often meet two policy principles: the realization of universal access and universal service.

Universal access

Universal access* simply means the *availability* of a connection to a computer and a network in equal terms for anyone. Universal service* is the availability or supply of *services* everyone needs on this physical infrastructure. Universal access is a condition for universal service. Universal access and universal service taken together may be defined as 'access to a defined minimum service of specified quality to all users independent of their geographical location and, in the light of specific national conditions, at an affordable price' (European Commission, 1996). This telecommunications principle could be extended to the Internet, specifically email, and, within a reasonable term, to broadband connections (Anderson et al., 1995; van Dijk, 1997b). However, up to now, this principle has not been realized anywhere completely. As realization seems to be impossible in the short term, all countries step back to achieve principles of public access. In the developed countries, this means access in schools, libraries, and other public buildings, and in many developing countries, it comes down to an attempt to connect at least every village or city neighborhood in telecentres, kiosks, or Internet cafés.

Universal access to homes is a realistic prospect in most developed societies; here public access (as the only type of physical access for people) can be considered to be a second-hand option that does not enable full participation in the network society. However, in developing countries public access might be the only option for the large majority of the population. Here, places of public access might be fully appropriate as locations to teach digital skills and organize community activities.

Universal service

The telecommunication services needed to use the connection are the first services required for using the physical infrastructure. The other services are those of content. Together, these services can be considered the *basic provisions* of information and communication that every inhabitant of a network society needs:

1   Basic connections: extending universal service of telecommunications to Internet connections, email, and (in a reasonable amount of time) broadband in all infrastructures (telephone systems, cable, and satellite)
2   Public information and communication: government information, vital community information services, and public broadcasting

3   Health information and communication, with basic alarm facilities
4   Compulsory education information: primary and secondary schools provided.

The United States is one of the few countries in the world that has a Universal Service Fund that subsidizes from a small part of the telecommunication tariffs (only) public *access* for schools and libraries – that is, only the connections described in item 1 above. The EU concentrates on public *service*, that is the provisions described in items 2, 3, and 4.

Ultimately, investment in the diffusion of digital skills and in the number and variety of network applications used is more important to improve equal access than realizing the necessary conditions (physical access and universal service). This investment requires a transformation of current educational programs at all levels (basic, secondary, higher and adult education). See Soloman et al. (2002) and van Dijk (2005) for concrete policy instruments in education.

Skills and usage access

Security

When networks become the nervous system of society, their breakdown will cause the organism, that is society, to come to a halt or at least enter a serious crisis. Perhaps the worst of nightmares for sociologists, the breakdown of society could even become real. However, this is only one side of the story. The other is the opportunity for networks to protect the safety of humans, organizations and society as a whole. Alarm and security systems may prove to be a great improvement for the ill, the handicapped and the elderly. Monitoring and registration systems can help to protect the ecological environment and the security of organizations in general and production processes in particular. Internal and external state security are improved by all sorts of registration systems.

Risks reduced

In many respects, we are heading for a society free of risks (Beck, 1992). Networks assist in reducing risks at all levels. States face less surprise (for instance rebellion) because they know more about the mood and the conduct of their subjects. Individual companies are confronted less with overproduction because they have more data about their stock and the daily demand of their customers. Finally, individuals need to communicate less with strangers and unwanted callers or writers because they have greater control over their contacts.

In other respects, the risks for society, organizations and individuals are increased by the use of network technology. This has both a technological and a social dimension. The technological dimension is the ubiquitous threat of a breakdown of critical connections. The social dimension is the potential lack of trust in each other and in network communication people might have when they use online instead of face-to-face communication.

Risks added

Networks prove to be a very vulnerable technology. This risk is clearly underestimated by contemporary governments and business leaderships. They do not take full precautions. Back-up systems are rarely available. In fact, they wait for the next disaster. After the leadership's choice to construct a network or to get access to collective networks, their social unit becomes dependent on a technology full of risks. The pressure of technology on communication processes may increase as well. Sometimes, if there is a malfunction, vital parts of messages are not transmitted and understood anymore.

In Chapter 6, I argued that measures to increase security often have contradictory effects: they might diminish security in other places. Another possibility is that these measures oppose other values. For example, attempts to bring more intelligence in public networks in order to trace the origins, destinations and kinds of messages contained in packets for security reasons (e.g. changing TCP/IP to include *IP Sec*; see Chapter 6) would completely change the character of the Internet as a relatively free and decentralized network. If we want to defend this character, security could best be protected by a connection that itself is as 'empty' as possible, and thus less vulnerable to technical failures, and that has most of its intelligence stored in the terminals. After all, they are interchangeable and they can be controlled locally. The same applies to small-scale networks that can be interconnected, instead of large-scale networks. It is doubtful whether current governments and business interests will choose the latter option. Anyway, this will make it perfectly clear that these apparent technical choices are in fact political decisions.

Design

Networks are not the inborn nervous system of societies as they are for human beings. They are more or less consciously constructed. Building a social network is at least partly a deliberative activity for humans. Constructing media networks always is a matter of technical and organizational design. However, they are not built like roads according to a (usually) well-considered local and national government plan. The infrastructure and architecture of media networks are rarely discussed in parliaments and other bodies of representation. Actually, this is a rather strange state of affairs for a technology that is so important for society. The two main reasons have been described above. First, this infrastructure of society was largely privatized and liberalized in the 1980s and 1990s. Second, the people in government and in parliaments usually do not have the expertise and vision needed.

The struggle for design   Previously, the telecommunication and mass communication networks were designed by both public and private organizations following the indications of far-reaching government regulation. Their design was centralized: the central exchanges of telecommunication and the downstream broadcasting of mass communication. Data-communication, originally designed by telecommunication operators, was decentralized with the rise of the Internet and of packet switching (Chapter 3). The Internet was designed by people in the US Departments of Defense, Education and Commerce in cooperation with people from American universities. The military and the academics preferred a decentralized network that would be resistant to attacks. The US Department of Commerce and the Telecommunication and Infrastructure Administration hoped this would boost further privatization and the liberalization of government regulation in the United States and the rest of the world.

With the tremendous growth of the World Wide Web, the Internet community took its chance to use and strengthen the decentralized and peer-to-peer nature of this network as an outstanding public network. However, since the end of the 1990s, governments, technicians and market interests have tried to regain a central hold on the Internet for reasons of security and commerce (marketing, reliable selling and billing and the protection of copyright). Currently, a fierce struggle for control over the Internet is being waged by businesses, governments, technicians and the Internet user community. This struggle was described in Chapter 6. It appears that the architectural design of the Internet is becoming increasingly important. Apparently technical discussions over 'codes', such as protocols and other standards, are in fact political discussions.

The first thing that should strike us here is that these discussions remain obscure and hidden from the vast majority of Internet users and the population at large. Only experts know about them. Even most political representatives in parliaments and governments do not know the stakes. This means that the design of the infrastructure of our future societies is completely undemocratic. A broad discussion in society, starting with the Internet community itself, is urgently required. **Obscure and private design**

The second observation is that after the privatization and liberalization of communication networks, the construction of this vital infrastructure for society has been completely left to the market. This goes for the technical infrastructure of the networks, their centres, wires and terminals, for the construction, maintenance and operation of these networks and for the vast majority of their content services. In Chapter 4, I showed that this leads to the construction of several information superhighways side by side. This may produce effective technical competition, but from the view of society as a whole it is also a waste. Moreover, the infrastructure will not be built according to design principles that prevent problems at the higher levels (operation and content services). At these levels appears the dilemma of having to weigh the rights of information and communication freedom, privacy, security and property rights against each other. This is the place where this is 'solved' by obscure decisions about protocols, encryption, access codes, filters, digital signatures and other codes.

The influence of the proprietary software and of the de facto standards of (mainly) US software companies such as Microsoft, Google, Yahoo and Computer Associates on the design of a public network such as the Internet also is extremely large. It has provoked an open-source movement developing open source and open code software within the Internet community itself. The result of the fight between proprietary and open software will be crucial for the future of the Internet. **Proprietary versus open-source software**

Would it not be better for democratic governments to design the basic network infrastructure of society after broad consultation with all interests, just **Policy suggestion** like they do for our roads systems? Subsequently, businesses can be tasked with building the infrastructure according to the principles set down by democratic decision-making. And all construction or maintenance and all content services, except for the basic public services could also be left to the market and the public contributions of the open-source movement.

Control

The struggle for the design of the nervous system of the network society is no less than a struggle for its control, which means future freedom and democracy. The result also sets down rules for the privacy and personal autonomy of network users.

Democracy   Almost every chapter in this book has pointed out that the design of computer networks can result in both centralization and decentralization. This applies to decision-making as well. However, as the initiative for the development and introduction of networks is usually taken entirely by central management, and because network technology is very complex (requiring network management and supervision) and since it is suitable for central registration and control, the centralizing effect of networks is at first stronger than the decentralizing effect. Nevertheless, large organizational units soon meet the limits of central control. Furthermore, it is well known that employee, citizen and consumer motivation is stimulated by local execution with wider margins. This is why all kinds of flexible control and controlled or guided decentralization are gaining popularity in business organizations and political systems.

In terms of *economic* democracy, government and legislation should deal with the rise of large private oligopolies in tele-, data and mass communication (Chapter 4). The technical convergence of tele-, data and mass communication is a stimulus to corporate concentration within and between these three sectors. Very soon, fewer than ten companies will dominate the world market in each of them. They will obtain a disproportionate grip on the communication policies of countries, companies and households. From a democratic point of view, this does not mean progress. The public monopolies at least were under some sort of democratic control.

Considering *political democracy*, it has become evident that information and communication networks are a lethal threat to traditional totalitarian rule. However, in Chapter 5 I argued that more ingenious ways to exercise control, to rule and to supervise with these technologies are appearing. They enable states to gain control over their citizens coupling all kinds of registrations and practising data mining. On the other hand, the same networks can be used by citizens themselves to ask for better information and to become more involved in political decision-making.

Politicians and civil servants use the new media for different strategic orientations. In Chapter 5, I explained that some are using them for the reinforcement of institutional politics and the state. Their perspective is to create a strong and efficient state that is able to compete with international crime and terrorism, that costs less and that performs better. Others use the new media or networks as means to spread politics and democracy into civil society and to empower individual citizens. Which strategic orientation is the best cannot be determined because it completely depends on the view of democracy one holds.

The *social democracy* of new media use will be decided by the evolution of the digital divide, as portrayed in Chapter 7. Most likely, information inequality will increase in the network society. However, the tripartite network society sketched in this book – a society of a relatively small information elite, a more or less participating majority and a relative large minority of excluded people – must be prevented at all costs from becoming a structural aspect of society and creating first, second and third class citizens, workers, students and consumers. See van Dijk (2005) for the policy instruments I would suggest.

Because networks are systems, they automatically take away part of the autonomy of those connected. Citizens, employees, clients and consumers as individuals usually have little choice as to whether they are to be connected to such networks. And once they are connected, they have little control over usage. One way to solve this problem is to increase users' choice opportunities; another is to grant the bodies representing these individuals more control and to extend the area in which they have a say. In particular, this applies to employee organizations. Networks will be a structuring part of any organization, not merely a technical instrument. However, in the few cases where employee organizations have been allowed to interfere in the fields of network technology, they have had little knowledge of issues such as organization structure, management strategy and information control. **Personal autonomy**

The second class of organizations that should organize personal autonomy and choice are consumer and citizen organizations. They should not only comment on final products and prices, but also on the design and regulation of these products, in this case e-commerce and e-government networks, and on the availability of the remaining non-electronic alternatives. The third class, of course, are individual users and user groups themselves. Is it not astonishing that user groups of frequently used and perhaps crucially important web sites rarely have any say in their design and services despite all apparent interactivity? When they are not satisfied, the only option they usually have is to click away and go to a competing web site.

The introduction of networks implies a greater threat to the informational and relational privacy of individuals than the preceding information and communication techniques. The threat comes from the coupling and the integration of files and the traceability of individuals' daily routines. **Privacy**

Most countries in the world have no comprehensive privacy law. The EU has one, that, in theory, is the best (see Chapter 6) and that serves as an example for many other countries, but it remains to be seen how it will work in practice. Network traffic remains elusive. This applies in particular to the Internet, which crosses every border and is barely regulated. When legal options do not offer adequate solutions, forms of individual and collective self-regulation and technical options of protection will come to the fore. The self-regulation of codes of conduct and (privacy) rating systems should be stimulated, and research programs dealing with new techniques of encryption and digital anonymity should be funded. However, I have argued that a combination of legal, self-regulatory and technical solutions remains the only viable alternative in the long run.

Legality

Online and offline principles

We expect the law to offer some protection against the wrong use of network technology, but the tragedy is that the law itself, particularly existing legislation, is being undermined by this technology. The first reaction of governments and legislators is to declare that what goes offline should also go online. This might be a safe principle at the start of a new technology, but it does not do justice to the special characteristics of computer networks in the long run. These networks are passing all frontiers and jurisdictions, they show no clear demarcation line between public and private affairs or between collective and individual property rights and they primarily exchange virtual instead of physical goods and services.

Framework legislation

For these new online realities, each country will have to develop framework legislation that balances at least three fundamental rights against each other: information and communication freedom, the protection of society and of individuals, and the protection of property rights. This framework should first of all be based on the constitutions of the countries concerned. Subsequently, it should specify the meaning of public and private, collective and individual, virtual and physical, national and international in online environments for classes of applications: information, consultation, registration, transaction, conversation and entertainment. Within the confines of this framework (a series of political documents) formal laws related to the three rights just mentioned can be drafted or changed.

Legislation is not sufficient

Repeatedly, I have stressed that governments and legislation cannot solve the problems of legality in networks alone. Legislation has to be supplemented by all kinds of self-regulation created and maintained by businesses, user groups and individual users themselves. Additionally, to make national legislation effective across frontiers, international agreements between governments will have to be made in all kinds of international forums. As the third instrument are ways of technological protection using encryption and other codes in the software or operations built in the hardware. As technological protection is a double-edged sword, to be used by the good and the bad, it should be embedded in self-regulation and legislation.

Returns

Welfare

What are the returns of the production and use of media networks for society? I first deal with the material returns such as economic welfare and employment. In the next section the immaterial returns are discussed.

As far as economic prosperity is concerned, the new communication technology seems to have a positive effect in both the short and the long term. In this book, I have observed that it helps solve bottlenecks of a general nature in the economy and society: bureaucratic organization; a jamming and polluting infrastructure of transportation and regional planning; and a continuing lack of communication in an increasingly differentiated, fragmented and individualized society. In the short term, the powerful communication capacities of the new media (speed, few restrictions on place and time, large storage and processing potential, accuracy and interactivity) will cause an increase in the effectiveness and efficiency of production and distribution processes and office work.

These capacities are crucial to the process innovations I have summarized in the term 'flow economy'. Apart from improving effectiveness and efficiency, they also help to save on production factors, among them the use of energy and materials. So, they might have a role to play in environmental protection. Furthermore, control of production processes as a whole will increase. Media networks have become indispensable in controlling the widespread chains of companies and other organizations and the increasing division of labour within these organizations.

The main problem of this general rise in economic prosperity is its increasingly unequal division. Network technology is highly selective in its diffusion, application and effects on the social and economic environment. Globally, it supports a tendency for the combined and uneven development of countries. Locally, it helps to create dual economies of parts directly linked to the global information infrastructure and parts that are not. **Global and local inequality**

This state of affairs touches every regional and national economic policy. Policy makers believe companies can be persuaded by local authorities to set up facilities in their region, and this will have positive effects on activities in the entire region/state. In fact, however, the international companies determine their own priorities and preferences on a global scale. They are indifferent to the general organic development of a particular region/state and contribute to one specific economic field of activity only. These specific assets of regions and states will be of far greater importance in the future. It will result in uneven development barely controlled by local authorities, except perhaps by stressing the region's strong assets. The problem of uneven development can be solved in the long term only by strengthening international political and economic bodies and regulatory agreements.

On balance, few jobs are created by ICT in the short term. In the network sector itself, the new services, transport, operations and the manufacture of equipment cannot balance the loss of jobs in the old services and the declining labour costs of support and maintenance of new infrastructures and equipment, primarily in telephony and cable networks. On the other hand, the network sector does cause the reduction of a lot of existing activities in production, distribution and administration, mainly through labour-saving data communications. Yet existing authorities do not really have the option to refuse to stimulate this technology. To an increasing extent, network technology is the backbone of any technological innovation considered necessary for lasting economic growth. **Employment**

All observers and policy makers agree that the future is innovation in content services and a knowledge economy. This will bring the vast majority of **Innovation perspectives** future new employment. The countries discussed in the previous section pursue different policies concerning innovation. Up to now, the United States has been the most successful country, because it has the most competitive market and because it has a very liberal immigration policy inviting ICT specialists and students across the world to work and study in the country. However, the United States risks creating too narrow a base for innovation among its own population, because it is cutting back on public education and because bridging the digital divide is not considered to be a priority.

The ageing continent of Europe has problems in keeping up with the United States and East Asia in the field of innovation. Europe has good assets for innovation because of its rich and varied cultural heritage. However, it has difficulties in organizing these assets because it is stuck in regulation, national protectionism and fragmentation of activities. East Asia still focuses on hardware innovation. Innovation in software, in content services and in a creative knowledge economy in general appears to be difficult. This might lead to stagnation in the future. The Third World is experiencing a brain drain of young innovative scholars and students to the developed world. Fortunately, many return to their home countries later on. However, there they tend to stay in the enclaves of a dual economy that are directly linked to the global information infrastructure that is primarily serving the developed countries.

Content

Face-to-face and mediated communication

Can networks also satisfy social and individual needs: in other words, can they add to our intangible welfare? They seem to intensify the rationalization and commodification of social relations, already characteristic of modern western culture. They do not score too well on communication capacities such as inter-activity (relatively low levels), stimuli richness (some sensorial decay compared with face-to-face communication, even in multimedia), complexity (of appropriate communication activities) and privacy. The last of these capacities applies in particular in comparison with face-to-face communication.

A comparison between mediated and face-to-face communication will be made with respect to increasing numbers of activities. In this book, I have argued that it is not right to think that face-to-face communication is superior to mediated communication in all respects. Moreover, ten to 20 years of CMC research have indicated that computer-mediated communication largely equals face-to-face communication after some time. The basic reason is the amazing human creativity and imagination involved in communication. So, the future is all kinds of links and interplay between online and offline communication.

Richness of the human mind

The new media intensify the historical process of replacing direct experience with mediated perception. The new media may enrich direct experience because they can help overcome barriers of distance, time and lack of information. On the other hand, they may also rob this experience of its 'total' character, its freedom and its ability to take its own initiatives.

Since direct action and experience will remain the basis for human experience in general, excessive and one-sided use of the new media will result in a decaying of human experience. This is all the more reason to combine their use with natural experience, learning and action and communication.

The optimum use of new media capacities requires people to develop themselves visually, verbally, auditively, logically and analytically. For most people, this is too much to ask. So, in fact, the optimum use of the new media requires a many-sided mental development and a multifunctional use of people's capacities. The truth is, the new media do not really have to be used optimally. Simple and superficial uses are also possible. Thus the paradoxical situation may arise of new media making human perception and mental processing more complicated on the one hand, and simpler on the other. People with high education are most likely to use the former, while people with low education will probably choose the latter. In this way, a usage gap will appear that is difficult to resolve (van Dijk, 2005). **Optimum use requires full mental development**

Information overload seems to be one of the main substantial problems in the information and network society. I have emphasized that this only becomes a real problem when people are forced to deal with this overload in conditions of work, study and family life. Additionally, being reachable at all times and places and with an increasing number of communication means may create what I have called over-communication. This is a problem when we are not strict enough in the selection of conversations and messages. The obvious solution are the different kinds of information agent that are available. According to Donald Norman (1999) and others, they should become invisible to users. I have second thoughts about that. Invisibility might be very user-friendly, but it also means that we no longer see (and often do not know) what the technology is doing. We might lose control and our own ability to judge. **Information overload and over-communication**

If we ignore, or no longer see the fundamental differences between human cognition and computer or medium processing discussed in Chapter 9, the richness of the human mind will be at stake. This could happen if typical human perception and cognition are subjected or adapted to the workings of hardware and software. Perhaps human beings will then even turn into cyborgs – creatures that are half computer and half human. This could happen earlier than we think, namely as soon as information technology and biotechnology are linked via the connection of chips to human cells and the implantation of chips in the human body. **Who adapts: people or technology?**

Probably, or perhaps fortunately, these links will not create a balanced unity. The differences between humans and computers or other new media most likely will remain and will cause friction in human–medium/computer interaction. Education, including media education, and experience at work should be directed towards learning how to handle such friction, not denying it. People in the network society will have to learn how to mentally integrate the various impressions and relations offered by mediated and face-to-face communication. Otherwise, they will change into tragic personalities torn apart by their fragmented experiential and technological environment.

GLOSSARY

ADSL (Asymmetrical Digital Subscriber Line). A digital broadband connection into the home at the end of a telephone line. Asymmetrical because download capacity is much higher than upload capacity. Also see DSL.

allocution See p. 10

analogue Through direct and continuing creation or transmission of natural signals, for instance vibrations in the air.

asynchronous transfer mode (ATM): network protocol based on cell switching, dividing data into small equal cells of 53 bytes for the most efficient, that is not synchronous, transmission. Particularly suited for broadband networks as it is able to combine text, voice, video and data on high-speed channels. Competitor of TCP/IP as a protocol for the Internet.

bit Binary digit: smallest unit of information in digital data (a 1 or a 0). Series of eight bits is a byte.

broadband/wideband Property of a communication channel offering high-frequency space for fast transmission, generally 1 million bits per second (Mb/s) or more; high-quality moving pictures require 2 Mb/s.

browser Program to move through electronic channels such as Internet sites and pages or channels of interactive TV.

bus structure See p. 49

CD-I Compact disk–interactive: optical readable disk for the storage, reading or presentation and interactive use of all data kinds, mainly designed for the consumer market; surpassed by CD-ROM and DVD.

CD-R, CD-RW Compact disk for one-time recording (CD-recordable) or recording many times (CD-rewritable) of all data kinds.

circuit switching See p. 46

communication (social) Transfer and/or exchange of symbolic information by senders with interpretation of its meaningful context and with attention to the presence of receivers.

communication capacity Desired characteristic of a communication kind. Nine new media communication capacities are given in Chapter 1.

communication kind/type Communication with a common character, filled with communication modes and shaped by data kinds. Examples: face-to-face communication, telecommunication, data communication and mass communication.

communication mode   Way of communication using particular signs or symbols (words, images, speech acts, gestures, formulas etc.). Alternative terms: symbol systems and sign systems. Examples: linguistic, iconic, musical, gestural.

communication network   Network, the main function of which is to supply facilities of communication; the most important information traffic patterns are allocution and conversation.

communications revolution   See p. 4

compression   Technique condensing or compacting large amounts of data for bigger and faster storage or transmission.

conditional access system   System requiring a username and password, or another access code or card to use it as a proof of membership, subscription or payment.

consultation   See p. 10

conversation   See p. 12

cookie   See p. 115

CSCW   Computer-supported collaborative work: computer-programmed tools and working methods to support teamwork in organizations using computer networks.

data   Numerical, alphanumerical and other notational signs or symbols rendered in bits and bytes and serving as the raw material for information.

databank   Collection of data managed by a particular organization.

database   Systematically composed and retrievable file of data in a computer (network).

data communication   See p. 48

data kind/type   A form data can take by means of various notational signs or symbols. In this book: sound/speech, text, images and numerical data.

digital   Through the creation, transmission or simulation of artificial signs in the form of binary digits (ones and zeros).

digital code   See p. 9

digital watermark   See p. 148

distribution network   Point-to-multipoint connection from a central unit to local units unable to connect among each other (e.g. broadcasting).

DSL   (Digital Subscriber Line). A digital broadband connection into the home at the end of a telephone line. Symmetrical because upload capacity is equal to download capacity; usually with more capacity than ADSL. Compare ADSL.

DVD   Digital video/versatile disk: compact disk with high capacity and high-quality images; able to contain movie pictures of two hours; successor of the videotape and recorder (with DVD player) and the CD-ROM; in its first design it was only able to read, not to write.

electronic billboard   Central file or medium storing and forwarding messages of electronic mail to be retrieved at any time; also called bulletin board system (BBS).

electronic commerce   Formal transaction of buying and selling goods and services on proprietary or open networks like the Internet.

electronic mail   Conversation with (mainly) messages of text, asynchronously sent and received in computer networks and stored in an electronic mailbox on a computer (server).

encryption   Encoding of messages to protect them from unwanted access; to be decoded for reception by a legitimate user.

emoticons or smileys   See p. 233

fax (facsimile)   Photocopying at a distance by means of electronic signals on telephone lines.

fibre-optic cable   See p. 45

Fordism   Economic mode of production based on a conveyor belt system and mass production, distribution and consumption.

full service network (FSN)   Integrated network for consumers offering all kinds of services of communication, information, transaction and entertainment, designed as a prototype of the information superhighway in a number of American cities from 1994 onwards.

GSM   Global system for mobile communications. European-made standard for digital mobile communications using personal codes for better security.

GPRS   (General Packet Radio Service). Second generation of digital mobile telephony. Five times faster than GSM. Particularly appropriate for sending and receiving data (such as text, picture and web pages) in parallel to or instead of speech. Uses packet switching as technique.

Guilder's law   See p. 59

HDTV   High definition television: television system with digital sound and wide screens offering high-resolution images, advanced colour rendition and quality sound.

HTML   HyperText Markup Language: graphic code to edit WWW pages.

hybrid media   Combination of heterogeneous media, not actually belonging to one another.

hypertext/hypermedia   Text and other contents edited and to be received and read in a non-linear way, jumping from one source, page, image etc. to another; typical way to design and consume multimedia content.

information   Data and other signals interpreted by humans and animals with sufficient capacities of perception and cognition.

information network   Network, the main function of which is to supply facilities of information retrieval; the most important information traffic patterns are consultation and registration.

information richness Extent of information a medium is able to process and transmit objectively; contained in the concept of communication capacity.

information society Society in which information has become the dominant source of productivity, wealth, employment and power.

information superhighway Projected future communication network(s) with a broadband capacity high enough to integrate current networks of tele-, data and mass communication; also see broadband.

innovation See p. 6

integrated network Network characterized by an integration of infrastructure and/or transport, management, services, kinds of data.

integration Accomplishing a unity; here in the field of infrastructure, transport, management and services of media networks and the kinds of communication called tele-, data and mass communication.

interactive television (ITV) Television channels and programmes offering viewers the chance to react to the source, ask questions, participate in discussions, quiz, game and talk shows, order products and fill in questionnaires.

interactivity Sequence of action and reaction.

interactivity levels (1) Two-way connection; (2) synchronicity; (3) control (4) mutual understanding. See pp. 8–9

Internet Global connection of hundreds of thousands of public and private computer networks by means of public exchanges, that is nodes, gateways and computer centres using the TCP/IP protocol. Both broadband and narrowband connections are available.

ISDN Integrated services digital network: narrowband, digital network offering integrated services of (mainly) digital telephony (e.g. videophony), data communication (file transfer) and relatively fast Internet connections – faster than a classic 56 Kb modem – to be used alongside each other as the network is based on two lines to the subscriber. Overruled by broadband connections.

Knowledge See p. 203

Knowledge management See p. 71

Knowledge networks See p. 70

local area network (LAN) See p. 49

logistics Principles of the most logical and efficient (di)versions, connections, structures, divisions etc. in a given situation.

log file Computer file automatically storing the date, time, backups and connections (Internet addresses or IP numbers) of every operation on the computer.

mass communication See p. 51

media network Connection between senders and receivers made of material means of transmission.

Metcalfe's law See p. 59

mesh structure   See p. 49

microwave   Electromagnetic (short) wave of length 0.1 mm to 1.0 cm, used in air connections and cooking devices.

modem   Modulator and demodulator: a device connecting a digital computer to analogue media like the traditional telephone.

Moore's law   See p. 58

multimedia   Used with two meanings: (1) a connection or system of a number of devices (media); (2) a single device integrating several functions formerly used separately, like a multimedia PC (computer, VCR, audio, photo-editing and telephone in a single machine).

multi-user network   Network in which a multitude of local units (workstations) use the same central facilities (servers, programs etc.).

nanotechnology   See p. 58

narrowband   Property of a communication channel offering low-frequency space, generally less than 1 Mb/ps and often even less than 64,000 bit/s; sufficient for speech telephony, low amounts of data and text and low-quality images.

net-PC   Personal computer with limited own storage and other capacities included in a computer network.

network   See p. 24

network computer (NC)   Computer terminal included in and completely dependent upon network distributing programs and storage or processing capacities.

network society   Society in which social and media networks are shaping its prime mode of organization and most important structures.

neural network   Network consisting of several processors switched in parallel (hardware) and working with unifying programs (software). In its structure resembling a primitive nervous system; mainly used for pattern recognition (vision) and as an alternative for single-expert systems.

new medium   Medium at the turn of the millennium using digital code, integrating infrastructures, transport, management, services and kinds of data in tele-, data and mass communications and being interactive at a particular level.

online learning communities   See p. 71

open code   Public domain software that is free for distribution and for change under a so-called General Public License. The source code is publicly available and alterable. An example is the operating system Linux.

open source   Free software (freeware) with a publicly available source code. However, exploitation and change are not entirely free; they may be charged and not all changes are allowed.

open systems   Systems or networks designed in such a way that they can be easily connected to or integrated in other networks, among other reasons because the standards of the OSI-model are used.

optical computer   Future computer not working on electronic circuits, chips that currently are of made of silicium with electricity running through its micro transistors, but on materials such as fibre or glass transmitting very small beams of light.

OSI-model   (Open Systems Interconnection reference model). Model designed by the International Standards Organization dividing a network in seven layers with protocols (rules) for every level. From the lowest (physical) layer of a network to the highest (application) layer. Every higher layer uses the functionality of lower levels.

organic (community etc.)   Tied to a particular time, place and physical reality.

packet switching   See p. 47

pay-per-view   Commercial supply of television and video programmes, paid for by the piece, whole programme or unit of time: also *see* video/audio on demand.

registration   See p. 10

relay   Electrical switch opening or closing with a weak current and a stronger circuit.

resolution   Resolving capacity of a screen; increases as the screen contains more picture lines or points.

ring structure   See p. 49

set-top box   Device connecting a television and a broadcasting centre (to demand particular channels or programmes) or connecting to another network of tele- and data communication.

smileys or emoticons   See p. 233

social presence   Attention to the presence of communication partners in media use; contained in the concept of communication capacity.

social network   Connection between social units made of interactions.

spam   See p. 142

spyware   See p. 137

star structure   See p. 49

switching network   Point-to-point connection between local units made by central switching of connections (e.g. telephony).

symbol system   See communication mode.

Taylorism   Referring to a labour organization with far-reaching division of tasks, first separating executive tasks and management or conceptual tasks, subsequently dividing them 'endlessly'.

TCP/IP   Network protocol based on packet switching; basic protocol of the Internet.

tele-CD   Device connecting a CD player to a network.

telecommunication   See p. 46

teledemocracy See p. 102

teletext Information service transmitting pages with text and simple standing images together with broadcasting signals.

telex Teleprinter exchange: oldest form of electronic mail, first using telegraph lines, then telephone lines.

time–space distantiation See p. 157

tree structure See p. 50

two-way cable TV Cable connection with feedback channel to be used for interactive TV or video/audio on demand.

ubiquitous computing See p. 58

UMTS (Universal Mobile Telephone System). So-called third generation broadband system for mobile communications. Facilitating moving video, sounds and data on a cellular phone, PDAs and laptops.

universal access See p. 254

universal service See p. 254

value-added network (VAN) Network offering so many extra services of information or communication that it reaches independence from the basic network it serves.

video/audio on demand Service offering viewers and listeners separate programmes, films and music according to their own choice as a pay-per-view using a set-top box.

videotex Interactive electronic information and communication system offering various services; data kinds are text, data and images. In transmission, use can be made of tele-, data and mass communication networks. In the 1990s gradually replaced by the Internet, leaving only a few advanced information services (business, finance) for this medium.

virtual Not tied to a particular place and time and not directly to a physical reality.

virtual reality media Multimedia switched in parallel creating three-dimensional artificial environments to be perceived and experienced with a plurality of senses and offering the opportunity to interact with this simulated and pre-programmed environment.

voice mail See p. 48

Voice over IP Telephony (voice over) the Internet and Local Area Networks using the IP protocol. Will gradually replace traditional analogue and digital telephony as it is much cheaper, especially when two PLs are linked. However, security is still interior to traditional telephony.

web-casting Broadcasting information and television channels on the Internet (e.g. receiving TV on a multimedia PC).

web log Personal web site with (almost) daily updates of pages containing news and opinions

web portal Opening menu of an Internet access or service provider or a search engine offering a variety of daily services (news, entertainment, shopping etc.).

web TV Broadcasting Internet sources/sites on a television using a set-top box as a switch between a telephone or cable TV line and a television device offering interactive services from the Internet; one of the steps on the way to interactive television.

wide area network (WAN) See p. 49

WiFi (Wireless Fidelity). Standard for wireless communications, most often in a local area network that uses high frequency radio signals to transmit and receive data over distances of a few hundred feet.

World Wide Web (www) Collection of graphically designed Internet sites and pages, between 2000 and 2005 mainly using HTML.

REFERENCES

Abrahamson, J.B., Arterton, F. and Orren, G. (1988) *The Electronic Commonwealth: the Impact of New Technologies upon Democratic Politics*. New York: Basic Books.

Adoni, H. and H. Nossek (2001) 'The New Media Consumers: Media Convergence and the Displacement Effect', *European Journal of Communication Research*, 26 (1): 59–83.

Aglietta, M. (1979) *A Theory of Capitalist Regulation: the US Experience*. London: Verso.

Albert, Réka, Hawoong, J. & Barabási, A. (1999) 'Diameter of the World-Wide Web', *Nature*, 401: 130–1.

Anderson, P. (1983) *Imagined Communities*. London: Verso.

Anderson, Peter R. (2002) 'Critical Infrastructure Protection' in R. Mansell, R. Samarajiva and A. Mahan (eds), *Networking Knowledge for Information Societies: Institutions and Intervention, Essays in Honour of Willam Melody*. Delft: Delft University Press. pp. 188–194.

Anderson, R., Bikson, T., Law, S.-A. and Mitchell, B. (eds) (1995) *Universal Access to e-mail: Feasibility and Societal Implications*. Santa Monica, CA: Rand. www. rand.org/publications/MR/MR650.

Applegate, Lynda (1999) 'In Search for a New Organizational Model', in G. DeSanctis and J. Fulk (eds), *Shaping Organizational Form: Communication, connection and community*. Thousand Oaks, CA: Sage.

Arterton, Christopher F. (1987) *Teledemocracy: Can Technology Protect Democracy?* Newbury Park, CA: Sage.

Axelrod, Robert and Cohen, Michael D. (1999) *Harnessing Complexity, Organizational Implications of a Scientific Frontier*. New York: The Free Press.

Badaracco, J.L. (1991) *The Knowledge Link: How firms compete through strategic alliances*. Boston, MA: Harvard University Press.

Balance, R.H. and Sinclair, S.W. (1983) *Collapse and Survival: Industry Strategies in a Changing World*. London: Allen and Unwin.

Baldwin, T., McVoy, D. and Steinfield, C. (1996) *Convergence: Integrating Media, Information and Communication*. Thousand Oaks, CA: Sage.

Bannon, L.J. (1986) 'Computer-mediated communication', in D.A. Norman and S. Draper (eds), *User Centered System Design: New Perspectives on Human–Computer Interaction*. Hillsdale, NJ: Erlbaum.

Barabási, Albert-László (2002) *Linked, The New Science of Networks*. Cambridge, MA: Perseus.

Barabási, Albert-László and Albert, Réka (1999) 'Emergence of Scaling in Random Networks', *Science*, 286: 509–12.

Barber, B.J. (1984) *Strong Democracy: Participatory Politics for a New Age*. Berkeley, CA: University of California Press.

Barber, Benjamin (1996) *Jihad versus McWorld: How the Planet is both Falling Apart and Coming Together*. New York: Ballantine.

Barnett, G.A., Salisbury, J., Kim, C.W. and Langhorne, L. (1998) 'Globalization and international communication: an examination of monetary, telecommunications and trade networks'. Paper presented to International Communication Association, Annual Conference, Jerusalem, 20–24 July.

Beck, Ulrich (1992) *Risk Society: Towards a New Modernity*. London: Sage.

Becker, T.L. (1981) 'Teledemocracy: bringing power back to the people', *Futurist*, 15 (6): 6–9.

Becker, T.L. and Slaton C. (2000) *The Future of Teledemocracy*. Westport, CT: Praeger.

Beniger, J.R. (1986) *The Control Revolution: Technological and Economic Origins of the Information Society*. Cambridge, MA: Harvester.

Beniger, J.R. (1987) 'Personalization of mass media and the growth of pseudo-community', *Communications Research*, 14 (3): 352–71.

Beniger, J.R. (1996) 'Who shall control cyberspace?', in L. Strate, R. Jacobson and S. Gibson (eds), *Communication and Cyberspace*. Cresskill, NJ: Hampton. pp. 49–58.

Benjamin, Walther (1968) 'The work of art in an age of mechanical reproduction', in W. Benjamin (ed.), *Illuminations*. London: Fontana.

Bikson, T.K., Eveland, J. and Gutek, B. (1989) 'Flexible interactive technologies for multi-person tasks: current problems and future prospects', in M.H. Olson (ed.), *Technological Support for Work Group Collaboration*. Hillsdale, NJ: Erlbaum.

Biocca, Frank (1992) 'Communication within virtual reality: creating a space for research', *Journal of Communication*, 42 (4): 5–22.

Bolter, J.D. (1984) *Turing's Man: Western Culture in the Computer Age*. Chapel Hill, NC: University of North Carolina Press.

Boogers, Marcel and Voerman, G. (2002) 'Who Visits Political Websites, and Why?' Paper presented at the Euricom Conference, Electronic Networks and Democratic Engagement, Nijmegen 9–12 October.

Boneva, B. and Kraut, R. (2002) 'Email, gender, and personal relationships', in B. Wellman and C. Haythornthwaite (eds), *The Internet in everyday life*. Oxford: Blackwell. pp. 372–403.

Bordewijk, J.L. and Van Kaam, B. (1982) *Allocutie: Enkele gedachten over communicatievrijheid in een bekabeld land*. Baarn: Bosch and Keuning.

Brass, D. (1995) 'A Social Network Perspective on Human Resources Management', *Research in Personnel and Human Resources Management, Vol. 13*. Greenwich, CT: JAI Press. pp. 39–79.

Brenner, Robert (1998) 'Uneven development and the long downturn: the advanced capitalist economies from boom to stagnation, 1950–1998, *New Left Review*, 229, May/June: 1–264.

Brown, D. (1997) *Cybertrends: Chaos, Power and Accountability in the Information Age*. London: Viking.

Brown, J.S. (1986) 'From cognitive to social ergonomics and beyond', in D.A. Norman and S. Draper (eds), *User Centered System Design: New Perspectives on Human–Computer Interaction*. Hillsdale, NJ: Erlbaum.

Brown, J.S. and Duguid, P. (2000) *The Social Life of Information*. Boston, MA: Harvard Business School Press.

Bruner, J.S. and Olson, D.R. (1973) 'Learning through experience and learning through media', in G. Gerbner, L. Gross and W. Melody (eds), *Communications Technology and Social Policy*. New York: Wiley.

Bryan, C., Tsagarousianou, R. and Tambini, D. (1998) 'Electronic democracy and the civic networking movement in context', in R. Tsagarousianou, D. Tambini and C. Bryan, *Cyberdemocracy, Technology, Cities and Civic Networks*. London/New York: Routledge.

Bryant, J. and Zillman, D. (eds) (1991) *Responding to the Screen*. Hillsdale, NJ: Erlbaum.

Buchanan, Mark (2002) *Nexus, Small Worlds and the Groundbreaking Science of Networks*. New York, London: W.W. Norton.

Burgers, J. (1988) *De Schaal van Solidariteit: Een studie naar de sociale constructie van de omgeving*. Leuven: Acco.

Burnham, D. (1983) *The Rise of the Computer State*. London: Weidenfeld and Nicolson.

Cairncross, Francis (2001) *The Death of Distance, How the Communications Revolution Is Changing our Lives*. Boston, MA: Harvard Business School Press.

Castells, Manuel (1989) *The Informational City: Information Technology, Economic Restructuring, and the Urban–Regional Process*. Oxford: Blackwell.

Castells, Manuel (1994) 'European cities, the informational society and the global economy', *New Left Review*, 204: 18–32.

Castells, Manuel (1996) *The Information Age: Economy, Society and Culture. Vol. I: The Rise of the Network Society*. Oxford: Blackwell.

Castells, Manuel (1997) *The Information Age: Economy, Society and Culture. Vol. II: The Power of Identity*. Oxford: Blackwell.

Castells, Manuel (1998) *The Information Age: Economy, Society and Culture. Vol. III: End of Millennium*. Oxford: Blackwell.

Castells, Manuel (2000) Materials for an exploratory theory of the network society. *British Journal of Sociology*, 51 (1): 5–24.

Castells, Manuel (2001) *The Internet Galaxy, Reflections on the Internet, Business and Society*. Oxford, New York: Oxford University Press.

Catinat, Michel (1997) *The 'National Information Infrastructure Initiative' in the US: Policy or Non-Policy?* Cambridge, MA: Harvard University, Center for International Affairs.

Chaum, David (1992) 'Achieving electronic privacy', *Scientific American*, August: 96–8.

Chaum, David (1994) 'Towards an open and secure payment system'. Speech at the 16th International Conference on Data Protection, 6 September, The Hague.

Chen, Wenhong, Boase, J. and Wellman, B. (2002) 'The Global Villagers: Comparing Internet Users and Uses Around the World', in B. Wellman and C. Haythornthwaite (eds), *The Internet in Everyday Life*. Malden, MA, Oxford: Blackwell Publishing. pp. 74–113.

Cho, J., de Zúñiga, H., Rojas, H. and Shah, D. (2003) 'Beyond access: the digital divide and Interest uses and gratifications', *IT & Society*, 1 (4): 46–72.

Chun, K.J. and Park, H.K. (1990) 'Examining the conflicting results of GDSS research', *Information Management*, 33: 313–325.

Coolen, Maarten (1986) 'Artificiële Intelligentie als de metafysica van onze tijd', in P. Hagoort and R. Maessen (eds), *Geest, Computer, Kunst*. Amsterdam: Stichting Grafiet. pp. 124–149.

Coolen, Maarten (1997) 'Totaal verknoopt', in Ymke deBoer and J. Vorstenbosch (eds), *Virtueel Verbonden: Filosoferen over cyberspace*. Amsterdam: Parresia. pp. 28–59.

Cornfield, M., Rainie, L. and Horrigan, J. (2003) *Untuned Keyboards, Online Campaigners, Citizens and Portals in the 2002 Elections*. Washington, DC: Pew Internet & American Life Project and Institute for Politics, Democracy, and the Internet.

Cummings, J., Butler, B. and Kraut, R. (2002) 'The Quality of Online Social Relationships', *Communications of the ACM*, 45 (7): 103–8.

Cyberatlas (1996) *Internet Demographics: Usage Patterns*. www.cyberatlas.com/demographics.html en . ... /usage patterns.html.

Daft, R.L. and Lengel, R.H. (1984) 'Information richness: a new approach to managerial behavior and organization design', in L. Cummings and B. Staw (eds), *Research in Organizational Behavior. Vol. 6*. Greenwich, CT: JAI Press. pp. 191–233.

Damasio, Antonio (1995) *Descartes' Error: Emotion, Reason and the Human Brain*. New York: Avon.

Damasio, Antonio (1999) *The Feeling of What Happens, Body and Emotion in the Making of Consciousness*. New York: Harcourt Brace.

Damasio, Antonio (2003) *Looking for Spinoza, Joy, Sorrow and the Feeling Brain*. Orlando, FL: Harcourt.

Datamation (1998) 'The Datamation Global 100, Calendar Year 1997'. www. datamation.com.

Davenport, Thomas and L. Prusak (1997) *Working Knowledge: How Organizations Manage What They Know*. Boston, MA: Harvard University Press.

Davidow, W.H. and Malone, M.S. (1992) *The Virtual Corporation*. New York: Harper Collins.

Davies, A. (1994) *Telecommunications and politics: the Decentralized Alternative*. London: Pinter.

De Sitter, L.U. (1994) *Simple Organizations, Complex Tasks: the Dutch Sociotechnical Approach*. Maastricht: MERIT.

Debord, G. (1996) *The Society of the Spectacle*. London: Verso.

Delli Carpini, M. and Keeter, S. (2003) 'The Internet and an Informed Citizenry', in D. Anderson and M. Cornfield (eds), *The Civic Web, Online Politics and Democratic Values*. Lanham, MD: Rowman & Littlefield. pp. 129–54.

Dennett, D. (1986) 'Information, technology, and the virtues of ignorance', *Deadalus*, 115 (3): 135–53.

Dennis, A. and Kinney, S. (1998) 'Testing media-richness theory in the new media: The effects of cues, feedback and task equivocality', *Information Systems Research*, 9: 256–74.

Dordick, H. and Wang, G. (1993) *The Information Society: A Retrospective View*. Newbury Park, CA, London, New Delhi: Sage.

Dyson, Esther (1995) 'Intellectual value', *Wired*, July: 136–41, 182–4.

Dyson, Esther (1997) *Release 2.0: a Design for Living in the Digital Age*. New York: Broadway.

Edelman, Gerald (1991) *Bright Air, Brilliant Fire: On the Matter of the Mind*. New York: Basic Books.

Edelman, Gerald M. and Tononi, G. (2000) *A Universe of Consciousness: How matter becomes imagination*. New York: Basic Books.

Edinger, J.A. and Patterson, M. (1983) 'Non-verbal involvement and social control', *Psychological Bulletin*, 93: 30–56.

European Commission (1995) *The Protection of Individuals with Regard to the Processing of Personal Data and the Free Movement of Such Data*. Directive. Brussels: Official Journal no. L 281, 23/11/1995. www.ispo.cec.be.

European Commission (1996) *On Standardisation and the Global Information Society: The European Approach*. COM (96) 359. Brussels: Office for Official Publications of the European Communities. www.ispo.cec.be.

European Commission (2000) *The EU-Economy 2000 Review*. Luxembourg: Office for Official Publications of the European Communities.

European Commission (2001) *On the Harmonization of Certain Aspects of Copyright and Related Rights in the Information Society*. Directive 2001/29/EC. Brussels: Office for Official Publications of the European Communities. www. ispo.cec.be.

European Commission (2004) *The EU-Economy 2003 Review*. Luxembourg: Office for Official Publications of the European Communities.

Featherstone, M. and Burrows, R. (eds) (1996) Introduction to *Cyberspace/Cyberbodies/Cyberpunk: Cultures of Technological Embodiment*. London: Sage.

Featherstone, M., Lash, S. and Robertson, R. (1995) *Global Modernities*. London: Sage.

Ferguson, M. (1990) 'Electronic media and the redefining of time and space', in M. Ferguson (ed.), *Public Communication: the New Imperatives*. London: Sage.

Ferguson, D.A. and Perse, E.M. (2000) 'The World Wide Web as a Functional Alternative to Television', *Journal of Broadcasting & Electronic Media*, 44 (2): 155–74.

Fidler, Roger (1997) *Mediamorphosis: Understanding New Media*. Thousand Oaks, CA: Pine Forge Press/Sage.

Fielding, G. and Hartley, P. (1987) 'The telephone: a neglected medium', in A. Cashdan and M. Jordin (eds), *Studies in Communication*. Oxford: Basil Blackwell.

Finholt, T. and Sproull, L. (1987) 'Electronic groups at work'. Research paper, Carnegie Mellon University.

Finn, S. and Korukonda, A. (2004) 'Avoiding computers: Does personality play a role?', in E. Bucy and J. Newhagen (eds), *Media Access: Social and Psychological Dimensions of New Technology Use*. London: LEA. pp. 73–90.

Flanagin, A. and Metzger. (2001) 'Internet Use in the Contemporary Media Environment', *Human Communication Research*, 27 (1): 153–177.

Fodor, J. (1986) 'Minds, machines and modules: an interview of Brown, C., Hagoort, P. and Maessen, R. with J. Fodor', in P. Hagoort and R. Maessen (eds), *Geest, Computer, Kunst*. Amsterdam: Stichting Grafiet. pp. 90–117.

Forrester, J. (1976) 'Business Structure, Economic Cycles and National Policy', *Futures*, 1976: 195–214.

Fountain, Jane (2001) *Building the Virtual State, Information Technology and Institutional Change*. Washington, DC: The Brookings Institution.

Freese, J. (1979) *International Data Flow*. Lund: Studentliteratur (Swedish University of Lund edition).

Frissen, P.H.A. (1989) *Bureaucratische cultuur en informatisering: Een studie naar de betekenis van informatisering voor de cultuur van een overheidsorganisatie*. Contains a summary in English. The Hague: SDU.

Frissen, P.H.A. (1999) *Politics, Government, Technology: a Postmodern Narrative on the Virtual State*. London: Edward Elgar.

Fulk, J. and G. DeSanctis (1999) 'Articulation of communication technology and organizational form', in G. DeSanctis and J. Fulk (eds), *Shaping Organizational Form: Communication, connection and community*. Thousand Oaks, CA: Sage. pp. 5–32.

Fulk, J. and Steinfield, C. (1990) *Organizations and Communication Technology*. Newbury Park, CA, London, New Delhi: Sage.

Fulk, J., Steinfield, C., Schmitz, J. and Power, J.G. (1987) 'A social information processing model of media use in organizations', *Communication Research*, 14 (5): 529–52.

Gandy, Oscar (1994) *The Panoptic Society*. Boulder, CO: Westview.

Garfinkel, Simson (2000) *Database Nation: The Death of Privacy in the 21st Century*. Sebastopol, CA: O'Reilly.

Garnham, N. (1997) 'Europe and the global information society: the history of a troubled relationship', *Telematics and Informatics*, 14 (4): 323–7.

Gates, Bill (1995) *The Road Ahead*. New York: Viking Penguin.

Gere, Charlie (2002) *Digital Culture*. London: Reaktion Books.

Gershuny, J. and Miles, I. (1983) *The New Service Economy: the Transformation of Employment in Industrial Societies*. London: Pinter.

Giddens, A. (1984) *The Constitution of Society: Outline of the Theory of Structuration*. Cambridge: Polity.

Giddens, A. (1991a) *The Consequences of Modernity*. Stanford, CA: Stanford University Press.

Giddens, A. (1991b) *Modernity and Self-Identity: Self and Society in the Late Modern Age*. Cambridge: Polity.

Goldsmith, S. and Eggers, W. (2004) *Governing by Network, The New Shape of the Public Sector*. Washington DC: Brookings Institution Press.

Goodman, N. (1968) *Languages of Art*. Indianapolis, IN: Hacket.

Graham, S. and Marvin, S. (1996) *Telecommunications and the City: Electronic spaces, urban places*. London/New York: Routledge.

Granovetter, M. (1973) 'The Strength of Weak Ties', *American Journal of Sociology*, 78: 1360–80.

Green, Nicola (2002) 'On the Move: Technology, Mobility and the Mediation of Social Time and Space', *The Information Society*, 18: 281–92.

Greiff, I. (ed.) (1988) *Computer Supported Co-operative Work: a Book of Readings*. Cambridge, MA: Kaufmann.

Gross, L.P. (1973) 'Modes of communication and the acquisition of symbolic competence', in G. Gerbner, L.P. Gross and W. Melody (eds), *Communications Technology and Social Policy*. New York: Wiley.

Guéhenno, Jean-Marie (1993) *La Fin de la Démocratie*. Paris: Flammarion. Translation: *The End of the Nation State*. Minneapolis, MN: University of Minnesota Press, 1995.

Gumpert, G. (1987) *Talking Tombstones and Other Tales of the Media Age*. New York: Oxford University Press.

Habermas, J. (1981) *Theorie des kommunikativen Handelns*. Vols I and II. Frankfurt: Suhrkamp.

Hacker, K. and van Dijk, J. (eds) (2000) *Digital Democracy: Issues of Theory and Practice*. London: Sage.

Hagel, H. and Armstrong, A. (1997) *Net Gain: Expanding Markets through Virtual Communities*. Boston, MA: Harvard Business School Press.

Hain, T. (2000) *Architectural Implications of NAT, RFC2993, 2000*. ftp://ftp.isi. edu/in-notes/rfc2993.txt.

Hakken, David (2003) *The Knowledge Landscapes of Cyberspace*. London, New York: Routledge.

Hamelink, C. (1994) *The Politics of World Communication*. London: Sage.

Hampton, K. and Wellman, B. (2002) 'The Not So Global Village of Netville', in B. Wellman and C. Haythornthwaite (eds), *The Internet in Everyday Life*. Malden, MA, Oxford: Blackwell. pp. 345–71.

Harrison, Bennett (1994) *Lean and Mean: the Changing Landscape of Corporate Power in the Age of Flexibility*. New York: Guilford.

Harvey, D. (1989) *The Condition of Postmodernity: an Enquiry into the Origins of Cultural Change*. Oxford: Polity.

Hawryskiewicz, I. (1996) *Designing the Networked Enterprise*. Norwood, MA: Artech.

Heim, M. (1987) *Electric Language: a Philosophical Study of Word Processing*. New Haven, CT: Yale University Press.

Held, David (1987) *Models of Democracy*. Cambridge: Polity Press.

Henten, A. and Kristensen, T. (2000) 'Information society visions in the Nordic countries', *Telematics and Informatics*, 17: 77–103.

Herring, Susan (2004) 'Slouching toward the ordinary: current trends in CMC', *New Media & Society*, 6: 26–36.

Holmes, Robert (1995) 'Privacy: philosophical foundations and moral dilemmas', in P. Ippel, G. de Heij and B. Crouwers (eds), *Privacy Disputed*. The Hague: SDU. pp. 15–30.

Hongladarom, Soraj (2002) 'The Web of Time and the Dilemma of Globalization', *The Information Society*, 18: 241–9.

Horrigan, J. and Rainie, L. (2002) *The broadband difference: How online behavior changes with high-speed Internet connections*. Washington, DC: Pew Internet and American Life Project. www.pewinternet.org.

Howard, P., Rainie, L. and Jones, S. (2002) 'Days and nights on the Internet: The impact of a diffusing technology', in B. Wellman and C. Haythornthwaite (eds), *The Internet in Everyday Life*. Oxford: Blackwell. pp. 45–73.

Hudiberg, R. (1999) 'Preliminary investigation of computer stress and the big five personality factors', *Psychology Reports*, 85: 473–480.

Huysmans, F., de Haan, J. and van de Broek, A. (2004) *Achter de schermen, Een kwart eeuw lezen, luisteren, kijken en internetten*. Contains a summary in English. The Hague: Sociaal en Cultureel Planbureau.

IDC (1996) *Telework and Mobile Computing 1996–2000*. Amsterdam: IDC-Benelux.

Information Society Forum (1996) *Building Networks for People and their Communities*. First annual report, June. Brussels: ISPO. www.cec.be/infoforum/pub/inrep1/html.

Issing, L. and Strebkowski, R. (1995) 'Lernen mit Multimedia', *Empirischen Medienpsychologie*, 4: 115–35.

ITU (International Telecommunication Union) (2003) *Birth of Broadband.* ITU Internet reports. Geneva: ITU.

Ivry, R. and Robertson, L. (1998) *The Two Sides of Perception.* Cambridge, MA: MIT Press.

James, J. (2003) *Technology, Globalization and Poverty.* Cheltenham, UK: Edward Elgar.

Jankowski, N. and van Selm, M. (2000) 'The Promise and Practice of Public Debate in Cyberspace', in K. Hacker and J. van Dijk (eds), *Digital Democracy, Issues of Theory and Practice.* London, Thousand Oaks, New Delhi: Sage. pp. 149–65.

Jensen, Jens (1999) '"Interactivity" – Tracking a New Concept in Media and Communication Studies', in P.A. Mayer (ed.), *Computer Media and Communication.* Oxford: Oxford University Press. pp. 160–88. Elaborated as 'The concept of '"Interactivity"', in J. Jensen and C. Toscan (eds), (1999) *Interactive Television, TV of the Future or the Future of TV?* Aalborg: Aalborg University Press. pp. 25–66.

Jensen, Jens and Toscan, C. (1999) 'Introduction', in J. Jensen and C. Toscan (eds), *Interactive Television, TV of the Future or the Future of TV?* Aalborg: Aalborg University Press. pp. 11–23.

Jerome, H. (1934) *Mechanization in Industry.* New York: Publications of the National Bureau of Economic Research.

Johansen, R., Vallee, J. and Spanger, K. (1979) *Electronic Meetings: Technical Alternatives and Social Choices.* Reading, MA: Addison-Wesley.

Joinson, A. (1998) 'Causes and Implications of Disinhibited Behavior on the Internet', in J. Gackenbach (ed.), *Psychology and the Internet: Intrapersonal, interpersonal and transpersonal implications.* San Diego CA: Academic Press. pp. 43–58.

Joinson, A. (2001) 'Self-disclosure in computer-mediated communication: the role of self-awareness and visual anonymity', *European Journal of Social Psychology,* 31 (2): 177–92.

Katz, J.E. (1997) 'Social and organizational consequences of wireless communications: a selective analysis of residential and business sectors in the US', *Telematics and Informatics,* 14 (3): 233–56.

Katz, J.E. and Rice, R.E. (2002) *Social Consequences of Internet Use, Access, Involvement, and Interaction.* Cambridge MA, London: The MIT Press.

Katz, Jon (1997) *Media Rants: Postpolitics in a Digital Nation.* San Francisco: Hardwired.

Kauffman, S.A. (1993) *The Origins of Order: Self-organizing and Selection in Evolution.* New York: Oxford University Press.

Kavanaugh, A. and Patterson, S. (2002) 'The Impact of Community Computer Networks on Social Capital and Community Involvement in Blacksburg', in B. Wellman and C. Haythornthwaite (eds), *The Internet in Everyday Life.* Malden, MA, Oxford: Blackwell Publishing.

Keane, J. (1995) 'Structural Transformations of the Public Sphere', *The Communication Review,* 1 (1): 1–22.

Kelly, Kevin (1998) *New Rules for the New Economy.* New York: Viking Press.

Kenny, C. (2002) *The Internet and Economic Growth in Least Developed Countries: A Case of Managing Expectations.* World Institute for Development Economics Research Discussion Paper No 2002175. www.wider.unu.edu/ publications/dps/dps2002/dp2002-75.pdf

Kerckhove, Derrick de (1998) *Connected Intelligence, The Arrival of the Web Society.* London: Kogan Page.

Kiesler, S. and Sproull, L. (1992) 'Group decision making and communication technology', *Organizational Behavior and Human Decision Processes,* 6: 96–123.

Kiesler, S., Siegel, J. and McGuire, T. (1984) 'Social-psychological aspects of computer-mediated communication', *The American Psychologist,* 39 (10): 1123–1143.

Koestler, A. (1967) *The Ghost in the Machine*. London: Hutchinson.

Kondratieff, N.D. (1929) 'Die langen Wellen in der Konjunktur', *Archiv für Sozialwissenschaft und Sozialpolitik*, 56, Band 1929: 573–609.

Kontopoulos, Kyriakos (1993) *The Logics of Social Structure*. Cambridge, NY: Cambridge University Press.

Konvit, M. (1998) 'Regulatory strategies in Central and Eastern-Europe and the former Soviet Union'. Paper presented at the Beyond Convergence: ITS-98 Conference, Stockholm, 14–21 June. www.ITS98.org/conference.

Kraut, R., Kiesler, S., Mukhopadhyay, T., Scherlis, W. and Patterson, W. (1998) 'Social impact of the Internet: what does it mean?' *Communications of the ACM*, 41 (12): 21–2.

Kubey, R. and Csikszentmihalyi, M. (1990) *Television and the Quality of Life: How Viewing Shapes Everyday Experience*. Hillsdale, NJ: Erlbaum.

Kubicek, H. (1988) 'Telematische Integration: Zurück in die Sozialstructuren des Früh-Kapitalismus?', in W. Steinmüller (ed.), *Verdatet und Vernetzt Sozialökologische Handlungsspielraüme in der Informationsgesellschaft*. Frankfurt: Fischer. pp. 17–42.

Kubicek, H. and Rolf, A. (1985) *Mikropolis, mit Computernetzen in die 'Informationsgesellschaft'*. Hamburg: VSA.

Kundera, M. (1986) *Life is Elsewhere*. London: Faber and Faber.

La Porte, T.M. (1999) 'National Differences in How Governments Use Websites.' in T. Sprehe (ed.), *The Internet Connection: Your Guide to Government Resource*. Washington, DC: Thomas Sprehe. pp. 21–28.

La Porte, T.M., Demchak, T. and Frijs, C. (1999) 'Webbing Governance: National Differences in Constructing the Public Face' in G.D. Garson (ed.), *Handbook of Public Information Systems*. New York: Marcel Dekker. pp. 179–96.

Lasch, C. (1977) *Heaven in a Heartless World*. New York: Basic Books.

Lash, S. and Urry, J. (1994) *Economies of Signs and Space*. London: Sage.

Lea, M. (ed.) (1992) *Contexts of Computer-Mediated Communication*. New York: Harvester.

Lee, H. and Liebenau, J. (2000) 'Time and the Internet at the Turn of the Millennium', *Time & Society*, 9 (1): 43–56.

Lee, H. and Whitley, E. (2002) 'Time and Information Technology: Temporal Impacts on Individuals, Organizations and Society', *The Information Society*, 18: 235–40.

Lessig, L. (1999) *Code, and other laws of cyberspace*. New York: Basic Books.

Lessig, L. (2001) *The Future of Ideas: The Fate of the Commons in a Connected World*. New York: Vintage Books.

Lévy, Pierre (1997) 'The aesthetics of cyberspace', in T. Druckery (ed.), *Electronic Culture*. New York: Aperture. pp. 358–372.

Loudon, K. (1986) *The Dossier Society: Comments on Democracy in an Information Society*. New York: Columbia University Press.

Lux Wigand, Dianne (1998) 'Information technology, organization structure, people, and tasks'. Paper presented to International Communication Association, Annual Conference, Jerusalem, 20–24 July.

Lyon, D. (1995) *The Electronic Eye: the Rise of the Surveillance Society*. Cambridge: Polity.

Lyon, D. (2001) *Surveillance Society: Monitoring Everyday Life*. Buckingham/ Philadelphia: Open University Press.

Lyon, David (2003) *Surveillance after September 11*. Cambridge: Polity.

Maclean, P. (1978) 'A mind of three minds: educating the triune brain', in National Society for the Study of Education, *Education and the Brain*. Chicago.

Magder, T. (1996) 'The information superhighway in Canada'. Paper presented at Virtual Democracy: 9th Colloquium on Communication and Culture of the European Institute for Communication and Culture, 'Virtual Democracy', Piran, 10–14 April.

Mandel, E. (1980) *Long Waves of Capitalist Development*. Cambridge: Cambridge Univesity Press.

Mansell, Robin (1993) *The New Telecommunications: a Political Economy of Network Evolution*. London: Sage.

Mansell, R. and When, U. (eds) (1998) *Knowledge Societies: Information Technology for Sustainable Development*. Oxford: Oxford University Press.

Mantovani, Guiseppe (1996) *New Communication Environments: from Everyday to Virtual*. London: Taylor and Francis.

Martin, James (1978) *The Wired Society*. Englewood Cliffs, NJ: Prentice-Hall.

Maturana, H. and Varela, F. (1980) *Autopoiesis and Cognition*. Boston, MA: D. Reidel.

Maturana, H. and Varela, F. (1984) *The Tree of Knowledge: the biological roots of human understanding*. Boston, MA: Shambala.

McLaughlin, M., Osborne, K. and Smith, C. (1995) 'Standards of conduct on Usenet', in S. Jones (ed.), *Cybersociety: Computer-mediated communication and Community*. Thousand Oaks, CA: Sage. pp. 90–111.

McLean, I. (1989) *Democracy and New Technology*. Cambridge: Polity.

McLuhan, M. (1966) *Understanding Media: the Extensions of Man*. New York: Signet.

McNeill, J.R. and McNeill, W.H. (2003) *The Human Web: A Bird's-eye View of World History*. New York, London: W.W. Norton.

McQuail, D. and Windahl, S. (1993) *Communication Models for the Study of Mass Communications*. London/New York: Longman.

Merton, R. (1968) 'The Matthew effect in science', *Science*, 159: 56–63.

Metcalfe, S. (1986) 'Information and some economics of the information revolution', in M. Ferguson (ed.), *New Communications Technologies and the Public Interest*. Beverly Hills, CA: Sage.

Meyrowitz, J. (1985) *No Sense of Place: the Impact of Electronic Media on Social Behavior*. New York: Oxford University Press.

Meyrowitz, J. (1997) 'Shifting worlds of strangers: medium theory and changes in "Them" versus '"Us"', *Sociological Inquiry*, 67 (1): 59–71.

Meyrowitz, J. and Maguire, J. (1993) 'Media, place and multiculturalism', *Society*, 30 (5): 41–8.

Midorikawa, M. et al. (1975) 'TV conference system', *Review of the Electrical Communication Laboratories*, 23: 5–6.

Milgram, Stanley (1967) 'The Small World Problem', *Psychology Today*, 2: 60–7.

Milgram, Stanley (1970) 'The experience of living in the cities', *Science*, 13 March: 1461–8.

Miller, J. and Schwarz, M. (eds) (1998) *Speed-Visions of an Accelerated Age*. London: The Photographers Gallery.

Miller, S. (1996) *Civilizing Cyberspace: Policy, Power and the Information Superhighway*. New York: Addison-Wesley.

Mintzberg, H. (1979) *The Structuring of Organizations: a Synthesis of the Research*. Englewood Cliffs, NJ: Prentice-Hall.

Monge, Peter R. and Contractor, Noshir S. (2003) *Theories of Communication Networks*. New York: Oxford University Press.

Moore, Barrington (1984) *Privacy: Studies in Social and Cultural History*. Armonk, NY: Sharpe.

Morley, D. (1986) *Family Television: Cultural Power and Domestic Leisure*. London: Comedia Publishing Group.

Mowshowitz, A. (1992) 'Virtual feudalism: a vision of political organisation in the information age', in P. Frissen, A. Koers and I. Snellen (eds), *Orwell of Athene? Democratie en informeedtiesamenleving*. The Hague: NOTA/SDU. pp. 285–300.

Mowshowitz, A. (1994) 'Virtual organization: a vision of management in the information age', *The Information Society*, 10 (4): 267–88.

Mowshowitz, A. (1997) 'On the theory of virtual organization', *Systems Research*, 14 (6): 373–84.

Moyal, A. (1992) 'The gendered use of the telephone: an Australian case study', *Media, Culture and Society*, 14: 51–72.

Mulgan, G.J. (1991) *Communication and Control: Networks and the New Economies of Communication*. Cambridge: Polity.

Mulgan, Geoff (1997) *Connexity, How to Live in a Connected World*. Boston, MA: Harvard Business School Press.

Murray, F. (1983) 'The decentralization of production: the decline of the mass-collective worker?', *Capital and Class*, 19: 74–99.

Nabben, P.F.P. and van de Luytgaarden, H. (1996) *De Ultieme Vrijheid: Een rechtstheoretische analyse van het recht op privacy*. Deventer: Kluwer.

Nahuis, Richard and de Groot, Henri (2003) *Rising Skill Premia, You ain't seen nothing yet?* CPB Discussion Paper No. 20. The Hague: CPB, Netherlands Bureau for Economic Policy Analysis. www.ideas.repec.org/s/cpb/discus.html.

Naisbitt, J.R. (1982) *Megatrends: Ten New Directions Transforming Our Lives*. New York: Macdonald.

Negroponte, Nicholas (1995) *Being Digital*. New York: Knopf.

Neisser, Ulric (1976) *Cognition and Reality*. New York: Freeman.

Newman, B.I. (1994) *The Marketing of the President: Political Marketing as Campaign Strategy*. Thousand Oaks, CA: Sage.

Nicol, L. (1985) 'Communications technology: economic and spatial aspects', in M. Castells (ed.), *High Technology, Space and Society*. Beverley Hills, CA: Sage.

Nie, N.H. (2001) 'Sociability, interpersonal relations and the Internet: reconstructing conflicting findings', *American Behavioral Scientist,* 45 (3): 420–35.

Nie, N.H. and Erbring, L. (2000) *Internet and society: A preliminary report.* www.stanford.edu/group/siqss.

Nie, N., Hillygus, D. and Erbring, L. (2002) 'Internet Use, Interpersonal Relations, and Sociability: A Time Diary Study', in B. Wellman and C. Haythornthwaite (eds), *The Internet In Everyday Life*. Malden MA, Oxford: Blackwell. pp. 215–243.

Nielsen Media Research (1996) *Home Technology Report*, July. New York: Nielsen Media Research Interactive Services. www.nielsenmedia.com/news/hotech-summary.html.

Noam, E. (1992) *Telecommunications in Europe*. London: Erlbaum.

Nonaka, I. and Takeuchi, H. (1995) *The Knowledge-Creating Company: How Japanese Companies Create the Dynamics of Innovation*. New York: Oxford University Press.

Norman, D.A. (1991) 'Cognitive artifacts', in J.M. Carroll (ed.), *Designing Interface: Psychology of the Human–Computer Interface*. Cambridge: Cambridge University Press. pp. 17–39.

Norman, D.A. (1993) *Things that Make Us Smart*. Reading, MA: Addison-Wesley.

Norman, D.A. (1999) *The Invisible Computer*. Cambridge, MA, London: The MIT Press.

Norman, D.A. and Draper, S. (1986) *User-centered System Design: New Perspectives on Human–Computer Interaction*. Hillsdale, NJ: Erlbaum.

Norris, P. (2001) *Digital Divide, Civic Engagement, Information Poverty and the Internet worldwide*. Cambridge, UK: Cambridge University Press.

O'Harrow, R. (2005) *No Place to Hide*. New York, London: Free Press.

O'Sullivan, P. and Flanagin, A. (2003) 'An interactional reconceptualizing "flaming" and other problematic communication', *New Media and Society*, 5 (1): 67–93.

OECD (2000) *A New Economy? The changing role of innovation and information technology in growth*. Paris: OECD.

OECD (2003) *Communications Outlook 2003*. www.oecd.org/documents.

Ornstein, R.E. (1986) *The Psychology of Consciousness*. Harmondsworth: Penguin.

Palvia, S., Palvia, P. and Zigli, R. (eds) (1992) *The Global Issues of Information Technology Management*. Harrisburg, PA: Idea Group.

Park, H. (2002) 'The Digital Divide in South Korea: Closing and Widening Divides in the 1990s', *Electronic Journal of Communication* 12 (182), www.cios.org/ejc.

Perritt, Henry (1996, 1998) *Law and the Information Superhighway*. New York: Wiley.

Peters, Jean-Marie (1989) *Het Filmisch Denken*. Amersfoort: Acco.

Peters, Jean-Marie (1996) *Het beeld: Bouwstenen van een algemene iconologie*. Baarn: Hadewijch.

Piore, M. and Sabel, C. (1984) *The New Industrial Divide*. New York: Basic Books.

Pool, I. de Sola (1983) *Technologies of Freedom*. Harvard, MA: Belknap.

Pool, I. de Sola, Inose, H., Takasaki, N. and Hunwitz, R. (1984) *Communication Flows: a Census in the US and Japan*. Amsterdam: North-Holland.

Postmes, T. and Spears, R. (1998) 'Breaching or building social boundaries? Side-effects of computer-mediated communication'. Paper presented to International Communication Association, Annual Conference, Jerusalem, 20–24 July.

Powell, W. (1990) 'Neither Market nor Hierarchy: Network Forms of Organizations', in B. Slaw (ed.), *Research in Organizational Behavior*, Vol. 12. Greenwich, CT: JAI Press. pp. 295–336.

Press, L., Foster, W. and Goodman, S. (1999) 'The Internet in India and China', *First Monday: Peer-Reviewed Journal on the Internet*, 7(10). www.firstmonday.dk/issues/issue7_10/press/

Prigogine, I. and Stengers, I. (1984) *Order out of Chaos, Man's new dialogue with nature*. Toronto: Bantam Books.

Putnam, Robert (2000) *Bowling Alone: the collapse and revival of American community*. New York: Simon and Schuster.

Quan-Haase, A. and Wellman, B. with Witte, J.C. and Hampton, K. (2002) 'Capitalizing on the Net: Social Contact, Civic Engagement, and Sense of Community', in B. Wellman and C. Haythornthwaite (eds), *The Internet in Everyday Life*. Malden, MA, Oxford: Blackwell. pp. 291–324.

Rada, J. (1980) 'Micro-electronics, information technology and its effects on developing countries', in J. Berting, S. Mills and H. Winterberger (eds), *The Socio-Economic Impact of Micro-electronics*. Oxford: Oxford University Press.

Rash, Wayne (1997) *Politics on the Nets: Wiring the Political Process*. New York: Freeman.

Rayport, Jeffrey and Sviokla, John (1999) 'Exploiting the Virtual Value Chain', in D. Tapscott (ed.), *Creating Value in the Network Economy*. Boston, MA: Harvard Business Review.

Reagan, E.J. (1989) 'The strategic importance of telecommunications to banking', in M. Jussawalla, T. Okuma and T. Araki (eds), *Information Technology and Global Interdependence*. New York: Greenwood.

Reeves, B. and Nass, C. (1996) *The Media Equation*. Cambridge, MA: Cambridge University Press.

Reichman, R. (1986) 'Communication paradigms for a window system', in D.A. Norman, and S. Draper (eds), *User-Centered System Design: New Perspectives on Human–Computer Interaction*. Hillsdale, NJ: Erlbaum.

Reidenberg, J.R. (1998) 'Lex Informatica. The Formulation of Information Policy Rules Through Technology', *Texas Law Review*, 3: 553–94.

Rheingold, Howard (1993a) 'A slice of life in my virtual community', in L.M. Harasim (ed.), *Global Networks: Computers and International Communication*. Cambridge, MA: MIT Press. pp. 57–82.

Rheingold, Howard (1993b) *The Virtual Community: Homesteading on the Electronic Frontier*. Reading, MA: Addison-Wesley.

Rice, R.E. (1998) 'Computer-mediated communication and media preference', *Behavior and Information Technology*, 17 (3): 164–74.

Rice, R.E. and Love, G. (1987) 'Electronic emotion: socio-emotional content in a computer-mediated communication network', *Communication Research*, 14: 85–108.

Rifkin, J. (1987) *Time Wars*. New York: Holt.

Roberts, J.M. and Gregor, T. (1971) 'Privacy: a cultural view', in J.R. Pennock and J. Chapman (eds), *Privacy*. New York: Atherton Press.

Robinson, J. and Nie, N.H. (2002) 'Issue Introduction of IT and Sociability', *IT & Society*, 1 (1): i–xi.

Robinson, J., DiMaggio, P. and Hargittai, E. (2003) 'New Social Survey Perspectives on the Digital Divide', *IT & Society*, 1 (5): 1–22.

Rojo, A. and Ragsdale, R. (1997) 'Participation in electronic forums', *Telematics and Informatics*, 13 (1): 83–96.

Roszak, T. (1986) *The Cult of Information: the Folklore of Computers and the True Art of Thinking*. New York: Pantheon.

Rothfelder, J. (1992) *Privacy for Sale*. New York: Simon and Schuster.

Rutter, D.R. (1984) *Looking and Seeing: the Role of Visual Communication in Social Interaction*. Chichester: Wiley.

Sabbah, F. (1985) 'The new media', in M. Castells (ed.), *High Technology, Space and Society*. Beverly Hills, CA: Sage.

Salomon, G. (1979) *Interaction of Media, Cognition and Learning*. San Francisco, CA: Jossey-Bass.

Samuelson, Pamela (1996) 'Intellectual property, at your expense', *Wired*, January: 135–8, 188–91.

Saunders, C.S., Robey, D. and Vaverek, K. (1994) 'The persistence of status differences in computer conferencing', *Human Communication Research*, 20 (4): 443–72.

Saunders, R.J. and Warford, G. (1983) *Telecommunications and Economic Development*. Baltimore, MD: World Bank and Johns Hopkins University Press.

Sayer, A. (1986) 'New developments in manufacturing: the just-in-time system', *Capital and Class*, 30: 43–72.

Schenk, David (1997) *Data Smog: Surviving the Information Glut*. New York: HarperEdge.

Schneider, S. (1997) 'Expanding the public sphere through computer-mediated communication: political discussion about abortion in a Usenet newsgroup'. Phd dissertation, MIT, Cambridge, MA.

Schumpeter, J.A. (1942) *Capitalism, Socialism and Democracy*. New York: Harper & Row.

Scott, C. and Easton, A. (1996) 'Examining equality of influence in group decision support system interaction', *Small Group Research*, 37 (3): 360–82.

SCP (Social and Cultural Planning Agency) (2001) Breedveld, K. and van den Broek, A. (eds), *Trends in de tijd* (Trends in time). SCP: The Hague.

Selnow, G.W. (1994) *High-Tech Campaigns: Computer Technology in Political Communication*. Westport, CT: Praeger.

Sennett, R. (1974) *The Fall of Public Man: on the Social Psychology of Capitalism*. New York: Vintage.

Shapiro, Carl and Varian, Hal R. (1999) *Information Rules – A Strategic Guide to the Network Economy*. Boston, MA: Harvard Business School Press.

Shils, E. (1975) *Center and Periphery: Essays in Macro-sociology*. Chicago: University of Chicago Press.

Short, J., Williams, E. and Christie, B. (1976) *The Social Psychology of Telecommunications*. New York: Wiley.

Silverstein C., Henzinger, H., Marais, H. and Moricz, M. (1999) 'Analysis of a Very Large Web Search Engine Query Log', *SIGIR Forum*, 33 (1): 6–12.

Silverstone, R. and Hadden, J. (1996) 'Design and domestication', in R. Mansell and R. Silverstone (eds), *Communication by Design*. Oxford: Oxford University Press.

Slaughter, A.-M. (2004) *A New World Order*. Princeton, NJ: Princeton University Press.

Smith, N., Bizot, E. and Hill, T. (1988) *Use of Electronic Mail in the Research and Development Organization*. Tulsa, OK: University of Tulsa Press.

Soloman, G., Allen, N. and Resta, P. (2002) *Toward Digital Equity: Bridging the Divide in Education*. Boston, MA: Allen and Bacon.

Spears, R. (1994) 'Panacea or panopticon? The hidden power of computer-mediated communication', *Communication Research*, 21 (4): 427–59.

Spears, R. and Lea, M. (1992) 'Social influence and the influence of the "Social" in computer-mediated communication', in M. Lea (ed.), *Contexts of Computer-Mediated Communication*. Hemel Hempstead: Harvester Wheatsheaf. pp. 30–65.

Spears, R., Lea, M. and Postmes, T. (2001) 'Social Psychological Theories of Computer-Mediated Communication: Social Pain and Social Gain', in W. Robinson and H. Giles (eds), *The New Handbook of Language and Social Psychology*. Chichester: Wiley.

Spink, A., Jansen, B., Wolfram, D. and Saracevic, T. (2002) 'From E-Sex to E-Commerce: Web Search Changes', *IEEE Computer*, 35 (3): 107–109.

Sproull, L. and Kiesler, S. (1986) 'Reducing social context cues: electronic mail in organizational communication', *Management Science*, 32: 1492–512.

Sproull, L. and Kiesler, S. (1991) *Connections: New Ways of Working in the Networked Organization*. Cambridge, MA: MIT Press.

Steijn, Bram (2001) *Werken in de informatiesamenleving*. Assen: Koninklijke van Gorcum.

Steinberg, S. (1996) 'Netheads vs bellheads', *Wired*, 4 (10).

Steinmüller, W. (2001) 'ICTs and the possibilities of leapfrogging by developing countries', *International Labour Review*, 140 (2): 193–210.

Stewart, James (1998–99) 'Interactive television at home: Television Meets the Internet', www.itvnews.com/. Published later in J. Jensen and C. Toscan (eds), *Interactive Television, TV of the Future or the Future of TV?* Aalborg: Aalborg University Press. pp. 231–260.

Stone, A.R. (1991) 'Will the real body please stand up?', in M. Benedict (ed.), *Cyberspace: First Steps*. Cambridge: Cambridge University Press. pp. 81–118.

Street, John (1997) 'Remote Control? Politics, Democracy and "Electronic Democracy"', *European Journal of Communication*, 12: 27–42.

Strickland, L.H., Guild, P., Barefoot, J. and Patterson, S. (1975) *Teleconferencing and Leadership Emergence*. Carleton: Carleton University.

Suchman, L.A. (1987) *Plans and Situated Actions: the Problem of Human–Machine Communication*. Cambridge, NY: Simon and Schuster.

Sunstein, Cass (2001) *Republic.com*. Princeton, NJ: Princeton University Press.

Sussman, G. (1997) *Communications Technology and Politics in the Information Age*. Thousand Oaks, CA: Sage.

Thomas, David (1996) 'Feedback and cybernetics: reimaging the body in the age of the cyborg', in M. Featherstone and R. Burrows (eds), *Cyberspace/Cyberbodies/Cyberpunk: Cultures of Technological Embodiment*. London: Sage.

Thurlow, C., Lengell, L. and Tomic, A. (2004) *Computer Mediated Communication: Social Interaction and the Internet*. London: Sage Publications.

Tichenor, P. Donohue, G. and Olieh, C. (1970) 'Mass media flow and the differential growth in knowledge', *Public Opinion Quarterly*, 34: 159–170.

Tracey, Michael (1998) *The Decline and Fall of Public Broadcasting*. Oxford: Oxford University Press.

Tsagarousianou, R. (1999). Electronic democracy: Rhetoric and reality. *Communications: The European Journal of Communication Research*, 24 (2): 189–208.

Turkle, Sherry (1984) *The Second Self: Computers and the Human Spirit*. London: Granada.

Turkle, Sherry (1995) *Life on the Screen: Identity in the Age of the Internet*. New York: Simon and Schuster.

Turkle, Sherry (1996a) 'Who am we?', *Wired*, January: 149–52, 194–9.

Turkle, Sherry (1996b) 'Parallel lives: working on identity in virtual space', in D. Grodin and T. Lindlof (eds), *Constructing the Self in a Mediated World*. Thousand Oaks, CA: Sage.

Turoff, M. (1989) 'The anatomy of a computer application innovation: computer-mediated communications', *Technological Forecasting and Social Change*, 36: 107–22.

Turow, Joseph (1997) *Breaking up America: Advertisers and the New Media World.* Chicago: University of Chicago Press.

UCLA, Center for Communication Policy (2003) *The UCLA Internet Report, Surveying the Digital Future, Year Three.* Los Angeles: UCLA, Center for Communication Policy. www.ccp.ucla.edu/pages/internet-report.asp.

US Copyright Office (1998) *Digital Millennium Copyright Act.* www.copyright.gov/.

Urry, John (2003) *Global Complexity.* Cambridge, UK: Polity Press.

Vallee, J. (1978) *Group Communication through Computers. Vol. 4: Social, Managerial and Economic Issues.* Report R-40. London: Institute for the Future.

Vallee, J., Johansen, R. and Lipinski, H. (1975) *Group Communication through Computers, Vol. III: Pragmatics and Dynamics. Institute for the Future.* Report R-35. London: Institute for the Future.

van Cuilenburg, J. and Noomen, G. (1984) *Communicatiewetenschap.* Muiderberg: Coutinho.

van Dijk, Jan A.G.M. (1991, 1994, 1997, 2000) *De Netwerkmaatschappij: Sociale aspecten van nieuwe media,* 1st–4th edns. Houten: Bohn Staflen van Loghum.

van Dijk, Jan A.G.M. (1993a) 'Communication networks and modernization', *Communication Research,* 20 (3): 384–407.

van Dijk, Jan A.G.M. (1993b) 'The mental challenge of the new media', *Medienpsychologie,* 1: 20–45.

van Dijk, Jan A.G.M. (1996) 'Models of democracy behind the design and use of new media in politics', *The Public/Javnost,* III (1): 43–56.

van Dijk, Jan A.G.M. (1997a) 'The reality of virtual communities', *Trends in Communication,* 1: 39–63.

van Dijk, Jan A.G.M. (1997b) *Universal Service from the Perspective of Consumers and Citizens.* Report to the Information Society Forum. Brussels: European Commission/ISPO.

van Dijk, Jan A.G.M. (1999) 'The one-dimensional network society of Manuel Castells', *New Media and Society,* 1 (1): 127–38.

van Dijk, Jan A.G.M. (2000a) 'Models of democracy and concepts of communication', in K. Hacker and J. van Dijk (eds), *Digital Democracy: Issues of Theory and Practice.* London, New Delhi, Thousand Oaks, CA: Sage. pp. 30–53.

van Dijk, Jan A.G.M. (2000b) 'Widening information gaps and policies of prevention', in K. Hacker and J. van Dijk (eds), *Digital Democracy: Issues of Theory and Practice.* London: Sage.

van Dijk, J.A.G.M. (2001) *Netwerken, het zenuwstelsel van onze maatschappij,* Oratie (Networks, the nervous system of our society, inaugural lecture). Enschede: University of Twente, Department of Communication.

van Dijk, J. and de Vos, L. (2001) 'Searching for the Holy Grail: Images of interactive television'. *New Media and Society,* 3 (4): 443–65.

van Dijk, Jan A.G.M. (2005) *The Deepening Divide, Inequality in the Information Society.* Thousand Oaks, CA, London, New Delhi: Sage.

van Dijk, Jan, Heuvelman, A. and Peters, O. (2003) 'Interactive Television or Enhanced Television?, The Dutch users' interest in ITV via set-top boxes'. Paper presented at the 53rd Annual Conference of the International Communication Association, 27 may–4 june 2003, San Diego, CA.

van Dijk, J.A.G.M. (2004) 'Divides in succession: Possession, skills and life of new media for societal participation', in E. Bucy and J. Newhagen (eds), *Media Access: Social and Psychological Dimensions of New Technology Use.* London: LEA. pp. 233–258.

van Dijk, J.A.G.M. and Hacker, K. (2003) 'The digital divide as a complex and dynamic phenomenon', *Information Society,* 19: 315–326.

van Duijn, J.J. (1979) *De lange golf in de economie.* Assen: Van Gorcum.

van Rossum, H., Gardeniers, H. and Borking, J. (1995a) *Privacy-Enhancing Technologies: The Path to Anonymity,* Vol I. TNO Physics and Electronics Laboratory. Rijswijk: Registratiekamer.

van Rossum, H., Gardeniers, H. and Borking, J. (1995b) *Privacy-Enhancing Technologies: The Path to Anonymity*, Vol II. TNO Physics and Electronics Laboratory. Rijswijk: Registratiekamer.

van Tulder, R. and Junne, R. (1988) *European Multinationals in Core Technologies*. Chichester: Wiley.

Vartanova, P. (1998) 'New communication technologies and information flows in Russia'. Paper presented at Beyond Convergence: ITS-98 Conference, Stockholm, Sweden, 14–21 June. www.ITS98.org/conference.

Venturelli, Shalini (1998) *Liberalizing the European Media: Politics, Regulation and the Public Sphere*. Oxford: Oxford University Press.

Venturelli, Shalini (2002) 'Inventing e-regulation in the US, EU and East Asia: conflicting social visions of the Information Society', *Telematics and Informatics*, 19: 69–90.

Vickers, G. (1965) *The Art of Judgment*. London: Chapman and Hall.

Virilio, P. (1988) *La Machine de Vision*. Paris: Galilée. Translation: *The Vision Machine*. Bloomington, IN: Indiana University Press, 1994.

Walden, Ian (1997) 'Data protection issues across the Internet', *Electronic Intellectual Property Right (EIPR)*, 13: 50–5.

Wallace, Patricia (1999) *The Psychology of the Internet*. Cambridge: Cambridge University Press.

Walther, J. (1992) 'Interpersonal effects in computer-mediated communication', *Communication Research*, 19 (1): 52–90.

Walther, J. (1995) 'Relational aspects of computer-mediated communication: experimental observations over time', *Organization Science*, 6: 186–203.

Walther, J. (1996) 'Computer-mediated communication: impersonal, interpersonal and hyperpersonal interaction', *Communication Research*, 23 (1): 1–43.

Walther, J. (1997) 'Group and Interpersonal Effects in International Computer-Mediated Collaboration', *Human Communication Research*, 23 (3): 442–69.

Wang, G. (1998) 'Regulating network communication in Asia: a different balancing act?'. Paper presented at Beyond Convergence: ITS-98 Conference, Stockholm, Sweden, 14–21 June. www.ITS98.org/conference.

Warschauer, Mark (2003) *Technology and Social Inclusion: Rethinking the Digital Divide*. Cambridge, MA, London: The MIT Press.

Watts, Duncan (2003) *Six Degrees: The Science of a Connected Age*. New York: Norton.

Watts, Duncan J. and Strogatz, Steven (1998) 'Collective Dynamics of "Small World" Networks', *Nature*, 393: 440–2.

Webber, M. (1963) 'Order in diversity: community without propinquity', in L. Wingo (ed.), *Cities and Space*. Baltimore, MD: Johns Hopkins University Press.

Weber, Max (1922) *Gesammelte Politische Schriften*. Tübingen: Mohr.

Webster, Frank (2001) 'The Information Society Revisited', in L. Lievrouw *Handbook of the New Media*, London, Thousand Oaks, CA, New Delhi: Sage. pp. 22–33.

Weingarten, R. and Fiehler, R. (eds) (1988) *Technisierte Kommunikation*. Opladen: Westdeutscher Verlag.

Wellman, B. (2000) 'Changing connectivity: A future history of Y2.03K', *Sociological Research Online*, 4 (4). www.socresonline.org.uk/4/4/wellman.html.

Wellman, Barry (2001) 'Computer Networks As Social Networks', *Science*, 293, 14 September: 2031–4.

Wellman, Barry and Berkowitz, S.D. (eds) (1988) *Social Structures: A Network Approach*. Greenwich CT, London: JAI Press.

Wellman, Barry and Haythornthwaite, Caroline (eds) (2002) *The Internet in Everyday Life*. Malden, MA, Oxford: Blackwell.

Wellman, B. and Leighton, B. (1979) 'Networks, neighbours and communities. Approaches to the study of the community question', *Urban Affairs Quarterly*, March.

Westin, A.F. (1987) *Privacy and Freedom*. London: Bodley Head.

Weston, J.R., Kristen, C. and O'Connor, S. (1975) *Teleconferencing*. Ottawa: Social Policy and Programmes Branch, Department of Communications.

Whisler, T.L. (1970) *The Impact of Computers on Organizations*. London: Praeger.

Williams, F. (1982) *The Communications Revolution*. Beverly Hills, CA: Sage.

Wilhelm, Anthony (2003) 'Civic Participation and Technology Inequality: The "Killer Application" is Education', in D. Anderson and M. Cornfield (eds), *The Civic Web, Online Politics and Democratic Values*. Lanham, MD: Rowman and Littlefield. pp. 113–28.

Wilhelm, Anthony (2004) *Digital Nation, Towards an Inclusive Information Society*. Cambridge, MA, London: The MIT Press.

Winston, Brian (1998) *Media Technology and Society: A History from the Telegraph to the Internet*. London: Routledge.

Wong, P.-K. (2002) 'The impact of IT investment on income and wealth inequality in the post-war US economy', *Information Economics and Poverty*, 14: 233–251.

Working Party on the Protection of Individuals with Regard to the Processing of Personal Data (1997) *Anonymity on the Internet*. European Commission, Directorate General XV, D/5022/97 final recommendation 3/97. Brussels: European Commission.

Wright, E.O. (1985) *Classes*. London: Verso.

Yao, Dennis (2003) 'Non-Market Strategies and Regulation in the United States' in B. Kogut (ed.), *The Global Internet Economy*. Cambridge MA, London: The MIT Press. pp. 407–35.

Zuboff, S. (1988) *In the Age of the Smart Machine: the Future of Work and Power*. New York: Basic Books.

Zuurmond, A. (1994) *De infocratie*. Contains a summary in English. The Hague: Phaedrus.

Zuurmond, A. (1996) 'Informatisering: technocratisering of democratisering?', *Beleid en Maatschappij*, 3: 134–44.

Zuurmond, A. (1998) 'From bureaucracy to infocracy: are democratic institutions lagging behind?', in I. Snellen and W. Van de Donk (eds), *Public Administration in the Information Age: A Handbook*. Amsterdam: IOS Press. pp. 78–95.

INDEX

Access, 98, 103, 178, 179 (table), 250, 253–5
  motivational, 179–80, 254
  physical, 180–1, 254
  public, 254–5
  skills, 181–2, 255
  usage, 182–3
Access systems, 88–9
(A)DSL, 51, 57
Agents: *see* information/personal agents
Allocution, 10, 132, 195, 197
Anthropomorphization of technology, 233–4
Art, 192
ATM (asynchronous transfer mode), 50, 135
Authors' right, 145, 146, 147; *see also* property right, intellectual

Beniger, James, 4, 63–5, 170, 243
Biometrics, 113, 135, 154
Biotechnology, 58, 81, 113
Broadband (networks), 7, 47–8, 51, 57–8, 59–60, 88, 254
Broadcasting, 33, 52, 84, 132, 171–3, 208
Broadcasting model, 131–2, 139
Browsers, 88–9
Bureaucracy, 64, 75, 76, 108–110; *see also* infocracy
Bus structure, 49

Camera surveillance, 113–14
Canada, 248
Capitalism, 20, 74, 76, 77, 79–80, 128, 187, 244, 250
Castells, Manuel, 18, 20, 28, 240, 250
CD-I, 91
Cell-switching, 50
China, 2, 88, 250, 252
Circuit switching (networks), 46–7, 50
Citizenship, 102, 103, 124
Civil rights, 98–9, 249, 251
Class structure, 175–7, 185–6

CLI (Calling Line Identification), 115–16
Codes of conduct, 141, 142, 148, 149, 153
Cognition and new media, 217–24
Communication, 23, 199, 203
  quality of, 163, 164, 165
  quantity of, 163, 164, 165
Communication capacities, 6, 13–16, 18, 206
Communication overload/overcommunication, 116, 200, 204, 263
Communication revolution, 3–6, 64–5, 243
  structural, 4–5
  technical, 5–6
Communications Decency Art, 141, 143, 247
Communities, 165–7, 173; *see also* organic communities; virtual communities
  communities online, 167
  online communities, 167
Complex adaptive systems, 30–2, 199–200
Computer conferencing, 230
Computer gaming, 53
Computer-integrated manufacturing, 68
Computer-mediated communication (CMC), 41, 210, 226–33
Computer-supported co-operative work (CSCW), 70, 71, 75
Conditional access systems, 45, 88–9, 132, 180
Connectivity, 1, 31, 36, 38, 59, 187–8
Consultation, 10, 132, 195, 197
Contagion, 187
Contractor, Noshir, 27
Control crisis, 63
Convergence, 7, 42, 46, 49, 52, 54, 87, 92, 129, 204–5, 258
Conversation, 12, 132, 195, 197, 232–3
Cookies, 115, 119, 136
Copyright, 145, 147; *see also* property right, intellectual

Costa Rica, 253
Creativity, 192, 195
Critical mass, 31, 59, 78
Culture of collage, 192–3
Culture of speed, 193–4
Cyborgs, 211, 237–8, 263

Data (broad)casting, 51, 54
Data metering, 148
Data mining, 116, 258
Data warehousing, 116
Democracy, 101, 258–9
   definition of, 104
   digital, 103–8
   views/models of, 101–3
Design, 91–3, 111, 120,
   244–5, 256–8
Developmental states, 20, 250–1
De Vos, Loes, 8
Digital code, 9
Digital culture, 190, 191–9
Digital democracy: see democracy
Digital divide, 40, 91, 169, 177–86,
   253, 259
Digital Millennium Copyright Act, 146
Digital pseudonym, 121
Digital radio and television, 53, 89
Digital rights management, 146
Digital signature, 122
Digital skills, 176, 181–2,
   215–16, 252, 255
Digital telephony, 48, 54
Digital watermark, 148
Digitalization, 43–4, 48, 53, 190,
   191, 192
Direct marketing, 172–3
Distance education, 163–4; see
   also telestudy
Distribution networks, 90
Domestication, 91–2
Dyson, Esther, 143

East Asia, 250–1, 262
Eastern Europe, 248, 250
Ecology, 2, 244, 261
E-commerce, 79, 119, 134, 139
Edelman, Gerald, 218–19, 221–2
E-government, 103–8
   definition of, 104
Electronic debate/discussion, 106, 167,
   230, 231
Email, 5, 136, 140, 153, 182, 196, 228,
   230, 231, 254
Embedded technology, 58–9
Encryption, 121–3, 136, 153–4, 249
Environmental protection: see ecology

Ethical minorities and ICT, 177, 186
European Union, 118, 141, 142, 143,
   146, 147, 150–2, 248–50,
   255, 262
EU Copyright Directive, 146–7
EU Directive of Minors and Content, 141
EU Privacy Directive, 118, 119, 150–2
Extranet, 55

Face-to-face communication, 34, 36, 166,
   168–9, 195, 224, 227, 229, 231,
   233, 236, 243, 255, 262
Fiber-optic cable, 120
File coupling, 116–17, 258
Flaming, 230
Fordism, 67
Freedom, 3, 99, 112, 113, 137–43
   of choice, 124–4, 191–2, 208
   of communication, 137–43, 250
   of information, 137–43, 250
Full service networks, 91

Gender and ICT, 177, 180, 181, 182–3
Globalization, 244
Google, 85, 134, 184
Granovetter, Mark, 30, 31
Groupware, 70
Group dynamics in CMC, 229–30
Guilder, George, 59
Guilder's law, 59

HDTV, 53
Heterarchy, 27–8, 36
Hierarchy, 27–8, 37, 72–6
House systems, 55
Human–computer communication/
   interaction, 211–24
Hypermedia, 9, 207, 225–6

Identity, 237
India, 2, 88, 252, 253
Individualization, 35, 63, 93, 160, 161,
   165, 198
Inequality: see information (in)equality;
   network individualization;
   social (in)equality
Infocracy, 40, 75, 109
Information, 199, 202 (figure)
   quality of, 202–3
   quantity of, 199–207
Information agents/personal agents,
   201, 235, 263
Information appliances, 58–9
Information elite, 107, 185–6, 252
Information (in)equality, 174–86, 244,
   259; see also social (in)equality

Information overload, 201–2, 207
Information richness, 13
Information society, 19, 20, 21, 244–53
  definition, 19
  models of, 244–253
Information superhighway, 2, 7, 84, 86,
  88, 245–6
Information traffic patterns, 10–13, 129
Innovation, 4, 6, 64, 81, 249, 262
  process innovation, 80, 94
  product innovation, 94
Integration, 6–8, 12, 53–5, 56, 97, 225;
  see also convergence
Intellectual property right: see
  property right, intellectual
Interactivity, 8–9, 16, 39–40,
  106, 224–5
  levels of, 8–9, 56
Interactive television, 52–3, 89, 92
Interconnectivity, 84, 97, 98,
  207–8, 250
Internet, 18, 28, 49, 54, 81, 93, 103, 106,
  107, 130–7, 139, 140, 152, 167, 169,
  171, 174, 184, 187, 193, 205, 206,
  254, 256–7, 259
Internet Architecture Board (IAB), 133
Internet Corporation for Assigned Names
  and Numbers (ICANN), 133
Internet Engeneering Taskforce
  (IETF), 133
Internet Service Providers, 133, 134,
  141, 142
Internet Society (ISOC), 133
Intranet, 55, 103, 105
ISDN, 51, 54

Japan, 250
Jensen, Jens, 8

Knowledge, 70, 144, 183, 199, 202,
  203, 207
Knowledge management, 71
Knowledge networks, 70, 75
Knowledge society, 19
Kontopoulos, Kyriakos, 27

LAN (Local Area Network), 49–50, 54
Learning with new media, 212–13,
  222–3, 224–6
Legislation and networks, 128–30, 140–2,
  145–7, 260
Lessig, Lawrence, 132, 135
Liberalization of telecommunication, 86,
  87, 245, 248, 251, 256–7
Logistics, 67
Loneliness, 235–6
Long waves of the economy, 80–1

Malaysia, 250
Marketing: see direct marketing
Markets, 72–6
Mass society, 19, 20, 23, 34 (figure), 39
  characteristics of, 32, 33 (table), 33–4
  definition of, 20
Matthew effect, 183–4
Mansell, Robin, 87
McNeill, I.R. and W., 21–3, 29, 32
Media concentration, 65, 82, 83,
  84–7, 176
Media replacement, 205–6
Media use, 204–8, 206 (table)
Mediated communication, 34, 36, 39, 44,
  51–3, 166, 168–9, 195, 196, 211,
  224, 233, 236, 243, 262
Medium theory, 18, 171, 242
Mental development, 263
Mesh structure, 49
Metcalfe's law, 59
Meyrowitz, Joshua, 171–3
Microsoft, 78, 83, 88, 97, 134,
  137, 250
Milgram, Stanley, 31, 38
Millennium problem: see year 2000
  problem
Mobile telephone, 47–8, 59
Modernity, 29
Modernization theory, 18
Modes of experience, 212–13
Modes of (symbolic) communication,
  213; see also symbol systems
Monopolization/oligopolization, 82, 83,
  84–5, 87–8, 258
Monge, Peter, 27
Moore's law, 58
MUD (Multi-user Dungeon or Domain),
  140, 237
Multimedia, 7, 55–6, 192
  CD, 56
  PC, 56

Nanotechnology, 58
Natural monopoly, 83–4
Netherlands, 107, 183, 206
Netiquette, 232–33
Networks
  as an economic form, 72–6
  broadband, 7, 12, 55, 57–8, 86, 88
  causes of the rise of, 29–32
  definition of, 24, 29–30, 38, 123–4
  global, 27
  history of, 21–3
  individual, 25
  levels of, 24–28
  organizational, 25–6
  random, 184

Networks *cont.*
  scale-free, 184
  societal, 26, 29
  types of, 24–5, 25 (table)
Network approach, 17, 24, 28, 38
Network architecture, 49–50, 111, 132,
    135–7, 257
Network economy, 26, 77–9, 175
Network effects or externalities, 78, 178
Network government/state, 26, 37,
    101, 103
Network individualization, 29, 38, 58,
    168, 169, 236
Network layers, 45, 50, 81–2, 129, 135–7
Network operators, 83–4, 135
Network organizations, 26, 29, 61,
    71, 75–6
Network services, 85
Network society, 19, 20, 21, 23, 25, 32,
    35 (figure), 37–41, 101, 156, 157,
    185–8, 206, 240–1, 243, 244–53
  characteristics of, 33 (table), 35–6
  definition of, 20
Network theory, 17, 27, 29–32
Network topology, 49–50
Network vulnerability, 95–8, 120,
    227, 255–6
Network warfare, 139
New economy, 26, 37, 61–2, 76–81
New media, 4
  characteristics of, 6–12
  definition of, 4, 9
  dystopian views, 2
  utopian views, 2
Norman, Donald, 59, 220, 263

Office work, 68, 69–70
Online dating, 169, 235
Online forums, 106, 107; *see also*
    electronic debate
Online groups, 170–1
Online learning communities, 71
Open code (public domain software),
    147, 257
Open source (freeware), 134, 147,
    246, 257
Open system, 50
Optical techniques, 46, 58
Organic communities, 166–7
OSI Model, 45, 50, 112, 135–6

Packet switching, 47, 50
Participation in society, 178–9,
    184–6, 254
Patriarchy, 244
Perception and new media, 211–16
Personal autonomy, 112, 123–5, 259

Personal digital assistant (PDA), 57
Personality and new media, 233–8
PGP (Pretty Good Privacy),
    122, 153
Policies for the network society, 253–63
Policy perspectives, 245–253
Press model, 131–2, 139
Privacy, 16, 44, 112–23, 149–54,
    161, 259–60
  definition of, 112–3
Privacy Directive EU, 150–2, 259
Privacy enhancing technologies, 121–3
Privacy law, 118–9, 149–52, 249
Privacy principles OECD, 150, 151
Privatization
  economic, 84–6, 131, 245, 257
  social, 158, 160, 161
Productivity, 77
Productivity paradox, 77, 199
Profiling (computer), 117
Property right
  intellectual, 144, 145–8, 249
  material, 148–9
Public domain software, 141, 147
Public information systems, 105
Public sphere, 161, 173–4

Rating and filtering systems, 142–3
Registration, 10, 100, 121, 132, 195,
    197, 255
Regulation of tele- and mass
    communication, 87–9, 131, 256–7
Reidenberg, J.R., 143
Relationship management, 155
Ring structure, 49
Risk society, 41, 255

Salomon, Gavriel, 214–6
Satellites, 46, 47, 52, 54
Scale extension/reduction, 29, 63, 65–8,
    158, 160, 171, 186, 241
Schumpeter, J.A., 81
Search engines, 134, 184
Security, 41, 96–8, 102, 114,
    120, 255–6
Self-regulation, 140, 141, 142,
    147–8, 152–3
Service providers, 81, 82, 85, 88
Singapore, 250
Six degrees of separation, 31, 38
Small world, 31, 32
Smart cards, 112
SMS, 13, 47, 53
Sociability, 167–9
Social capital, 168, 169
Social cohesion, 39, 171–4, 175, 198
Social exclusion, 184–6, 254

Social (in)equality, 40, 174–7, 261;
    see also information (in)equality
Social isolation, 163, 164, 167
Social presence, 13, 14
Social relationships, 168, 235; see also
    sociability; social capital; ties
Socialization
    of knowledge, 144, 148
    of space and time, 160–1
South Korea, 183
Space and time in networks, 157
Spam, 142
Spyware, 119, 137
Standardization, 78, 83, 192
State autonomy, 138–9
Steganography, 123, 154
Store-and-forward principle, 44
Structuration theory, 17–8, 242
Suchman, Lucy, 219
Surveillance, 99, 114–15, 117
Symbol systems, 213; see also modes of
    (symbolic) communication
Systems theory, 29–32
Switching methods, 46–7

Taylorism, 67, 69
TCP/IP, 50, 135–6, 256
Technology
    enabling and defining, 14, 17, 171, 242
    mutual shaping, 17, 156
    view of, 17
Technology push, 91, 125, 245
Tele-activities, 161–5; see also
    telestudy; telework
Telecommunications model, 131–2, 139
Teledemocracy, 102–3
Teleshopping, 183, 198
Telestudy, 163–4; see also
    distance education
Teletext, 52, 197
Telework, 162–3
Third World, 252–3, 262

Ties, 30, 36, 37, 38
    strong, 30, 185
    weak, 30, 31, 169, 185
Time–space distantiation, 157
Tree structure, 50
Turkle, Sherry, 233, 236, 237

UMTS, 47–8, 51
Uneven and combined development,
    174–5, 252
United States, 65, 102, 107, 118,
    141, 142, 143, 146, 150, 152,
    169, 174, 183, 195, 246–8,
    255, 262
Universal access/service, 247, 249, 254–5
Usage gap, 183, 207, 263

Value added networks (VAN), 45
Van Dijk, Jan, 8, 177
Veturelli, Shalini, 245–51
Video conferencing, 48, 53, 91,
    228, 230
Videophone, 48, 91, 198, 228, 229
Videotex, 91
Virtual communities, 36, 166–7
Virtual organization, 61, 71–2
Virtual reality, 57
Visual culture, 194–9
Voice over IP, 50

Walther, Joseph, 14
Web logs, 170
Web organization, 72
WEB TV, 89
Wide area network (WAN), 49
Williams, Frederick, 4
Winston, Brian, 243
Wireless connections, 47–8, 59
Workflow, 69

Yahoo, 85, 134
Year 2000 problem, 97